Me MONEY EDUCATION

CASES IN FINANCIAL PLANNING

Analysis and Presentation

FIRST EDITION

Michael A. Dalton
James F. Dalton
Katheleen F. Oakley

CASES IN FINANCIAL PLANNING

Analysis and Presentation

FIRST EDITION

Me

115 James Drive West
Suite 140
St. Rose, LA 70087
888-295-6023

Printed in the U.S.A.

ISBN: 978-1-936602-08-7

Library of Congress Card Number: 2012943232

About the Authors

Michael A. Dalton, Ph.D., JD, CPA, CLU, ChFC, CFP®

- Former Chair of the Board of Dalton Publications, L.L.C.
- Associate professor of Accounting and Taxation at Loyola University in New Orleans, Louisiana (retired)
- Adjunct faculty in Financial Planning at Georgetown University in Washington, D.C.
- Former Senior Vice President, Education at BISYS Group
- Ph.D. in Accounting from Georgia State University
- J.D. from Louisiana State University in Baton Rouge, Louisiana
- MBA and BBA in Management and Accounting from Georgia State University
- Former board member of the CFP Board's Board of Examiners, Board of Standards, and Board of Governors
- Former member (and chair) of the CFP Board's Board of Examiners
- Member of the Financial Planning Association
- Member of the *Journal of Financial Planning* Editorial Advisory Board
- Member of the *Journal of Financial Planning* Editorial Review Board
- Member of the LSU Law School Board of Trustees (2000 - 2006)
- Author of *Dalton Review for the CFP® Certification Examination: Volume I – Outlines and Study Guides, Volume II – Problems and Solutions, Volume III - Case Exam Book, Mock Exams A-1 and A-2 (1st - 8th Editions)*
- Author of *Retirement Planning and Employee Benefits for Financial Planners (1st - 8th Editions)*
- Author of *Estate Planning for Financial Planners (1st - 6th Editions)*
- Author of *Fundamentals of Financial Planning (1st - 2nd Edition)*
- Author of *Fundamentals of Financial Planning Insurance Supplement (1st -2nd Edition)*
- Co-author of *Income Tax Planning for Financial Planners (1st - 5th Editions)*
- Co-author of *Dalton CFA® Study Notes Volumes I and II (1st - 2nd Editions)*
- Co-author of *Dalton's Personal Financial Planning Series – Personal Financial Planning Theory and Practice (1st - 3rd Editions)*
- Co-author of *Dalton's Personal Financial Planning Series – Personal Financial Planning Cases and Applications (1st - 4th Editions)*
- Co-author of *Cost Accounting: Traditions and Innovations* published by West Publishing Company
- Co-author of the *ABCs of Managing Your Money* published by National Endowment for Financial Education (NEFE)

James F. Dalton, MBA, MS, CPA/PFS, CFA®, CFP®

- Adjunct faculty member at Georgetown University
- Former Executive Vice President, Assessment Technologies Institute LLC
- Former Senior Vice President, Kaplan Professional
- Former President, Dalton Publications LLC
- Former Senior Manager of KPMG, LLP, concentrating in personal financial planning, investment planning, and litigation consulting
- MBA from Loyola University New Orleans
- Master of Accounting in Taxation from the University of New Orleans
- BS in accounting from Florida State University in Tallahassee, Florida
- Member of the CFP Board of Standards July 1996, Comprehensive CFP® Exam Pass Score Committee
- Member of the AICPA and the Louisiana Society of CPAs
- Member of the Financial Planning Association
- Member of the *Journal of Financial Planning* Editorial Review Board
- Member of the New Orleans Estate Planning Council
- Author of Kaplan Schweser's Personal Financial Planning Understanding Your Financial Calculator
- Author of Kaplan Schweser's Understanding Your Financial Calculator for the CFA® Exam
- Co-author of BISYS CFA® Study Notes Volumes I and II
- Co-author of Kaplan Schweser's Personal Financial Planning Cases and Applications
- Co-author of the Kaplan Schweser Review for the CFP® Certification Examination, Volumes I–VIII and Kaplan Schweser's Financial Planning Flashcards

Katheleen F. Oakley, MBS, CPA, CFP®

- Former director of financial planning for the Houston office of Lincoln Financial Advisors
- Former vice president and chief financial planning officer with Kanaly Trust Company (Houston, Texas)
- Member of the Financial Planning Association
- Former board member of the Pearland Economic Development Corporation
- Former Vice-Chair of two committees for the Houston Chapter of CPAs
- BS in Finance and an MBA from the University of New Orleans
- Insurance license in the state of Texas and formerly held securities licenses, including the NASD Series 7 and 63
- Academic Program Director for classroom and web-based CFP Certification Education programs in the Susanne M. Glasscock, School of Continuing Studies at Rice University
- Author of the Martin case published in Dalton's Personal Financial Planning Cases and Applications, 3rd edition textbook and instructor manual
- Taught financial planning education as well as review classes in General Principles of Financial Planning along with the Case Studies class
- Editor of practice questions and answers contained in the Dalton CFA® Review, Volumes I and II Study Notes and is a contributing author to the Dalton CFA® Review Testbank

Acknowledgements & Special Thanks

We are most appreciative for the tremendous support and encouragement we have received throughout this project. We are extremely grateful to the instructors and program directors of CFP Board-Registered programs who provided valuable comments during the development stages of this text. We are fortunate to have dedicated, careful readers at many institutions who were willing to share their needs, expectations, and time with us.

We owe a special thanks to all the students in the Rice University and Georgetown University Case Analysis and Presentation classes who worked diligently on these cases. Their thorough editing, detailed calculations, reviews, suggestions and other valuable comments improved this textbook. We also owe a special thanks to the faculty who ran these classes and provided great assistance in the development of this textbook. To each of these individuals we extend our deepest gratitude and appreciation.

We would also like to pay special thanks to **Donna Dalton** and **Robin Meyer** for their significant contribution to this textbook. Developing a textbook that is aesthetically pleasing and easy to read is a difficult undertaking. They worked diligently with the authors and reviewers to manage the project, performed numerous reviews, and provided invaluable feedback throughout the entire project. This book would not have been possible without their extraordinary dedication, skill, and knowledge.

We also owe thanks to Cody Cadella for his constructive feedback and thorough editing. His helpful suggestions and other valuable comments have improved this textbook. A special thank you also goes out to Desktop Miracles for designing our cover and chapter title artwork.

We have received so much help from so many people, it is possible that we have inadvertently overlooked thanking someone. If so, it is our shortcoming, and we apologize in advance. Please let us know if you are that someone, and we will make it right in our next printing.

PREFACE

Cases in Financial Planning: Analysis and Presentation is written for graduate and upperdivision undergraduate level students interested in acquiring an understanding of comprehensive financial planning from a professional financial planning viewpoint. The textbook is intended to be used in a case course as part of an overall curriculum in financial planning. The textbook is also intended to serve as a reference and resource for practicing professional financial planners.

This textbook was designed to meet the educational requirements for a Case Analysis and Presentation Course in a CFP Board-Registered Program. Therefore, one of our goals is to assure CFP Board-Registered Program Directors, instructors, students, and financial planners that we have addressed every relevant topic covered by the CFP Board Exam Topic List and the most recent model curriculum syllabus for this course. The book will be updated, as needed, to keep current with any changes in the law, exam topic list, or model curriculum.

TO THE STUDENT

Welcome to your comprehensive case course. This book aims to assist you in developing or refining your methodology for approaching financial planning clients. The book is structured as follows:

- Part 1: Case Analysis and Presentation
- Part 2: Mini Cases Examples & Exercises
- Part 3: Comprehensive Case Example
- Part 4: Comprehensive Cases
- Appendices

The first part of the textbook provides an introduction on how to approach financial planning cases. There are many techniques that you may find useful in assessing a client's situation. The second part of the textbook illustrates how to address issues in the major areas of financial planning, including insurance, investments, tax, retirement and estate planning. It also provides you with an opportunity to practice what was learned in the first part of the textbook and in the mini case examples. The third part of the textbook is an example of how to analyze a comprehensive case. The fourth part of the textbook includes comprehensive cases that deal with various financial planning issues. The last part of the textbook is the appendix, which includes reference materials for each of the functional areas of financial planning. This appendix will prevent having to look up information in other textbooks and will be a great resource for you when practicing financial planning.

IMPORTANT INFORMATION REGARDING APPENDICES (STUDENTS AND INSTRUCTORS SHOULD READ!)

The appendices includes a separate appendix for each of the major financial planning topics. We are confident you will find these helpful both during your case analysis and as a resource in future practice. The Insurance Appendix includes estimated premiums for life, health, disability, long-term care, property, and liability insurance. We are fully aware that you may find other premium amounts on the internet or from other sources. However, unless your instructor assigns an exercise involving the research of premiums, we encourage you to use the provided premiums, as they will impact cash flows. The premiums provided in the Insurance Appendix were used by the authors to develop our model solutions for the Instructor Manual.

Additional resources can be found at www.money-education.com.

This book is dedicated to

Robin Delle Meyer

for providing the glue that keeps Money Education together.

She is the inspiration to our creativity and

she is the guardian of our culture and high quality

commitment to our customers.

Visit our website at money-education.com for updates to the textbook & information on our Quick Sheets!

Table of Contents

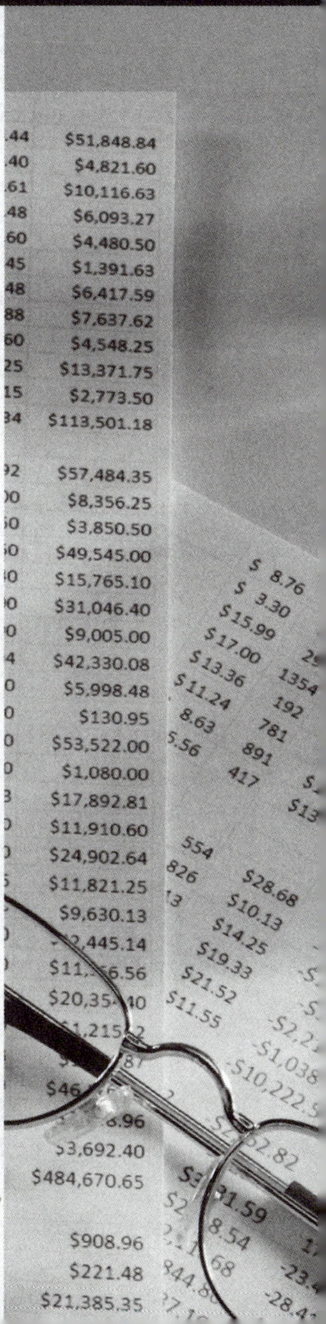

PART 1: CASE ANALYSIS AND PRESENTATION

Chapter 1: Case Analysis and Presentation

Chapter 2: Financial Planning Approaches: Analysis & Recommendations

Chapter 3: Personal Financial Statements: Preparation & Analysis

PART 2: MINI CASES: EXAMPLES & EXERCISES

Mini Case 1: Risk Management

Mini Case 2: Short-Term Goals and Obligations

Mini Case 3: Education and Education Funding

Mini Case 4: Retirement Needs and Capital Needs Analysis

Mini Case 5: Present Value Approach

Mini Case 6: Tax Analysis

Mini Case 7: Risk Tolerance

Mini Case 8: Estate Planning

PART 4: COMPREHENSIVE CASES

Case 1: Grayson and Tally Alexander Case

Case 2: George and Laura Freeman Case

Case 3: Trevor and Linda Gates Case

Case 4: Alvin and Fran Jackson Case

Case 5: Sharon Laynee Case

Case 6: Argo and Marie Merritt Case

Case 7: The Berry Case

Case 8: John and Jackie Griffin Case

Case 9: Bob and Candi Sweet Case

Case 10: Elvis and Adele Singer Case

APPENDICES

Appendix A: Fundamentals

Appendix B: Insurance

Appendix C: Investments

Appendix D: Income Tax

Appendix E: Retirement & Social Security

Appendix F: Estates

Part 1

Case Analysis & Presentation

CHAPTER 1

Case Analysis and Presentation for Personal Financial Planning

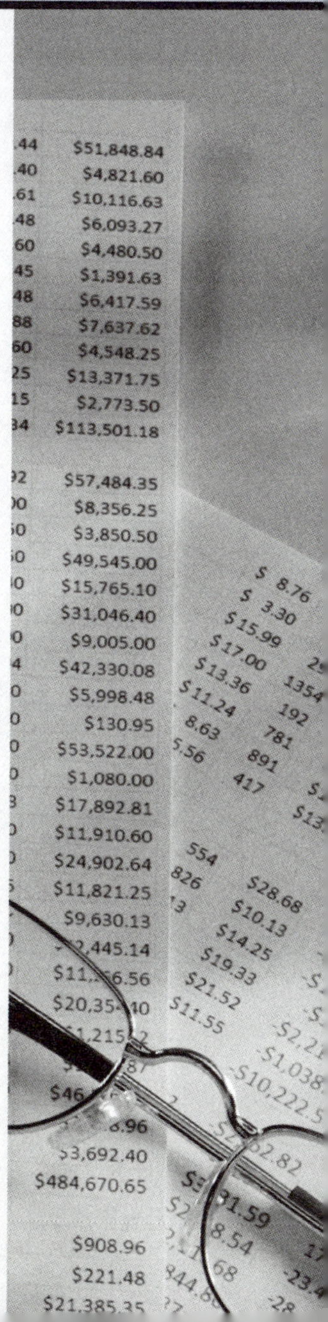

INTRODUCTION

This textbook is a valuable resource for financial planning students and practitioners, including those with either limited or substantial experience, and those who are interested in improving their financial planning skills. The text covers the financial planning process from the initial contact with a client to the presentation of the plan itself. Case studies are included in the textbook that cover a range of scenarios from basic to more complex. Varied financial planning approaches are provided to ensure that the financial planner has the appropriate planning methodologies necessary to arrive at logical and substantiated planning recommendations. This textbook should remain an important reference tool for the financial planner seeking knowledge and assistance in the preparation of professional comprehensive personal financial plans.

PERSONAL FINANCIAL PLANNING

Personal financial planning (financial planning) is the process of formulating, implementing, and monitoring financial decisions into an integrated plan that guides an individual or a family to achieve their financial goals.

The Process

The process of financial planning includes, but is not limited to:

Establishing and defining the client relationship

- the introductory meeting
- identifying general goals and objectives
- formulating an engagement letter

Gathering client data

- gathering internal client data, including goals
- determining relevant external data

Analyzing and Evaluating Client's Financial Status

- preparing data analysis including an evaluation of the client's risk management portfolio, financial statement analysis, and the external economic environment
- establishing alternative options (plans) to achieve financial goals including time frames

Developing and Presenting Financial Plan Recommendations

- selecting one set of recommendations from the alternative options

Implementing Financial Plan Recommendations

- defining the planner's responsibilities separately from the client's responsibilities
- guiding the implementation of the plan

Monitoring the Plan

- setting a schedule for the periodic review and adjustment of the agreed to plan

Exhibit 1.1 provides a visual representation of the financial planning process.

EXHIBIT 1.1 FINANCIAL PLANNING PROCESS[1]

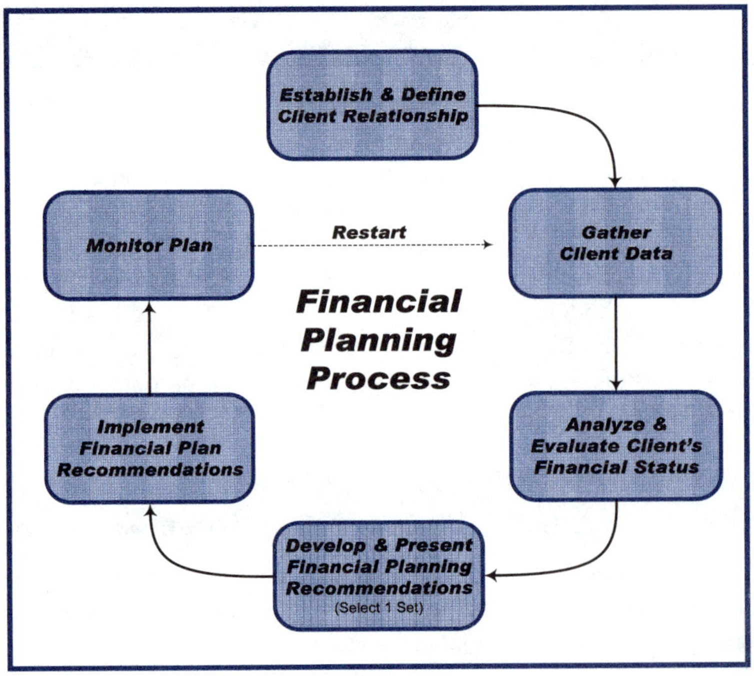

CONTENTS OF THE FINANCIAL PLAN

A financial plan is a written document that generally sets out a list of recommendations to achieve a set of goals and objectives based on an understanding of a client's current financial situation. A financial plan is the work product and result from the application of several financial planning concepts to a client's current and prospective financial situation. The application of the concepts (listed below) considers the client's financial goals and values (internal data) and the external environment (external data). The external environment includes current and expected future income, gift and estate taxes, investment returns, inflation and interest rates.

1. Abbreviated from the CFP Board's Financial Planning Practice Standards.

Financial planning concepts applied include:

- an evaluation of the client's risk management portfolio (includes risks retained and risks transferred through the use of insurance contracts)
- financial statement preparation and analysis including cash flow analysis and budgeting
- emergency fund and debt management (short-term goals)
- long-term goal planning including:
  - achieving financial security (retirement planning)
  - education planning for children's or grandchildren's college or private secondary education
  - planning for lump-sum purchases (major expenditures)
  - legacy planning (estate planning)
- income tax planning is integrated throughout all aspects of the plan
- the investment planning portfolio is used to fund many of the client's short and long-term goals

In order to apply each of these concepts to a client's current and prospective financial status, the financial planner uses tools such as financial statement preparation and analysis, cash flow analysis, and budgeting. This chapter introduces the first two steps in the financial planning process including: (1) establishing the relationship and (2) gathering client data. The entire financial planning method is comprehensively reviewed in Chapter 2 (Financial Planning Approaches) and then applied in the Burke Case in Part 3 of the textbook.

Key Concepts

Underline/highlight the answers to these questions as you read:

1. What are the steps in the financial planning process?
2. What is the difference between internal and external data collected as part of the financial planning process?
3. What are the subject matter areas that are applied to a client's financial plan considering the client's profile, financial goals, and values?
4. What should the financial planner attempt to accomplish during the client introductory meeting?

Establish and Define the Client Relationship

Communication with Client

The role of the financial planner is to educate the client, gather relevant information, analyze that information, and assist the client in preparing and implementing a financial plan that will achieve the client's financial goals within the desired time frame.

In order to educate the client and gather relevant information, the financial planner must be able to communicate effectively with the client. The planner must respect the client and establish a relationship of trust. The planner must be empathetic and assess the attitudes and values of the client as well as the client's risk tolerance and views regarding savings, spending, taxation, and financial discipline. Issues such as the importance of work versus leisure time, job security, community service, attitudes regarding children from previous marriages, former spouses, and the client's extended family all are important in understanding and assisting the client to achieve their goals.

Key Concepts

Underline/highlight the answers to these questions as you read:

1. What are the elements of the financial planning engagement letter?
2. What is the purpose of a financial planning client questionnaire?
3. What are types of necessary quantitative and qualitative data that is collected from the client?
4. What are examples of external environment data that a financial planner needs to know in order to properly analyze, evaluate, and make recommendations related to a comprehensive financial plan?

How does a planner effectively communicate with a client? From the onset, the financial planner should address the client formally (Mr., Mrs., Dr., etc.) using the appropriate salutation. This formality can be relaxed later in the relationship if the client is more comfortable with first names. The planner should actively listen to the client and especially to the verbs the client uses. This often indicates the client's learning style. Use of phrases such as "see what I mean," "imagine that," and any other words that imply that the client is a visual learner suggests that the planner should use examples including charts, graphs, and other visual aids to make the client more comfortable. If the client appears to pay attention to every spoken word or is asking for an explanation of words, the client's learning style is likely that of a verbal learner and graphics may be supplemented with carefully selected words. There is some data that suggests that up to 65 percent of people are visual learners. A generous use of pictures, graphs, and charts is always helpful in the communication process.

As a matter of professional courtesy, the financial planner should respect the client's time. This means being punctual, starting on time, ending on time, and telling the client how long each meeting will last. In order to establish a trusting relationship, the planner can generally share prior experiences. However, the planner must ensure that the client knows that client information is confidential by not identifying details about other clients.

The planner can show empathy by use of nonverbal pacing and showing a genuine interest in the hobbies, activities, vacations, and children of the client. To make communication effective, the financial planner can use restatement, paraphrasing, summarizing, open ended questions, and questions that show interest. This can assure minimal miscommunication allowing the planner to reach the pertinent details.

Introductory Meeting

If there has been little communication before the first meeting, the financial planner should at least provide the client with a list of documents and information that the client needs to provide for the first meeting (e.g., get to know each other, collect some data, answer questions, clarify goals, reduce fears). At the first meeting, the financial planner should assist the client with establishing defined goals and discuss how the client's values fit into those goals. There will also be a general discussion of the client's personal data and family data. Typically the planner will meet with either one, or preferably both spouses to get an overview of the family and extended family (e.g., ages, marital status, children, grandchildren, net worth, income, self employment). From this basic information the planner can make a preliminary assessment of the general risks and goals of the client.

The financial planner and client should mutually agree as to how they will communicate (e.g., email, office telephone, cell phone) and how often they will meet (e.g., 2 hours per week for 10 weeks). The client should be given a time frame for when the plan will be completed (e.g., 3 months). The financial planner should discuss the planning process, fees, and answer questions that the client is likely to have. The planner should effectively manage the client's expectations and have a remedy for instances when the client is dissatisfied. At the end of the introductory meeting, an engagement letter should be prepared and sent to the client for approval.

Engagement Letter

An engagement letter is a legal agreement (a contract) between a professional organization and a client that defines their business relationship. The engagement letter should define the parties to the agreement, the specific services to be provided, the duration of the agreement, the methods of communication (email, meetings), and the expected frequency of contact. The letter should also specify the conditions under which the agreement can be terminated.

Elements of an engagement letter:

- define the parties to the agreement
- a description of the mutually agreed upon services (the scope of work)
- the time horizon for the work to be completed
- a description of the fees and costs
- the obligation and responsibilities of each party (planner/client) regarding:
    - defining goals, needs, and objectives
    - gathering data
    - projecting the result of no action
    - formulating alternative possibilities
    - selecting from those alternatives
    - establishing who is expected to implement which elements of the plan (this can be subject to revision at the implementation phase of the process)
    - defining who has monitoring responsibilities
    - delineating services that are not provided, such as legal documents or income, gift, or estate tax return preparation

In addition to the above, there should be a mutual understanding regarding the use of proprietary products and/or other professionals or entities in meeting any of the service obligations in the engagement agreement.

Exhibit 1.2 Sample Engagement Letter

Sample Engagement Letter

Dear Client:

This letter will confirm the terms of our agreement regarding the financial planning services we will provide for you.

Engagement Objectives

The primary objective of our engagement is to review and analyze your personal financial situation and make recommendations for your financial plan. This review will identify your personal financial goals and objectives, and will include possible strategies to achieve them. Our analysis and recommendations are based on information provided by you that will be relied upon for representations.

Activities

The initial phase involves accumulating and organizing facts about your current financial status, identifying specific goals and objectives, and agreeing upon planning assumptions. This information will be obtained during an initial meeting or conversation with you and/or from the use of a financial planning data questionnaire. We will also review copies of pertinent documents, such as wills, company-provided fringe benefit booklets, prior tax returns, investment account statements, and insurance documents.

After the information has been received, the data will be analyzed and projections will be made. A subsequent meeting will be held to verify the accuracy of the data and will allow you to validate the assumptions used. Alternative courses of action to meet goals and address any issues will be comprehensively discussed.

The projections will then be updated for any required changes and a comprehensive financial planning report containing recommendations in all relevant areas of your financial situation will be presented. We will work with you to finalize the choice of strategies, to set time goals, and to establish responsibilities for your implementation of the plan.

The methods that you choose to follow for the implementation of the financial planning recommendations are at your discretion. You will be responsible for all decisions regarding implementation of the recommendations.

We are available, via a separate engagement, to assist you with implementation of your chosen strategies or to coordinate implementation with other financial professionals of your choosing. As part of this separate engagement, we can answer questions, monitor activities, or make new recommendations regarding your financial matters as circumstances change. In addition, we do not offer legal services such as will or trust preparation; however, we will be happy to refer you to a legal professional.

Your plan should be reviewed with us informally on a semiannual basis and more formally on an annual basis. These update sessions are essential so that adjustments can be made for changes in circumstances, economic conditions, and income, gift, or estate tax law revisions.

Sample Engagement Letter Continued

Fees

The fee for your Comprehensive Financial Plan has been determined by our mutual agreement and is $_________ which is due and payable upon return of this Engagement Letter. Please note that this fee is for the written financial plan alone and the plan shall contain all of our recommendations to you through the date of its delivery.

This agreement and fee does not provide for any product sales that may be offered at no obligation to you. This is a separate service that may be considered a conflict of interest because commissions and/or additional fees may be paid in connection with products purchased. We will inform you if there is any conflict of interest.

If additional conferences and interactions are beyond the scope of the services stated above, our fee for this service is based upon the time necessary to complete the additional agreed upon tasks. The agreed time allocated to accomplish additional tasks will be billed at our rate of $____ per hour.

We reserve the right to discontinue services if billings are not paid when due.

If at any time you are dissatisfied with our services, you may terminate this agreement. If you do so within three business days of your acceptance, you will receive a full refund. Subsequently, any fees that you have paid to us in advance will be charged for the time and effort that has been devoted, up to that termination time, to prepare your written report and any remaining balance will be refunded.

We anticipate beginning the engagement immediately. If this letter meets with your approval, please sign the enclosed copy in the space provided and return it to us in the enclosed envelope.

We thank you for the opportunity to be of service, and we welcome you as a valued client.

Sincerely,

Financial Planner

I/We agree to the above terms & conditions:

Client Signature: ______________________________ Date: ________________________

Client Signature: ______________________________ Date: ________________________

The Scope of the Engagement

A financial planning engagement can be very narrow or fully comprehensive. Activities that are typically part of a comprehensive plan include:

- Preparation and analysis of personal financial statements;
- A review of all risk management policies (including life, health, disability, long-term care, property and liability insurance) and what to do about any uncovered areas of risk;
- An evaluation of short-term financial goals including the emergency fund and debt management;
- The establishment of long-term goals including retirement, education funding, lump-sum (major) expenditures, and legacy planning including documents;
- An evaluation of the current investment portfolio with the objective of creating a new investment approach that helps to achieve the client's goals within the risk tolerance of the client; and
- An examination and recommendation regarding any special needs situation of the client (divorce, elderly parent, special needs child).

> ## *Quick Quiz 1.1*
>
> **Highlight the answer to these questions:**
>
> 1. Personal financial planning is the comprehensive process of formulating, implementing, and monitoring financial decisions that guide the client to achieve financial goals.
>   a. True
>   b. False
>
> 2. Long-term goal planning includes emergency funding, financial security planning, education planning, lump-sum purchase planning, and legacy planning.
>   a. True
>   b. False
>
> 3. At the introductory meeting, the financial planner will collect data, come to understand the client's values and goals, establish the scope of the engagement, and discuss fees.
>   a. True
>   b. False
>
> 4. Examples of internal data include current interest rates, housing market status, job market status, local cost of living, and the expected inflation rate.
>   a. True
>   b. False
>
> True, False, True, False.

GATHER CLIENT DATA

The Internal Data Collection Process

The planner must obtain sufficient information (both quantitative and qualitative) from the client in order to assess and analyze the client's financial situation. Quantitative information is measurable and includes the client's age, income, number of children, death benefit of life insurance policies, and much more. Qualitative information is how the client feels about something, or their attitude or belief, including working versus retiring and spending versus saving. The information includes client provided documents and may be obtained by the planner through the use of questionnaires and/or interviews. See Exhibit 1.3 for a basic sample of a client questionnaire. The planner will need to explore and evaluate the client's values, attitudes, expectations, and time horizons as they affect client goals, needs, and priorities.

Quantitative information collected must be complete, accurate, verifiable, and free from bias. The information to be collected will include:

- The family - list of members, their age, health, education, income, financial competence, and any special situations (e.g., special needs child, aging parents who are or may become dependents).
- The insurance portfolio - collect all insurance policies and a detailed description of any employer provided or sponsored insurance. Make sure to identify the premiums paid by the client (life, health, disability, long-term care, property including homeowners, flood, auto, boat, etc., and whether the client has a personal or professional liability policy).
- Banking and investment information - collect current statements on all bank accounts and investment accounts including qualified plans (IRAs, SEPs, SIMPLEs, 403(b)s, 457s). Obtain from the client any other investment information and their valuation, amount of debt and cash flows, such as rental property or business interests.
- Taxes - all income, gift and trust tax returns for the last five years if available.
- Retirement and Employee Benefits - all retirement information including Social Security statements or benefits, employer sponsored retirement plans, and employee benefits (get a copy of the booklets and summary description of plan).
- Estate Planning - all wills, durable powers of attorney for health care decisions, all advance medical directives and any trust documents.
- All personal financial statements if available including any recently used to obtain debt (balance sheet and income statement) - a list of debt with original amount, date of inception, interest rate, term of repayment and current balance. Most clients will not have financial statements and either the planner or a CPA will have to prepare them.

The financial planner also needs to collect qualitative information from the client. Qualitative information includes the client's attitude and beliefs regarding:

- Education goals,
- Retirement goals,
- Employment goals,
- Savings goals,
- Risk tolerance,
- Charitable goals, and
- General attitude towards spending.

The financial planner will request that the client bring all of the above information to the first meeting. Frequently, the client will not have all the quantitative information (such as insurance policies and employee benefits brochures) and rarely do clients have properly prepared personal financial statements. The engagement letter may be modified to include an addendum of missing information needed for later meetings.

EXHIBIT 1.3 SAMPLE FINANCIAL PLANNING QUESTIONNAIRE

Sample of a Financial Planning Client Questionnaire*

General Information:		**General Information:**	
Client 1 Full Name:		Client 2 Full Name:	
Home Address:		Home Address	
City, State, Zip:		City, State, Zip:	
Home Phone:		Home Phone:	
Work Phone:		Work Phone:	
Mobile Phone:		Mobile Phone:	
Occupation:		Occupation:	
Employer:		Employer:	
Annual Earned Income:		Annual Earned Income:	
Fax:		Fax:	
Email:		Email:	
Social Security #:		Social Security #:	
Birth date:		Birth date:	
Prior Marriage(s):		Prior Marriage(s):	
Family/Dependent Information:		**Family/Dependent Information:**	
Name:		Name:	
Relationship:		Relationship:	
Date of Birth:		Date of Birth:	
Social Security #:		Social Security #:	
Dependent:		Dependent:	
Resides:		Resides:	
Assets:	**Ownership: Client 1 or 2**	**Assets:**	**Ownership: Client 1 or 2**
Bank Account:		**Bank Account:**	
Account Number & Type:		Account Number & Type:	
Average Balance:		Average Balance:	
CD – Held:		**CD – Held:**	
Maturity:		Maturity:	
Value:		Value:	
Primary Residence:		**Secondary Residence:**	
Value:		Value:	
Automobile 1:		**Automobile 2:**	
Value:		Value:	
Retirement Accounts:		**Retirement Accounts:**	
Type/Ownership:		Type/Ownership:	
Held by:		Held by:	
Account Number:		Account Number:	
Value:		Value:	
Other Account:		**Other Account:**	
Account Number & Type:		Account Number & Type:	
Value:		Value:	

SAMPLE FINANCIAL PLANNING QUESTIONNAIRE CONTINUED

Insurance:	Ownership: Client 1 or 2	Insurance:	Ownership: Client 1 or 2
Health/Company:		**Health/Company:**	
Coverage/Cost:		Coverage/Cost:	
Disability/Company:		**Disability/Company:**	
Coverage/Cost:		Coverage/Cost:	
Life/Company:		**Life/Company:**	
Type/Coverage/Cost:		Type/Coverage/Cost:	
Homeowners:		**Homeowners:**	
Type/Coverage/Cost:		Type/Coverage/Cost:	
Auto:		**Auto:**	
Type/Coverage/Cost:		Type/Coverage/Cost:	
Umbrella Liability:		**Umbrella Liability:**	
Type/Coverage/Cost:		Type/Coverage/Cost:	
Professional Liability		**Professional Liability:**	
Type/Coverage/Cost:		Type/Coverage/Cost:	
Long Term Care:		**Long Term Care:**	
Type/Coverage/Cost:		Type/Coverage/Cost:	
Liabilities:	Client 1 or 2	**Liabilities:**	Client 1 or 2
Credit Card:		**Credit Card:**	
Monthly Pmt. /Balance:		Monthly Pmt. /Balance:	
Residence Loan:		**Residence Loan:**	
Monthly Pmt. /Balance:		Monthly Pmt. /Balance:	
Auto Loan:		**Auto Loan:**	
Monthly Pmt. /Balance:		Monthly Pmt. /Balance:	
Other Debt:		**Other Debt:**	
Monthly Pmt. /Balance:		Monthly Pmt. /Balance:	
Estate Issues:	Client 1 or 2	**Estate Issues:**	Client 1 or 2
Current Will: Y N		Current Will: Y N	
Living Will: Y N		Living Will: Y N	
Medical Power of Attorney: Y N		Medical Power of Attorney: Y N	
General Power of Attorney: Y N		General Power of Attorney: Y N	

Items that may be needed:
Prior Year Tax Returns
Brokerage Account Statements
Trust account Statements
Retirement Plan Account Statements
Loan Documents
Insurance Policies
Legal Documents

Current Advisors:
Attorney: ____________________
Accountant: ____________________
Insurance Agent: ____________________
Stockbroker: ____________________

Comment on advice you are seeking:
____
____
____

The External Data Collection Process

It is important that the planner is cognizant of the current external environmental data including the economic, legal, political, sociological, taxation and technological environment. This general knowledge may be obtained by taking various university courses, attending professional conferences, and reading professional and news related journals.

The financial planner should identify and document the following external information at the inception of the engagement:

- Interest rates
  - the current and prospective outlook including savings rates and mortgage rates
- Housing market - housing is a major asset but markets are local
  - what is the stock of available housing
  - is it a buyer's or seller's market
- Job market
  - what is the unemployment rate
- Investment market
  - current and prospective outlook
- Business cycle
  - peak, contraction, trough, expansion
  - where are we now
- Local insurance costs
  - housing, auto, liability
- Local cost of living
- Expected inflation rate, both short and long term
- Expected rate of increase in the prices of education and medical care
- Legislation that may impact certain industry sectors (e.g., healthcare)
- Current and expected income, gift, and estate tax rates

Analyzing and Evaluating the Client's Financial Status

Once the planner has collected internal and external data and mutually established the goals, needs, and priorities of the client, the planner will begin the analysis phase. This textbook goes into great detail using many financial planning approaches to analyze, evaluate, and make recommendations to the client. Specifically, Chapter 2 covers additional steps of the financial planning process including the analysis of the client's financial situation and the development and presentation of recommendations.

CHAPTER

Financial Planning Approaches: Analysis and Recommendations

2

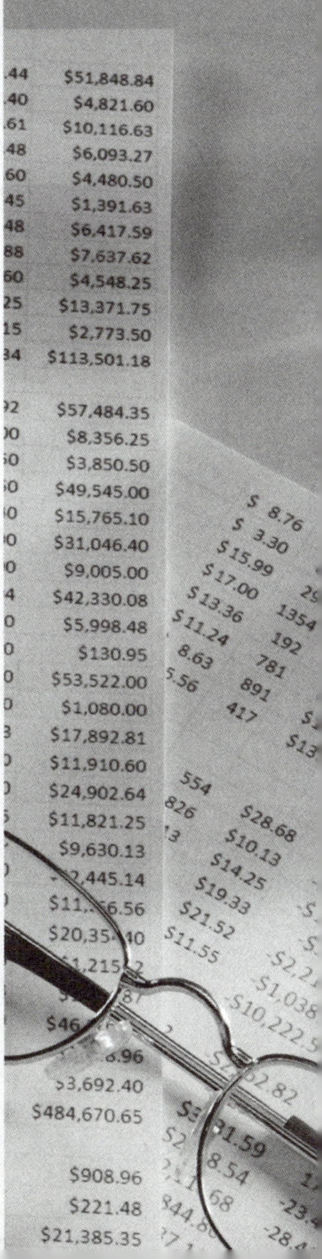

INTRODUCTION

Prior to developing and presenting financial plan recommendations to the client, the planner and client should mutually define the client's personal and financial goals, needs and priorities. The planner must keep the client's values, attitudes, expectations, and time horizons in mind as they affect the goals, needs, and priorities of the client.

Goals and objectives provide a roadmap for the financial planning process. Goals tend to be broad (such as having sufficient assets to retire), while objectives are more narrow and can effectively be subjected to measurement (e.g., $1,000,000 in investment assets by age 45).

In order to evaluate the extent to which the client's goals, needs, and priorities can be met by the client's current and future financial resources, the planner must collect and analyze both internal and external data.

REASONABLE ASSUMPTIONS

The planner, in consultation with the client, must establish reasonable assumptions, especially where projections will be used to determine if a goal can be achieved. Some of these assumptions include information about:

- What constitutes an adequate emergency fund (e.g., savings provisions).
- What is an appropriate emergency fund ratio (the number of months of coverage by cash and cash equivalents of non-discretionary cash flows).
- What are appropriate debt ratios - what is an appropriate benchmark for this client. When will the client be out of debt.
- What are the personal, property, and liability risks that the client faces and how best to cover those risks.
- What retirement benchmarks are to be used, including the retirement age, the percentage of pre-retirement income needed to maintain the retirement lifestyle, the retirement life expectancy, any legacy requirements, inflation rates, income tax

rates, and expected investment returns consistent with the client's risk tolerance and actual portfolio asset allocation.

- What estimates will be used to provide for any college education goals - ages of children, education inflation rate, current costs of relevant education.
- What estimates will be used to provide for any lump-sum funding goals - today's cost, the inflation rate, the amount needed to provide an adequate down payment.
- What estimates will be used to provide for legacy goals - defined in dollars (today's), the inflation rate, earnings rate, the expected estate and gift tax rates, exclusions, and exemptions (state and federal).

THE ANALYSIS

Once the financial planner has completed the initial financial planning process steps where the client relationship is established and the required data is collected, the practitioner can begin analyzing and evaluating the client's situation. Agreed upon assumptions can be taken into consideration, and financial planning approaches can be applied to arrive at plan recommendations. This chapter will focus on the following two steps of the financial planning process: (1) analyzing and evaluating the client's financial status and (2) developing and presenting financial planning recommendations.

EXHIBIT 2.1 **FINANCIAL PLANNING PROCESS**[1]

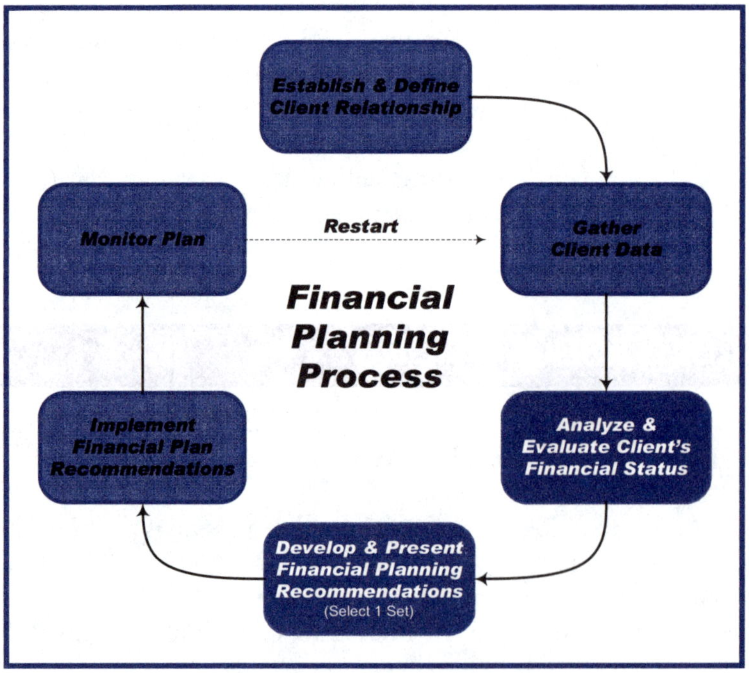

The purpose of the analysis is to identify any weaknesses in the plan and make recommendations which will assist the client to achieve their goals.

1. Abbreviated from the CFP Board's Financial Planning Practice Standards.

THE APPROACHES TO FINANCIAL PLANNING ANALYSIS AND RECOMMENDATIONS

There are a wide variety of possible approaches to analyzing, evaluating, and developing recommendations in the financial planning process. Each approach by itself is useful and provides the planner and client with a slightly different perspective of the collected data. Several of these approaches are identified and the benefits of each approach are briefly described below.

- The **life cycle approach** - Data collection is quick and simple and relatively non-threatening to the client. It provides the planner with a brief overview of the client's financial profile permitting the planner to have a relatively focused conversation with the client. It is generally used very early in the engagement.
- The **pie chart approach** - This approach provides a visual representation of how the client allocates financial resources. It provides a broad perspective on the client's financial status and it is generally used after the collection of internal data and the preparation of financial statements. For example, the balance sheet pie chart illustrates the relative size of liabilities and net worth to total assets, the relative size of cash/cash equivalents, and investment assets to total assets, and personal use assets to total assets. If a benchmark comparison pie chart from the metrics approach (discussed below) is added, it is often revealing for the client.
- The **financial statement and ratio analysis approach** - This approach helps to establish where the client is today. The ratio analysis provides an opportunity to assess the client's strengths, weaknesses, and deficiencies when the client's ratios are compared to benchmark metrics. The ratio approach usually follows the pie chart approach and provides the planner with the actual financial ratios with which to compare the benchmarks in the metrics approach.
- The **two-step/three-panel approach** - A step-by-step approach where the client's actual financial situation is compared against benchmark criteria. This approach is relatively thorough and presents a manageable approach to the client. It stresses the management of risk, seeks to avoid financial dependence, and promotes savings and investing to achieve financial independence.
- The **present value of goals approach** - This approach takes each short-term, intermediate-term, and long-term goal, determines its present value, then sums all of these together and treats them as an obligation to be reduced by current resources of investment assets and cash and cash equivalents. The resultant is the net future obligation to be retired over the remaining work life expectancy at the expected rate of return using an ordinary annuity. This annuity is then compared to the current annual savings amount post any implemented risk management and other recommendations, to determine whether the current savings amount is adequate to fund all goals. As part of determining the ability to save, a pre and post recommendations tax analysis must be preformed to determine whether the client is properly, over, or under withheld on income taxes.
- The **metrics approach** - This approach uses qualitative benchmarks which provide rules of thumb for a measurement of where a client's financial profile should be.

When combined with the two-step/three-panel approach, metrics help establish objectives that are measurable compared to ratio analysis.

- The **cash flow approach** - This approach takes an income statement approach to recommendations. It uses the three-panel approach and uses a pro forma approach (as if) "to purchase" the recommendations thus driving down the discretionary cash flow. Next, positive cash flows or the sale of assets are identified to finance the recommendations.
- The **strategic approach** - This approach uses a mission, goal, and objective approach considering the internal and external environment and may be used with other approaches.

Using any single approach described above will not likely be adequate to develop a comprehensive financial plan. Employing all of the approaches will likely create some redundancy but considered together will probably produce a comprehensive financial plan that is effective for the client. While a beginner planner may want to use all of the approaches, an experienced financial planner will find it sufficient to use a select few. For example, it is usually essential in any comprehensive plan to use the cash flow approach because it requires the client to prioritize and monetize each recommendation and determine the overall financial impact of the recommendation on the financial statements. Also, the cash flow approach clarifies the resources to be used and whether they are currently sufficient to implement the recommendations or whether some recommendations will have to be deferred until additional resources are available. Experienced financial planners will combine approaches depending on the preferences of the planner and the needs of the client.

Key Concepts

Underline/highlight the answers to these questions as you read:

1. What are the assumptions that the financial planner and client need to consider when developing a comprehensive financial plan?
2. Identify the seven approaches to financial planning analysis and recommendations.
3. What are the types of information the financial planner gathers and analyzes using the life cycle approach?
4. Identify the three phases of the life cycle approach along with each phase's likely risks and goals.

Exhibit 2.2 portrays common characteristics, by age group, of individuals with typical financial risks and goals. Financial planners should be familiar with these typical characteristics so that their particular client's financial wants, needs, and goals can be anticipated.

Common Client Profiles and Their Typical Life Cycle Factors, Financial Risks, and Goals (These are selected and not intended to be exhaustive)

Exhibit 2.2

Life Cycle Factors							
Age	22-30	25-35	25-35	35-45	45-55	55-65	65-75
Marital Status	Single	Married**	Married	Married	Married	Married	Married
Children* **	No	No	Yes	Yes	Yes	Yes	Yes
Grandchildren* **	No	No	No	No	No	Yes	Yes
Income	$35-$75k	$35-$75k	$45-$100k	$50-$150k	$75-$200k	$100-$200k	$50-$200k
Net Worth	$10-$20k	$10-$20k	$15-$25k	$20-$40k	$50-$100k	$500-$1,200k	$400-$1,500k
Self Employed	No	No	No	No	Yes	Maybe	No
Typical Risks/Insurance Coverage Needs							
Life Insurance	No	Maybe	Yes	Yes	Yes	Yes	No
Disability	Yes	Yes	Yes	Yes	Yes	Yes	No
Health	Yes	Yes	Yes	Yes	Yes	Yes	Yes
Long-Term Care*	No	No	No	No	No	Maybe Yes	Maybe Yes
Property	Yes	Yes	Yes	Yes	Yes	Yes	Yes
Liability	Yes	Yes	Yes	Yes	Yes	Yes	Yes
Typical Goals							
Retirement Security	Yes	Yes	Yes	Yes	Yes	Yes	In Retirement
Education Funding	No	No	Yes	Yes	Yes	No	No
Gifting	No	No	No	No	No	Yes	Yes
Lump-Sum Expenses	Yes	Yes	Yes	Yes	Yes	Yes	No
Legacy	No	No	No	No	No	Maybe	Maybe

* While younger clients will not typically require long-term care insurance, in some circumstances long-term care may be appropriate.

** Married could be married, divorced, or widow(er).

*** Children and grandchildren are always yes, no, or maybe.

THE LIFE CYCLE APPROACH

Using this approach, the planner gathers and analyzes the following information:

- the ages of client and spouse;
- the client's marital status;
- the number and ages of children and grandchildren;
- the family income by each contributor;
- the family net worth; and
- whether the client is employed, unemployed, self-employed, or retired.

The life cycle approach is a very broad view of the client financial profile and is best employed to provide general information with which to focus a financial discussion with the client when the financial planner only has partial information. For example, a married couple with small children will probably have a goal to save for the college education of their children. Meanwhile they should be concerned about certain other risks such as their untimely death or disability. The life cycle approach gives the planner a 60-75 percent perspective of the risks the client is likely to be concerned about and their likely goals and serves as a foundation for a dialog with the client.

It should be emphasized that there are no absolutes in personal financial planning. Each client is unique. Having said that, many clients fit into similar profiles (see Exhibit 2.2). The ages of the spouses may give an indication as to what phase of life the client is in, as defined below.

- The **asset accumulation phase** usually occurs in the early 20s to mid 50s when discretionary cash flow for investing is low and the debt to net worth ratio is high.
- The **conservation (risk management) phase** usually occurs from the late 20s to the early 70s, where cash flow, assets, and net worth have increased and debts have decreased somewhat. In addition, risk management of events like unemployment, disability due to illness or accident, and untimely death become a priority.
- The **distribution (gifting) phase** usually occurs from the mid 40s to the end of life and is characterized by the individual having high cash flow, low debt, and high net worth.

The client's life cycle phase helps the planner to understand the client's risks and likely goals. It is entirely possible for a given client to be in two or even all three of these phases at the same time. When special circumstances occur, such as the untimely death of a spouse, the conservation phase may come before the asset accumulation phase for a particular client.

Life Cycles

Exhibit 2.3

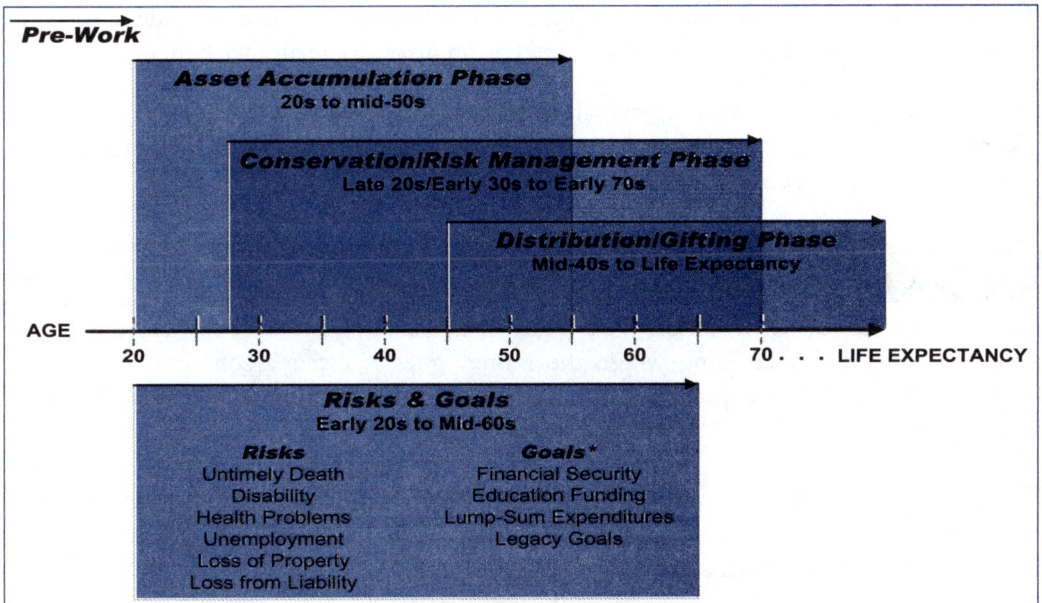

*Financial security means retirement with adequate income to maintain lifestyle.

If the client is married, the couple typically files a joint income tax return and relies on both incomes for the payment of family expenses (such as a home mortgage, auto loans, etc.). This situation creates a life insurance and disability insurance need for each spouse. The fact that a client has young children signals a need for life insurance and disability insurance, regardless of the parent's marital status. Young children may also indicate a client's need for college education funding. If a client has grandchildren, gifts, tuition payment plans, and other transfers during life (gifts) or at death (bequests) to or for grandchildren may be a consideration. Older clients may also be thinking about estate planning needs.

The planner should conduct a comprehensive review of the insurance portfolio for all clients (especially for those in the risk management phase), including the use of life insurance, health insurance, disability insurance, long-term care insurance, and property and liability insurance.

Other client profile characteristics that give insight into the client's needs include:

- Any client that is simultaneously in the accumulation and conservation phase has financial security (retirement) as a long-term goal.
- Generally, the higher a client's net worth and the greater a client's income, the more interest that client has in income tax minimization.
- If a client is self-employed, it creates opportunities to use employer-sponsored retirement plans to assist that client in accomplishing long-term financial security goals.

Analyzing client data to achieve long-term financial goals takes time. Achieving those financial goals takes persistent savings, and good investment returns. Unfortunately, risks that are insured against like untimely death, disability, health issues, and loss of property or personal liability are unexpected events that can occur at any time. An uninsured loss can destroy even the best conceived savings and investment plan. Therefore, clients need to make risk management their top priority. A great retirement investment plan with a time horizon of 30 years that relies on persistent savings and investment returns can be derailed if the client becomes disabled before retirement and has no disability insurance benefits.

The life cycle approach provides financial planners a broad overview of the client's probable risks and likely goals. It is a good place to start, but it lacks the specifics to direct the planner to develop a detailed, comprehensive financial plan.

THE PIE CHART APPROACH

A pie chart focuses the client on the relative size of financial variables. People can only spend what they have and visualizing where the money goes is often a sobering, but helpful experience. The pie chart approach is an effective analytical and illustrative tool for financial planning clients.

The pie chart approach provides the planner and the client with separate pictorial representations of the balance sheet and the statement of income and expenses. These financial statements are discussed in detail in Chapter 3.

The financial statements are prepared first and then depicted in pie charts. One set of pie charts is for the statement of income and expenses (income statement) and the other set is for the balance sheet (statement of financial position). Note that the statement of income and expenses (income statement) is also referred to as the cash flow statement. For purposes of this textbook, it is not referred to as the cash flow statement because not all cash flows are included in the statement (such as inheritance of cash). The pie chart approach generally uses percentages of the whole, but can use a dollar approach. The percentage approach is usually more effective for comparison purposes.

INCOME STATEMENT PIE CHART

The questions that the pie chart approach addresses are:

- What percentage of gross pay is the client paying in taxes (income and Social Security)?
- What percentage of the client's gross pay are they saving?
- What percentage of the client's gross pay goes to protection (insurance)?
- What percentage of the client's gross pay is spent on basic housing costs (principal, interest, tax, and insurance or rent plus insurance)?
- What percentage of the client's gross pay is spent on debt repayments both excluding housing costs and including housing costs?
- What percentage of the client's gross pay is left to live on?

Key Concepts

Underline/highlight the answers to these questions as you read:

1. Identify the financial planning usefulness of the income statement pie chart.
2. What are the questions that the balance sheet pie chart should answer and illustrate?
3. Identify the reason for creating benchmark pie charts.

For example, the following sample income statement pie chart reflects total living expenses of 54 percent (housing costs 25% plus other living expenses). This is useful information for the planner to analyze considering a client's other characteristics (e.g., age, gross pay, risks, etc.). To build the pie chart, the planner calculates the client's expenses from the income statement as a proportion of the client's gross pay and portrays them in the income statement pie chart.

INCOME STATEMENT PIE CHART

EXHIBIT 2.4

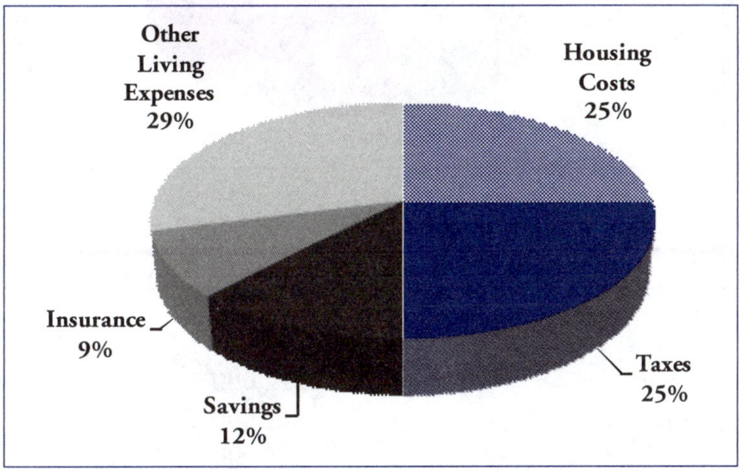

There are many flexible and creative ways to make a pie chart. One useful way is total income arrayed by percentage of:

- savings,
- housing costs,
- other debt payments (ODP),
- insurance other than property insurance,
- all other living costs (OLC),
- taxes other than property taxes, and
- net discretionary cash flows (DCF), presuming that they are positive.

One shortcoming of the pie chart approach, however, is that it is difficult to depict negative cash flows in pie charts.

EXAMPLE 2.1

Assume a client has gross pay of $100,000 and expenses as listed in the table below. The data can be reflected in an income statement pie chart, allowing the client to visualize his financial situation as pertains to income and expenses.

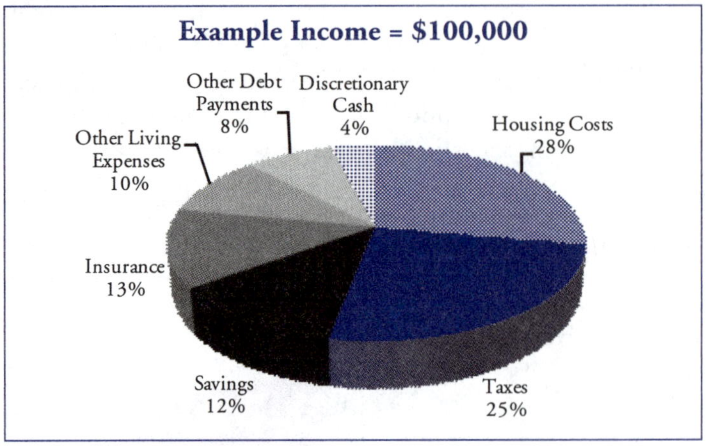

	Amount	Percentage
Gross Income	$100,000	100%
Taxes	$25,000	25%
Savings	$12,000	12%
Insurance	$13,000	13%
Housing Costs	$28,000	28%
Other Debt Payments (ODP)	$8,000	8%
Other Living Costs (OLC)	$10,000	10%
Discretionary Cash Flow (DCF)	$4,000	4%

It is easy to depict on an income statement pie chart with the percentages that a client is paying for taxes, saving for the future, and paying insurance premiums (25% + 12% + 13% = 50%) to protect the client's assets that have or will be accumulated. That leaves approximately 50 percent of the current income for current living expenses, 10-28 percent of which is typically allocated to housing or shelter costs. Exhibit 2.5 gives targeted example benchmarks for various income statement items.

The pie chart approach assists the planner and client by illustrating if the client is spending too much on debt repayment or too much on housing that may result in either undersaving or being underinsured. The financial planner can then present benchmark pie charts that illustrate where a client should be in order to meet typical goals and objectives.

Income Statement Targeted Example Benchmarks

Exhibit 2.5

	Targeted Example Benchmarks
Taxes (income and payroll)	15 - 30%
Savings (future asset protection)	10 - 18%
Protection (insurance) (past and future asset protection)	5 - 12%
Living - Present	40 - 60%
Housing (Rent or Mortgage Payment)	≤ 28%
Housing and Other Debt Payments	≤ 36%

*These are very general and vary widely among individuals.

The pie chart depiction of the income statement provides the planner with an opportunity to discuss with the client where the client is currently from a financial point of view. If the benchmark pie chart is agreed to, a step by step plan to get from the current situation to the benchmark can be established.

> *Quick Quiz 2.1*
>
> **Highlight the answer to these questions:**
>
> 1. The life cycle approach utilizes liquidity ratios to analyze the client's financial situation.
>   a. True
>   b. False
>
> 2. The pie chart approach provides a pictorial representation of the balance sheet and the statement of income and expenses.
>   a. True
>   b. False
>
> False, True.

Balance Sheet Pie Chart

The questions that the pie chart approach addresses include, what percentage of total assets are in the form of:

- cash and cash equivalents?
- investment assets?
- personal use assets?
- current liabilities?
- long-term liabilities?
- net worth?

The balance sheet pie chart is portrayed in two pie charts, one for the asset side of the balance sheet and the other for the liabilities and net worth side of the balance sheet. The asset pie chart is broken down into three categories: cash and cash equivalents, investment assets, and personal use assets.

EXHIBIT 2.6 **BALANCE SHEET PIE CHART**

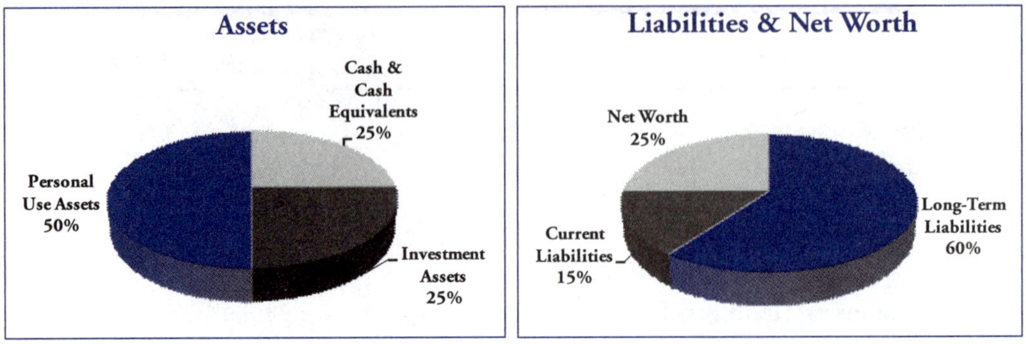

Assume a client has assets (and liabilities and net worth) totalling $300,000. The balance sheet data can be reflected in the following pie charts.

EXHIBIT 2.7 **CLIENT SAMPLE BALANCE SHEET PIE CHART**

Assets = 100%		
Cash & Cash Equivalents	$30,000	10%
Investment Assets	$120,000	40%
Personal Use Assets	$150,000	50%
	$300,000	100%

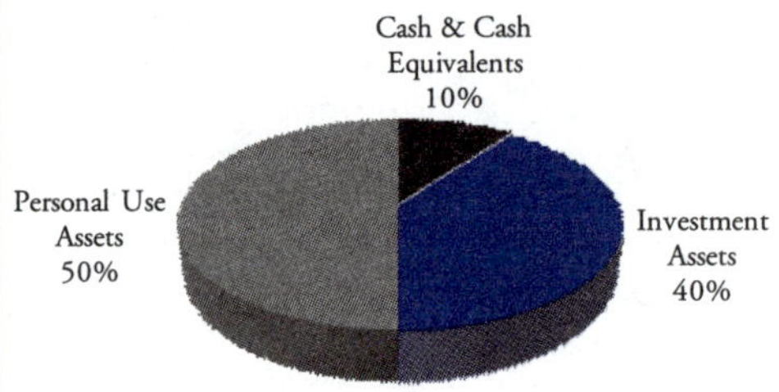

Liabilities & Net Worth = 100%		
Current Liabilities	$75,000	25%
Long-Term Liabilities	$150,000	50%
Net Worth	$75,000	25%
	$300,000	100%

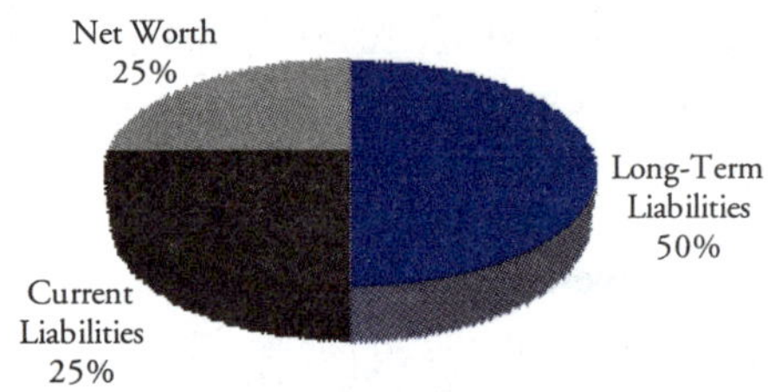

Regardless of the amount of total assets, a portion of assets should be in cash and cash equivalents and a portion should be in investment assets. The percentage needed in cash and cash equivalents is functionally related to the non-discretionary cash outflows on the income statement. The percentage that should be in investment assets is functionally related to the age of the client and the gross pay (See Exhibit 2.8).

The liabilities (both short term and long term) are then integrated into a separate pie chart opposite the assets, along with the client's net worth. If net worth is negative, the client is technically insolvent and the pie charts for the balance sheet may be unreliable.

The planner can compare the age of the client, the gross pay, and non-discretionary cash flows to create additional information from the pie chart. However, even before creating a benchmark pie chart for the example client, we already know that cash and cash equivalents are only 40 percent of current liabilities (10% ÷ 25%) and total debt represents 75 percent of all assets (25% + 50%) with net worth representing only 25 percent of assets (See Exhibit 2.7).

Keeping benchmarks in mind, given a client's characteristics, the financial planner can develop balance sheet benchmark pie charts to use to compare to the client's actual pie charts. This creates the opportunity to have a quick and high level discussion of where the client is currently and where the client should be based on appropriate benchmarks.

The following exhibit provides typical benchmark goals by age range for a client's balance sheet.

An Estimate of Balance Sheet Targeted Benchmarks by Ages

Exhibit 2.8

		20s - 30s	40s - 50s	60s - 70s
Assets*	Cash & Cash Equivalents	5 - 20%	5 - 20%	5 - 20%
	Investment Assets	0 - 30%	30 - 60%	60 - 70%
	Personal Use Assets	55 - 90%	25 - 60%	15 - 30%
Liabilities*	Current Liabilities	10 - 20%	10 - 20%	0 - 10%
	Long-Term Liabilities	40 - 72%	16 - 48%	8 - 24%
Net Worth*	Net Worth	8 - 50%	32 - 74%	66 - 82%

* A more detailed description of each category is provided in Chapter 3. These can vary widely.

Financial Planning Assumptions for Exhibit 2.8

Assumptions	
Inflation and Raises	3%
Investment Returns	8.5%
Savings Rate	11.5%*
Retirement Accumulation	18 times pre-retirement income**

*Average Savings Rate = 10-13%; Savings Rate = 11.5% of gross pay.

**Produces an initial wage replacement ratio of 72% of pre-retirement income at retirement at a 4% withdrawal rate (a 4% withdrawal rate is considered a relatively safe withdrawal rate as determined by current research).

Pie charts are very effective tools for helping the client to see pictorially and to understand (especially if the client is a visual learner) where their assets are deployed in cash, in investment assets, or for maintaining their current lifestyle (personal use assets) in retirement.

Summary Regarding the Life Cycle and Pie Chart Approaches

The life cycle and pie chart approaches are generally used in the preliminary stages of an engagement to get a general idea of the client and/or to present, in the case of the pie chart approach, a graphical picture of the current and general benchmark situation. These are generally not used for detailed analysis.

THE FINANCIAL STATEMENT AND RATIO ANALYSIS APPROACH

The purpose of calculating and presenting financial ratios is to provide useful planning information to the user. The financial statement and ratio analysis approach uses financial ratios to help clarify and reveal the true financial situation of a client. The approach uses four types of ratios:

- **Liquidity ratios:** measures the client's ability to meet short-term obligations.
- **Debt ratios:** indicates how well the client manages debt.
- **Ratios for financial security goals:** indicates the progress that the client is making toward achieving long-term financial security goals.
- **Performance ratios:** indicates the adequacy of returns on investments, given the risks taken by the client.

Key Concepts

Underline/highlight the answers to these questions as you read:

1. Identify the purpose of evaluating liquidity ratios used in the financial statement and ratio analysis approach.
2. Identify the difference between discretionary and non-discretionary cash flows.

The information covered in this section is an overview and introduction to financial statement and ratio analysis as one method of analyzing, evaluating, and making financial planning recommendations to a client. **A more detailed explanation of financial statements and financial statement analysis is covered in Chapter 3.** For now, a high level overview of this approach is discussed in this chapter.

Key Concepts

Underline/highlight the answers to these questions as you read:

1. What information is provided by housing ratio 1 and housing ratio 2 and what are the benchmarks for both ratios?
2. How is the savings rate calculated and what are the typical benchmarks for this ratio?
3. Identify the usefulness of the performance ratios.

LIQUIDITY RATIOS

The emergency fund ratio and the current ratio are the two most common financial ratios used to provide meaningful information for measuring the ability to meet short-term obligations.

Emergency Fund Ratio

$$\text{Emergency Fund Ratio} = \frac{\text{Cash \& Cash Equivalents}}{\text{Monthly Non-Discretionary Cash Flows}} = 3 - 6 \text{ Months}$$

The emergency fund ratio determines the number of months of non-discretionary cash flows (income statement items) the client can pay with current liquidity. The risks covered by an emergency fund are those arising from loss of employment, injury, or some other unexpected occurrence. The benchmark is three-to-six months of non-discretionary cash flow coverage. However, this benchmark is highly dependent on the individual client's situation and the job market at the time of the financial emergency. Therefore, the benchmark should be used cautiously and revised accordingly for a particular client and a particular economic climate. For example, a specialty job may require more than six months for a job seeker to replace, especially for an older worker. On the other hand, a tenured faculty member at a university may be in a low risk situation and would not necessarily need an emergency fund of three months of non-discretionary cash flows. The elimination period of a client's disability policy should also be considered when selecting an emergency fund ratio target.

Definition of Terms

An evaluation of a client's monthly expenses is necessary for the calculation of emergency fund coverage. Discretionary versus non-discretionary cash flows must be identified to estimate the monthly expenses that must be met. Discretionary cash flows are those expenses that can be avoided in the event of loss of income, whereas non-discretionary cash flows are mostly fixed monthly obligations and expenses that are required to be met regardless of the loss of income.

DISCRETIONARY CASH FLOWS VS. NON-DISCRETIONARY CASH FLOWS — **EXHIBIT 2.9**

Common Non-discretionary Cash Flows	Common Cash Flows that may be either Discretionary or Non-discretionary	Common Discretionary Cash Flows
Mortgage Loan	Charitable Contributions	Entertainment
Auto Loan	Church Donations	Vacations
Credit Cards	Lawn Service	Satellite or Cable TV
Life Insurance	Child Care	
Health Insurance		
Auto Insurance		
Homeowners (or Renters) Insurance		
Tuition and Education Expenses		
Property Taxes		
Food		
Auto Maintenance		
Utilities		
Clothing		

While many costs may have both a fixed and variable (controllable) component (e.g., utilities), what the financial planner is looking for is an idea of how many months of coverage exists for those costs that the client considers to be non-discretionary. Ordinarily, income taxes and payroll taxes are not included in the determination of discretionary versus non-discretionary cash flows because the most likely risk triggering the use of the emergency fund is the loss of employment income. However, the financial planner calculating non-discretionary expenditures should consider whether the client is unemployed and if the client is receiving unemployment benefits (unemployment benefits are subject to federal income tax, but not payroll taxes). In addition, some clients who have lost jobs have either outstanding 401(k) plan or other qualified plan loans, which will be treated as a taxable distribution if the loan is not repaid shortly after termination. Still some clients who find themselves unemployed exhaust their qualified plan balance in such a way as to make the distributions subject to both federal and state income tax. The planner should decide whether any of the above should be considered in the determination of non-discretionary expenses.

Current Ratio

$$\text{Current Ratio} = \frac{\text{Cash \& Cash Equivalents}}{\text{Current Liabilities}}$$

The current ratio provides insight into the client's ability to meet short-term obligations as they come due. Current liabilities represent those liabilities that will be paid within the next year. A larger current ratio implies more liquidity and thus a greater ability to pay current liabilities as they come due. It may appear that there is a liquidity problem when the current ratio is less than 1. However, most individuals pay their current liabilities and associated interest out of their current income (statement of income) and not out of their cash and cash equivalents (balance sheet). Therefore, to the extent this is true, a current ratio that is less than 1 may be adequate.

It also should be noted that the current ratio can be modified by adding the net positive discretionary cash flow to the numerator, which should provide a better measure of liquidity over a period of time. Of course if net expected discretionary cash flow from the projected income statements is negative, it would have to be subtracted from cash and cash equivalents to provide a clearer picture of liquidity using the current ratio.

Debt Ratios

There are four debt ratios used in the financial statement and ratio analysis approach to help the planner determine how well the client manages debt:

- the housing ratio 1 (basic),
- the housing ratio 2 (broad),
- the debt to total assets ratio, and
- the net worth to total assets ratio.

Housing Ratio 1 (Basic)

$$\text{Housing Ratio 1} = \frac{\text{Housing Costs}}{\text{Gross Pay}} \leq 28\%$$

Housing costs include principal payment on the mortgage (or alternately rent), interest, homeowners insurance, property taxes, and association dues, if applicable.

The purpose of housing ratio 1 (HR1) is to calculate the percentage of gross pay that is devoted to basic housing. It does not include utilities, lawn care, maintenance, etc. The benchmark for housing ratio 1 is less than or equal to 28 percent. Generally, a housing ratio 1 of 28 percent or less is the initial ratio necessary for a first time home buyer to qualify for a conforming (best) rate mortgage. The conforming rate mortgage generally requires a 20 percent down payment and good credit. Assuming that the mortgage interest rate is fixed and amortized over 15 or 30 years, then as inflation causes salaries and housing values to increase, housing ratio 1 should decline gradually.

The housing ratio 1 benchmark is used traditionally by mortgage lenders to issue conforming (best) rate mortgages. Note that the ratio should decline to roughly five percent (although not in a state with very high property taxes, such as Texas) at retirement, when the mortgage is assumed to be completely paid off and only taxes, association dues, and insurance expenses continue.

Housing Ratio 2 (Broad)

$$\text{Housing Ratio 2} = \frac{\text{Housing Costs + Other Debt Payments}}{\text{Gross Pay}} \leq 36\%$$

Housing ratio 2 (HR2) combines basic housing costs (HR1) with all other monthly debt payments, including payments for automobile loans, student loans, bank loans, revolving consumer loans, credit card payments, and any other debt payments made on a recurring basis. The housing ratio 2 benchmark is less than or equal to 36 percent of gross pay. The planner should be cautious when considering the client's credit card payments for purposes of this ratio. If the client is only making minimum payments on credit cards, the payback period for such debt could be 17 years or longer, depending on the relationship between the interest rate, the minimum payments, and the original balance. In the situation where a client is only making minimum credit card payments, then the planner should calculate a payment using the interest rate on the card that would retire the credit card debt in 36 to 60 months. The planner can then use that payment for this calculation, rather than the minimum payment the client is actually making, so as to avoid underestimating the relevant ratio. Credit card statements are now required to disclose this type of comparison and may save the planner time and effort.

Debt to Total Assets Ratio

$$\text{Debt to Total Assets Ratio} = \frac{\text{Total Debt}}{\text{Total Assets}} = \text{Benchmark Depends on Client Age}$$

The debt to total assets ratio is essentially a leverage ratio. It reflects what portion of assets owned by a client are financed by creditors. Usually, young people establishing themselves have relatively high debt ratios due to the presence of automobile and student loans. First time home buyers generally have high ratios, even with a 20 percent down payment (implying an 80% mortgage). This ratio, like all other ratios, is best considered over time to monitor the client's progress. This ratio is commonly as high as 80 percent for young people and as low as 10 percent or less for those near retirement age.

Net Worth to Total Assets Ratio

$$\text{Net Worth to Total Assets Ratio} = \frac{\text{Net Worth}}{\text{Total Assets}} = \text{Benchmark Depends on Client Age}$$

The net worth to total assets ratio is the complement of the debt to assets ratio described above. The two add up to one (i.e., as debt declines as a percent of total assets, net worth rises). This ratio provides the planner with the percentage of total assets owned or paid for by the client. It is not surprising that this would be 20 percent for young people and up to 90 to 100 percent for retirement age clients. This ratio once again is best observed over time. Note that the net worth increases as assets increase in value (home and investments) and also increases with additional savings and with the payoff of obligations (liabilities).

RATIOS FOR FINANCIAL SECURITY GOALS

Ratios for financial security goals help the financial planner to assess the progress that the client is making toward achieving long-term goals. The two most common ratios used to assess that progress are the savings rate and the investment assets to gross pay ratio.

Savings Rate

$$\text{Savings Rate} = \frac{\text{Savings + Employer Match}}{\text{Gross Pay}} = \begin{matrix}\text{Benchmark Depends}\\ \text{on Client Goals}\end{matrix}$$

An appropriate savings rate is critical to achieving long-term goals including retirement, education funding, large lump-sum expenditures (e.g., second home), and legacy plans. The savings rate is calculated by dividing gross savings in dollars, employee elective deferrals into 401(k), 403(b), and 457 plans plus any employer match), and any other savings, by gross pay. The savings rate benchmark depends on the number of long-term goals of the client. If the only goal of the client is financial security (retirement) the benchmark savings rate should be 10 to 13 percent of gross pay. The persistent savings rate needed for a 25-year old with retirement as his only goal should be 10 to 13 percent, excluding Social Security contributions.

If the client has multiple long-term goals, the savings rate must be greater than 10 to 13 percent to meet those goals. For example, a couple, both age 25, earning $75,000 annually with newborn twins who they plan to send to an in-state college for four years, would need a savings rate of 10 to 13 percent for retirement plus an additional two to three percent for education for a combined savings rate of 12 to 16 percent. The education savings rate is dependent on the type of school their children will attend (in-state / lower costs, private / medium costs, or private / higher costs) and the income level of the client because the savings rate for tuition declines as income increases because tuition is a fixed dollar amount.

Relationship Between Time, Savings, and Withdrawal Rates on Retirement Planning

The following three scenarios will help to illustrate the intricate nature of the savings rate on the retirement capital balance and how they impact the withdrawal rate and the required rate of earnings needed during retirement. The first scenario assumes the client saves for 40 years, while the second scenario assumes 30 years of savings and finally, the third scenario assumes 20 years of savings.

Each of the scenarios assumes a **real rate of return** while saving of 5%, which is reasonable over a long period of time. However, adjusting this rate up or down will have a significant effect on the final result. These scenarios also assume a retirement life expectancy of 30 years, which is very conservative for most of the population.[1]

The first scenario assumes a wage replacement ratio of 80%. The wage replacement ratio for scenarios 2 and 3 have been reduced from the original 80% to 70% and 60% respectively, to make the models work with a reasonable required **real rate of return** during retirement. Effectively, clients who begin saving later in life are less likely to be able to fund a larger annual withdrawal amount as compared to someone who begins saving at an earlier age. Social Security has purposely been left out of this analysis.

1. Scenarios 1, 2, and 3 assume that savings are made at the end of the year (ordinary annuity) and that withdrawals are made at the beginning of the year (annuity due).

Scenario 1

Annual Savings	Annual Savings Rate	Retirement Capital Balance	Annual Needs at Retirement	Required Withdrawal Rate	Required Real Rate of Return
$18,000	18%	$2,174,396	$80,000	3.68%	0.70%
$16,000	16%	$1,932,796	$80,000	4.14%	1.57%
$14,000	14%	$1,691,197	$80,000	4.73%	2.62%
$13,000	**13%**	**$1,570,397**	**$80,000**	**5.09%**	**3.24%**
$12,000	**12%**	**$1,449,597**	**$80,000**	**5.52%**	**3.93%**
$11,000	11%	$1,328,798	$80,000	6.02%	4.73%
$10,000	10%	$1,207,998	$80,000	6.62%	5.65%

Scenario 1 illustrates a person 25 years of age saving about 12% to 13% of his income for 40 years and accumulating approximately $1.5 million. The result is that he is able to meet an 80% wage replacement ratio with a reasonable required real rate of return during retirement. At a 13% savings rate, the $80,000 needs at retirement translate to a 5.09% withdrawal rate. To maintain this withdrawal throughout retirement, a real return of 3.24% would have to be earned. If inflation were 3%, this would equate to a 6.3% nominal return, still quite conservative. The calculation of the required real return assumes he has spent all of his capital at the end of the 30 year period.

Scenario 2

Annual Savings	Annual Savings Rate	Retirement Capital Balance	Annual Needs at Retirement	Required Withdrawal Rate	Required Real Rate of Return
$25,000	25%	$1,660,971	$70,000	4.21%	1.71%
$24,000	24%	$1,594,532	$70,000	4.39%	2.02%
$23,000	23%	$1,528,093	$70,000	4.58%	2.36%
$22,000	22%	$1,461,655	$70,000	4.79%	2.72%
$21,000	**21%**	**$1,395,216**	**$70,000**	**5.02%**	**3.11%**
$20,000	**20%**	**$1,328,777**	**$70,000**	**5.27%**	**3.52%**
$19,000	19%	$1,262,338	$70,000	5.55%	3.98%

Scenario 2 illustrates a person 35 years of age required to save closer to 20% of his income to drive a retirement plan with a 70% wage replacement ratio. It appears that the 20% savings rate is adequate to drive a reasonable withdrawal rate and required rate of return. Note that this person has started saving 10 years later and can only sustain an annual retirement annuity of $70,000, which is $10,000 less than the result in scenario 1.

Scenario 3

Annual Savings	Annual Savings Rate	Retirement Capital Balance	Annual Needs at Retirement	Required Withdrawal Rate	Required Real Rate of Return
$30,000	**30%**	**$991,979**	**$60,000**	**6.05%**	**4.77%**
$29,000	**29%**	**$958,913**	**$60,000**	**6.26%**	**5.10%**
$28,000	28%	$925,847	$60,000	6.48%	5.44%
$27,000	27%	$892,781	$60,000	6.72%	5.80%
$26,000	26%	$859,715	$60,000	6.98%	6.19%
$25,000	25%	$826,649	$60,000	7.26%	6.60%
$24,000	24%	$793,583	$60,000	7.56%	7.04%

Scenario 3 illustrates a person 45 years of age with only 20 years to save for retirement. In this scenario, 20 years of savings is driving a 30 year withdrawal period. The result of this scenario is that the required savings rate is very high and the wage replacement ratio is significantly less than the results in scenario 1 or 2.

The above three scenarios clearly illustrate the importance of the timing of savings and the duration of savings. These scenarios were based on a constant real rate of return of 5%, however investment returns are not constant or linear in financial markets. Rather, there are ups and downs and when returns are down, the account balance at retirement (e.g., if negative returns occur for the three years preceding retirement) can be significantly impacted.

Negative portfolio returns can also seriously damage an investment plan if they occur shortly after retirement when there are no additional savings to be added to the plan. In such a case, there are both withdrawals and negative portfolio returns exacerbating the reduction in the account balance of the retirement fund. This kind of situation increases the probability of running out of money before the end of life (superannuation).

There are a few ways to mitigate the risk of superannuation. Options before retirement include saving more and beginning to save at an earlier age. Saving more means saving based on a model such as the purchasing power preservation model or working a few extra years to make certain that the capital balance is sufficient to adequately fund retirement. In addition, it is important to have investment returns that provide a sufficient real rate of return. Equities are an important element of a portfolio that is attempting to generate a positive real rate of return. Once in retirement, the primary way to mitigate the risk of superannuation is to maintain a relatively low withdrawal rate and have a balanced portfolio that can withstand unexpected fluctuations in the investment markets.

Social Security and part-time work in retirement has not been included in this analysis. Social Security, for average income workers, provides as much as 42% of wage replacement and for higher income workers provides as low as 26% of wage replacement (this assumes a same age non-working spouse who is entitled to a 50% benefit based on the working spouse's earnings history). To adjust these amounts for a single individual, divide the wage replacement percentage by 150 percent (e.g., 42% ÷ 150% = 28%).

Investment Assets to Gross Pay

Saving 10 to 13 percent of gross pay is sufficient only if the client begins saving at age 25. Therefore, it is necessary to calculate a second ratio. The combination of these two ratios provides the planner with a better understanding of the progress toward achieving retirement goals. The investment assets to gross pay ratio is the second ratio used to assess a retirement plan that persistently has clients saving 10 to 13 percent of gross pay. As used in this textbook, all investment assets are considered, including cash and cash equivalents and education savings. If the client wants to measure retirement assets separately, the planner can redefine the ratio for retirement assets only by leaving out nonretirement savings (e.g., cash and cash equivalents and education savings).

$$\text{Investment Assets to Gross Pay} = \frac{(\text{Investment Assets}) + (\text{Cash} + \text{Cash Equivalents})}{\text{Gross Pay}} = \text{Benchmark Depends on Client Age}$$

For this ratio to be effective, the financial planner needs to make sure that all personal use assets are classified correctly (e.g., most homes and various collectibles are not investment assets for this purpose). In the event that a client has multiple goals such as college education for children, lump sum, retirement, and legacy goals, the investment assets used in this calculation should be reduced by those devoted to the other goals.

The investment assets to gross pay benchmark is calculated according to age and is generally reliable for a wide range of income levels (e.g., $40,000 to $400,000 annual income).

Exhibit 2.10 **Investment Assets to Gross Pay Benchmarks**

Benchmark for Investment Assets as a Ratio of Gross Pay by Age	
25	0.2:1
30	0.6 - 0.8:1
35	1.6 - 1.8:1
45	3 - 4:1
55	8 - 10:1
65	16 - 20:1

*A continued savings rate of 10 to 13% of gross pay until retirement age 65 will achieve these ratios if invested in a balanced fund that produces reasonable returns. Inflation and pay raises are included in the analysis.

For example, the above information indicates that a client age 35 should have 1.6 to 1.8 times his annual gross pay in investment assets as savings for retirement. A savings rate of 10 to 13 percent of gross pay will facilitate achieving the financial security (retirement) goal. This table of investment asset ratios is consistent with a four to five percent withdrawal rate at retirement that will mitigate the risk of superannuation.

A frequent question regarding the above benchmark data table is how a defined benefit plan or employer-provided pension plan fits into this analysis. A financial planner has two alternatives to address the additional retirement funding provided by the defined benefit plan. The first is to calculate the present value of the benefit and include that amount on the client's balance sheet under investment assets. The second alternative is to reduce the wage replacement needs amount at retirement for the expected pension benefit and then recalculate the client's adjusted needs for the amount of savings necessary to drive the wage replacement ratios (as adjusted by the portion provided by the pension). In either case, the planner should only include these adjustments when there is reasonable certainty that the client will receive the benefit. The first approach is preferred because it only includes the present value of vested benefits, without making any assumptions about whether the client will remain with his current employer to retirement.

EXAMPLE 2.2

Cindy, age 45, is expecting to receive an annual pension of $23,400 at her normal retirement age of 65.

The present value of the pension is:

N = 20 (life expectancy at 65 to 85)

i = 4 (the riskless rate if a strong company)

PMT_{AD} = $23,400

FV = $0 (a single life annuity)

PV_{65} = $330,734 (to age 65)

PV_{45} = $150,943 (to age 45)

The $330,734 represents the lump-sum amount needed at age 65 to pay Cindy $23,400 per year during her retirement. The $150,943 represents the lump-sum amount set aside today that will grow to $330,734 at age 65.

Cindy can put the $150,943 on her balance sheet or reduce her retirement needs by $23,400 annually at age 65. The balance sheet approach is preferred because many defined benefit pensions are not adjusted for inflation making the needs approach more difficult.

Note that if Cindy remains with the company until age 65 and her salary grows by 3% per year, the present value of her pension will be $1,261,058 at age 65, calculated as follows:

N = 20 (life expectancy at 65)

i = 4 (the riskless rate if a strong company)

PMT_{AD} = $89,222 (annual pension payment based on company's pension formula)

FV = $0 (a single life annuity)

PV_{65} = $1,261,058 (at age 65)

Another important point to consider when evaluating the investment assets to gross pay ratio is the context of this ratio within the entire set of ratios. For example, if the client is fairly young, owns a principal residence that is debt free, but has an investment assets to gross pay ratio that is low for his age, this may not be a problem. It may be that a similarly situated person with debt on a principal residence has a higher investment assets to gross pay ratio, but a lower savings rate. As long as the client, who is not servicing debt on a residence, has a current and future increasing savings rate, then the investment asset to gross pay ratio should grow quickly.

PERFORMANCE RATIOS

Return on investments, return on assets, and return on net worth are the most common performance ratios used to determine the adequacy of returns on investments for the risks taken.

Return on Investments (ROI)

The Return on Investments (ROI) ratio calculates the rate of return on invested assets. The ratio is calculated by taking the ending balance of investments (I_1) minus the beginning balance of investments (I_0) plus the annual savings (S), divided by the beginning balance of investments.

$$\text{Return on Investments (ROI)} = \frac{I_1 - (I_0 + \text{Savings})}{I_0}$$

This ratio is an appropriate measure of the return on investments made during a year. There is an implicit assumption that savings are made in equal monthly deposits during the year. This calculation produces what is referred to as an arithmetic return (AR), which is appropriate for a one-year period. However, for measuring returns over a long period of time, the arithmetic mean is not as accurate as the geometric average, and will generally overstate the return. The geometric average is equivalent to the internal rate of return, while the arithmetic return is a simple average.

For example, assume that a client had \$100 at I_0 and \$120 at I_1 and that the client had also saved \$10 during the year. The ROI would be \$120 - (\$100 + \$10) ÷ \$100 = 10%. However, if the ROI was calculated exactly using a geometric mean return it would actually be 9.173 percent.

Geometric Return (GR) Calculation

N	=	12 months
PV	=	\$100
FV	=	(\$120)
Payments	=	0.8333 per month (\$10 ÷ 12)
i	=	0.76442 per month x 12 = 9.173% (GR)

The ROI of 9.173 percent is the geometric return. The ten percent return as calculated by the initial formula produces the arithmetic return. In order to calculate the ROI we need two balance sheets. Once again, ROI is best calculated over time and geometric returns are more useful to the financial planner than arithmetic returns.

Quick Quiz 2.2

Highlight the answer to these questions:

1. The savings rate is measured to help clients achieve long-term goals including retirement funding, education funding, lump-sum expenditures, and legacy plans.
   a. True
   b. False

2. The savings rate benchmark is client goal oriented, while the investment assets to gross pay benchmark is client age dependent.
   a. True
   b. False

3. Common performance ratios include net worth to total asset ratio, return on investments, and return on assets.
   a. True
   b. False

4. Debt ratios utilized in the financial analysis include housing ratio 1, housing ratio 2, debt to total assets ratio, and net worth to total assets ratio.
   a. True
   b. False

True, True, False, True.

The ROI benchmark comparison should be made using the same asset class returns as the actual investments. For example, it would be inappropriate to compare a balanced fund to the S&P 500 index. Instead, the investment should be compared to a blended index that includes equities and fixed income.

Return on Assets (ROA)

The Return on Assets (ROA) ratio measures total asset returns by calculating the difference between ending assets (A_1) less beginning assets (A_0) plus any savings (S), divided by beginning assets.

$$\text{Return on Assets} = \frac{A_1 - (A_0 + \text{Savings})}{A_0}$$

This ratio must be used cautiously when the client is adding assets that are leveraged with debt. In the event new assets are added to the balance sheet and they are highly leveraged, the financial planner may consider simply adding the net equity to the year-end assets (A_1) for purpose of calculating ROA.

Return on Net Worth (RONW)

The Return on Net Worth (RONW) ratio further refines the performance set of ratios by calculating the rate of return on net worth. The calculation takes ending net worth (NW_1) less the sum of beginning net worth (NW_0) and savings (S), divided by beginning net worth.

$$\text{Return on Net Worth} = \frac{NW_1 - (NW_0 + \text{Savings})}{NW_0}$$

If the client is adding assets with debt, this ratio should help to clarify the ROA ratio.

EXHIBIT 2.11 SUMMARY OF FINANCIAL STATEMENT RATIOS

LIQUIDITY RATIOS			
RATIO	**FORMULA**	**MEASURES**	**BENCHMARK**
Emergency Funds	$\frac{\text{Cash \& Cash Equivalents}}{\text{Monthly Non-Discretionary Cash Flows}}$	The number of months of non-discretionary expenses in the form of cash and cash equivalents.	3 - 6 months
Current Ratio	$\frac{\text{Cash \& Cash Equivalents}}{\text{Current Liabilities}}$	The number of times a client can satisfy their short-term liabilities.	1.0 - 2.0
DEBT RATIOS			
Housing Ratio 1 (Basic)	$\frac{\text{Housing Costs}}{\text{Gross Pay}}$	The percentage of income spent on housing debt.	≤ 28%
Housing Ratio 2 (Broad)	$\frac{\text{Housing Costs + Other Debt Payments}}{\text{Gross Pay}}$	The percentage of income spent on housing and all other recurring debt.	≤ 36%
Debt to Total Assets	$\frac{\text{Total Debt}}{\text{Total Assets}}$	The percentage of assets being provided by creditors.	As a person ages, this ratio should decline.
Net Worth to Total Assets	$\frac{\text{Net Worth}}{\text{Total Assets}}$	The percentage of total assets owned or paid for by client.	Depends on age. 20% for young client and 90-100% for retirement age client.
RATIOS FOR FINANCIAL SECURITY GOALS			
Savings Rate	$\frac{\text{Savings + Employer Match}}{\text{Gross Pay}}$	The percentage of income saved towards a retirement goal.	10 – 13% assuming the client starts early, ages 25-35.
Investment Assets to Gross Pay	$\frac{\text{Investment Assets + Cash \& Cash Equivalents}}{\text{Gross Pay}}$	The progress towards a retirement goal.	Depends upon age. At retirement age – 16:1
PERFORMANCE RATIOS			
Return on Investments	$\frac{I_1 - (I_0 + \text{Savings})}{I_0}$	The growth rate of a client's investment assets.	8 – 10%
Return on Assets	$\frac{A_1 - (A_0 + \text{Savings})}{A_0}$	A blended growth rate of all assets.	2 – 4%
Return on Net Worth	$\frac{NW_1 - (NW_0 + \text{Savings})}{NW_0}$	The growth rate of net worth.	The higher the better. This ratio is likely to become smaller as the client's net worth increases.

Guide for Calculating Financial Ratios

Financial ratios can be created and defined using different criteria according to a particular client's situation. For example, one client's non-discretionary spending (e.g., charitable contributions, church donations, etc.) may be defined by different values as compared to another client's non-discretionary spending.

The following exhibit reflects common financial ratios along with an indication of which financial statements contain the data necessary to calculate each ratio. Some ratios may be calculated using both historical and current financial statements. The same ratios can also be calculated using projected financial statements based on a financial planner's recommendations.

This textbook reflects the reality of various client scenarios and calculates ratios based on current information and in some cases based on projected financial statements. Some ratios can be calculated using only one (current) balance sheet and other ratios (performance ratios) require two balance sheets. The calculated ratios in this textbook are reflective of the particular client's scenario and whether one balance sheet or two balance sheets are available. The financial planner should view a ratio as one part of a mosaic; by itself the ratio does not portray the entire financial picture. Ratios should be viewed individually and then as part of the whole financial "mosaic" to obtain a true understanding of a client's entire financial situation.

Financial Statements Needed to Calculate Ratios

Exhibit 2.12

Liquidity Ratios			
Ratio	Formula	Balance Sheet[1]	Income Statement
Emergency Funds Ratio[2]	Cash & Cash Equivalents / Monthly Non-Discretionary Cash Flows	✓	✓
Current Ratio	Cash & Cash Equivalents / Current Liabilities	✓	

1 Balance sheet ratios may use beginning balance sheet, one year projected, or both.

2 Client must determine non-discretionary payments based on personal values (charitable contributions, church donations, etc.).

EXHIBIT 2.13 FINANCIAL STATEMENTS NEEDED TO CALCULATE RATIOS (CONTINUED)

DEBT RATIOS			
RATIO	FORMULA	BALANCE SHEET[3]	INCOME STATEMENT
Housing Ratio 1 (Basic)	$\frac{\text{Housing Costs}}{\text{Gross Pay}}$		✓
Housing Ratio 2 (Broad)	$\frac{\text{Housing Costs + Other Debt Payments}}{\text{Gross Pay}}$		✓
Debt to Total Assets	$\frac{\text{Total Debt}}{\text{Total Assets}}$	✓	
Net Worth to Total Assets	$\frac{\text{Net Worth}}{\text{Total Assets}}$	✓	

3 *Balance sheet ratios may use beginning balance sheet, one year projected, or both.*

RATIOS FOR FINANCIAL SECURITY GOALS			
RATIO	FORMULA	BALANCE SHEET	INCOME STATEMENT
Savings Rate[4]	$\frac{\text{Savings + Employer Match}}{\text{Gross Pay}}$		✓
Investment Assets to Gross Pay[5/6]	$\frac{\text{Investment Assets + Cash \& Cash Equivalents}}{\text{Gross Pay}}$	✓	✓

4 *Include any employer matches for retirement funds.*
5 *Can be separated by goal. If retirement only, use retirement committed investment assets. Education assets and cash and cash equivalents are not included. If calculating total investment assets to gross pay then: All Investment Assets + Cash and Cash Equivalents ÷ Gross Pay.*
6 *Use all Investment Assets and Cash and Cash Equivalents also in the ratio calculation.*

PERFORMANCE RATIOS			
RATIO	FORMULA	BALANCE SHEET	INCOME STATEMENT
Return on Investments - Retirement	$\frac{I_1 - (I_0 + \text{Savings})}{I_0}$	✓	✓
Return on Investments - Education	$\frac{I_1 - (I_0 + \text{Savings})}{I_0}$	✓	✓
Return on Investments - Total	$\frac{I_1 - (I_0 + \text{Savings})}{I_0}$	✓	✓
Return on Assets	$\frac{A_1 - (A_0 + \text{Savings})}{A_0}$	✓	✓
Return on Net Worth	$\frac{NW_1 - (NW_0 + \text{Savings})}{NW_0}$	✓	✓

HESS CASE EXAMPLE OF APPLYING THE PIE CHART, FINANCIAL STATEMENT, AND RATIO ANALYSIS APPROACH

The purpose of this case is to illustrate how the pie chart approach and the ratio analysis approach may be applied to a client scenario. A more detailed application of these approaches will follow in subsequent chapters.

Jack Hess is a 45-year old marketing manager for a national pharmaceutical company. His annual salary is $73,000. He participates in his company's 401(k) retirement plan and his employer matches three percent of his salary. Jack's wife, Marilyn, is a 43-year old make-up artist with an annual salary of $36,000. There are no company retirement plans available for Marilyn. Jack and Marilyn have been married for 18 years and plan to retire in 20 years. They have a 13-year old daughter, Melba, who is in the 8th grade at a private school in their area. Jack and Marilyn anticipate that Melba will attend a private university with tuition of $21,000 annually in today's dollars. Jack and Marilyn have a moderate level of risk tolerance and rank their financial objectives, by priority, as follows:

1. save for retirement,
2. save for private college education for Melba, and
3. have an adequate insurance portfolio.

FINANCIAL STATEMENTS: BALANCE SHEET (12/31/2012)

Statement of Financial Position
Jack and Marilyn Hess
Balance Sheet as of 12/31/2012

ASSETS[1]			LIABILITIES AND NET WORTH		
Current Assets			**Current Liabilities[2]**		
Checking Account	$18,000		Credit Card Balances	$11,000	
Money Market Account	$12,000		**Total Current Liabilities**		**$11,000**
Total Current Assets		**$30,000**			
Investment Assets			**Long-Term Liabilities[2]**		
401(k) Plan	$86,000		Mortgage Balance (Residence)[3]	$145,000	
IRA	$16,000		Auto Loans	$16,000	
CDs	$15,000		**Total Long-Term Liabilities**		**$161,000**
Growth Mutual Fund	$20,000				
Stock Portfolio[4]	$40,000				
Total Investment Assets		**$177,000**	**Total Liabilities**		**$172,000**
Personal Use Assets					
Personal Residence	$155,000				
Personal Property	$57,000		**Total Net Worth**		**$280,000**
Automobiles	$33,000				
Total Personal Use Assets		**$245,000**			
Total Assets		**$452,000**	**Total Liabilities & Net Worth**		**$452,000**

1. Assets are stated at fair market value.
2. Principal balance only.
3. The mortgage is a 30-year note at 8% with an original balance of $145,000. They just purchased the home.
4. Publicly-traded stock.

Financial Statements: Statement of Income and Expenses

Statement of Income and Expenses Mr. and Mrs. Hess Statement of Income and Expenses for 2012 and Expected (Approximate) For 2013		
CASH INFLOWS[1]		**Totals**
Salaries		
Jack's Salary	$73,000	
Marilyn's Salary	$36,000	
Total Cash Inflows		$109,000
CASH OUTFLOWS		
Savings[1]		
Employee - Elective Deferral	$14,600	
Total Savings		$14,600
Ordinary Living Expenses		$26,000
Debt Payments		
Credit Card Payments	$3,300	
Mortgage Loan	$12,768	
Auto Loans	$5,400	
Total Debt Payments		$21,468
Insurance Premiums		
Life Insurance	$1,900	
Health Insurance	$500	
Auto Insurance	$800	
Homeowners Insurance	$1,600	
Total Insurance Premiums		$4,800
Charitable Contributions		$935
Tuition & Education Expenses		$10,000
Entertainment & Vacations		$2,000
Taxes		
Federal Income Taxes	$16,220	
State Income Taxes	$3,175	
Social Security Taxes	$8,033	
Property Tax (Residence)	$2,895	
Total Taxes		$30,323
TOTAL CASH OUTFLOWS		$110,126
NET DISCRETIONARY CASH FLOW		($1,126)

1. Reinvested earnings are not included in gross pay or the savings rate because they are included in the overall expected portfolio rate of return.

FINANCIAL STATEMENTS: PROJECTED BALANCE SHEET (12/31/2013)

Statement of Financial Position
Jack and Marilyn Hess
Projected Balance Sheet as of 12/31/2013

ASSETS[1]			LIABILITIES AND NET WORTH		
Current Assets			**Current Liabilities[2]**		
Checking Account	$16,174		Credit Card Balances	$11,000	
Money Market Account	$12,000		**Total Current Liabilities**		**$11,000**
Total Current Assets		**$28,174**			
Investment Assets			**Long-Term Liabilities[2]**		
401(k) Plan	$89,600		Mortgage Balance (Residence)[3]	$143,789	
IRA	$17,000		Auto Loans	$10,600	
CDs	$15,000		**Total Long-Term Liabilities**		**$154,389**
Growth Mutual Fund	$18,000				
Stock Portfolio[4]	$36,000				
Total Investment Assets		**$175,600**	**Total Liabilities**		**$165,389**
Personal Use Assets					
Personal Residence	$160,000				
Personal Property	$57,000		**Total Net Worth**		**$285,385**
Automobiles	$30,000				
Total Personal Use Assets		**$247,000**			
Total Assets		**$450,774**	**Total Liabilities & Net Worth**		**$450,774**

1. Assets are stated at fair market value.
2. Principal balance only.
3. The mortgage is a 30-year note at 8% with an original balance of $145,000.
4. Publicly-traded stock.

Pie Chart Analysis for Hess Case

From the balance sheet and income statement data, the financial planner can then create pie charts as shown below.

Balance Sheet Data and Pie Charts (12/31/2012)

Assets = 100%		
Cash & Cash Equivalents	$ 30,000	7%
Investment Assets	$177,000	39%
Personal Use Assets	$245,000	54%
	$452,000	100%

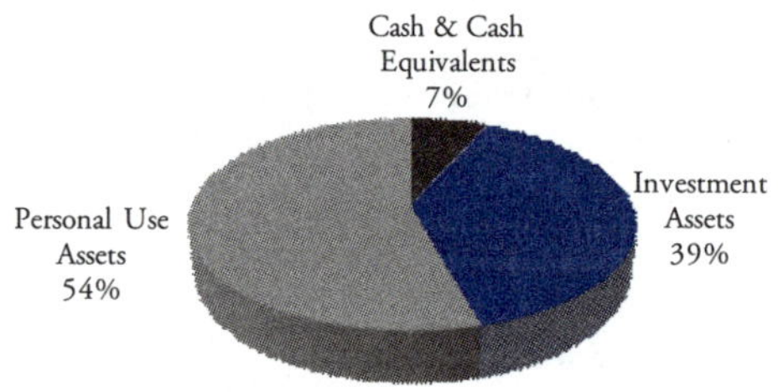

Liabilities & Net Worth = 100%		
Current Liabilities	$ 11,000	2%
Long-Term Liabilities	$161,000	36%
Net Worth	$280,000	62%
	$452,000	100%

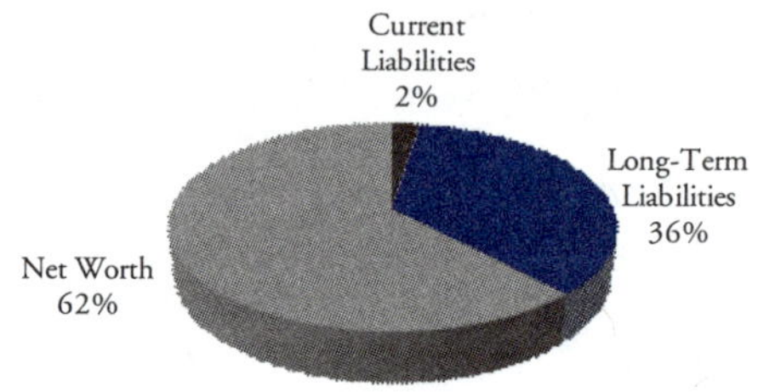

Income Statement Data (For Year 2013)

	Amount	Percentage
Gross Income	$109,000	100%
Taxes	$30,323	27.8%
Savings	$14,600	13.4%
Insurance	$4,800	4.4%
Ordinary Living Expenses	$26,000	23.8%
Other Debt Payments (ODP)	$21,468	19.7%
Charitable, Tuition, Entertainment	$12,935	11.9%
Discretionary Cash Flow (DCF)	($1,126)	(1%)

Income Statement Pie Chart

Income = $109,000

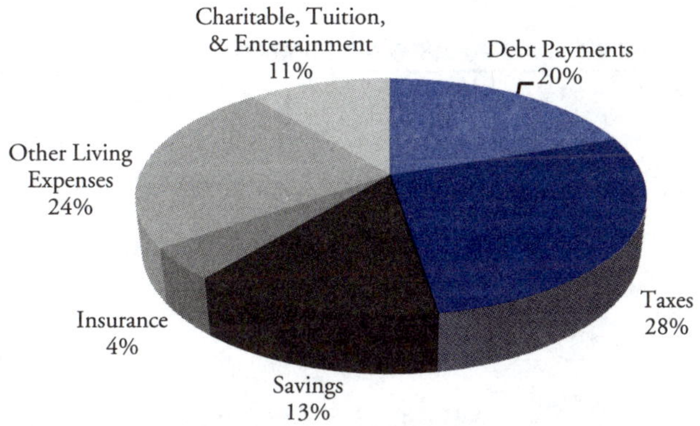

Note: Discretionary cash flow is not listed because it is negative $1,126 or -1%.

FINANCIAL RATIOS FOR HESS CASE

The ratios below are based on the year beginning balance sheet (2012) except for the performance ratios, that are based on the year-end values (2013).

Liquidity Ratios

$$\text{Emergency Fund Ratio} = \frac{\$30{,}000}{(\$66{,}098 \div 12) = \$5{,}508.17} = 5.44 \text{ Months Coverage (Good)}$$

$26,000	Ordinary Living Expenses
$21,468	Total Debt Payments
$4,800	Total Insurance Payments
$10,000	Tuition & Education Expenses
$2,895	Residence Property Taxes
$935	Charitable Contributions*
$66,098	Total Non-Discretionary Cash Flows

* Charitable contributions are considered non-discretionary by the client.

$$\text{(2012) Current Ratio} = \frac{\$30{,}000}{\$11{,}000} = 2.73 \text{ (Good)}$$

$$\text{(2013) Current Ratio} = \frac{\$28{,}174}{\$11{,}000} = 2.56 \text{ (Good)}$$

Debt Ratios

$$\text{Housing Ratio 1} = \frac{\$12{,}768 + \$1{,}600 + \$2{,}895}{\$109{,}000} = 15.8\% \text{ (Very Good)}$$

$$\text{Housing Ratio 2} = \frac{\$12{,}768 + \$1{,}600 + \$2{,}895 + \$3{,}300 + \$5{,}400}{\$109{,}000} = 23.8\% \text{ (Very Good)}$$

$$\text{Debt to Total Assets Ratio} = \frac{\$172{,}000}{\$452{,}000} = 38.1\% \text{ (Good) (2012)}$$

$$\text{Debt to Total Assets Ratio} = \frac{\$165{,}389}{\$450{,}774} = 36.7\% \text{ (Good) (2013)}$$

$$\text{Net Worth to Total Assets Ratio} = \frac{\$280{,}000}{\$452{,}000} = \text{62\% (Good) Benchmark Depends on Age (2011)}$$

$$\text{Net Worth to Total Assets Ratio} = \frac{\$285{,}385}{\$450{,}774} = \text{63\% (Good) Benchmark Depends on Age (2012)}$$

Ratios for Financial Security Goals

$$\text{Savings Rate*} = \frac{\$2{,}190 + \$14{,}600}{\$109{,}000} = 15.4\% \text{ (Good) (\$2,190 = employer match)}$$

(* Excludes reinvestments)

$$\text{Investment Assets to Gross Pay} = \frac{\$177{,}000 + \$30{,}000}{\$109{,}000} = 1.90 \text{ times (Weak)}$$

401(k) Plan Savings	
Employee Elective Deferral	$14,600
Employer Match	$2,190
Total	$16,790

Performance Ratios

$$\text{Return on 401(k)} = \frac{\$89{,}600 - (\$86{,}000 + \$16{,}790)}{\$86{,}000} = -15.5\% \text{ (Very Poor)}$$

$$\text{Return on Total Investments} = \frac{\$175{,}600 - (\$177{,}000 + \$16{,}950 + \$2{,}190)}{\$177{,}000} = -11.6\% \text{ (Very Poor)}$$

Overall, the ratio approach suggests the Hess' only have two major weaknesses in the amount of savings to gross pay and return on investments. Additional approaches should be applied to reveal a more comprehensive analysis of the Hess financial position. The additional approaches are covered during the remainder of this chapter.

THE TWO-STEP / THREE-PANEL / METRICS APPROACH

Two-Step Approach

The two-step approach to financial planning recommends covering the risks and saving and investing. The two-step approach considers personal risks as potentially leading to catastrophic losses or dependence on someone else for their financial well being. The two-step approach regards savings and investments as the path to financial security or independence. Dependence on others can be caused by a single catastrophic event that can occur unexpectedly. Financial independence, however, is achieved over a long period of time by saving and investing. In summary, the two-step approach focuses on risk management and appropriate saving and investing.

> *Key Concepts*
>
> **Underline/highlight the answers to these questions as you read:**
>
> 1. What are the two focuses of the two-step approach and the financial categories analyzed by the three-panel approach?
> 2. Identify the purpose of the example benchmarks used in the metrics approach.

Three-Panel Approach

The three-panel approach is a slight refinement of the two-step approach. It divides saving and investing into short and long-term objectives. The three-panel approach provides the planner and the client with a methodology for financial planning in order to achieve the goals of covering the risks, saving, and investing. The exhibit below outlines the three-panel methodology.

Three-Panel Methodology

Exhibit 2.14

Panel 1	Panel 2	Panel 3
Risk Management of Personal, Property, and Liability Risks	**Short-Term Savings and Investments & Debt Management**	**Long-Term Savings and Investments**
Evaluate the need for and quality of personal insurance:	**Evaluate the adequacy of:**	**Evaluate the adequacy of progress toward:**
1. Life Insurance 2. Health Insurance 3. Disability Insurance 4. Long-Term Care Insurance 5. Property Insurance: • Homeowner's Insurance • Auto Insurance • Other Property Insurance 6. Liability Insurance	1. The emergency fund 2. The proportion of income spent on housing 3. The proportion of income spent on debt other than housing debt repayments	1. The retirement goal • the savings rate • investment assets 2. The education funding goal 3. Any large purchase goal 4. Legacy goals • documents • financial

Panel 1 is used to evaluate each of the risks listed and then evaluates the client's actual portfolio of insurance to determine the adequacy of current insurance coverage. The focus is on covering catastrophic risk exposures.

Panel 2 is used to calculate the emergency fund ratio (which is also available from using the financial statement analysis approach). Next, the planner calculates housing ratio 1 and housing ratio 2 and evaluates the quality of client debt. The focus is on meeting short-term obligations and evaluating how well the client is managing debt.

Panel 3 focuses on long-term goals. To meet the financial security goal (ability to maintain the pre-retirement lifestyle throughout retirement) requires persistent savings, adequate investment performance, and investment assets appropriate for the age and gross pay of the client. If the client also expects or wants to provide a college education for children, the savings rate must be increased. If the client also has lump-sum goals (second home, very expensive trip, boat, airplane) the savings rate should increase at least sufficiently to provide a down payment on the lump-sum asset of 20 percent. Finally, all clients need basic estate planning documents (will, durable power of attorney for health care, advance medical directive). If, in addition to the other goals, the client wants to leave a financial legacy, even more savings is required.

As shown in Exhibit 2.15, client A has no children. Client B has two children and plans to send them to an in-state college. Client C plans to send two children to a good private school and plans to buy a second home at the beach in ten years (current cost $250,000). Client D plans to send the children to an exclusive private school and buy a second home for $350,000 in ten years and leave $1,000,000 in purchasing power to the children at death (age 65). Expected earnings is eight percent and inflation is expected to be three percent. The wage replacement ratio is approximately 90 to 100 percent of pre-retirement income.

Exhibit 2.15 **Savings Rate Necessary for Various Clients / Scenarios**

	A **Single Age 25** **(0 children)**	**B** **Married Age 35** **(2 children)**	**C** **Married Age 40** **(2 children)**	**D** **Married Age 40** **(2 children)**
Income	$100,000	$100,000	$150,000	$200,000
Retirement Goal Savings Rate (as a % of gross pay)	10 - 13%	10 - 13%	10 - 13%	10 - 13%
Investment Assets	$2,000	$150,000	$365,000	$500,000
Education Goal	0	3%	5%	7%
Lump-Sum Goal	0	0	3%	3.3%
Legacy Goal	0	0	0	6.30%
Overall Savings Rate Needed (as a % of gross pay)	10 - 13%	13 - 16%	18 - 21%	26.6 - 29.6%

The point is not necessarily how much a person needs, but rather whether the retirement goal is being met by: (1) a savings rate of 10 to 13 percent and (2) investment assets of a certain amount that are an appropriate percentage of gross pay depending on the age of the client. If the client has goals other than retirement (education, lump sum, and/or legacy) the overall savings rate will have to be increased to meet those additional goals.

The three-panel approach is like a recipe or a checklist. An advantage of this approach is that it is easy to follow by both the planner and the client. Keep in mind this methodology does not answer every question in financial planning, nor does it require the analysis of rates of return on investments or evaluate investment risk.

Once the three-panel approach is understood, the financial planner can overlay it with quantitative and qualitative metrics that provide benchmarks to compare to the client's actual financial situation. The result of this analysis will determine deficiencies in the client's risk management portfolio, short-term savings and investing (plus debt management), and long-term savings and investing (to determine if adequate progress is being made towards long-term goals).

Metrics Approach

The metrics approach provides quantitative example benchmarks for the financial planner and client to use as guidance for necessary comprehensive financial goals and objectives. Once the practitioner has analyzed and evaluated the client's actual financial situation, the metrics can be applied to establish financial planning recommendations.

Quick Quiz 2.3

Highlight the answer to these questions:

1. The two-step approach considers savings and investments as the financial plan leading to financial security (and independence).
   a. True
   b. False

2. The three-panel approach provides a plan for risk management of personal, property, and liability risks, along with both short-term and long-term savings.
   a. True
   b. False

3. The metrics approach provides finite benchmarks for the financial planner to use as a comparison of client actual to client goal.
   a. True
   b. False

True, True, False.

EXHIBIT 2.16 EXAMPLE BENCHMARKS (METRICS)

	Metric	Comment / Recommendation
RISK MANAGEMENT DATA		
Life Insurance	12 - 16 times gross pay, if needed.	
Health Insurance	Lifetime benefit ≥ $1,000,000.	
Disability Insurance	60 - 70% of gross pay and at least guaranteed renewable.	Covering both sickness and accident and a hybrid or own occupation definition and appropriate elimination period.
Long-Term Care Insurance	If needed, daily or monthly benefits ≥ average for appropriate facility.	Benefits inflation adjusted and a benefit period ≥ 36 - 60 months.
Homeowners Insurance	≤ full replacement value on both dwelling and content and coverage for open perils.	
Automobile Insurance	≤ full fair market value for comprehensive and collision.	
Liability Insurance	At least a $1,000,000 personal liability policy.	Need sufficient underlying homeowners and auto liability to satisfy PLUP issuer.
SHORT-TERM SAVINGS AND INVESTING GOALS		
Emergency Fund	Equal to 3 - 6 times the monthly non-discretionary cash outflows.	
Housing	Housing ratio1 should be ≤ 28% of gross pay.	Housing ratio 1 should decline to ≤ 5% of gross pay at retirement.
Housing and Debt	The total paid for housing costs and other debt payments ≤ 36% of gross pay.	Other debt payments include, but are not limited to, credit cards, auto loans, and student loans.
LONG-TERM SAVINGS AND INVESTMENT GOALS		
Financial Security (Retirement)	Save 10 - 13% of gross pay (include employer match).	Have an appropriate amount of investment assets relative to gross pay for the client's age.
College Education Funding	Save $3,000/$6,000/or $9,000 per child per year for 18 years in a balanced portfolio (60% stocks/40% fixed income).	Savings is dependent on where the child is expected to attend college (in state/mid-private/elite-private).
Lump-Sum Goals	Goals like 2nd home, airplane, or boat require savings of at least 20% of the total price as a down payment.	This additional goal will increase the overall savings rate required to achieve all the goals.
Legacy Goals	Every client under age 50 needs basic documents. Those 50 and over may also need trusts and estate planning.	Basic documents include a will, durable power of attorney for healthcare, advanced medical directive (living will), and durable power of attorney for financial matters.

Risk Tolerance and Asset Allocation

The three-panel approach and the metrics approach are very helpful in providing a framework and benchmarks for the client and planner. However, clients and planners need tools to develop an investment plan. A proper investment plan is a critical element in the pursuit of most financial planning goals, including retirement and education. The investment plan is a bit like the engine in a car – without it, you cannot reach the destination.

In financial planning, calculating savings for retirement or education is sometimes performed without a significant amount of thought and consideration given to a proper expected investment rate of return. However, this "variable" or "input" is an extremely important factor in determining the amount that needs to be accumulated or saved.

Investing is a challenging component of financial planning as certainty resides only in past and not in future investment performance. However, it is generally accepted that asset allocation is the largest contributor to investment performance over time and the two key components of asset allocation are risk tolerance and time horizon.

As part of the investment planning process, the financial planner evaluates the client's goals in terms of both dollar value and time. The client's goals are assessed together with risk tolerance in designing the appropriate investment strategy. The client's risk tolerance is a combination of both the ability and the willingness to accept investment risk. The planner will develop an investment plan considering the client's investment ability (an objective state of being, based on the client's financial profile) and the client's willingness (a subjective state of being) to take on investment risk and to commit dollars over time to reach the investment goals. The ability and willingness of the client to accept risk can be gauged by various factors. For example, the longer the time horizon of a client, the more risk that the client is able to accept in the investment portfolio. The client's ability to accept risk is associated with time horizon, liquidity needs, tax conditions, and unique financial and personal circumstances. The client's willingness to accept risk is associated with the psychological condition of risk tolerance. The risk tolerance questionnaire provides both the planner and the client with a clear understanding of the client's psychological tolerance (willingness) for taking risk.

Financial planners employ tools to assess the client's willingness to accept investment risk, thus helping to determine the client's risk tolerance as part of the investment planning process. Dr. William Droms, CFA, the Powers Professor of Finance in the McDonough School of Business at Georgetown University and a principal at in Droms Strauss Advisors, Inc. has granted us permission to use his Global Portfolio Allocation Scoring System (PASS) in this text.[2] PASS considers both time horizon and risk tolerance in determining an appropriate asset allocation. Step one is to have the client answer the following questions, which have scores ranging from 5 to 1. Once the questions are answered, each of the point values is summed and is used as part of determining the asset allocation.

2. More information can be found on Dr. Droms at http://www.droms-strauss.com, as well as the complete article from the Journal of Financial Planning.

Global Portfolio Allocation Scoring System (PASS) for Individual Investors[1]						
Questions		Strongly Agree	Agree	Neutral	Disagree	Strongly Disagree
1	Earning a high long-term total return that will allow my capital to grow faster than the inflation rate is one of my most important investment objectives.	5	4	3	2	1
2	I would like an investment that provides me with an opportunity to defer taxation of capital gains to future years.	5	4	3	2	1
3	I do not require a high level of current income from my investments.	5	4	3	2	1
4	I am willing to tolerate some sharp down swings in the return on my investments in order to seek a potentially higher return than would normally be expected from more stable investments.	5	4	3	2	1
5	I am willing to risk a short-term loss in return for a potentially higher long-run rate of return.	5	4	3	2	1
6	I am financially able to accept a low level of liquidity in my investment portfolio.	5	4	3	2	1

1. More information can be found on Dr. Droms at http://www.droms-strauss.com, as well as the complete article from the Journal of Financial Planning.

The next step is to determine the time horizon of the investment goal and then to use the PASS score to determine the appropriate asset allocation. The higher the score, the more tolerance for risk the client has shown and the more the portfolio can be aggressively allocated.

	Short-Term Horizon				Intermediate-Term Horizon				Long-Term Horizon			
	RT1 Target	RT2 Target	RT3 Target	RT4 Target	RT1 Target	RT2 Target	RT3 Target	RT4 Target	RT1 Target	RT2 Target	RT3 Target	RT4 Target
PASS Score	6 - 12	13 - 18	19 - 24	25 - 30	6 - 12	13 - 18	19 - 24	25 - 30	6 - 12	13 - 18	19 - 24	25 - 30
Cash and Money Market Fund	40%	30%	20%	10%	5%	5%	5%	5%	5%	5%	3%	2%
Treasury Bonds/ Bond Funds	40%	30%	30%	20%	60%	35%	20%	10%	30%	20%	12%	0%
Corporate Bonds/ Bond Funds	20%	30%	30%	40%	15%	15%	15%	10%	15%	10%	10%	4%
Subtotal	**100%**	**90%**	**80%**	**70%**	**80%**	**55%**	**40%**	**25%**	**50%**	**35%**	**25%**	**6%**
International Bond Funds	0%	0%	0%	0%	0%	5%	5%	5%	0%	5%	5%	4%
Subtotal	**0%**	**0%**	**0%**	**0%**	**0%**	**5%**	**5%**	**5%**	**0%**	**5%**	**5%**	**4%**
Index Fund	0%	10%	10%	10%	10%	15%	20%	20%	20%	20%	20%	25%
Large Cap Value Funds/Stocks	0%	0%	5%	5%	5%	5%	10%	10%	10%	10%	5%	5%
Large Cap Growth Funds/Stocks	0%	0%	0%	0%	5%	5%	5%	10%	15%	10%	10%	5%
Mid/Small Growth Funds/Stocks	0%	0%	0%	0%	0%	0%	5%	5%	0%	0%	5%	10%
Mid/Small Value Funds/Stocks	0%	0%	0%	5%	0%	5%	5%	5%	0%	5%	5%	10%
Subtotal	**0%**	**10%**	**15%**	**20%**	**20%**	**30%**	**45%**	**50%**	**45%**	**45%**	**45%**	**55%**
International Stock Funds	0%	0%	0%	5%	0%	5%	5%	10%	0%	5%	10%	15%
Subtotal	**0%**	**0%**	**0%**	**5%**	**0%**	**5%**	**5%**	**10%**	**0%**	**5%**	**10%**	**15%**
Real Estate Funds	0%	0%	5%	5%	0%	5%	5%	10%	5%	10%	15%	20%
Subtotal	**0%**	**0%**	**5%**	**5%**	**0%**	**5%**	**5%**	**10%**	**5%**	**10%**	**15%**	**20%**
Total	**100%**	**100%**	**100%**	**100%**	**100%**	**100%**	**100%**	**100%**	**100%**	**100%**	**100%**	**100%**

PASS defines short-term as three years or less, intermediate-term as three to seven years and long-term as more than seven years. With the PASS score and the time horizon, the asset allocation can be determined. There are other models that can be used to assess risk tolerance and determine an appropriate asset allocation. However, Dr. Drom's PASS is a valid model and his article in the Journal of Financial Planning can be used as an additional reference on the subject.

To simplify and to help determine expected return and to consider risk of asset classes, the asset classes above have been condensed into the following asset classes with corresponding expected returns and expected standard deviations:

	Expected Rates of Return	Standard Deviation of Returns
Cash and Money Market Fund	2.5%	2.0%
Treasury Bonds / Bond Fund	4.0%	4.0%
Corporate Bonds / Bond Fund	6.0%	5.0%
International Bond Funds	7.0%	6.0%
Index Funds	9.0%	14.0%
Large Cap Funds / Stocks	10.0%	16.0%
Mid / Small Funds / Stocks	12.0%	18.0%
International Stock Funds	13.0%	22.0%
Real Estate Funds	8.0%	12.0%

These asset classes are used in the cases included in this text. In practice, some of these asset classes might be excluded while other asset classes might be included.

The following chart reflects the condensed asset classes and weightings with the corresponding expected return and estimated standard deviation for each portfolio.[3]

	Short-Term Horizon				Intermediate-Term Horizon				Long-Term Horizon			
	RT1 Target	RT2 Target	RT3 Target	RT4 Target	RT1 Target	RT2 Target	RT3 Target	RT4 Target	RT1 Target	RT2 Target	RT3 Target	RT4 Target
PASS Score	6 - 12	13 - 18	19 - 24	25 - 30	6 - 12	13 - 18	19 - 24	25 - 30	6 - 12	13 - 18	19 - 24	25 - 30
Cash and Money Market Fund	40%	30%	20%	10%	5%	5%	5%	5%	5%	5%	3%	2%
Treasury Bonds/ Bond Funds	40%	30%	30%	20%	60%	35%	20%	10%	30%	20%	12%	0%
Corporate Bonds/ Bond Funds	20%	30%	30%	40%	15%	15%	15%	10%	15%	10%	10%	4%
International Bond Funds	0%	0%	0%	0%	0%	5%	5%	5%	0%	5%	5%	4%
Index Fund	0%	10%	10%	10%	10%	15%	20%	20%	20%	20%	20%	25%
Large Cap Funds/Stocks	0%	0%	5%	5%	10%	10%	15%	20%	25%	20%	15%	10%
Mid/Small Funds/Stocks	0%	0%	0%	5%	0%	5%	10%	10%	0%	5%	10%	20%
International Stock Funds	0%	0%	0%	5%	0%	5%	5%	10%	0%	5%	10%	15%
Real Estate Funds	0%	0%	5%	5%	0%	5%	5%	10%	5%	10%	15%	20%
Total	**100%**	**100%**	**100%**	**100%**	**100%**	**100%**	**100%**	**100%**	**100%**	**100%**	**100%**	**100%**
Expected Return	3.80%	4.65%	5.30%	6.50%	5.33%	6.78%	7.73%	8.58%	6.93%	7.73%	8.51%	9.77%
Expected Standard Deviation (est)	2.79%	3.85%	4.84%	6.40%	5.13%	7.26%	8.73%	10.25%	7.75%	8.94%	10.12%	12.20%

The information in the chart above can be used to support the required returns in the comprehensive cases in the text and can be used to comment on both diversification and risk. In practice, this analysis will often be conducted using a software package that incorporates mean variance optimization. However, the above approach is effective for the included cases.

THE PRESENT VALUE OF GOALS APPROACH

The present value of goals approach takes each short, intermediate, and long-term goal, determines each individual present value, then sums these together and reduces them by current resources (investment assets and cash and cash equivalents).

Refer back to Hess Goal (slightly modified for our purposes here). **Note**: New details for example purposes. They now have three goals.

Goal 1: Retire

Both retire at Jack's age 65 with an 80% wage replacement ratio with inflation projected to be 3%, an earnings rate to and through retirement of 8.0% and life expectancy of 25 years for both spouses (e.g., to 90 and 88 respectively). Assume Social Security will pay $25,000 in today's dollars at age 67 for Jack and $20,000 for Marilyn.

3. The standard deviation for each portfolio has been estimated. To calculate it as accurately as possible, a correlation matrix would be needed.

Wage Replacement Calculation

Income	$109,000	
WRR%	x 0.80	
Total Needs in Today's Dollars	$87,200	
Jack's Social Security	($21,667)	$25,000 (0.8666)
Marilyn's Social Security	($15,000)	$20,000 (0.75)
Adjustable Needs in Today's Dollars	$50,533	

Retirement Calculation

Step 1		Step 2		Step 3	
N	= 20 (45-65)	PMT_{AD}	= $91,268.21902	$FV_{@65}$	= $1,368,681.23
i	= 3	N	= 25	N	= 20
PV	= $50,333	i	= (1.08 ÷ 1.03 - 1) x 100	i	= 8
PMT	= 0	FV	= 0	$PV_{@45}$	= $293,648.10
FV	= $91,268.21902	$PV_{@65}$	= $1,368,681.23		

Goal 2: Education for Melba, age 13

Facts: $21,000 per year, 5 years (added), education inflation 6%.

Step 1		Step 2	
N	= 5	$FV_{@18}$	= $101,182.46
PMT_{AD}	= $21,000	N	= 5 (18 - 13)
i	= (1.08 ÷ 1.06 - 1) x 100	i	= (1.08 ÷ 1.06 - 1) x 100
$PV_{@18}$	= $101,182.46	PMT	= 0
FV	= 0	$PV_{@13}$	= $92,154.34

Goal 3: Created for this example.
Assume they want to buy a second home for $300,000 in today's dollars 11 years from now.

Step 1			**Step 2**		
N	=	11	FV	=	$415,270.16
i	=	3	N	=	11
PV	=	$300,000	i	=	8
PMT	=	0	PV		$178,102.25
FV	=	$415,270.16			

Note: This calculation can also be done in one step using an inflation adjusted discount rate.

The summation of the goals in present value terms:

Retirement	$293,648.10	
Education	$92,154.34	
Second Home	$178,102.25	
Total PV of all Goals	$563,904.69	
Current Resources	$207,000.00	(Investment assets and cash)
Short Fall / PV	$356,904.69	
i	8%	(the earnings rate)
N	20	(to retirement)
FV	0	
PMT_{OA}	$36,351.53	

Once the present value of the goals are summed and then reduced by current resources, the remaining present value of goals can be determined and treated hypothetically as a mortgage at the expected earnings rate to determine how much they need to be saving annually, at year end, to achieve all their goals. That resultant ($36,351.53) can then be compared to the current savings amount to determine its adequacy.

Current savings amount	$14,600
Plus the employer match	$2,190
Total current savings	$16,790
The $16,950 on the income statement includes reinvestment which is included in the overall portfolio rate and should not be counted in the savings rate.	

They are $19,561.53 in annual savings short of meeting all goals ($36,351.53 - $16,790). Consider some of their alternatives:

1. Do they have additional discretionary cash flow they can save? No!
2. Are they over withheld on taxes? The answer to this requires a tax analysis (see below).

Tax Analysis (2012)

Itemized Deductions

Mortgage Interest	$11,556
Charitable Contribution	$935
State Income Tax	$3,175
Property Tax	$2,895
	$18,561

Income	$111,350	
401(k)	$14,600	
AGI	$96,750	
P&D	$11,400	3 personal and dependency exemptions
ID	$18,561	MFJ / itemized deduction - assumed
Taxable	$66,789	
Tax	$9,148	Tax income / Appendix A - www.money-education.com
Child Credit	$1,000	
Tax Liability	$8,148	
Tax withheld	$16,220	
Over withheld	$8,072	

It is not uncommon that clients are over-withheld. The problem is these same over withholders spend rather than save the refund check. So, if we, as planners, can get them to increase their 401(k) or other savings during the year by changing the with-holdings form (W-4), we can increase their savings by $8,072 ÷ 0.85 (the marginal tax rate) and they will be just as well off except they will have no refund.

Below is the revised savings amount resulting from the tax analysis (this amount is calculated without grossing up the over withholding).

401(k) deferral	$14,600	
Employer match	$2,190	
Addition 401(k) deferral	$2,400	(to get to $17,000)
Traditional spouse IRA	$5,000	
Roth IRA	$672	
New Total Savings	$24,862	

While this amount is still far from the $36,351.53 needed, the wage replacement ratio can be adjusted to reflect the new savings amount. The wage replacement ratio was 80% or $87,200 in today's dollars but with the above additional savings, they currently are living on:

Gross pay	$109,000	
Less savings	$22,672	(excluding employer match)
Less Social Security taxes	$8,033	
Net	$78,295	(which is a WRR of 71.83%, not 80%)

* While they wanted an 80% wage replacement ratio, they can maintain their lifestyle with a WRR of approximately 72%.

Consider the following adjustments:

1. Delay retirement to normal age retirement of age 67 (2 more years) and reduce the wage replacement ratio to 72% from 80%.
2. Leave all other goals the same.

Impact on calculations:

	$109,000.00	Income
	0.72	WRR
	$78,480.00	Needs in today's dollars
Social Security (Jack)	($25,000.00)	normal age retirement
Social Security (Marilyn)	($17,333.33)	2 years early, not 4 (13.33% reduction)
Needs	$36,146.67	Retirement needs in today's dollars

Step 1		**Step 2**		**Step 3**	
N	= 22	PMT_{AD}	= $69,260.76	FV	= $993,168.10
i	= 3	i	= (1.08 ÷ 1.03 - 1) x 100	i	= 8
PV	= $36,146.67	N	= 23	N	= 22
FV	= $69,260.76	$PV_{@67}$	= $993,168.10	PV	= $182,683.84

New calculation of PV of all goals:

PV of retirement	$182,683.84	
PV of education	$92,154.34	
PV of second house	$178,102.25	
PV	$452,940.43	
Less resources:	$207,000.00	
Short fall PV	$245,940.43	
N	22	(note 2 more years)
i	8%	
PMT_{OA}	$24,110.05	(new savings calculations)
FV_0	0	

It is clear from the revised calculation of the savings and wage replacement ratio that they can meet all their goals by delaying retirement by two years and revising their wage replacement needs to 72% from 80%. The amount needed to be saved is $24,110.05 and they are currently saving $24,862 (assuming the Form W-4 changes). But what if they do not like this idea? The client can consider other choices in various combinations.

1. Only pay for 4 years of education.
2. Reduce the price of the second home to $200,000 from $300,000 or do not buy a second home.
3. Use a 72% WRR.
4. Delay retirement one year instead of two.
5. Perhaps refinance.
6. Save more and spend less.

THE CASH FLOW APPROACH

> ***Key Concepts***
>
> **Underline/highlight the answers to these questions as you read:**
>
> 1. What is the usefulness of the cash flow approach?
> 2. Identify the three focus areas being managed under the cash flow approach.
> 3. What is the strategic approach to financial planning?

The cash flow approach takes the annual current income statement and adjusts the cash flows by forecasting what they would be after implementing all of the planning recommendations. This approach begins with the discretionary cash flows at the bottom of the income statement and accounts for each of the recommendations in the order of priority. The annual cost of each recommendation is charged against the discretionary cash flows regardless of any negative cash flow impact. The approach separates the recommendations into four impact categories:

1. No cash flow impact.
2. Annual recurring positive (very few) or negative cash flow impact.
3. One-time non-recurring positive (sale of an asset) or negative (pay off debt) cash flow impact.
4. Impact that affects the client in a positive or negative way, but does not affect his cash flow on the income statement (an increase in the employer match in the 401(k) plan as a result of increased employee deferrals or the employer no longer matches thus causing a decrease).

RISK MANAGEMENT

The immediate risk management recommendations are usually related to insurance portfolio changes because perils (the cause of a loss) are event driven (e.g., untimely death) or unpredictable, and can occur at any time. It takes a long time for an implemented financial plan to provide financial security for a client, with both savings and investing potentially taking 25 to 40 years to be successful. However, a catastrophic loss caused by a peril associated with personal risks (life, health, disability, or long-term care), property loss, or liability can occur suddenly and completely destroy an otherwise well thought out financial plan. Hence, the importance of implementing insurance portfolio recommendations as the first priority.

Insurance recommendations may have annual recurring positive, negative, or no cash flow impact. Insurance recommendations involve adding, deleting, changing, or replacing some aspect of the insurance portfolio so as to improve the overall catastrophic protection for the client and maximize premium efficiency. The following provides examples of insurance recommendations impact (or lack of) on cash flows.

Exhibit 2.17 **Insurance Recommendations and Their Impact on Cash Flows**

1	**No Cash Flow Impact** • Change name of beneficiary • Assign policy to another • Stop driving uninsured vehicle • Clarify the lifetime benefits of an employer provided health plan
2A	**Positive Annual Cash Flow Impact** • Raise deductibles (e.g., auto) • Eliminate duplicate coverage (e.g., disability) • Reduce coverage (e.g., home value declined) • Replace one policy for another (e.g., term life)
2B	**Negative Annual Cash Flow Impact** • Purchase life, health, disability, long-term care, property, or liability insurance • Increasing the amount of current coverage • Lowering deductibles

Insurance recommendations follow the three-panel and metrics approach when a detailed analysis of the insurance portfolio needed for a particular client is conducted. The estimated cash flow impact resulting from changes described in cash flow categories 2A and 2B above can be determined by contacting an insurance agent who sells the product type that is being changed, added, deleted, or replaced (and may also be estimated by a thorough internet search). For purposes of this chapter and the textbook, assume that the planner has previously investigated the costs and/or savings from changing, adding, deleting, or replacing an insurance policy. Therefore, when the planner implements these recommendations into the cash flow statement, it is an accurate estimate of the cost (e.g., the annual per $1,000 cost of term life insurance for a male age 30 is about 70 cents for a 30-year term policy).

Exhibit 2.18 provides an illustration of risk management recommendations for a client along with the cash flow impact and implementation responsibility.

Examples of Risk Management Recommendations

Exhibit 2.18

	Recommendation	Annual Recurring Cost <Negative> + Positive*	Non-Recurring Cost	Other	To Be Implemented by Client or Planner
1	Change the beneficiary on life insurance Policy A to wife	None			Client
2	Purchase a $500k 30-year term life insurance policy on husband	<$350.00>			Client
3	Purchase disability insurance for wife 60% of pay, benefits to 65, guaranteed renewable	<$360.00>			Client
4	Change homeowners policy to reflect a decline in value and raise the homeowner's deductible	+$250.00			Client

** For the purpose of this textbook, cash flow impacts are estimated.*

Debt Management

The next area of recommendations will either involve debt management or savings and investing depending on the client's priorities. Since debt management has an impact on savings and investments, debt management will be covered first.

Frequently, people have too much debt, have debt with high interest rates, and/or have debt that is not well managed. The analysis of debt includes calculating housing ratios 1 and 2 and comparing those to the well established benchmarks (metrics) of 28% / 36%. In addition, the financial planner should evaluate the quality and the cost of each client's individual debt. Good debt tends to have two components: (1) the interest rate is relatively low in comparison to expected inflation and expected investment returns, and (2) the expected debt repayment period is substantially less than the expected economic life of the asset. An example of good debt is a fixed 15-year mortgage on a home with an economic life of the home in excess of 40 years, a house payment that fits within the housing ratios, and an interest rate of five percent (and the lowest rate available) when the client's raise rate is expected to be four percent, inflation is expected to be three percent, and the client's expected investment return is 8.5 percent. Another example of good debt is a student loan used to provide education tied to a profession (e.g., medicine, law, financial planning, accounting, or engineering) for a person with a reasonable work life expectancy. This type of education is essentially an investment that can provide returns well in excess of the capital cost and over a period much longer than the debt repayment period. It remains important that debt is incurred at a reasonable interest rate.

In addition to good debt, there is also reasonable debt where the debt repayment period is longer or the returns on the debt are positive, but less certain than for good debt. Examples of reasonable debt include 30-year home mortgages at conforming interest rates and student loans that are for general education.

Bad debt is associated with: (1) high interest rates, or (2) when the economic life of the purchase is exceeded by the associated debt repayment period. An example of bad debt is an automobile loan with a small down payment and a 72-month term where the economic life of the automobile is three to five years. Another example of bad debt involves debt with high interest rates, (which includes most credit cards). Consider the following credit card debt and associated pay off schedule ramifications:

Alternative	Balance	Minimum Payment Due	Term to Pay-Off Balance	Implied Interest Rate	Total Estimated Payments
A	$1,912.78	$39.13	16 years	24%	$7,512.79
B	$1,912.78	$75.04	3 years	24%	$2,701.58
C	$1,912.78	$106.26	1.5 years	0%*	$1,912.78

* The rate is 0% interest because it is a promotional program with 18-months free interest but only if the account is completely paid off by the promotional code expiration date.

Note in the above example that if the client only pays the minimum monthly payment (Alternative A), it will take 16 years and cost $7,512.79 to pay for $1,912.78 of debt.

For Alternative C, note that retailers using promotional rates of zero percent, also use low minimum payments that creates a balloon payment at the end of the promotional term. Retailers expect that most consumers will violate the agreement resulting in them having to pay all of the interest from the original date of purchase.

EXHIBIT 2.19 CHARACTERISTICS OF VARIOUS TYPES OF DEBT

Classification of Debt	Interest Rates	Nature of and Economic Life of Asset Purchased	Repayment Period	Examples
Good Debt	Relatively Low	Typically Long Lived	Substantially less than economic life of asset	• Home purchase with 15-year mortgage • Student loan with vocation • Car loan with repayment period of 3 years or less
Reasonable Debt	Competitive	Typically Long Lived	Less than the economic life of asset	• Home purchase with 30-year mortgage • Student loan for general higher education • Car loan with repayment period of 4-5 years
Bad Debt	High	Short or Long Lived or Consumed Expenditure	Longer than economic life of purchase	• Minimum payments on credit card debt • Car loan with repayment period longer than economic life of car

The following table outlines example debt management recommendations for a client, including the cash flow impact and implementation responsibilities.

Debt Management Recommendations

Exhibit 2.20

	Recommendations	Annual Recurring Cost <Negative> + Positive	Non-Recurring Cost (Savings)	Other	To Be Implemented by Client or Planner
A	Refinance a home for 15 years at 5% (current loan at 7.5% on $300,000). 3% closing included in mortgage	+ $4,049.73			Client
B	Pay off balance of credit cards (also eliminates recurring payment)	+ $2,150.00	<$9,000> to pay off		Client
C	Pay off furniture loan	+ $1,802.00	<$3,115> to pay off		Client

Savings and Investing Management

Savings and investing management recommendations require both an increase in savings and an increase in the emergency fund. Once the planner has calculated the savings rate (savings and reinvestment of dividends, interest, and capital gains, plus any employer match/gross pay), the rate should equal 10 to 13 percent if the client only has one financial goal, that being financial security. As previously stated, if the client and family have multiple financial goals including retirement, college education, and lump-sum goals (e.g., new house or second home) the savings rate must be increased from the 10 to 13 percent to a savings rate necessary to achieve all of the goals. It is possible that the client can be more tax efficient by saving on a pre-tax rather than post-tax basis. Recall that the 10 to 13 percent savings rate is for a client who is between ages 25 and 35 years old.

The rule of thumb for an emergency fund is three to six months of non-discretionary cash flows. The astute planner understands however, that there are no absolutes in financial planning. The more difficult the labor market and the more unique the worker, the longer the worker may be out of work, which is one of the most significant risks addressed by the emergency fund. The following exhibit contains both savings and investing management recommendations. The cash flow impact is listed along with implementation responsibilities.

Saving and Investing Recommendations

Exhibit 2.21

	Recommendation	Annual Recurring Cost <Negative> + Positive	Non-Recurring Cost	Other	To Be Implemented by Client or Planner
A	Increase the 401(k) plan employee deferral by $1,000 from $2,000 to $3,000 (note that there is a tax savings of 15% and an increased employer match	<$1,000> + $150		+ $500 Employer Match	Client
B	Add to the emergency fund to get to 3 months coverage		<$5,000>		Client

Other approach recommendations may include:

- executing estate planning documents (e.g., will, durable power of attorney for health care, advanced medical directive),
- managing the withholding of taxes (W-4),
- planning for income from part time jobs or changing jobs to earn more,
- annuitizing an annuity to create recurring income,
- planning to take required minimum distributions from IRAs and qualified plans, or
- deciding to begin drawing Social Security retirement benefits.

These additional recommendations require an analysis of any impact on cash flow and should be implemented in order of priority.

Ultimately, the cash flow approach yields a net recurring cash flow number and a net non-recurring cash flow number. If the cash flow impact is positive, all is well, but if the cash flow impact is negative (as it usually is), then the planner will need to look for the money with which to fund the client's recommendations. There are usually three possible sources of funding that may be available:

- savings from refinancing of a home mortgage,
- increased cash flows from adjusting the W-4 exemptions upward, and
- cash flows from the sale of assets on the balance sheet.

These may also be additional cash flows from raising deductibles on insurance policies.

A lack of funding availability will limit the ability to immediately implement recommendations. However, since the recommendations are already prioritized, the planner can simply cut off implementing recommendations at the point where there is no additional funding remaining and later fund the remainder of the recommendations.

The cash flow approach should include:

- a mortgage refinance calculation, both pre and post recommendations;
- a current and projected tax analysis pre and post recommendations;
- a present value analysis of all needs pre recommendations; and
- a consideration of alternatives (e.g., delay retirement, include Social Security).

THE STRATEGIC APPROACH

The strategic approach is characterized by a client mission statement (e.g., to achieve financial security), a set of goals, and a set of objectives. Specifically, the planner can construct a plan driven by the client's mission statement. Then, a needs-driven list of client goals is created. From the list of goals, a detailed list of objectives is created that will all together result in the accomplishment of the mission of the client's financial planning. The planner creates a plan by reviewing relevant internal and external data and produces a plan for the long-run (the mission) with both short and intermediate accomplishment of goals and objectives. The plan incorporates capitalizing on a client's strengths (e.g., good salary or savings rate), overcoming a client's weaknesses (e.g., insufficient insurance), taking advantage of external opportunities, and mitigating external threats.

Note that the strategic approach takes into consideration needs versus wants. Needs are defined as those objectives required by law (e.g., auto liability insurance) or essential to make the financial plan successful (e.g., savings). Wants on the other hand are somewhat discretionary (e.g., purchase a new home). Planning using the strategic approach focuses on the needs-driven versus wants-driven priorities that can be successfully implemented following the design of a financial planning mission, goal and objective oriented arrangement.

The typical structure of the strategic approach to financial planning includes:

Mission Statement (An Enduring Long-Term Statement)

- Financial Security – A formal statement of the purpose of the client's financial planning.

Goals (Broadly Conceived Goals)

- Adequate risk management portfolio
- Adequate savings rate for retirement and education
- Adequate emergency fund
- Adequate debt management
- Adequate investment portfolio
- Adequate estate plan

> *Quick Quiz 2.4*
>
> **Highlight the answer to these questions:**
>
> 1. The cash flow approach adjusts the cash flows on the balance sheet by forecasting what they would be after implementing all client recommendations.
>   a. True
>   b. False
>
> 2. The three areas the cash flow approach focuses on are the risk management, the debt management, and the savings and investment management cash flow areas of the client's financial planning.
>   a. True
>   b. False
>
> 3. The strategic approach is a needs versus wants directed financial plan based on the client's mission statement and goals.
>   a. True
>   b. False
>
> False, True, True.

Objectives (Narrow Measurable Objectives)

- **Risk Management** – A risk management objective may include the purchase or increase or decrease in coverage of life, disability, liability, or personal property insurance. In addition, the client may need to sell a liability associated asset that is either uninsured or uninsurable.
- **Debt Management** - Objectives associated with debt management may include reducing or eliminating high interest debt, paying off credit card debt, and reducing housing ratios to appropriate levels (HR1 = $\leq$ 28% and HR2 = $\leq$ 36%).
- **Tax Management and Emergency Fund** - For tax management purposes, the client may need to adjust income tax over withholding as an objective in order to meet other cash-required objectives. The client's emergency fund balance may need to be increased to meet at least a three to six month balance objective.
- **Savings and Investments** - Savings objectives may include creating, adjusting, or increasing amounts associated with retirement, education, or housing funding.

Changing the risk of an investment portfolio or either buying or selling existing investments to fit the financial planning mission are possible investment objectives.

- **Estate Plan** - Having estate documents prepared (will, durable power of attorney for financial matters and healthcare, advanced medical directive etc.) is an important objective.

If the planner chooses to start the financial planning process using the strategic approach method, it is likely that this approach will be followed by the use of the cash flow approach and recommendations. This ensures that implementation of the mission, goals, and objectives are feasible.

Investment Analysis

- Risk tolerance analysis comparison of current implicit rate of return tool with PASS score.
- Investment performance analysis compares current rate of return to the expected rate of return based on the risk tolerance profile applied with the PASS score.

PRESENTATION OF THE PRESENT VALUE APPROACH

When presenting the present value approach, it is useful to present values at various times and both the overall savings requirements and specific goal savings requirements. As an example, presume the following:

Table 1

Goal	Present Value	Annual Savings Required*	Annual Savings Required**
# 1 - Retirement	$300,000.00	$28,926.65	$28,926.65
# 2 - Education	$195,000.00	$18,802.32	$23,652.89****
# 3 - Second Home	$100,840.00	$9,723.21	$9,732.21
Total	$595,840.00	$57,452.18	N/A
Current Resources***	($200,000.00)	($19,284.43)	N/A
Net Needs	$395,840.00	$38,167.75	N/A

* Savings on an annual ordinary annuity basis over the remaining work life expectancy.

** Savings required to the beginning of the draw down.

Other Assumptions:

- Earnings Rate 8% / Inflation 3% / Age 42 / Retire at 65
- Educate 3 children 2, 4, and 6 years old. Education inflation 5%.
- Purchase second home 23 years from now for $300,000.

*** Current resources include investment assets and cash and cash equivalents.

**** Assume the money is needed in 14 years.

By presenting the present value in current real dollar terms, the net needs can be hypothetically treated as an obligation (mortgage) to be repaid at the expected rate of return (in this case, 8%) over the work life expectancy (in this case, 23 years). The resultant ($38,167.75) can then be compared to the current actual savings rate to determine whether current savings are adequate to pay for all goals. Presuming annual savings are not adequate, it is relatively easy to see the cost of each goal in terms of annual required savings and consider priorities. For example, in this case, the client might decide the second home is not important or a less expensive one could suffice. The client could decide that one or two more years of working would be preferable to changing other goals. Keep in mind that an additional year of working: (1) increases Social Security benefits up to age 70, (2) increases savings years by one, (3) increases compounding by one, and (4) decreases consumption by one year. One to two years of delayed retirement can be very significant.

In addition to the Table 1 presentation, it may also be useful to present the values in nominal dollars for each goal at the start of the draw down as in Table 2.

TABLE 2

Goal	Present Values	Future Values	
# 1 - Retirement	$300,000.00	$1,761,439.09	Value at the beginning of retirement
# 2 - Education	$195,000.00	$572,752.76	Value at the start of education*
# 3 - Second Home	$100,840.00	$592,078.39	Value in 23 years
Income**	$170,000	$335,509.71	Value in 23 years

* Assume in 14 years.

** Assume raises are at 3%.

Table 2 data provides a perspective of both the present and future (nominal) dollars required to achieve the financial goals. The current and projected income also provides a relative perspective as between today and the future costs of goals.

In the Table 1 example, it is notable that education (which is sometimes the most important goal) could be fully funded by utilizing all of the current resources. If the goal of the second home were abandoned the required savings rate would decline from approximately 22.5% to 17%. Table 3 depicts various changes and the impact of each change on the required savings rate.

TABLE 3

Alternatives	Current Savings Rate Required	New Savings Rate Required
# 1 - Abandon 2nd home, fully fund education now, retire on time	22.5%	17%
# 2 - Abandon 2nd home, fully fund education now, delay retirement 2 years	22.5%	12.77%*
# 3 - Fully fund education now, delay retirement 2 years	22.5%	18.324%

Ultimately, the questions are "What are the priorities of the client" and "How much (savings % or dollars) are they willing to sacrifice to achieve the goals and over what time frame?"

The present value approach assists the planner in understanding the requirements of the goals that the client has specified in present and future dollar terms as well as the corresponding savings required to achieve those goals.

CHAPTER

Personal Financial Statements: Preparation and Analysis

3

INTRODUCTION

Personal financial statements are essential for the financial planner to evaluate a client's financial position and to review changes or trends in the client's financial position and financial performance. The planner can use the financial statements to prepare a financial statement analysis, which is the process of calculating financial ratios and comparing the actual ratios to industry established benchmarks. Financial statement analysis helps to reveal:

- how well a client is managing debt,
- whether the client is saving enough for retirement or education goals,
- whether the client's risks are adequately covered, and
- how well is the client able to meet short-term financial obligations.

The process of conducting financial statement analysis permits the financial planner to identify weaknesses in the client's financial position and performance. The planner can then develop an appropriate set of actions to respond to and improve upon those weaknesses.

Clients rarely have well prepared personal financial statements. A financial planner should be prepared to assist the client in the preparation of basic financial statements, including a balance sheet and a statement of income and expenses. This chapter explores the preparation and presentation of a client's financial statements. Financial statement analysis is also covered in this chapter so that the planner is prepared to evaluate the client's financial position and determine trends in the client's financial position and financial performance.

Preparing financial statements is the process of accounting for asset and liability balances, as well as for income and expenses for a client. For personal financial planning purposes, there are two principal financial statements and two supplementary financial statements.

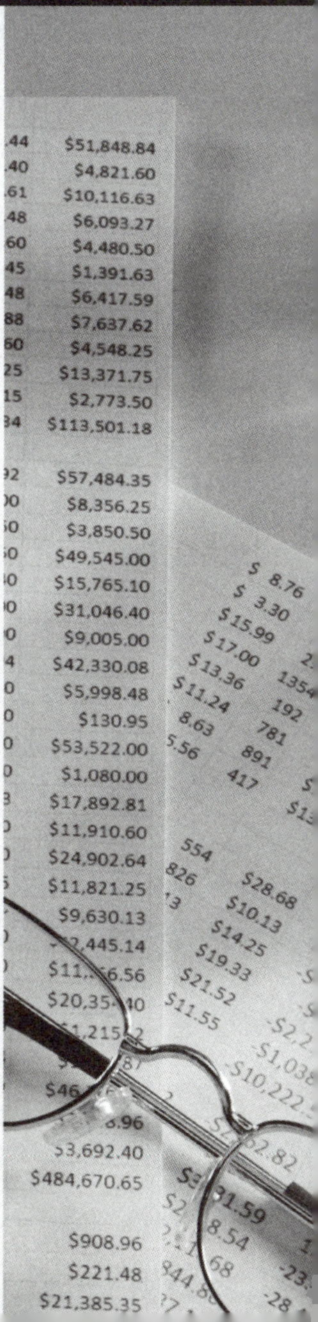

Principal Financial Statements

- The Balance Sheet (A Statement of Financial Position or A Statement of Assets, Liabilities and Net Worth)
- The Income Statement (A Statement of Income and Expenses)

Supplementary Financial Statements

- The Statement of Net Worth
- The Cash Flow Statement

Key Concepts

Underline/highlight the answers to these questions as you read:

1. Identify the process and purpose of financial statement analysis.

2. Identify the common principal and supplementary financial statements used as part of the financial planning process.

This chapter primarily focuses on the balance sheet and income statement. Although the statements of net worth and cash flow provide useful information, in practice they are rarely prepared for individuals. This chapter also builds on and expands the approaches and analysis discussed in Chapter 2, including the financial statement and ratio analysis, the pie chart approach, and the two-step / three panel approach.

BALANCE SHEET (STATEMENT OF FINANCIAL POSITION)

A balance sheet, or as commonly referred to, a statement of financial position, represents the accounting for items the client "owns" (assets) and items that are "owed" (liabilities). The difference between the value of assets and liabilities is the owner's equity (net worth). The balance sheet provides a snapshot of the client's assets, liabilities, and net worth as of a stated date. Typically, a balance sheet is dated "as of 12/31/xx", which represents the value of assets owned, liabilities owed, and resulting net worth at that particular moment in time.

Assets represent anything of economic value that can ultimately be converted into cash. Depending upon the client's intent regarding disposition of an asset, the asset is further classified into one of the following three categories as reflected on the balance sheet:

- Cash and Cash Equivalents (Current Assets)
- Investment Assets
- Personal Use Assets

Key Concepts

Underline/highlight the answers to these questions as you read:

1. Identify the main categories listed on a balance sheet.

2. Distinguish between cash and cash equivalents, investment assets, and personal use assets.

3. Distinguish between short-term liabilities and long-term liabilities.

CASH AND CASH EQUIVALENTS

Cash and cash equivalents (current assets) represent assets that are highly liquid, which means they are either cash or can be converted to cash (within the next 12 months) with little to no price concession from their current value. Cash and cash equivalents also represent very safe investments that are unlikely to lose value. An example of a current asset that can be converted to cash within the next 12 months is a certificate of deposit that matures in six months.

Typical assets included in cash and cash equivalents are:

- cash,
- checking accounts,
- money market accounts,
- savings accounts, and
- certificates of deposit (maturity is ≤ 12 months).

Since cash and cash equivalents represent highly liquid "safe" investments, it is important to the client's financial position and financial performance to maintain sufficient levels of cash and cash equivalents to meet liabilities that are due within the next 12 months. Benchmarks and ratios (discussed later in this chapter) assist the planner in determining whether the client is maintaining sufficient levels of cash and cash equivalents.

Investment Assets

Investment assets include appreciating assets or those assets being held to accomplish one or more financial goals. Typical assets included in this category are:

- retirement accounts (401(k) plans, profit sharing plans, IRAs, annuities),
- brokerage accounts,
- education funds,
- cash value in life insurance,
- business ownership interests, and
- the vested portion of any pension plan.

Investment assets are listed on the balance sheet at their current fair market value. As a financial planner, there are important issues to consider when preparing the investment assets section, including:

- ensuring that all investment assets are included (e.g., stock certificates sitting in a safety deposit box), and
- making sure that the current fair market value of the investment is properly determined.

One of the most difficult investment assets to value is ownership in a privately-held business. Unlike a publicly-traded company, there is no established market value for a privately-held company:

- whether the basis for valuation is a professional opinion versus the owner's opinion,
- if a professional valuation, is it current (completed in the last six to nine months),
- a determination of whether goodwill is associated specifically with the business or with the owner (in the event that the owner leaves the business), and
- Whether the business will be sold to fund retirement and if so, what will be the characteristics of the funding (e.g., short versus long-term funding arrangement).

Important questions to consider with regard to the valuation of a private business include:

- Who prepared the valuation? The valuation may have been prepared by the owner himself, which could result in the value of the business being significantly overstated or understated. Alternatively, a professional valuation expert may have valued the business. However, it is important to understand the purpose of the valuation and to understand important assumptions of the valuation.
- How current is the valuation? The valuation may be accurate or it may be understated or overstated if the underlying assumptions no longer apply.
- Is goodwill associated with the business or with the owner? Some businesses are critically dependent on the owner and founder of the business and can be negatively impacted upon the owner's departure.
- Will the business be sold to fund retirement? It is important to understand how the owner is planning on selling a business and over what time period he expects the proceeds. This information will assist the planning in a conversation about any risks associated with the exit strategy.

For small business owners, a large portion of their net worth is usually invested in the business. Financial planners should be very cautious and conservative when valuing business ownership interests on the balance sheet. If the business is valued too high, the client's financial position will be too optimistic, perhaps resulting in a shortfall at retirement. If the business is valued too low, the client's financial resources may be improperly allocated, jeopardizing other financial goals.

Personal Use Assets

Personal use assets are those assets that maintain the client's lifestyle. Examples of assets included in personal use assets are:

- personal residences
- automobiles
- furniture
- clothing
- boats
- jet skis
- vacation homes
- electronics (television, stereo, iPod, etc.)
- collectibles (art, antiques)

The value of personal use assets is usually determined by client estimation as opposed to appraisal. Anytime a financial planner is estimating the value of assets, it is always better to be conservative and not overvalue the assets. Financial statements and financial statement analysis provides insight into the client's financial position, performance, strengths and weaknesses, so accurately valuing assets is an important part of the process.

Although the value of personal use assets will impact net worth, financial planners are more concerned with cash, cash equivalents and investment assets when conducting financial statement analysis. As previously discussed, a properly valued business ownership interest is important, especially if the client is relying on the business to accomplish a retirement goal. However, the **exact** economic or fair market value of personal use assets is less important than the exact fair market value of investment assets. Reasonable and conservative estimates are usually adequate when valuing personal use assets, because the client will likely continue to use their personal use assets to maintain their lifestyle through the retirement years. It is important to periodically determine if there are any major changes in the value of personal use assets, such as the appreciation or depreciation of the primary residence, vacation property, and other high dollar amount items. Also, a question may arise as to whether an item is a personal use asset or an investment asset.

EXAMPLE 3.1

Holly purchases a $50,000 painting and hangs it on her wall. Is it a personal use asset or an investment asset? The determination is dependent on Holly's intent. Does she intend to leave it on her wall to show her family and friends or does she intend to hold it as an appreciating asset to be sold for a profit? If Holly's intent is to leave the painting on the wall to enjoy, then the painting should be classified as a personal use asset on the balance sheet. If Holly's intent is to hold the painting to advance future profit, then the painting should be classified as an investment asset.

LIABILITIES

Liabilities represent financial obligations that the client owes to creditors. To satisfy a liability, either a client-owned asset or some other economic benefit must be transferred to the creditor. A liability may be either a legal obligation or moral obligation that resulted from a past transaction. A legal obligation may be a mortgage or a car payment. If a client borrows money from the bank to purchase a house or a car, then there is a legal obligation to repay the loan (a liability). A moral obligation can result from the pledging of a donation to a charity or a not-for-profit entity. A pledge is not necessarily a legal obligation, but if intended to be honored, it does represent a financial liability.

EXAMPLE 3.2

Ivan is an alumnus of Florida State University and is a football season ticket holder. In April each year, Ivan pledges to contribute $1,000 to the boosters association in return for parking privileges at the football games. Ivan does not have to pay the $1,000 pledge until the end of the year. Ivan has a moral obligation to pay the $1,000, and it should be reflected as a liability on his balance sheet until the $1,000 pledge is paid (assuming he intends to pay the pledge). In some states, pledges to charitable organizations are legally enforceable debts.

Other types of liabilities include unpaid utility bills, credit card bills, insurance premiums that are due and any other debt obligations. Liabilities are valued at their current outstanding balance as of the date of the balance sheet. The current outstanding balance represents the amount owed to the creditor, including amounts for any bills that have been received but not yet paid. Liabilities are categorized according to the timing of when the liability is due or expected to be paid. The categories of liabilities are:

- short-term or current liabilities (expected to be paid within one year), and
- long-term liabilities (expected to be paid beyond one year).

Short-Term (Current) Liabilities

Short-term liabilities represent those obligations that are "current" in nature that are due or expected to be paid within the next 12 months (≤ 12 months). Examples of liabilities that are included in short-term or current liabilities are:

- Electric, gas, water, garbage, and sewage bills incurred, but not yet paid
- Principal portion of any debt obligations due within the next 12 months (mortgage and auto loan)
- Unpaid credit card bills
- Outstanding medical expenses
- Insurance premiums due
- Unpaid taxes

When reporting debts such as a mortgage or a car loan, only the principal portion of the loan that is due in the next 12 months is reported as a short-term or current liability. This treatment is the correct accounting methodology, **but is rarely used by individuals in preparation of personal financial statements.** Interest expense for the next 12 months is not reported on the balance sheet. If a loan is paid off today, the payoff amount would include the interest expense incurred since the last payment (plus the outstanding principal) because the interest expense is calculated for having a loan outstanding for the previous month. Liabilities only reflect the amount currently owed by the client. Since interest expense for the next 12 months has yet to be incurred, it is not reflected on the balance sheet.

Long-Term Liabilities

Long-term liabilities are financial obligations owed that are due and expected to be paid beyond the next 12 months. Long-term liabilities are usually the result of major financial purchases and resulting obligations that are amortized over multiple years. Examples of liabilities that are included under long-term liabilities are:

- primary residence loans (mortgage),
- vacation home loans (mortgage),
- automobile loans,
- student loans, and
- any other type of loan or promissory note.

When reporting the outstanding balance of a loan, the current portion of the liability should be reported separately from the long-term portion of the liability. This allows the financial planner to make a comparison between current assets and current liabilities and to evaluate the client's liquidity status and ability to meet short-term financial obligations.

Quick Quiz 3.1

Highlight the answer to these questions:

1. The client's balance sheet represents all income earned less expenses incurred for the period being covered.
   a. True
   b. False

2. Cash and cash equivalents are assets that are highly liquid and are either cash or can be converted to cash within the next 12 months.
   a. True
   b. False

3. Investment assets are those assets that help to maintain the client's lifestyle.
   a. True
   b. False

4. Long-term liabilities represent client financial obligations that are owed to creditors beyond the next 12 months.
   a. True
   b. False

False, True, False, True.

EXAMPLE 3.3

Lisa has a $300,000 mortgage on her house, with a 30-year term at 6% interest. She expects to pay a total of $21,583.81 this upcoming year, including $3,684.04 in principal reduction and $17,899.77 in interest expense. The loan should be properly categorized as a liability on the balance sheet as follows:

Short-Term Liabilities

Mortgage on Primary Residence = $3,684.04

Long-Term Liabilities

Mortgage on Primary Residence = $296,315.96

Total Liabilities = $300,000.00

Note: Even though Lisa knows how much interest expense she will be paying in the next 12 months ($17,899.77), it is not reported as a liability until the interest expense is incurred. If the interest is paid as incurred, it will not be recorded as a liability but rather simply be reflected in the monthly or annual income statement. She is not legally obligated to pay the interest until it accrues each month. Another way to think about this is to consider that she could pay $300,000 today to retire the debt and thus, avoid the interest during the year.

VALUING ASSETS AND LIABILITIES

As previously stated, it is important that assets reflect their fair market value and that liabilities are stated at their current outstanding principal balance as of the date of the balance sheet.

NET WORTH

The net worth of the client as reflected on the balance sheet represents the amount of total equity (assets - liabilities = net worth) a client has accumulated as of the date of the balance sheet. When evaluating a client's financial position, net worth is an important consideration because it represents an absolute dollar amount reflective of a client's financial position. A positive net worth may imply the client has done a good job of saving, investing, and managing debt. A negative net worth implies that the client is insolvent and potentially facing bankruptcy.

Unfortunately, due to the real estate crisis in years 2008 to 2010 and the high home foreclosure rate, a negative net worth is a reality for many households. In 2009 alone, California experienced a 20 percent decline in real estate values, which was in addition to the 19 percent decline in 2008. For many homeowners this collapse has led to the value of their homes declining significantly below the outstanding debt on the homes. In other words, they are "upside down" on their mortgage (also known as underwater). For some clients who have accumulated savings and investment assets of $200,000 to $300,000, it is possible to have a negative net worth simply due to the decline in real estate values.

Exhibit 3.1 illustrates a balance sheet for Mr. and Mrs. Zacker that reflects the three types of assets, short-term liabilities, long-term liabilities and the resulting net worth.

BALANCE SHEET EXAMPLE

EXHIBIT 3.1

Statement of Financial Position
Mr. and Mrs. Zacker
Balance Sheet as of 12/31/12

Assets				**Liabilities and Net Worth**			
Current Assets				**Current Liabilities**			
JT	Cash & Checking	$5,000		W	Credit Cards	$5,000	
JT	CD Maturing in 6 months	$25,000		H	Auto # 1	$5,000	
JT	Money Market	$50,000		W	Auto # 2	$6,000	
				JT	Personal Residence	$10,000	
Total Current Assets			$80,000	**Total Current Liabilities**			$26,000
Investment Assets				**Long-Term Liabilities**			
H	401(k) Plan	$30,000		H	Auto # 1	$14,000	
W	IRA	$50,000		W	Auto # 2	$17,000	
JT	Brokerage Account	$100,000		JT	Personal Residence	$450,000	
W	Value of Business Interests	$500,000					
W	Education Savings	$75,000		**Total Long-Term Liabilities**			$481,000
Total Invested Assets			$755,000				
				Total Liabilities			$507,000
Personal Use Assets							
JT	Personal Residence	$500,000		**Total Net Worth**			$1,008,000
JT	Furniture, Clothing	$125,000					
H	Auto # 1	$25,000					
W	Auto # 2	$30,000					
Total Personal Use Assets			$680,000				
Total Assets			$1,515,000		**Total Liabilities and Net Worth**		$1,515,000

H = Husband Owns
W = Wife Owns
JT = Jointly owned by husband and wife

The balance sheet formula is: Assets = Liabilities + Net Worth.

Alternatively, we can restate the formula, such that: Assets – Liabilities = Net Worth.

These formulas help us understand how financial transactions impact a client's net worth.

EXAMPLE 3.4

Lisa buys a house for $400,000. She makes a $50,000 down payment and finances the balance with a mortgage. How is her net worth impacted from this transaction?

	Assets	-	Liabilities	=	Net Worth
Cash and Cash Equivalents	($50,000)				($50,000)
Personal Use Assets	+ $400,000				+ $400,000
Mortgage on New House			$350,000		($350,000)
Net Impact	$350,000	-	$350,000	=	$0

Lisa exchanges one asset ($50,000 cash) for another ($400,000 home) and increases her liabilities ($350,000 mortgage). Therefore, her net worth is not impacted by purchasing the house. However, as time goes by, the increase or decrease in the value of the house will impact her net worth as will the reduction in the principal obligation of the mortgage. The principal reduction is funded most by income that would otherwise have increased another asset category on the balance sheet, such as cash or investments.

EXAMPLE 3.5

One year ago, Elaine purchased a house for $400,000. Today, the house is worth $425,000 and she has reduced her outstanding mortgage principal by $10,000. What is the impact to Elaine's net worth?

	Assets	-	Liabilities	=	Net Worth
Personal Use Assets	+ $25,000				$25,000
Reduction in Outstanding Mortgage Balance			($10,000)		+ $10,000
Net Impact	$25,000	-	($10,000)	=	$35,000

Elaine's net worth increased as a result of the value of her house increasing ($25,000), plus she has paid down her mortgage throughout the year. Since her liabilities have decreased by $10,000, the two actions result in Elaine's net worth increasing by a total of $35,000.

EXAMPLE 3.6

Laureen, her husband and 5 children went on vacation to Disney World for one week. Laureen spent $7,000 on the family vacation and paid for it with money in her savings account. What is the impact to her net worth?

	Assets	-	Liabilities	=	Net Worth
Cash and Cash Equivalents	($7,000)				($7,000)
Net Impact	($7,000)	-		=	($7,000)

Laureen's net worth has decreased by the $7,000 she spent on the vacation. Although they are certainly priceless, she cannot capture the good times and memories she has from the vacation and report them on her balance sheet.

SOURCES OF INFORMATION

In order to properly and accurately prepare personal financial statements, the financial planner needs source documents from the client to properly value assets and liabilities. Source documents include:

- bank statements,
- brokerage statements,
- loan amortization schedules, and
- tax returns.

> *Key Concepts*
>
> **Underline/highlight the answers to these questions as you read:**
>
> 1. Distinguish between property owned fee simple and tenancy in common.
> 2. Distinguish between property owned JTWROS and tenancy by the entirety versus community property.
> 3. Identify the importance of footnotes to financial statements.

ACCOUNT OWNERSHIP

As part of the balance sheet presentation, it is important to disclose how an asset or liability is titled (owned). The most common forms of ownership are:

- Fee Simple
- Tenancy in Common
- Joint Tenancy with Right of Survivorship (JTWROS)
- Tenancy by the Entirety
- Community Property

Below is a brief explanation of the types of ownership.

Fee simple ownership is the complete ownership of property by one individual who possesses all ownership rights associated with the property, including the right to use, sell, gift, alienate, convey, or bequeath the property. Typically, a car is owned fee simple and is titled in the name of one person. When preparing a balance sheet for a husband and wife, (H) is used to designate the asset or liability belongs to the husband only and (W) is used if the asset or liability belongs to the wife only.

Tenancy in common is an interest in property held by two or more related or unrelated persons. Each owner is referred to as a tenant in common. Tenancy in common is the most common type of joint ownership between nonspouses. Each person holds an undivided, but not necessarily equal, interest in the entire property.

Joint Tenancy with Right of Survivorship (JTWROS) is typically how a husband and wife own joint property. Joint tenancy is an interest in property held by two or more related or unrelated persons called joint tenants. Each person holds an undivided, equal interest in the whole property. A right of survivorship is normally implied with this form of ownership, and at the death of the first joint tenant, the decedent's interest transfers to the other joint tenants outside of the probate process according to state titling law. Probate is the process whereby the probate court retitles assets and gives creditors an opportunity to be heard and stake a claim to any assets to satisfy outstanding debts. Because of this right of survivorship, joint tenancy is often called joint tenancy with right of survivorship.

Quick Quiz 3.2

Highlight the answer to these questions:

1. Fee Simple ownership is an interest in property held by two or more related or unrelated persons.
   a. True
   b. False

2. If property is owned tenancy by the entirety or as community property then probate is avoided.
   a. True
   b. False

False, False.

Tenancy by the entirety is similar to property owned as JTWROS between a husband and wife because property ownership is automatically transferred to the surviving spouse upon death. The two tenants own an undivided interest in the whole asset. However, the ownership cannot be severed without the consent of the other spouse.

Community property is a civil law statutory regime under which married individuals own an equal undivided interest in all property accumulated during their marriage. During marriage, the income of each spouse is considered community property. Property acquired before the marriage and property received by gift or inheritance during the marriage retains its status as separate property. However, if any separate property is commingled with community property, it is often assumed to be community property. The states following the community property regime are Arizona, California, Idaho, Louisiana, Nevada, New Mexico, Texas, Washington, and Wisconsin. Community property does not usually have an automatic right of survivorship feature although some states, including Texas and California, have a survivorship option.

As previously indicated, an important distinction between fee simple, tenants in common, and sometimes community property versus JTWROS and tenancy by the entirety is that property owned by the former will pass through probate at the death of the owner. Property owned JTWROS and tenancy by the entirety avoids probate and the decedent's interest transfers automatically. Property owned in a revocable trust would be listed on the balance sheet as trust assets.

Footnotes to the Financial Statements

Footnotes are an important source of information regarding the financial statements. Footnotes listed on financial statements can provide information such as how the asset or liability is owned. For example, it may state whether the asset is owned individually or jointly. In addition, footnotes can provide information regarding a client's purchase price of an asset, the date the asset or liability was acquired, how the value of an asset was determined and much more. When reviewing financial statements, it is important that the financial planner always read the footnotes.

STATEMENT OF INCOME AND EXPENSES

A statement of income and expenses (income statement) represents all income earned or expected to be earned by the client, less all expenses incurred or expected to be incurred during the time period being covered. The heading of the statement of income and expenses identifies the person or persons that the statement applies to, the type of financial statement, and the time period covered by the statement. To indicate the reporting period, the time period is generally listed as "For the Year Ended 12/31/xx" or for "January 1, 2012 – December 31, 2012." Although financial planners typically prepare and work with annual financial statements, the income statement can also be prepared for a monthly or quarterly period of time.

Key Concepts

Underline/highlight the answers to these questions as you read:

1. Identify the main categories listed on the statement of income and expenses.
2. Identify examples of recurring income.
3. Identify examples of savings contributions.
4. Distinguish between variable and fixed expenses.
5. Determine how net discretionary cash flow is calculated.

Income

Examples of recurring income accounts earned by the client are:

- Salary
- Interest
- Dividend
- Pension
- Retirement Account Withdrawal
- Business Income
- Alimony Received

Note:
Dividend and interest income may not be included on the Income Statement because they are often reinvested and included in the portfolio rate of return. Therefore, they are not included on the Income Statement or in the annual savings rate.

Savings Contributions

Along with expenses, recurring savings contributions must be reported on the statement of income and expenses. Examples include savings contributions to the following types of accounts:

- 401(k) plan
- 403(b) plan
- IRA (Traditional or Roth)
- Education Savings
- Any other type of savings account contributions

Expenses

Recurring expenses represent those items that are paid regularly by the client during the time period being presented. Examples of expense accounts include:

- Mortgage Principal and Interest
- Utilities
- Taxes
- Insurance
- Telephone
- Water
- Cable or Satellite
- Internet
- Cell Phone

Variable and Fixed Expenses

Expenses can be divided into variable and fixed expenses. There is less discretion over fixed expenses in the short term. Examples of fixed expense accounts include:

- Mortgage Payment
- Car Payment
- Boat Payment
- Student Loan Payment
- Property Taxes
- Insurance Premiums
- Federal and State Income Taxes Withheld
- Social Security Payments Withheld

Variable expenses are more discretionary than fixed expenses over the short term. A client has more discretion over the amount of variable expenses and this area often presents an opportunity for savings if variable expenses are closely monitored and controlled. Examples of variable expense accounts include:

- Entertainment Expenses
- Vacation Expenses
- Travel Expenses
- Charitable Contributions (may or may not be considered variable or discretionary)

The statement of income and expenses is a compromise in accounting. Note that cash transactions that are non-recurring are not included or reported on the statement of income and expenses. Examples of cash transactions that are non-recurring include:

- the sale of stock,
- an employer's contribution to a retirement plan,
- giving or receiving a gift of cash, or
- an inheritance.

In addition, transactions that are noncash, non-recurring changes in the balance sheet are not reported on the statement of income expenses. Noncash, non-recurring changes in the balance sheet include:

- gifting (or receiving) stock, and
- gifting (or receiving) personal use assets and would only be reported in a statement of changes in net worth.

It is precisely because of the lack of perfection in the income statement that a planner should consider the balance sheet and the income statement together. The two documents provide a significantly more complete picture of the client's financial situation than either document alone.

Quick Quiz 3.3

Highlight the answer to these questions:

1. Main categories listed on the income statement include income, savings contributions, assets, and expenses.
   a. True
   b. False

2. Net discretionary cash flow represents the amount of cash flow still available after all savings, expenses, and taxes have been paid.
   a. True
   b. False

3. The client's income statement can be prepared from the client's W-2 information, credit card statement, and other billing statement information.
   a. True
   b. False

False, True, True.

Net Discretionary Cash Flows

Net discretionary cash flow represents the amount of cash flow available after all savings, expenses, and taxes have been paid. The net discretionary cash flow formula is a result of the statement of income and expenses.

The net discretionary cash flow formula from the income statement is:

Income – Savings – Expenses – Taxes = Net Discretionary Cash Flow

Net discretionary cash flow is a critical item when analyzing the statement of income and expenses. Net discretionary cash flow can be positive, negative, or equal to zero. A positive discretionary cash flow indicates that income is greater than savings, taxes, and expenses. This financial situation creates an opportunity for additional savings to accomplish a financial goal, retire debt, or purchase more comprehensive insurance. A negative net discretionary cash flow is one of the most important weaknesses a financial planner must mitigate against. A negative discretionary cash flow indicates that gross income is less than savings, taxes, and expenses. This financial situation requires steps to reduce expenses, taxes, or savings or to increase income. While a client can likely tolerate a negative net discretionary cash flow for a short period of time, ultimately, a negative net discretionary cash flow can lead to financial disaster, including bankruptcy in the most extreme cases.

The following is a statement of income and expenses for Mr. and Mrs. Zacker as expected for a complete year. This statement provides an efficient method of determining where the Zacker's income is being spent or saved during the year.

INCOME STATEMENT EXAMPLE

EXHIBIT 3.2

Statement of Income and Expenses
Mr. and Mrs. Zacker
Statement of Income and Expenses
Expected (Approximate) for 2013

		Totals
CASH INFLOWS		
Salary - Husband	$58,000	
Salary - Wife	$100,000	
Total Cash Inflows		**$158,000**
CASH OUTFLOWS		
Savings		
Husband's 401(k) Plan	$5,000	
Wife's 401(k) Plan	$10,000	
IRA Contribution	$5,000	
Education Savings (529 Plan)	$8,000	
Total Savings		**$28,000**
Debt Payments		
Personal Residence (mortgage)	$35,000	
Auto - Husband	$7,000	
Student Loans	$2,500	
Total Debt Payments		**$44,500**
Living Expenses		
Utilities	$3,500	
Gasoline for Autos	$3,000	
Lawn Service	$3,000	
Entertainment	$6,000	
Vacations	$4,000	
Church Donations	$2,000	
Food	$8,000	
Auto Maintenance	$2,500	
Telephone	$3,000	
Clothing	$6,000	
Total Living Expenses		**$41,000**
Insurance Payments		
HO Personal Residence	$4,500	
Auto Premiums	$2,000	
Life Insurance Premiums	$1,000	
Personal Liability Umbrella Premium	$500	
Total Insurance Payments		**$8,000**
Taxes		
Federal Income Taxes Withheld	$15,000	
State Income Taxes Withheld	$7,500	
Social Security Taxes	$9,000	
Property Tax Personal Residence	$4,000	
Total Taxes		**$35,500**
Total Savings, Expenses and Taxes		**$157,000**
NET DISCRETIONARY CASH FLOW		$1,000

SOURCES OF INFORMATION

Preparing a statement of income and expenses during the initial meetings with a client can be difficult because all sources of information may not yet be available. During the initial or subsequent meetings with a client, the planner should obtain the following documents with which to prepare the statement of income and expenses:

- W-2s (reports income and deferred retirement savings),
- credit card statements (provides insight to expenses and spending, with year-end statements being especially informative),
- billing statements (such as utilities, telephone, satellite, internet, water),
- bank statements (especially those with bill payments), and
- Federal and state income statements.

Frequently, a client will not have all of the above documents and may not have complete records of expenses for an entire year. In these situations, financial planners may need to "back into" expenses over the time period being presented. In other words, if the planner knows the increase in cash and cash equivalents over the time period being presented, along with the client's income, the planner can calculate the total amount spent on taxes, savings, and expenses over that time period.

EXAMPLE 3.7

Jan's salary last year was $125,000. According to her bank statements dated 12/31 from the previous two years, her cash and cash equivalents increased by $5,000. Her financial planner can assume that $120,000 ($125,000 - $5,000) was spent by Jan on taxes, savings to retirement plans, education, variable, and fixed expenses. The planner's objective now is to fill in the details of the statement of income and expenses to determine how Jan spent the $120,000 last year.

PROJECTED INCOME STATEMENTS

It is extremely useful to clients that expect a change in life or lifestyle to have the financial planner prepare a projected income statement for the period just following the projected lifestyle change (i.e., children go to college or client retires). Projected financial statements of this sort can help identify shortfalls in cash or excess net-discretionary cash flows.

STATEMENT OF NET WORTH

The purpose of the statement of net worth is to explain changes in net worth between two balance sheets by reporting financial transactions that are not reported on the income statement or other financial statements. Example of transactions that would appear on the statement of net worth are:

- Giving or receiving property other than cash
- Inheriting property other than cash
- Employer contributions or matches to retirement savings accounts
- Appreciation or depreciation of assets such as a primary residence, investments, auto, jewelry, etc.

The formula for the statement of net worth is:

Beginning balance of net worth (from the January 1st balance sheet)
\+ additions (appreciation of assets, receiving a gift or inheritance)
\- subtractions (giving gifts other than cash)
= Ending balance of net worth (from the December 31st balance sheet)

Few clients will have a statement of net worth and very few financial planners will actually prepare a statement of net worth for a client. The statement of net worth is a supplementary financial statement that captures and reports transactions that affect net worth that are otherwise not reported on the two principal statements (balance sheet and statement of income and expenses).

> *Key Concepts*
>
> **Underline/highlight the answers to these questions as you read:**
>
> 1. Recognize the purpose of a statement of net worth.
> 2. Recognize the purpose of a cash flow statement.
> 3. Determine what forecasted financial statements should reflect.
> 4. Identify the importance of budgeting and the steps to the budgeting process.

CASH FLOW STATEMENT

The purpose of the cash flow statement is to explain how cash and cash equivalents were used or generated between the period of two balance sheets. The cash flow statement is a supplementary financial statement of non-recurring transactions not reported on the statement of income and expenses. Recall that the income statement only captures monthly or annually recurring income and expenses. The major sections of the cash flow statement includes how nonrecurring cash transactions were used or generated from investment activities and financing activities.

Cash Flow Statement Category Examples

Exhibit 3.3

Investing Activities
• Purchase or sale of a personal use asset, such as a car or house for cash (decrease in cash)
• Purchase or sale of an investment asset, such as a mutual fund or stock (increase or decrease)
• Contributing to a retirement or education savings account (decrease in cash)
• Receiving or making gifts of cash (increase or decrease)
• Cash inheritances (increase in cash)
Financing Activities
• Principal reduction of any loans (decrease in cash)
• Taking out any new loans (increase in cash)
• Paying off credit card balances (decrease in cash)

The result of all the transactions on the cash flow statement reflects how cash was used or generated between two balance sheets. Few clients will have a cash flow statement and very few financial planners will actually prepare a cash flow statement.

FORECASTING

After preparing the initial financial statements, the planner will work with the client to overcome any weaknesses and accomplish financial goals. Recommendations may include purchasing additional life insurance, contributing more to savings, or retiring debt. The planner should prepare forecasted balance sheets and a statement of income and expenses for next year, three years from now and five years from now. The forecasted financial statements should reflect the following:

- **Implementation of recommendations.** For example, if the planner recommends increasing 401(k) plan savings, the forecasted financial statements should indicate the amount of savings and balance of the 401(k) plan for the next year, the next three years, and the next five years.
- **Inflation adjustment for expenses.** Certain expenses are likely to increase over the next five years, such as insurance premiums, utilities, gasoline for autos, groceries, clothing, etc. The financial planner should prepare forecasted statements of income and expenses based on a historical inflation rate that is likely to continue for the next five years. Fixed interest rate debt payments are not impacted by inflation, so no inflation adjustments should be made to fixed rate loans. However, if the client has any variable interest rate loans that are likely to increase over the next five years, adjustments to the forecasted income statement should include increased debt payment for variable rate loans.
- **Inflation adjustment for income.** If the client expects to receive salary increases each year, those salary adjustments should be reflected in the forecasted statement of income and expenses.
- **Other adjustments.** Other adjustments to the forecasted financial statements may include:
    - Whether the client is retiring and experiencing major changes to their income in the next five years. The financial planner should prepare forecasted financial statements to reflect withdrawing retirement assets to generate income. The possibility of the client living on reduced income during retirement should be evaluated and forecasted in financial statements.
    - Whether the client is expected to retire debt in the next five years. The financial planner should reflect the retiring of debt on the balance sheet to determine the impact on the balance sheet, net worth, and discretionary cash flow on the statement of income and expenses.

- Whether the client expects to begin paying for college education expenses, and how the tuition payments and living expenses for the child impact the financial statements. The planner should reflect the draw down on any college savings and the increased expenses on the income statement associated with a child living away from home while at college.
- Whether the client expects to borrow money for a car, house, boat, college education, etc. The planner should incorporate the debt into the forecasted balance sheet and statement of income and expenses.

Once the financial planner has prepared forecasted financial statements, the planner can conduct financial statement analysis on the forecasted financial statements. Financial statement analysis is discussed later in this chapter.

Importance of Budgeting

The purpose in creating a financial budget is to evaluate the client's spending and savings behavior, and to establish a spending and savings plan to assist the client in achieving their financial goals. Typically, clients are resistant to preparing or using a budget because historically they have been unsuccessful at following budgets. Actual expenses turn out to be higher than they anticipated and they become frustrated by their inability to save or spend as anticipated.

> *Quick Quiz 3.4*
>
> **Highlight the answer to these questions:**
>
> 1. The statement of net worth explains changes to net worth such as employer contributions to retirement savings accounts.
>   a. True
>   b. False
>
> 2. The cash flow statement captures recurring income and expenses for the period being reported.
>   a. True
>   b. False
>
> 3. Forecasted financial statements should reflect recommendations and inflation adjusted income and expenses.
>   a. True
>   b. False
>
> True, False, True.

There are three important tips to being successful in preparing and using a budget.

- First, be realistic with spending behavior. It is easy to overlook credit card expenses for shopping or dining out. Credit cards are an easy way to "blow the budget."
- Secondly, budget a line item expense for miscellaneous expenses and unforeseen expenses. Miscellaneous expenses include gifts at the holidays, car repairs, house repairs, traffic tickets, kid's sporting events, etc. As clients get older, the miscellaneous expense item tends to grow.
- Finally, being successful with a budget takes practice. The more often a client prepares a budget and compares their actual spending to a budget, the better they will

become at budgeting. The first few budgets are likely to be unrealistic and not very accurate. Over time, the client will become more comfortable with budgeting and more realistic with their spending, savings, and miscellaneous expenses.

The budgeting process consists of the following steps:

- Establish goals with the client, such as saving for retirement, education, or a lump-sum purchase (a second home, new car, or boat).
- Determine the client's income for a time period, which could be monthly or annually. Income is based on a client's past earnings and expected income for the time period that is being budgeted.
- Determine expenses, both fixed and variable, for the time period of the budget.
- Determine whether the net discretionary cash flow is positive or negative. If net discretionary cash flow is positive, no immediate action is necessary. If net discretionary cash flow is negative, expenses must be reduced or income needs to increase.
- Present expenses as a percentage of income for the time period being presented. At this point, it is necessary to compare expenses as a percentage of income for previous budgets as well. Generally, the expenses as a percentage of income should be level or decreasing over time.

Financial Statement Analysis

Financial statements are designed to assist users in identifying key relationships and trends within the client's financial situation. Financial statement analysis is a critical part of the "analyze and evaluate" step of the financial planning process, as the financial planner is measuring a client's progress towards attaining financial goals, assessing the client's ability to meet short-term obligations, and overall debt management.

Financial statement analysis is accomplished by conducting vertical analysis, horizontal analysis, and ratio analysis. Trends will help the planner identify if the client is moving in the right direction and is making adequate progress towards attaining the financial goals. It also allows the planner to glean information that the client may not have communicated to the planner that is important to the overall financial plan and to the ability to meet future financial objectives.

> *Key Concepts*
>
> **Underline/highlight the answers to these questions as you read:**
>
> 1. Identify the purpose of financial statement analysis and the tools used in the comparative financial statement analysis.
> 2. Identify the purpose of ratio analysis.

Comparative Financial Statement Tools

Vertical Analysis

Vertical analysis lists each line item on the income statement as a percentage of total income and presents each line item on the statement of financial position (balance sheet) as a percentage of total assets. The restated percentage is known as a common size income statement or balance sheet. Vertical analysis compares each line item using a common size analysis and strips away the absolute dollar size of the line item. The financial planner is then able to compare trends for each percentage over time. Using the Zacker's statement of financial position from last year (Exhibit 3.1) and the current year (below), the planner is able to prepare a vertical analysis of their balance sheet (Exhibit 3.4).

BALANCE SHEET AS OF 12/31/2013

Statement of Financial Position
Mr. and Mrs. Zacker
Balance Sheet as of 12/31/13

Assets				**Liabilities and Net Worth**			
Current Assets				**Current Liabilities**			
JT	Cash & Checking	$5,025		W	Credit Cards	$4,985	
JT	CD Maturing in 6 months	$25,125		H	Auto # 1	$4,985	
JT	Money Market	$51,000		W	Auto # 2	$5,700	
				JT	Personal Residence	$9,700	
Total Current Assets			$81,150	**Total Current Liabilities**			$25,370
Investment Assets				**Long-Term Liabilities**			
H	401(k) Plan	$30,090		H	Auto # 1	$12,600	
W	IRA	$49,900		W	Auto # 2	$14,450	
JT	Brokerage Account	$106,000		JT	Personal Residence	$438,750	
W	Value of Business Interests	$475,000					
W	Education Savings	$77,250		**Total Long-Term Liabilities**			$465,800
Total Invested Assets			$738,240				
				Total Liabilities			$491,170
Personal Use Assets							
JT	Personal Residence	$505,000		**Total Net Worth**			$1,007,445
JT	Furniture, Clothing	$125,025					
H	Auto # 1	$22,500					
W	Auto # 2	$26,700					
Total Personal Use Assets			$679,225				
Total Assets			$1,498,615	**Total Liabilities and Net Worth**			$1,498,615

H = Husband Owns
W = Wife Owns
JT = Jointly owned by husband and wife

EXHIBIT 3.4 BALANCE SHEET VERTICAL ANALYSIS EXAMPLE

Mr. and Mrs. Zacker			
Current Assets	**12/31/12**	**12/31/13**	**Difference**
JT - Cash & Checking	0.33%	0.34%	+0.01%
JT - CD Maturing in 6 months	1.65%	1.68%	+0.03%
JT - Money Market	3.30%	3.40%	+0.10%
Total Current Assets	**5.28%**	**5.42%**	**+0.13%**
Investment Assets			
H - 401(k) Plan	1.98%	2.01%	+0.03%
W – IRA	3.30%	3.33%	+0.03%
JT - Brokerage Account	6.60%	7.07%	+0.47%
W - Value of Business Interests	33.00%	31.70%	-1.31%
W - Education Savings	4.95%	5.15%	+0.20%
Total Invested Assets	**49.83%**	**49.26%**	**-0.57%**
Personal Use Assets			
JT - Personal Residence	33.0%	33.7%	+0.69%
JT - Furniture, Clothing	8.25%	8.34%	+0.09%
H - Auto #1	1.65%	1.50%	-0.15%
W - Auto #2	1.99%	1.78%	-0.20%
Total Personal Use Assets	**44.89%**	**45.32%**	**-0.44%**
Total Assets	**100.00%**	**100.00%**	
Current Liabilities			
W - Credit Cards	0.33%	0.33%	-0.00%
H - Auto #1	0.33%	0.33%	-0.00%
W - Auto #2	0.40%	0.38%	-0.02%
JT - Personal Residence	0.66%	0.65%	-0.01%
Total Current Liabilities	**1.72%**	**1.69%**	**-0.02%**
Long-Term Liabilities			
H - Auto #1	0.92%	0.84%	-0.08%
W - Auto #2	1.12%	0.96%	-0.16%
JT - Personal Residence	29.70%	29.28%	-0.43%
Total Long-Term Liabilities	**31.74%**	**31.08%**	**-0.67%**
Total Liabilities	**33.46%**	**32.77%**	**-0.69%**
Total Net Worth	**66.54%**	**67.23%**	**+0.69%**

Statement of Income and Expenses Vertical Analysis Example

Exhibit 3.5

Mr. and Mrs. Zacker		
CASH INFLOWS	**For 2013**	**Totals**
Salary-Husband	36.71%	
Salary-Wife	63.29%	
Total Cash Inflows		**100%**
CASH OUTFLOWS		
Savings		
Husband's 401(k) Plan	3.16%	
Wife's 401(k) Plan	6.33%	
IRA Contribution	3.16%	
Education Savings (529 Plan)	5.06%	
Total Savings		**17.71%**
Available for Expenses		**82.29%**
Debt Payments		
Personal Residence (mortgage)	22.15%	
Auto-Husband	4.43%	
Student Loans	1.58%	
Total Debt Payments		**28.16%**
Living Expenses		
Utilities	2.22%	
Gasoline for Autos	1.90%	
Lawn Service	1.90%	
Entertainment	3.80%	
Vacations	2.53%	
Church Donations	1.27%	
Food	5.06%	
Auto Maintenance	1.58%	
Telephone	1.90%	
Clothing	3.80%	
Total Living Expenses		**25.96%**
Insurance Payments		
HO Personal Residence	2.85%	
Auto Premiums	1.27%	
Life Insurance Premiums	0.63%	
Personal Liability Umbrella Premium	0.32%	
Total Insurance Payments		**5.07%**
Taxes		
Federal Income Taxes Withheld	9.49%	
State Income Taxes Withheld	4.75%	
Social Security Taxes	5.70%	
Property Tax Personal Residence	2.53%	
Total Taxes		**22.47%**
Total Savings, Expenses and Taxes		**81.66%**
NET DISCRETIONARY CASH FLOW		**0.63%**

The vertical analysis for the Zackers (Exhibits 3.4 and 3.5) does not reveal any significant issues on the balance sheet or income statement. However, some important observations include a savings rate of 17.7 percent, debt payments of 28 percent and taxes of 22 percent.

Horizontal Analysis

Horizontal analysis lists each item as a percentage of a base year and creates a trend over time. For example, on the income statement, income may be stated over a six-year period from 2009 to 2014, but is reflected as a percentage of 2009 income. Expenses, taxes and savings are all stated as a percentage of a base year amount.

EXAMPLE 3.8

Eric earned $100,000 in 2009 and experienced salary increases each year for the past 6 years, such that his salary in 2013 is now $128,000.

Horizontal analysis of his income is as follows:

Year	2009	2010	2011	2012	2013	2014
Income	100%	105%	115%	125%	127%	128%

The horizontal analysis of income would indicate that Eric's income has increased each year for six years and income in 2014 is 28% more than it was in 2009. Horizontal analysis will be conducted for each line item on the income statement and balance sheet. This analysis provides the financial planner and client with a trend that identifies potential problems or demonstrates improved financial performance.

Consider an abbreviated horizontal analysis for Eric's income and golf expenses over the past five years.

Year	2009	2010	2011	2012	2013	2014
Income	100%	105%	115%	125%	127%	128%
Golf Expenses	100%	110%	120%	130%	140%	150%

Although Eric's income has increased 28% over the past 6 years, his golf expenses have increased 10% each year for the past 6 years (for a total increase of 50%). This past year, his golf expenses were 150% of his golf expenses five years ago. So, if Eric's golf expenses were $10,000 in 2009, he paid $15,000 in golf expenses in 2014. Considering that his income increased by $28,000 on a pre-tax basis, he has spent approximately 18% ($5,000 ÷ $28,000) of his additional income on this one expense item that increased $5,000 since 2009 Horizontal analysis may provide insight into a potentially problematic trend in income or expenses that needs to be addressed.

RATIO ANALYSIS

Ratio analysis is the process of calculating key financial ratios for a client, comparing those metrics to industry benchmarks and then evaluating possible deficiencies. Ratio analysis was introduced in Chapter 2 while discussing the financial statement analysis and the two step / three panel approach to evaluating a client's financial position. This section of Chapter 3 provides a more in-depth discussion of financial statement and ratio analysis. Some overlap exists with topics covered in Chapter 2, for the purpose of providing a thorough discussion of the benefits and application of ratio analysis. Ratio analysis provides a historical perspective of the client's financial position and performance because the ratios are calculated based on historical financial statements. Ratio analysis is both an art and a science. The art portion is being able to interpret the results that will become the basis for recommendations the financial planner makes to the client. The science portion is being able to calculate the financial ratios. When conducting ratio analysis, there is a need for a comparative analysis (benchmarks) to gain perspective about the client's ability to meet short and long-term obligations and goals.

Ratio analysis provides insight to underlying conditions that may not be apparent directly from the financial statements. This type of analysis expresses the relationship between selected items from the income statement and the balance sheet and provides additional information for the financial planner to use in building the client's financial plan.

Limitations

Any single financial ratio has limited use because a single ratio by itself has very little meaning. The ratio begins to take on meaning when it is used for comparison purposes over time to identify trends and when combined with information and insight from other ratios.

Ratios become more meaningful when compared to benchmarks. Benchmarks provide a rule of thumb for analyzing client status as it relates to industry standards. Note that the individual circumstances may cause any benchmark to be inappropriate for a given client. It is important that the financial planner recognize circumstances that may cause a benchmark to be inappropriate and to make adjustments accordingly.

Quick Quiz 3.5

Highlight the answer to these questions:

1. Vertical analysis is a tool for financial statement analysis using a common size comparison of a statement's line items.
   a. True
   b. False

2. Ratio analysis is the process of calculating financial ratios that are compared to example benchmarks for meaningful interpretation of the client's actual financial status.
   a. True
   b. False

3. The emergency fund ratio measure how many times the client can satisfy their short-term liabilities.
   a. True
   b. False

True, True, False.

FINANCIAL STATEMENT ANALYSIS - THE BOWDENS

BRANDON AND JILL BOWDEN

Brandon (age 40) and Jill (age 43) are married with two children, Cole (age 9) and Owen (age 5). Brandon is a vice president with a health care company and Jill manages their family and household. Brandon's salary is $124,000 per year and he contributes three percent of his salary to a 401(k) retirement plan while his employer matches $0.50 for every $1 contributed, up to three percent of his salary.

Bowden's Financial Goals

- Save for retirement.
- Save for their children's college education.
- Transfer all assets to their children at Brandon and Jill's death.

Brandon and Jill Bowden's balance sheets for the beginning of this year and the end of the current year are below.

EXHIBIT 3.6 BALANCE SHEET AS OF 12/31/2012

Statement of Financial Position
Brandon and Jill Bowden
Balance Sheet as of 12/31/2012

ASSETS				LIABILITIES AND NET WORTH			
Current Assets				**Current Liabilities (current portion of long-term debt)**			
JT	Cash & Checking	$3,500		W	Credit Cards	$20,000	
JT	Money Market	$6,650		W	Auto # 2	$4,588	
				JT	Personal Residence	$3,812	
Total Current Assets			$10,150	**Total Current Liabilities**			$28,400
Investment Assets				**Long -Term Liabilities**			
H	401(k) Plan	$61,800		W	Auto # 2	$16,176	
H	Education Savings	$11,500		JT	Personal Residence	$342,633	
H	High Tech Stock[1]	$7,500					
Total Investment Assets			$80,800	**Total Long-Term Liabilities**			$358,809
Personal Use Assets				**Total Liabilities**			$387,209
JT	Personal Residence[2]	$390,000					
H	Furniture, Clothing	$95,000		**Total Net Worth**			$222,241
H	Auto # 1	$9,000					
W	Auto # 2[3]	$24,500					
Total Personal Use Assets			$518,500				
Total Assets			**$609,450**	**Total Liabilities and Net Worth**			**$609,450**

1. Brandon and Jill intend to use this investment for retirement savings.
2. The house was purchased on 1/1/2012 for $375,000 with a loan for $350,000 financed over 30 years at 7%.
3. The car was purchased on 1/1/2012 for $30,000 with $5,000 down, financed over 5 years at 8%.

H = Husband Owns
W = Wife Owns
JT = Jointly owned by husband and wife

Loan Calculation Explanation to Exhibit 3.6

Auto Loan Calculation			Home Loan Calculation		
(Present Value) PV =	$25,000		(Present Value) PV =	$350,000	
(Term) N =	60		(Term) N =	360	
(Interest Rate) i =	$\frac{8\%}{12} = 0.666$		(Interest Rate) i =	$\frac{7\%}{12} = 0.583$	
(Future Value) FV =	0		(Future Value) FV =	0	
(Payment) PMT =	$506.91		(Payment) PMT =	$2,328.56	
12/31/11 Principal Balance =	$20,764		12/31/11 Principal Balance =	$346,444	
12/31/12 Principal Balance =	$16,176	(Long-Term Liability)	12/31/12 Principal Balance =	$342,632	(Long-Term Liability)
	$4,588	(Current Liability)		$3,812	(Current Liability)

Balance Sheet as of 12/31/2013

Exhibit 3.7

Statement of Financial Position
Brandon and Jill Bowden
Balance Sheet as of 12/31/2013

Assets				Liabilities and Net Worth			
Current Assets				**Current Liabilities**			
JT	Cash & Checking	$3,000		W	Credit Cards	$25,000	
JT	Money Market	$5,000		W	Auto # 2	$4,968	
				JT	Personal Residence	$4,088	
Total Current Assets			$8,000	**Total Current Liabilities**			$34,056
Investment Assets				**Long -Term Liabilities**			
H	401(k) Plan	$75,000		W	Auto # 2	$11,208	
H	Education Savings	$15,000		JT	Personal Residence	$338,544	
H	High Tech Stock[1]	$5,000					
Total Investment Assets			$95,000	**Total Long-Term Liabilities**			$349,752
Personal Use Assets				**Total Liabilities**			$383,808
JT	Personal Residence[2]	$400,000					
H	Furniture, Clothing	$100,000		**Total Net Worth**			$249,192
H	Auto # 1	$8,000					
W	Auto # 2	$22,000					
Total Personal Use Assets			$530,000				
Total Assets			**$633,000**	**Total Liabilities and Net Worth**			**$633,000**

1.Brandon and Jill intend to use this investment for retirement savings.
2.The house was purchased on 1/1/2012 for $375,000 with a loan for $350,000 financed over 30 years at 7%.
3.The car was purchased on 1/1/2012 for $30,000 with $5,000 down, financed over 5 years at 8%.

H = Husband Owns
W = Wife Owns
JT = Jointly owned by husband and wife

LOAN CALCULATION EXPLANATION TO EXHIBIT 3.7

AUTO LOAN CALCULATION				HOME LOAN CALCULATION			
(Present Value) PV	=	$25,000		(Present Value) PV	=	$350,000	
(Term) N	=	60		(Term) N	=	360	
(Interest Rate) i	=	$\frac{8\%}{12}$ = 0.666		(Interest Rate) i	=	$\frac{7\%}{12}$ = 0.583	
(Future Value) FV	=	0		(Future Value) FV	=	0	
(Payment) PMT	=	$506.91		(Payment) PMT	=	$2,328.56	
Principal Balance*	=	$16,176		Principal Balance*	=	$342,632	
Principal Balance*	=	$11,208	(Long-Term Liability)	Principal Balance*	=	$338,544	(Long-Term Liability)
12/31/13		$4,968	(Current Liability)	12/31/13		$4,088	(Current Liability)

* The principal balance includes both current and long-term liability for 2013.

STATEMENT OF INCOME AND EXPENSES

EXHIBIT 3.8

Statement of Income and Expenses Mr. and Mrs. Bowden Statement of Income and Expenses for Past Year and Expected (Approximate) For This Year		
CASH INFLOWS		**Totals**
Brandon's Salary	$124,000	
Total Cash Inflows		$124,000
CASH OUTFLOWS		
Savings		
Brandon's 401(k) Plan	$3,720	
Education Savings (529 Plan)	$2,000	
Total Savings		$5,720
Debt Payments		
Personal Residence (mortgage)	$27,943	
Jill's Auto	$6,083	
Credit Cards[1]	$7,000	
Total Debt Payments		$41,026
Living Expenses		
Utilities	$5,000	
Gasoline for Autos	$4,000	
Lawn Service	$1,500	
Entertainment	$3,000	
Vacations	$2,500	
Church Donations	$1,000	
Food	$6,000	
Auto Maintenance	$1,000	
Telephone	$2,660	
Clothing	$3,000	
Total Living Expenses		$29,660
Insurance Payments		
HO Personal Residence	$4,500	
Auto Premiums	$2,000	
Life Insurance Premiums	$1,000	
Total Insurance Payments		$7,500
Taxes		
Federal Income Taxes Withheld	$24,800	
State Income Taxes Withheld	$6,200	
Social Security Taxes	$8,420	
Property Tax Personal Residence	$3,500	
Total Taxes		$42,920
Total Savings, Expenses and Taxes		$126,826
NET DISCRETIONARY CASH FLOW		($2,826)

1. The Bowden's make the minimum monthly payments on some of their credit cards.

Categories of Financial Ratios

Financial statement ratios are classified according to the analysis and insight provided by calculating the ratio. Financial statement ratios are broken down into the following categories:

- **Liquidity Ratios** – Measures the amount of cash and cash equivalents relative to short-term liabilities.
- **Debt Ratios** – Measures how well the client is managing their overall debt structure.
- **Ratios for Financial Security Goals** – Measures the client's progress towards achieving long-term financial security goals.
- **Performance Ratios** – Measure the return a client is generating on assets.

The remaining portion of this chapter discusses the ratios within each category, how the ratio is calculated, associated ratio benchmarks, and how to interpret and apply meaning to each ratio.

> *Key Concepts*
>
> **Underline/highlight the answers to these questions as you read:**
>
> 1. Identify the key liquidity ratios used in financial planning ratio analysis.
> 2. Identify the key debt ratios used in financial planning ratio analysis.
> 3. Identify the key ratios for financial security goals used in financial planning ratio analysis.
> 4. Identify the key performance ratios used in financial planning ratio analysis.
> 5. Determine the various limitations on financial statement analysis.

Liquidity Ratios

Liquidity ratios provide the financial planner insight into the client's ability to meet short-term obligations with current assets. Liquidity ratios include the emergency fund and current ratio.

Emergency Fund Ratio

The emergency fund ratio measures how many months of non-discretionary expenses the client has in the form of cash and cash equivalents or current assets.

The formula for the emergency fund is:

$$\text{Emergency Fund} = \frac{\text{Cash and Cash Equivalents}}{\text{Monthly Non-discretionary Cash Flows}}$$

Current assets are represented by cash and cash equivalents on the balance sheet.

Non-discretionary cash flows are those expenses that exist even if a job or other income source is lost. Non-discretionary cash flows are typically fixed expenses. Examples of non-discretionary expenses include:

- All debt payments (mortgage, car loan, student loan, boat loan, credit cards)
- Utilities
- Insurance premiums
- Property taxes
- Food

Travel, entertainment, and payroll taxes are examples of expenses that would be minimized or eliminated if a job or other income source was lost.

The benchmark for the emergency fund is three to six months and is important to provide for the following risks:

- Job loss
- Elimination period on a disability policy
- Unexpected expenses

Job Loss

The emergency fund can be used to pay monthly non-discretionary expenses in the event of job loss. Often times, it can take months to find a job, especially during periods of a recession like recently experienced during 2008 – 2012 and also during periods of high unemployment.

For clients that have a one wage earner family, the client should be on the high end of the benchmark, such as five to six months. If a financial planner has a client in a two wage earner family, the client can be on the low end of the benchmark, such as three months. With a two wage earner family, if one spouse is still working, a three month emergency fund can pay 50 percent of the monthly non-discretionary expenses, while the working spouse can pay the other 50 percent of the monthly non-discretionary expenses. This assumes, of course, that the spouse that is still employed earns enough to pay 50 percent of the monthly non-discretionary expenses. The planner can help guide the client to an appropriate amount of emergency fund based on individual circumstances.

Elimination Period on a Disability Policy

It is also important for the financial planner to make sure the emergency fund is equal to the elimination period of any disability policy. A disability policy is designed to provide income replacement if the insured is unable to work because of sickness or accident. The elimination period of a disability policy is the amount of time the insured must wait before collecting benefits under the policy. If the elimination period is 180 days, the client must wait six months before collecting benefits under the policy. If the client is unable to work for six months, the emergency fund should be at least six months to satisfy the elimination period of the disability policy.

Unexpected Expenses

A comprehensive financial plan will also account for the unexpected. Often times it is the unanticipated risk that can cause the greatest problems. A financial plan that accounts for the unexpected will better position a client to achieve their financial goals. An emergency fund can help mitigate the impact of unexpected expenses. Examples of unexpected expenses that a planner should anticipate include:

- Large deductibles for a homeowners' insurance policy. Many earthquake and flood policies have the insured paying a percentage of the total loss as a deductible.
- Large deductibles for private health insurance. To help reduce the cost of health insurance, some families purchase high deductible health insurance policies ($5,000 or more deductible per person).
- House repairs or additions for dependent family members that may move into the client's home.
- Large auto repairs, household repairs, etc.

Mitigating Circumstances

Although the emergency fund is important, the planner should keep the emergency fund in perspective when evaluating the client's financial position. Many competing needs may arise, and the client will have limited financial resources to satisfy all of the needs. The financial planner and client must prioritize which competing needs to address first and which needs to postpone until a later time. If the client has access to a home equity line of credit or loan provisions as part of a 401(k) plan or other qualified retirement plan, contributing to the emergency fund may be a lesser priority than purchasing health insurance.

Brandon and Jill Bowden's Emergency Fund

The Bowden's monthly non-discretionary expenses (cash outflows) from the Income Statement are:

Property Tax on Personal Residence	$3,500
Debt Payments (Personal residence, auto, credit cards)	$41,026
Utilities	$5,000
Gasoline for Autos	$4,000
Church Donations	$1,000
Food	$6,000
Auto Maintenance	$1,000
Telephone	$2,660
Insurance Premiums	$7,500
	$71,686

$$\text{Emergency Fund} = \frac{\text{Cash and Cash Equivalents}}{\text{Monthly Non-discretionary Cash Flows}}$$

$$\text{Emergency Fund} = \frac{\$10{,}150}{(\$71{,}686 \div 12)} = \frac{\$10{,}150}{\$5{,}974} = 1.70 \text{ months (2012)}$$

$$\text{Emergency Fund} = \frac{\$8{,}000}{(\$71{,}686 \div 12)} = \frac{\$8{,}000}{\$5{,}974} = 1.34 \text{ months (2013)}$$

The Bowden's have an emergency fund of less than two months. This is a weakness that requires planning to overcome in order to have an emergency fund of three to six months. As a one-income family, the Bowden's should have a 6-month emergency fund. However, that would require them to increase their cash and cash equivalents from $8,000 to $35,844 (6 x $5,974 in monthly non-discretionary expenses). Initially a 3-month emergency fund may be the most appropriate recommendation because there may be other sources of emergency funding, such as a home equity line of credit or borrowing provisions from Brandon's 401(k) plan. In addition, it is likely there will be other financial weaknesses the financial planner must help Brandon and Jill overcome, so increasing the emergency fund to three months in the short term will be sufficient. As the financial planner works with Brandon and Jill in the coming years, an evaluation can be made as to when increasing their emergency fund to six months is an appropriate recommendation.

Current Ratio

The current ratio measures how many times the client can satisfy their short-term liabilities with cash and cash equivalents. The current ratio is:

$$\text{Current Ratio} = \frac{\text{Cash \& Cash Equivalents}}{\text{Current Liabilities}}$$

Current assets represent cash and cash equivalents on the balance sheet. Current liabilities represent short-term liabilities on the balance sheet.

For the current ratio the industry benchmark is 1.0 – 2.0, with the higher the ratio the better. It is also helpful if the financial planner tracks the current ratio over a period of years to determine the trend. If the ratio becomes too large, it could signify that the client needs to reallocate some current assets to more growth oriented investment assets. If the ratio is decreasing, it will likely lead to a lower emergency fund as well. If the planner addresses the emergency fund first, it will likely lead to an improved current ratio.

Brandon and Jill Bowden's Current Ratio

The current ratio is:

$$\text{Current Ratio} = \frac{\text{Cash \& Cash Equivalents}}{\text{Current Liabilities}} = \frac{\$10{,}150}{\$28{,}400} = 0.36 \text{ (2012)}$$

$$\text{Current Ratio} = \frac{\text{Cash \& Cash Equivalents}}{\text{Current Liabilities}} = \frac{\$8{,}000}{\$34{,}056} = 0.23 \text{ (2013)}$$

The Bowden's have approximately 20 percent (for 2013) of their current liabilities in the form of current assets. As the Bowden's begin to overcome their emergency fund deficiency, the current ratio will improve at the same time. For example, if the Bowden's increase their emergency fund to three months, they will have $17,922 (3 x $5,974 in monthly non-discretionary expense) in cash and cash equivalents. Assuming their current liabilities do not change, the new current ratio would be 0.53 ($17,922 ÷ $34,056). By increasing the Bowden's emergency fund from 1.34 to 3.0 months, the current ratio would almost double from 0.23 to 0.53.

DEBT RATIOS

The debt management section of ratio analysis provides insight into how well the client is managing debt (too much or the right amount) and the quality of that debt.

Housing Ratio 1 (Basic)

Housing ratio 1 was established by the banking industry to determine if the amount of income and housing debt that a client is carrying is appropriate and affordable. If a borrower meets housing ratio 1, he likely will qualify for a conventional mortgage loan at a favorable rate.

The formula for housing ratio 1 is:

$$\text{Housing Ratio 1} = \frac{\text{Housing Costs}}{\text{Gross Pay}} \leq 28\%$$

Housing Costs = PITI
P = Principal
I = Interest
T = Taxes
I = Insurance (home)
Gross Income = Gross pay (before taxes)

Note: The PITI and gross income can be stated on a monthly or annual basis. The PITI and gross income should be stated on the same terms, either both on a monthly basis or both an annual basis.

Brandon and Jill Bowden's Housing Ratio 1

The Bowden's housing costs (PITI and other debt) from the Income Statement are:

Principal and Interest on Personal Residence	$27,943
Property Taxes – Personal Residence	$3,500
Insurance HO Personal Residence	$4,500
	$35,943
Total monthly housing costs ($35,943 ÷ 12)	**$2,995.25**

Their monthly gross pay is:

Total monthly gross pay (Brandon's Salary $124,000 ÷ 12)	**$10,333**

$$\text{Housing Ratio 1} = \frac{\text{Housing Costs}}{\text{Gross Pay}} \leq 28\%$$

$$\text{Housing Ratio 1} = \frac{\$2{,}995.25}{\$10{,}333} = 28.9\%$$

The Bowden's housing ratio 1 is 28.9 percent, which is slightly above the industry benchmark of 28 percent. The actual ratio of 28.9 percent is near the benchmark of 28 percent, so the Bowdens may be able to wait one or two years and allow for Brandon's salary increases to bring the ratio down to the benchmark.

For example, if Brandon receives a five percent raise each year for the next two years, the Bowden's housing ratio 1 would be:

$$\text{Next Year} = \frac{\$2{,}995.25}{\$10{,}333 \times 1.05} = 27.6\%$$

$$\text{Next 2 Years} = \frac{\$2{,}995.25}{\$10{,}333 \times 1.05 \times 1.05} = 26.3\%$$

This is a good example of how forecasted financial statements provide the financial planner with insight as to how financial ratios will be impacted by salary adjustments, inflation, or the implementation of planning recommendations. Care must be exercised, however, when assuming the ratio will "fix itself" based on future salary adjustments. The client may not receive the salary adjustment, the salary adjustment may or may not be as much as forecasted, or increasing expenses may offset the increased salary. In this example, not only would the financial planner be concerned about Brandon actually receiving the salary adjustment, but there is also concern that the property taxes or insurance premiums may increase and offset the increased salary. In this situation, the front end ratio would continue being higher than 28 percent. It is important to monitor the ratio and consider other alternatives such as potentially decreasing the insurance premium or potentially refinancing the mortgage, if possible.

Housing Ratio 2 (Broad)

Housing ratio 2 is also referred to as housing ratio 1 plus all other debt. This ratio was established by the banking industry to determine if the total amount of debt that a client is carrying is appropriate for a given level of income. If housing ratio 2 is met, the borrower will likely qualify for a conventional loan at a favorable rate.

The formula for housing ratio 2 is:

$$\text{Housing Ratio 2} = \frac{\text{Housing Costs + Other Debt Payments}}{\text{Gross Pay}} \leq 36\%$$

Housing Costs = PITI
P = Principal
I = Interest
T = Taxes
I = Insurance (home)
Gross Income = Gross pay before taxes

All other debt payments include:

- Car loan payments
- Boat loan payments
- Student loan payments
- Credit cards payments
- Principal and interest on vacation or second homes
- Any other monthly recurring debt

Recurring debt payments do not include utilities, car insurance, property insurance on a second home, or property taxes on a second home.

Note: It is important that PITI, all other debt payments, and gross income are stated on the same terms, either all on a monthly basis or all on an annual basis.

Brandon and Jill Bowden's Housing Ratio 2
From their Statement of Income Expenses, this is the Bowden's PITI plus all other recurring debt:

The Bowden's housing costs (PITI) from the Income Statement are:

Principal and Interest on Personal Residence	$27,943
Property Taxes – Personal Residence	$3,500
Insurance HO Personal Residence	$4,500
Jill's Auto	$6,083
Credit Cards	$7,000
	$49,026
Total monthly PITI plus other debt payments ($49,026 ÷ 12)	**$4,086**

Their monthly gross pay is:

Total monthly gross pay (Brandon's Salary $124,000 ÷ 12)	**$10,333**

$$\text{Housing Ratio 2} = \frac{\text{Housing Costs + Other Debt Payments}}{\text{Gross Pay}} \leq 36\%$$

$$\text{Housing Ratio 2} = \frac{\$4{,}086}{10,333} = 39.5\%$$

The Bowden's housing ratio 2 of 39.5 percent is slightly above the industry benchmark of 36 percent. Since the housing ratio 1 of 28.9 percent is so close to the industry benchmark of 28 percent, the issue with the housing ratio 2 is related to all other recurring debt. The financial planner should make recommendations to reduce the all other debt payments by either using assets on the balance sheet to retire debt or by increasing monthly debt payments.

Debt to Total Assets Ratio

The debt to total assets ratio indicates the percentage of assets that is owned by creditors. The lower this ratio the better, as it indicates that the assets owned have a low amount of debt owed.

To calculate the debt to total assets ratio:

$$\text{Debt to Total Assets Ratio} = \frac{\text{Total Debt}}{\text{Total Assets}} = \text{Benchmark Depends on Client Age}$$

Brandon and Jill Bowden's Debt to Total Assets Ratio

As of 12/31/12

$$\text{Debt to Total Assets Ratio} = \frac{\$387{,}209}{\$609{,}450} = 0.6353$$

As of 12/31/13

$$\text{Debt to Total Assets Ratio} = \frac{\$383{,}808}{\$633{,}000} = 0.6063$$

The total debt to total assets ratio has improved for the Bowdens over the past year. The financial planner should continue monitoring the debt to total asset ratio trend which should continue decreasing. As housing ratio 2 decreases from retiring all other recurring debt, the debt to total assets ratio will continue to improve.

Quality of Debt

The quality of debt assessment is based on the relationship between the term of the debt and the useful life of the asset. The quality of debt can be classified into three categories: good, reasonable, and bad debt. Any time the useful life of the asset far exceeds the term of the debt, the debt is considered good debt. Examples of good debt include a 3-year car loan, a 15-year home mortgage or any type of debt from student loans. Reasonable debt includes obligations where the useful life of the asset equals the term of the debt. Examples of reasonable debt include a 5-year car loan or a 30-year mortgage. Bad debt implies that the term of the debt far exceeds the useful life of the asset. For example, if a client charges a two-week summer vacation on a credit card, then makes the minimum payments for the next 20 years, the term of the debt when making minimum payments far exceeds the two-week useful life of the vacation. When an assessment as to the quality of the debt has been made, the financial planner can develop recommendations for the client to implement (such as retiring the bad debt).

When working with a client who has bad debt, such as credit card or consumer debt, the planner should develop a plan to help the client retire the debt as soon as possible and within a reasonable amount of time. Consider a client who has $15,000 in credit card debt with an interest rate of 19 percent. The initial minimum payment may be $500, but as each month passes, the minimum payment will continue to decline. By simply making the minimum payment, it can take between 16 to 20+ years to retire this debt. Instead, the client should continue to make a level payment of $500 each month and will be able to retire the debt in less than five years. Another alternative to retiring bad debt includes using assets on the balance sheet to pay down debt. It is the financial planner's responsibility to evaluate the appropriate mix of using assets to pay down debt or retiring the debt within a reasonable amount of time by making monthly payments.

Quick Quiz 3.6

Highlight the answer to these questions:

1. The housing ratio 1 industry benchmark is less than or equal to 28 percent.
   a. True
   b. False

2. The savings rate calculation includes reinvestments and the employer match.
   a. True
   b. False

3. The quality of debt assessment is based on the comparison of the term of the debt on an asset and the useful life of the asset.
   a. True
   b. False

True, True, True.

An assessment of the quality of Brandon and Jill's debt reveals that their home is financed over 30 years and the car is financed over five years. The term of the debt on the house and car match the useful life of both assets, so those debt items are reasonable debt. However, according to the Statement of Income and Expenses, the Bowden's are making the minimum monthly payment on their credit cards. It will take almost 15 years to payoff the credit card balances by making the minimum monthly payment, which is clearly bad debt. An important recommendation for the Bowdens is to retire the credit card debt within a reasonable amount of time.

In the event a financial planner discovers that the client is making minimum payments on credit card debt, it would seem reasonable to recalculate housing ratio 2 using a payment more representative of a reasonable term (e.g., 36 months). Credit card minimum payments may require a payback period of 16 to 20+ years. If the credit card debt payment is understated in housing ratio 2, the ratio may indicate everything is below the benchmark when really this is a distortion.

For example, three alternatives for paying off a balance of $2,000 on credit cards charging 20 percent interest are:

Alternative	Balance	Payment	Years	Number of Payments	Total Paid Back
A	$2,000	$34.78	16	192	$6,677.76
B	$2,000	$52.99	5	60	$3,179.26
C	$2,000	$74.32	3	36	$2,675.78

It would seem prudent that if the client were actually paying under alternative A, the planner would recalculate housing ratio 2 using the payment under alternative C.

Net Worth to Total Assets Ratio

$$\text{Net Worth to Total Assets Ratio} = \frac{\text{Net Worth}}{\text{Total Assets}} = \text{Benchmark Depends on Client Age}$$

The net worth to total assets ratio is the compliment of the debt to assets ratio described above. These two should add up to one. This ratio provides the planner with the percentage of total assets owned or paid for by the client. It is not surprising that this would be 20 percent for young people and up to 90 to 100 percent for retirement age clients. This ratio once again is best observed over time. Note that the net worth increases as assets increase in value (home and investment), which increases in savings, and with the payoff of obligations (liabilities).

Brandon and Jill Bowden's Net Worth to Total Assets Ratio

$$\text{Net Worth to Total Assets Ratio} = \frac{\text{Net Worth}}{\text{Total Assets}} = \frac{\$249,191}{\$633,000} = 39.37\%\ (2013)$$

The Bowden's net worth to total assets ratio of 39.37 percent is low as compared to the benchmark for their age group. The ratio will improve as the Bowden's assets increase.

Ratios for Financial Security Goals

Ratios for financial security goals provide the planner with insight about the progress (adequate or not) that the client is making towards their long-term goals. For example, ratios can answer questions such as: Is the client earning an appropriate rate of return on retirement investments? Is the client saving an appropriate amount? How much has the client accumulated towards a goal based on age?

Savings Rate

The savings rate measures the amount a client is saving towards a retirement goal. If a client begins saving for retirement between ages 25 to 35, there is a need to save about 10 to 13 percent of annual gross income. However, if a client does not begin saving at an early age, then a greater percentage of annual income must be saved to overcome the lost years of contributions and compounding interest.

Age Beginning Regular and Recurring Savings*	Savings (as percent of gross pay) Rate Required to Create Appropriate Capital*
25 - 35	10 - 13%
35 - 45	13 - 20%
45 - 55	20 - 40%**

*Assumes appropriate asset allocation for reasonable-risk investor through accumulation years; also assumes normal raises and an 80 percent wage replacement ratio at Social Security normal retirement age and includes Social Security retirement benefits.

**At age 55 the person will have to delay retirement until age 70.

The formula for the savings rate is:

$$\text{Savings Rate} = \frac{\text{Savings + Employer Match}}{\text{Gross Pay}} = \text{Benchmark Depends on Client Goals}$$

Note: The savings rate includes any employee and employer contributions. It does not include reinvested earnings as they are included in the total portfolio rate of return.

Example 3.9

David's salary at United Technologies Industries is $100,000 per year. He contributes 8% of his compensation to his 401(k) plan and his employer matches his contributions dollar for dollar, up to 4% of his compensation. His total savings rate is:

$$\text{Savings Rate} = \frac{\text{Employee Contributions + Employer Contributions}}{\text{Gross Pay}}$$

$$\text{Savings Rate} = \frac{(\$100{,}000 \times 0.08) + (\$100{,}000 \times 0.04)}{\$100{,}000}$$

$$\text{Savings Rate} = \frac{\$8{,}000 + \$4{,}000}{\$100{,}000} = 0.12 \text{ or } 12\%$$

When calculating the savings rate for a husband and a wife, combine both their retirement savings amounts and combine their gross incomes.

Example 3.10

Jason and Sally are married. Jason has a salary of $45,000 and Sally has a salary of $75,000. Jason's employer regularly contributes $2,500 to his profit sharing plan. Sally does not participate in her employer's retirement plan, but contributes $5,000 per year to a Roth IRA. Jason and Sally's savings rate is:

$$\text{Savings Rate} = \frac{\text{Employee Contributions + Employer Contributions}}{\text{Gross Pay}}$$

$$\text{Savings Rate} = \frac{(\$2{,}500 + \$5{,}000)}{(\$45{,}000 + \$75{,}000)}$$

$$\text{Savings Rate} = \frac{\$7{,}500}{\$120{,}000} = 0.0625 \text{ or } 6.25\%$$

Brandon and Jill Bowden's Savings Rate

Recall that Brandon contributes three percent of his compensation to his 401(k) plan and that his employer matches $0.50 for each $1 contributed, up to three percent of his compensation.

Brandon's contribution to his 401(k) plan is 0.03 x $124,000 = $3,720
Brandon's employer match is 0.015 x $124,000 = $1,860

Brandon and Jill are also saving for education expenses in a 529 Plan.

$$\text{Savings Rate} = \frac{\text{Employee Contributions + Employer Contribution + 529 Savings}}{\text{Gross Pay}}$$

$$\text{Savings Rate} = \frac{(\$3{,}720 + \$1{,}860) + \$2{,}000 \text{ (education savings)}}{\$124{,}000}$$

$$\text{Savings Rate} = \frac{\$7{,}580}{\$124{,}000} = 0.0611 \text{ or } 6.11\%$$

The Bowden's savings rate of 6.11 percent is well below the industry benchmark of 10 to 13 percent. Recall that the 10 to 13 percent benchmark is to meet a retirement goal only. The retirement only savings rate for the Bowden's is 4.5% [($3,720 + $1,860) ÷ $124,000]. If Brandon increases his 401(k) plan deferral to six percent, his employer will match an additional three percent, bringing Brandon's total savings rate to 10.61 percent (6% + 3% + 1.61 percent (education savings). A 10.61 percent savings rate would be a significant improvement over his current total savings rate of 6.11 percent. The additional savings required by Brandon would only be another three percent of his compensation or $3,720 on a pre-tax basis. On an after tax basis, it would be closer to $3,000. Although the Bowdens have a negative discretionary cash flow of $2,826, this will turn positive once the credit card debt is retired. Once the credit card debt is retired, the Bowdens will have a positive discretionary cash flow of $4,174 ($7,000 - $2,826), which is more than enough to increase Brandon's 401(k) plan deferral by another three percent.

Investment Assets to Gross Pay

Investment assets to gross pay ratio measures progress towards a client's saving goal, based on the client's age and income. The benchmark (as shown in the following table) is a useful metric because it provides insight as to: (1) whether the client has saved enough towards the retirement goal and (2) how much the client needs in retirement assets to generate a certain level of income at retirement.

Age	Investment Assets as a Ratio to Gross Pay Needed at Varying Ages
25	0.20 : 1
30	0.6 - 0.8 : 1
35	1.6 - 1.8 : 1
45	3 - 4 : 1
55	8 - 10 : 1
65	16 - 20 : 1

The benchmark considers income between $50,000 and $250,000 and inflation at approximately two to three percent. It also considers a balanced investment portfolio of 60/40 (equities to bonds) returning five percent over inflation, a savings rate of 10 to 13 percent of gross pay, and a wage replacement ratio of 80 percent of gross pay.

This ratio can answer the question, "For his age, has the client saved enough towards retirement?"

EXAMPLE 3.11

Jan age 45 with an annual salary of $80,000, has saved $250,000 in her retirement accounts. Jan should have at least $80,000 x 3 = $240,000 towards her retirement goal.

How much does the client need in retirement assets to generate a certain level of income?

EXAMPLE 3.12

Peter, age 50, is looking to retire at age 65, with about $100,000 per year in retirement income. Peter will need $100,000 x 16 = $1,600,000 in retirement savings to generate $100,000 per year in retirement income.

Brandon and Jill Bowden's Investment Assets to Gross Pay Ratio

The ratio for Brandon (age 40) and Jill (age 43) is based on their age. They should have three times their gross pay in retirement savings using this calculation:
Savings Amount = Salary x Benchmark
Savings Amount = $124,000 x 3

Benchmark Amount of Investment Assets = \$372,000

The most current actual retirement savings for the Bowden's is:

Brandon's 401(k) Plan (2010)	\$75,000
High Tech Stock	\$5,000
Cash and Cash Equivalents	\$8,000
Total	\$88,000

$$\text{Actual Ratio} = \frac{\text{Investment Assets + Cash \& Cash Equivalents}}{\text{Gross Pay}} = \frac{\$88,000}{\$124,000} = 0.71{:}1$$

Their total retirement savings is \$88,000, which is well below what is needed based on the benchmark of \$372,000. This is a difficult deficiency to overcome in the short term. However, the Bowdens are young enough and have another 20+ years remaining to work and increase their retirement savings. The first step is to increase Brandon's saving ratio from 4.5 percent to nine percent. The financial planner should also recommend looking at additional savings opportunities once some of the Bowden's bad debt is retired. The Bowden's should also evaluate the feasibility of Jill taking on a part time or full time job to help overcome the savings amount shortfall. Note that because in this case the ratio is refined to measure progress towards the retirement goal only, education savings is not included in the calculation.

Performance Ratios

Performance ratios will provide the planner with information regarding the return the client is earning on assets, net worth, and investments. This section of the chapter provides the appropriate ratios and formulas to calculate the ratios. However, using a financial calculator will provide the most accurate, compounded rate of return.

Return on Investments (ROI)

Return on investments (ROI) ratio is a critical performance ratio, as it measures the compounded rate of return on a client's investments. If the client's ROI is too low over a number of years, it may result in the client not having sufficient capital to retire or pay for education.

$$\text{Return on Investments} = \frac{I_1 - (I_0 + \text{Savings})}{I_0}$$

I_0	=	Beginning Investments
I_1	=	Ending Investments
S	=	Savings (include employer match)

Beginning investment assets are the investment assets, typically from the preceding year, and ending investment assets are the investment assets on the balance sheet at the end of the current year. Savings includes any amount contributed to a retirement plan by the employee and employer. In addition, savings includes contributions to an education savings account. Average net worth represents an average net worth between two balance sheets. Alternatively, a financial calculator can be used to compute this ratio.

An appropriate benchmark for return on investments depends on the time horizon and risk tolerance of the client. Generally, a client with a long-term time horizon, such as 10 years or more, should have a portfolio more heavily weighted towards equities. A client with a long-term time horizon is expected to have a return on equity of eight to ten percent per year. A client with a shorter time horizon would have a portfolio with a higher weighting of bonds and a return on equity of six to eight percent per year.

Brandon and Jill Bowden's Return on Investment Ratio

$$\text{ROI} = \frac{\$95{,}000 - (\$80{,}800 + \$5{,}720 + \$1{,}860)}{\$80{,}800} = \frac{\$6{,}620}{\$80{,}800} = 0.0819 \text{ or } 8.19\%$$

Based on the age of the Bowdens, an ROI on retirement savings of eight to ten percent is expected, so they are within the ROI benchmark. However, the financial planner should review their High Tech Stock, as their portfolio does not appear to be well diversified and the High Tech Stock lost 33 percent of its value last year.

Return on Assets (ROA)

The return on assets ratio provides the planner with insight to the general growth rate of a client's assets.

$$\text{Return on Assets} = \frac{A_1 - (A_0 + S)}{A_0}$$

A_0	=	Beginning Assets
A_1	=	Ending Assets
S	=	Savings (include employer match)

Beginning total assets are the total assets, typically from the preceding year, and ending total assets are the total assets on the balance sheet at the end of the current year.

This measure of return is a blended growth rate of all assets a client owns because it considers returns on low yielding assets like savings and checking accounts, personal residence and auto (an asset declining in value), along with higher returning assets like retirement savings, stocks, and bonds. It is reasonable to expect the return on assets to be low, typically between two to four percent annually. The financial planner should monitor this return over time as it will provide insight to the client's mix of assets (cash and cash equivalents versus investment assets versus personal use assets). If the rate of return on assets begins to trend lower, or below three percent, it may indicate too many low returning assets like personal use assets or cash and cash equivalents.

Brandon and Jill Bowden's Return on Assets

$$\text{Return on Assets} = \frac{\$633{,}000 - (\$609{,}450 + \$5{,}720 + \$1{,}860)}{\$609{,}450} = \frac{\$15{,}970}{\$609{,}450} = 2.62\%$$

A return on assets of 2.62 percent is low in comparison to the typical three to four percent annual return expected on total assets. This return includes cash and cash equivalents that earn less than one percent and personal use assets (which include a house that may or may not increase in value), personal autos (that decline in value) and other personal use assets (such as furniture and clothing which do not increase in value each year). The financial planner should review the client's assets and recommend changes to increase the return.

Return on Net Worth (RONW)

The return on net worth ratio provides the planner with insight as to the average growth rate on net worth.

$$\text{Return on Net Worth} = \frac{NW_1 - (NW_0 + S)}{NW_0}$$

NW_0	=	Beginning Net Worth
NW_1	=	Ending Net Worth
S	=	Savings (include employer match)

Beginning net worth is the total net worth, typically from the preceding year, and ending net worth is the total net worth on the balance sheet at the end of the current year.

Brandon and Jill Bowden's Rate of Return on Net Worth

$$\text{Return on Net Worth} = \frac{\$249{,}191 - (\$222{,}241 + \$5{,}720 + \$1{,}860)}{\$222{,}241} = \frac{\$19{,}370}{\$222{,}241} = 0.0871 \text{ or } 8.71\%$$

A return on net worth of 8.71 percent is reasonable. A financial planner should calculate the return on net worth each year and develop a trend over time. The return on net worth is expected to be higher when a client is working, then begin to decline as the client enters retirement (as assets are drawn down to generate income).

EXHIBIT 3.9 BOWDEN RATIO ANALYSIS

LIQUIDITY RATIOS				
Ratio	**Formula**		**Comment**	**Benchmark**
Emergency Fund Ratio =	$\frac{\text{Cash \& Cash Equivalents}}{\text{Monthly Non-Discretionary Cash Flows}}$	$\frac{\$8{,}000}{\$5{,}974}$ = 1.34 months (2013)	Weak	3 - 6 months
Current Ratio =	$\frac{\text{Cash \& Cash Equivalents}}{\text{Current Liabilities}}$	$\frac{\$8{,}000}{\$34{,}056}$ = 0.23 (2013)	Low	1.0 - 2.0
DEBT RATIOS				
Housing Ratio 1 (HR 1)(Basic) =	$\frac{\text{Housing Costs}}{\text{Gross Pay}}$	$\frac{\$2{,}995.25}{\$10{,}333}$ = 28.9%	Slightly High	≤ 28%
Housing Ratio 2 (HR 2)(Broad) =	$\frac{\text{Housing Costs + Other Debt Payments}}{\text{Gross Pay}}$	$\frac{\$4{,}086}{\$10{,}333}$ = 39.5%	Slightly High	≤ 36%
Debt to Total Assets =	$\frac{\text{Total Debt}}{\text{Total Assets}}$	$\frac{\$383{,}808}{\$633{,}000}$ = 60.63% (2013)	High	As a person ages, this ratio should decline.
Net Worth to Total Assets =	$\frac{\text{Net Worth}}{\text{Total Assets}}$	$\frac{\$249{,}191}{\$633{,}000}$ = 39.37% (2013)	Low	Depends on age. 20% for young client and 90-100% for retirement age client.
RATIOS FOR FINANCIAL SECURITY GOALS				
Savings Rate =	$\frac{\text{Savings + Employer Match}}{\text{Gross Pay}}$	$\frac{\$2{,}000 + \$3{,}720 + 1{,}860}{\$124{,}000}$ = 6.11%	Low	10 – 13% assuming the client starts early, ages 25-35.
Investment Assets to Gross Pay =	$\frac{\text{Investment Assets + Cash \& Cash Equivalents}}{\text{Gross Pay}}$	$\frac{\$88{,}000}{\$124{,}000}$ = 0.71:1	Low	Depends upon age. At retirement age – 16:1
PERFORMANCE RATIOS				
Return on Investments =	$\frac{I_1 - (I_0 + \text{Savings})}{I_0}$	$\frac{\$6{,}620}{\$80{,}800}$ = 8.19%	Good	8 – 10%
Return on Assets =	$\frac{A_1 - (A_0 + \text{Savings})}{A_0}$	$\frac{\$15{,}970}{\$609{,}450}$ = 2.62%	Low	2 – 4%
Return on Net Worth =	$\frac{NW_1 - (NW_0 + \text{Savings})}{NW_0}$	$\frac{\$19{,}370}{\$222{,}241}$ = 8.71%	Good	The higher the better. This ratio is likely to become smaller as the client's net worth increases.

SUMMARY OF FINANCIAL STATEMENT RATIOS (GENERALIZED)

EXHIBIT 3.10

Ratio	Formula	Measures	Benchmark
LIQUIDITY RATIOS			
Emergency Funds	$\frac{\text{Cash \& Cash Equivalents}}{\text{Monthly Non-Discretionary Cash Flows}}$	The number of months of non-discretionary expenses in the form of cash and cash equivalents.	3 - 6 months
Current Ratio	$\frac{\text{Cash \& Cash Equivalents}}{\text{Current Liabilities}}$	The number of times a client can satisfy their short-term liabilities.	1.0 - 2.0
DEBT RATIOS			
Housing Ratio 1 (Basic)	$\frac{\text{Housing Costs}}{\text{Gross Pay}}$	The percentage of income spent on housing debt.	≤ 28%
Housing Ratio 2 (Broad)	$\frac{\text{Housing Costs + Other Debt Payments}}{\text{Gross Pay}}$	The percentage of income spent on housing and all other recurring debt.	≤ 36%
Debt to Total Assets	$\frac{\text{Total Debt}}{\text{Total Assets}}$	The percentage of assets being provided by creditors.	As a person ages, this ratio should decline.
Net Worth to Total Assets	$\frac{\text{Net Worth}}{\text{Total Assets}}$	The percentage of total assets owned or paid for by client.	Depends on age. 20% for young client and 90-100% for retirement age client.
RATIOS FOR FINANCIAL SECURITY GOALS			
Savings Rate	$\frac{\text{Savings + Employer Match}}{\text{Gross Pay}}$	The percentage of income saved towards a retirement goal.	10 – 13% Assuming the client starts early, ages 25-35.
Investment Assets to Gross Pay	$\frac{\text{Investment Assets + Cash \& Cash Equivalents}}{\text{Gross Pay}}$	The progress towards a retirement goal.	Depends upon age. At retirement age – 16:1
PERFORMANCE RATIOS			
Return on Investments	$\frac{I_1 - (I_0 + \text{Savings})}{I_0}$	The growth rate of a client's investment assets.	8 – 10%
Return on Assets	$\frac{A_1 - (A_0 + \text{Savings})}{A_0}$	A blended growth rate of all assets.	2 – 4%
Return on Net Worth	$\frac{NW_1 - (NW_0 + \text{Savings})}{NW_0}$	The growth rate of net worth.	The higher the better. This ratio is likely to become smaller as the client's net worth increases.

Limitations of Financial Statement Analysis

Estimating Fair Market Value

When preparing financial statements, the financial planner must estimate the fair market value of certain assets like the primary residence, second homes, boats, cars, and any collectibles. In addition, if the client owns a small business, it is likely the planner will have to estimate the value of the business as well. This becomes problematic when the client is planning to sell the asset and use the proceeds to fund a goal. The estimate of fair market value must be conservative enough so that the financial goal is not jeopardized because the value was overstated.

Inflation

The impact of inflation makes it very difficult to compare financial statements over multiple years. The financial planner needs to adjust investment returns for inflation to determine a real, after inflation, rate of return. The planner should also adjust income and savings into real, after inflation, dollars. Inflation of even a small rate (e.g., 3%) can have a very serious effect on financial statements over a long period of time (e.g., 10 to 30 years).

Hard to Value Assets

Some assets such as collectibles and private business interests are difficult to value. To the extent the asset is going to fund a financial goal, such as retirement, it is important for the financial planner to use an appraiser to determine an appropriate value of the asset. For example, if a client intends to sell a business ownership interest to fund retirement, the planner wants to make sure the client is going to be able to sell the business interest at the current value of the interest. The planner does not want to report the value of the business interest at $1 million on the balance sheet, only to find out years later that the client can only sell the interest for half of the value reported. If the client was including the business interest in the retirement amount calculation and now has a significant shortfall in retirement assets, it is likely to leave the client unable to retire and looking for a new planner.

Liquidity of Certain Assets

Other assets may be difficult to sell, such as a small business or collectible items. If a client is planning to use illiquid assets to fund a financial goal, the client and financial planner must carefully plan the timing of the sale of the asset, as it may not occur exactly as the client intends. For example, if the client is trying to sell a small business to fund retirement at age 62, the client may have to start looking for a buyer five years before the intended retirement date. It may also result in the client having to retire earlier or later than intended.

Uncertain Returns

Many of the benchmarks covered in this chapter assume a certain level of return. Returns are based on historical returns for asset classes such as stocks and bonds. As the markets continue to evolve over time, future returns may be higher or lower than historical returns, which could positively or negatively impact the financial planner's calculations and benchmarks.

Sensitivity Analysis

Financial statements and retirement and education needs that are projected over long periods of time employ many assumptions such as the rate of increase in income, the tax rate, the savings rate, the inflation rate, and the investment return rate. Retirement age and life expectancy are additional assumptions used for retirement projections. Assumptions made for education funding include the cost of education, when the cost will occur, and how many years the student will be in school. With all of these assumptions and variables, the financial planner needs to subject the plan to some sensitivity analysis. This involves slightly rotating the value of the variable toward the risk. For example, what if the client retires one year earlier than expected or inflation is 3.5 percent instead of the assumption used of three percent? Sensitivity analysis can also be used to illustrate to the client how the plan would be impacted if the client decides to pursue one or two years of additional work and savings (delayed retirement).

Conducting Sensitivity Analysis

Sensitivity analysis is the process of changing key variables in planning assumptions, to determine the overall impact of those changes on the plan. When a planner is calculating the amount needed to save towards an education goal, the financial planner must assume an investment rate of return, an inflation rate of return, and future cost of tuition. Sensitivity analysis involves calculating the amount needed to save for education, if the investment rate of return is two, three or more percentage points lower than the original assumption. The planner would also adjust the tuition inflation rate up and then calculate the amount needed to save for education. The planner would then adjust the tuition inflation rate down and recalculate the amount needed to save for education. Sensitivity analysis provides a range of savings required to meet a goal, based upon differing assumptions and the implications of the assumptions changing.

Conducting Monte Carlo Analysis

Monte Carlo analysis is a mathematical simulation to determine the probability of achieving a given outcome. Monte Carlo analysis is useful for financial planners to help measure the probability of our assumptions being true or false. Suppose a client, age 62, has $1 million in a retirement savings account and wants to know how much can be withdrawn each year for income. If a planner assumes a historical rate of return of eight percent on the investment assets, the planner may suggest $90,000 a year in withdrawals which should last for 30 years. However, if the client experiences negative returns during the first three to four years of retiring, then retirement savings will be depleted in less than ten years. By conducting Monte Carlo analysis, the planner may determine that there is a 20 percent probability of running out of money within ten years of retiring. Then appropriate steps can be taken to adjust the annual withdrawal amount to decrease the probability of running out of money to a more tolerable level.

MONEY EDUCATION

Part 2

Mini Cases: Examples & Exercises

MINI CASE

Risk Management Mini Case 1

Today is January 1, 2013

WILLIAM AND LUCY HAYES

THE FAMILY

William and Lucy Hayes have come to you, a financial planner, for help in developing a plan to accomplish their financial goals. From your initial meeting, you have gathered the following information.

William Hayes, age 37, is the owner and manager of a store that sells children's toys. He has Schedule C net income of $65,000. Lucy Hayes, age 37, is a paralegal with an income of $55,000. Their net worth is $300,000 consisting of $150,000 equity in their home and $150,000 of investments and cash and cash equivalents.

William and Lucy have been married for 15 years. They plan to retire in 25 years. They have two children, Taylor and Cavan, and do not plan to have any more children. Taylor, age 15, attends the local public high school and is in the ninth grade. Cavan, age 11, is in the sixth grade at the local grammar school.

FINANCIAL GOALS & CONCERNS

Their primary goal, for this example, is to develop an appropriate risk management portfolio. Their other goals and concerns are as follows:

1. The Hayes' want to provide a standard of living post retirement of 80% of their preretirement earnings.
2. They want to accumulate sufficient assets to send their children to a state university.
3. They want to minimize their current income liability.
4. They want to expand the toy store.
5. They want to be mortgage and debt free at retirement.
6. They want to purchase an airplane upon retirement.

External Information

Economic Information

- General inflation is expected to average 3.0% annually for the foreseeable future.

Bank Lending Rates

- 15-year conforming annual rate mortgages are 5.0%.
- 30-year conforming rate mortgages are 5.5%.
- Any closing costs associated with mortgage refinance are an additional 3% of the amount mortgaged and will be included in the mortgage or paid directly.

Insurance Information

Life Insurance

	Policy 1	Policy 2
Insured	Lucy	William
Policy Through	Employer	Private
Face Amount	$55,000	$150,000
Type	Term (group)	Term
Cash Value	$0	$0
Annual Premium	$102 (employer paid)	$1,000 (personally paid)
Beneficiary	William	Lucy
Contingent Beneficiary	Two children	None
Owner	Lucy	William
Settlement Options	None	Life Annuity

Lucy also has an accidental death and dismemberment policy through her employer. She is covered for $100,000 under this policy. She pays a premium of $68 per year for this coverage.

Health Insurance

All family members are covered by Lucy's employer under a group health plan with an annual per person deductible of $400. After the deductible is met, the plan pays 100% of the first $2,000 of covered hospital charges for each hospital stay and 80% thereafter. The policy features a $2,000 maximum annual out-of-pocket limit. The plan will then pay 100% of any other covered expenses. The family premium is $460 per month.

- $400 per individual deductible per year
- $1,000,000 lifetime benefit limit per person

The Hayes' have dental insurance. The premium is $216 annually.

Disability Insurance

William has a personal disability policy with an own-occupation definition that provides a monthly benefit of $2,800 and has a 30-day elimination period. The policy was purchased from a local insurance company. This policy covers both accidents and sickness, is guaranteed renewable, and has a benefit period of five years. His annual premium is $608.

Lucy has an own-occupation definition disability policy that provides an annual benefit of 65% of her gross pay and has a 90-day elimination period. The policy is provided through her employer. The policy covers both accidents and sickness and provides benefits until age 65. The annual premium is $460, and the employer and Lucy each pay half.

Homeowners Insurance

The Hayes' have a HO-3 policy (replacement value and open perils endorsement) with a $250 deductible, a dwelling value of $300,000, an 80% coinsurance requirement, and a current yearly premium of $2,400. There is a $100,000 liability coverage per occurrence. The home is worth $375,000 and the separate land value is $75,000 for a total value of $450,000. If they raise the deductible to $2,000 and increase coverage to $375,000 for the dwelling, they will save $675 per year.

Automobile Insurance (Personal Auto Package - PAP)

Both Cars	
Type	Personal Auto Policy
Liability	$100,000/$300,000/$50,000
Medical Payments	$5,000 per person
Physical Damage, Own Car	Actual Cash Value
Uninsured Motorist	$50,000 / accident
Collision Deductible	$100
Comprehensive Deductible	$250
Premium (per year)	$1,080

SUGGESTED SOLUTION

ANALYSIS

- Lifecycle: William (H) and Lucy Hayes (W)
- Ages 37 and 37
- Married
- Children: 2 - Taylor (age 15) and Cavan (age 11)
- Income: $65,000 (H) and $55,000 (W)
- Net Worth: $300,000
- Self-Employed: Yes, William (H) owns a toy store

RISK MANAGEMENT PORTFOLIO

		Metric	Actual	Recommendation	Cost to Implement
Life Insurance	H	12-16 x GP	2-3x	Buy $1M 30-year term	$750 annually*
	W	12-16 x GP	1 x	Buy $1M 30-year term	$375 annually*
Health Insurance		≥ $1M LTB	$1,000,000	Adequate	No Cost
Disability Insurance	H	60-70% GP	$2,800	Replace with a policy that has a longer elimination period and provides benefits until age 65.	No Cost
	W	60-70% GP	65%	Adequate	No Cost
Long-Term Care		None	None	Do Nothing Now	No Cost
Property Insurance - HO		≤ FMV	80%	Increase coverage to $375,000, revise deductible to $2,000	Savings approximately $675
Property Insurance - Auto		≤ FMV	ACV	Adequate but raise deductible and increase uninsured motorist to bodily injury limit	No net change
Liability - PLUP		$1-$3M	None	Add $1M PLUP	Cost $250
				Net Cost Change Annually	**$700**

** Used appendix rates interpolated for age 37 at 0.75 per $1,000 for male and ½ rate for female.*

Notes:

Life Insurance: Consider dropping Lucy's accidental death and dismemberment policy for $100,000 pick up $68 per year. The million on her may be excessive but is relatively inexpensive.

Health Insurance: Their policy looks to be inexpensive and adequate with a low out of pocket limit and lifetime benefits (LTB) of $1,000,000 per person. It is employer dependent.

Disability Insurance: William's disability policy is slightly more than 50% of his Schedule C net income. Because it is a personal policy, any benefits received are not taxable. The elimination period should be raised to 90-180 days to reduce the premium. The major deficiency is in the five year term of benefits since he is 37. They need to replace this policy with one that:

1. has a term of benefits to age 65;
2. has a 90-180 elimination period;
3. provides $3,750 per month benefit (approximately 70%);
4. is guaranteed renewable;
5. covers sickness and accidents;
6. has own occupation definition or hybrid (own 5 years/any for which educated, trained, or experienced for balance);
7. has a residual income feature; and
8. has a competitive premium.

Lucy's disability policy looks to be adequate. However, the planner will want to get a copy of the employer fringe benefit booklet or get written permission from Lucy to contact her employer's the fringe benefit officer to determine the definition of disability and any additional features or characteristics.

Long-Term Care Insurance: They currently have none and arguably have no current need.

Property Insurance - Home: The homeowners policy coverage for the dwelling is on the verge of them becoming a co-insurer. They should increase the dwelling coverage to $375,000 (replacement value) and increase the deductible to $2,000 (easily affordable). The net result is probably an overall decrease in premiums of $675 annually. The liability limit may have to be increased to satisfy the PLUP carrier but will have little impact on the premium.

Property Insurance - Auto: The liability limits are probably adequate for the PLUP carrier. However, the deductibles should be raised to $1,000 to $2,000 per car for both comprehensive and collision presuming the cars are valuable. The uninsured motorist coverage is inadequate if needed and should be changed to equal the bodily injury limits of $100,000/$300,000. The overall effect may be no change in overall premium.

Personal Liability Insurance: They should purchase a $1,000,000 PLUP costing about $250 annually.

MINI CASE

Short-Term Goals & Obligations Mini Case 2

Today is January 1, 2013

RYAN AND TIFFANY PIERCE

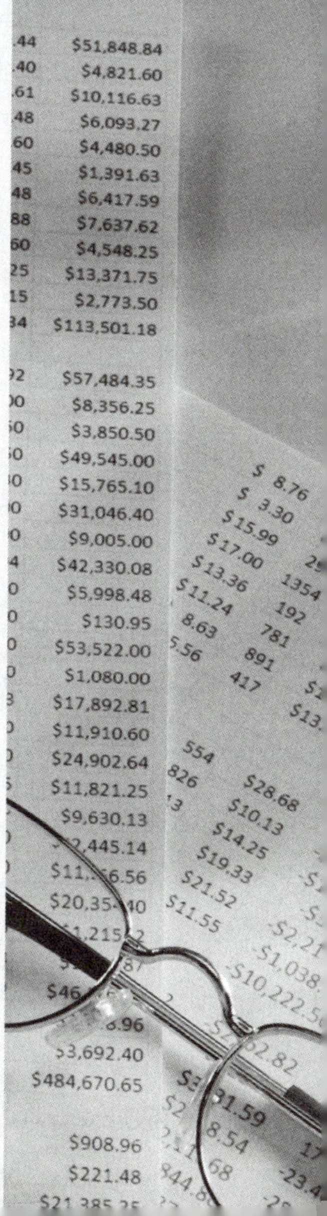

The Family

Ryan Pierce (age 47) is an executive with Crush Quota, a closely-held corporation focused on sales training. His salary is $100,000, and he expects raises of 5% per year. Tiffany Pierce (age 50) is an administrative assistant and has a salary of $36,000. She expects raises of 5% per year. They have three children: Dylan (age 16), Colin (age 12), and Madison (age 2). During the day, the children are cared for by their paternal grandmother who lives across the street. Ryan and Tiffany have been married for twenty years. They do not reside in a community property state.

Financial Goals & Concerns

Their primary goal, for this example, is to examine their short-term goals of emergency fund, housing ratio, and debt management. Their other goals and concerns are as follows:

1. They want to provide for their children's college education (5 years each), which is expected to cost $25,000 per year in today's dollars.
2. They want to retire debt free when he is age 65.
3. They initially define adequate retirement income as 80% of preretirement income.
4. They expect the retirement period to be 30 years.
5. They want to review life insurance needs and have wills drafted for both of them.
6. They want to minimize any estate tax liability.
7. They plan to travel extensively during retirement.

External Information

Economic Information

- General inflation has averaged 3.0% annually for the last 20 years.
- General inflation is expected to be 2.5% in the future.
- Education inflation is expected to be 6% annually.

Bank Lending Rates

- 15-year conforming annual rate mortgages are 3.50%.
- 30-year conforming rate mortgages are 3.80%.
- Any closing costs associated with mortgage refinance are an additional 3% of the amount mortgaged and will be included in the mortgage or paid directly.
- Bank unsecured loan is 7.5%.
- Credit card rates are 20%.
- Auto loan rates range from 0 - 5%.

Investment Information

They expect to have an 8% rate of return on investment assets.

Income Statement

Statement of Income and Expenses Ryan and Tiffany Pierce Statement of Income and Expenses for Past Year (2012) and Expected (Approximate) For This Year (2013)				
Cash Inflows				**Totals**
Ryan's Salary		$100,000		
Tiffany's Salary		$36,000		
ML Brokerage Account		$3,050		
Investment Portfolio		$4,771		
Savings Account		$618		
Education Fund		$1,062		
	Total Cash Inflows			$145,501
Cash Outflows				
Savings				
401(k) Plan		$15,000		
	Total Savings			$15,000
Taxes				
Federal Income Taxes Withheld		$37,200		
State Income Taxes Withheld		$4,000		
Property Tax Residence		$4,936	ND	
Payroll (FICA)		$10,404		
	Total Taxes			$56,540
Debt Payments (Principal & Interest)				
Principal Residence		$14,891	ND	
Auto Loan		$18,818	ND	
Credit Cards		$1,300	ND	
	Total Debt Payments			$35,009
Living Expenses				
Utilities for Residence		$5,000	ND	
Entertainment		$6,500		
Church Donations		$5,000	ND	
Clothing		$6,000	ND	
Auto Maintenance		$1,243	ND	
Food		$6,300	ND	
	Total Living Expenses			$30,043
Insurance Payments				
HO Insurance Principal Residence		$920	ND	
Health		$2,400	ND	
Auto Premiums		$2,660	ND	
Life Insurance #1		$520	ND	
Fur and Jewelry Endorsement		$30	ND	
Disability		$2,667	ND	
	Total Insurance Payments			$9,197
Total Cash Outflows				$145,789
Net Discretionary Cash Flows				($288)

ND = Non-Discretionary cash flows per mutual understanding between financial planner and client.

* Federal and state income taxes withheld and Social Security taxes are presumed to be discretionary as opposed to nondiscretionary because job loss is the greatest risk to the emergency fund and these expenses are not incurred in the event of a job loss.

Statement of Financial Position (Beginning of Year)

Statement of Financial Position Ryan and Tiffany Pierce Balance Sheet as of 1/1/2013						
ASSETS[1]				**LIABILITIES AND NET WORTH**		
Current Assets				**Current Liabilities[2]**		
JT	Cash & Checking[6]	$7,500		W Credit Cards	$4,300	
JT	Savings[7]	$15,450		**Total Current Liabilities**		$4,300
Total Current Assets			$22,950			
Investment Assets				**Long-Term Liabilities**		
H	First Mutual Growth Fund	$7,950		JT Principal Residence	$134,959	
W	Investment Portfolio	$210,000		JT Auto Loans	$40,069	
H	ML Brokerage Account[3]	$100,000		H Margin Loan[5]	$17,522	
W	Education Fund	$22,747		**Total Long-Term Liabilities**		$192,550
H	Profit Sharing Plan	$80,000				
W	Profit Sharing Plan	$12,000				
H	IRA[4]	$9,000				
Total Investment Assets			$441,697	**Total Liabilities**		$196,850
Personal Use Assets						
JT	Principal Residence	$185,000				
H	Automobile # 1	$32,000				
W	Automobile # 2	$21,000		**Total Net Worth**		$552,797
H	Boat	$10,000				
W	Furs and Jewelry	$10,000				
JT	Furniture and Household	$27,000				
Total Personal Use Assets			$285,000			
Total Assets			$749,647	**Total Liabilities & Net Worth**		$749,647

1. Assets are stated at fair market value.
2. Liabilities are stated at principal only as of January 1, 2013 before January payments.
3. ML Brokerage Account is stated at gross value, which does not include margin loan of $17,522.
4. IRA is currently invested in CDs at a local bank.
5. Margin loan is for ML Brokerage Account. Interest rate is currently 8% and deducted from account balance.
6. The checking account is a non-interest bearing account.
7. The savings account earns 4% per year.

Title Designations:
H = Husband (Sole Owner)
W = Wife (Sole Owner)
JT = Joint Tenancy with Survivorship Rights

Personal Residence - Purchased 1/1/2011	
FMV (Current)	$185,000
Original Loan	$148,000
Term	15 years
Interest Rate	5.9%
Payment	$1,240.93
Remaining Mortgage	$134,959
Remaining Term	13 years
Taxes on Home	$4,936
Homeowners Policy (with endorsements)	$920

	Auto #1 Ryan's 2011 Car	Auto # 2 Tiffany's 2010 Car
Purchase Price	$40,000	$35,000
Down Payment	$0	$10,000
Term	48 months	48 months
Interest Rate	7%	8%
Monthly Payment	$957.85	$610.32
Payments Remaining	33	20
Balance	$28,677.07	$11,392.23

SUGGESTED SOLUTION

ANALYSIS TOOLS

1. Calculate the emergency fund ratio.
2. Calculate the current ratio.
3. Calculate housing ratio 1.
4. Calculate housing ratio 2.
5. Analyze their debt.
6. Make recommendations.

Emergency Fund Ratio and Current Ratio

- Determine nondiscretionary cash flows.

Total Cash Out Flows	$145,799	
Less:		
Taxes except Property Taxes ($56,540 - $44,936)	$51,604	
Entertainment	$6,500	
Savings	$15,000	
Nondiscretionary Cash Flow	$72,695	
Divide by 12	$6,057.92	
Divide into Cash and Cash Equivalents (Balance Sheet)	$22,950.00	
Emergency Fund Ratio	3.8 months	(adequate)
The Current Ratio		
Cash and Cash Equivalents / Current Liabilities $22,950/$4,300	5.34	(Good)

Housing Ratio 1

$$\text{Housing Ratio 1} = \frac{\text{Housing Costs}}{\text{Gross Pay}} \leq 28\% \text{ Benchmark}$$

$$\$14{,}891 + \$4{,}936 + \$920 = \frac{\$20{,}747}{\$136{,}000} = 15.26\% \text{ (very good)}$$

Housing Ratio 2

$$\frac{\text{Housing Costs + Debt Payments}}{\text{Gross Pay}} \leq 36\% \text{ Benchmark}$$

$$\$20{,}747 + \$18{,}818 \text{ (auto)} + \$1{,}300 \text{ (credit cards)} = \frac{\$40{,}865}{\$136{,}000} = 30\% \text{ (good)}$$

Further Analysis

The credit cards will take approximately 5.5 years to pay off at 20% interest if no further charges are added and they continue to pay $1,300 per year. They should pay them off and always pay charges in full monthly.

Looking at the Debt

	Balance	Remaining Term	Interest Rate	PMT	Market Rate	Impact of Payoff (P) or Refinance (R)	
Housing	$134,959	156 months	5.9	$14,891	3.5%	+ $2,966	R*
Autos	$40,069	20 - 33 months	7 - 8%	$18,818	**	+ $18,818	P
Credit Cards	$4,300	66 months	20%	$1,300	***	+ $1,300	P
Margin Debt	$17,522	****	8%	0	****	0	P

** If the home is refinanced including closing costs, the new payment is $11,925 per year for the full 180 months or $13,325 for 156 months.*

*** For a market rate, consider their expected rate of return of 8%.*

**** It will take 5.5 years at 20% if no additional charges.*

***** This is accruing against the investment portfolio.*

Recommendations

	Recommendation	Cost	Impact on Annual Cash Flow
1.	Refinance Home	0	+ $2,966
2.	Pay off Cars	$40,069	+ $18,818
3.	Pay off Credit Cards	$4,300	+ $1,300
4.	Pay off Margin Loan	$17,522	+ 0
		$61,891*	$23,084

** Pay from investment assets.*

Impact of Implementing Recommendations

1. Emergency Fund Ratio Goes Up

   $$(\$72{,}695 - \$18{,}818 - \$1{,}300 - \$2{,}966) = \frac{\$49{,}611}{12} = \$4{,}134.25$$

   $$\frac{\$22{,}950}{\$4{,}134.25} = 5.51 \text{ months (excellent)}$$

2. Housing Ratio 1
   $11,925 + $4,936 + $920 = $17,781

   $$\frac{\$17{,}781}{\$136{,}000} = 13.1\% \text{ (excellent)}$$

3. Housing Ratio 2

   $$\frac{\$17{,}781}{\$136{,}000} = 13.1\% \text{ (excellent)}$$

4. They free up $23,084 per year for savings and can rebuild their costs of paying off the debt in only 2-3 years. If they implement our recommendations, they have no debt except the mortgage. They should avoid all long-term credit card debt and margin debt.

Presentation to the Pierce Family

1. You had debt of $196,850. You now owe $139,008.
2. You had discretionary cash flow of ($288). You now have $23,084 - $288 = $22,796 extra per year.
3. The only debt you owe is your mortgage.
4. The payoff of your debt effectively earned you your expected rate of return for the auto, credit cards, and margin interest.
5. You are now positioned to save for your retirement and education needs.

Education & Education Funding Mini Case 3

Today is August 15, 2013

WILLIAM AND KATE WINDSOR

Introductory Data

William and Kate came to you because their oldest child starts college tomorrow and they need help determining how to pay for it. They have done a good job of saving for retirement, but have not set aside any funds to pay for their children to attend college. They hope their children will qualify for scholarships and/or financial aid from the federal government and just submitted their first Free Application for Federal Student Aid (FAFSA). They have not received official word yet as to the type and amount of aid for which they may qualify, but the on-line FAFSA estimator indicated they would not be eligible for Federal Pell Grants or Subsidized Stafford Loans.

The Windsors believe they may benefit from meeting with a CERTIFIED FINANCIAL PLANNER™ practitioner. They arrived with the following information for you to assist them in creating a plan to meet their education funding goals.

The Family

William and Kate Windsor are both 42 years old and have been married for 22 years. William Windsor is an aircraft mechanic who works full-time for Southeast Airlines (SE) Company, a large publicly owned firm, which offers flights across the United States. William and Kate met and fell in love in high school while William's father was stationed at Fort Soldier. William's father was reassigned to another base at the end of William's senior year. William moved with his family but stayed in touch with Kate, and they eventually married.

Kate worked while William learned his craft at the local Technical school. After William began working for SE, they began their family and Kate became a stay-at-home mom. Kate returned to work about 8 years ago. She is employed by SE as a Gate Attendant. William and Kate have three children.

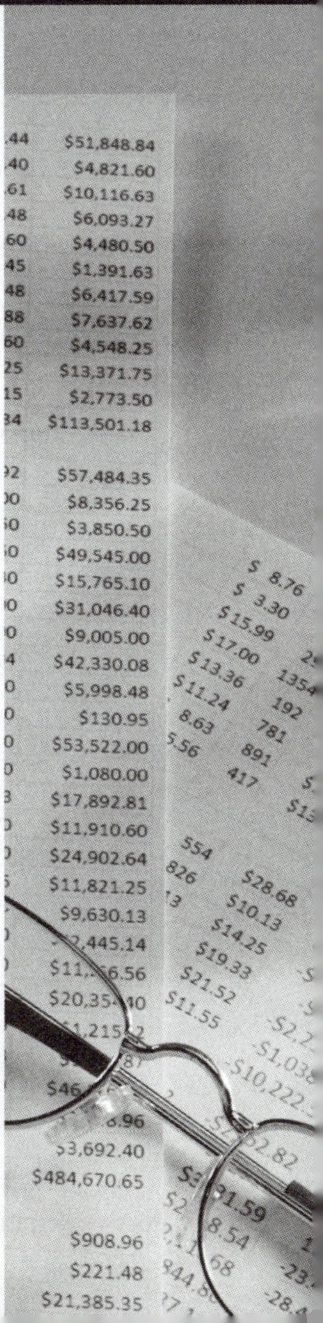

The Children

Kylie, age 18, who will begin college today. Tyler, age 12, is in sixth grade, and Trace, age 9, is in third grade. While all of the children are academically talented students with excellent grades, Kylie has shown exceptional athletic ability and Tyler has shown exceptional musical ability. Trace, the baby, exhibits a charming personality and winning smile, but no interest in sports or music. He considers himself a work in progress.

William and Kate have not saved any money to send any of the children to college. Their hope was that each child would qualify for financial aid. They believe it likely that Kylie will qualify for an athletic scholarship, or a combination of an athletic scholarship and financial aid, and Tyler will qualify for some sort of music scholarship and financial aid. As their thoughts turned to Trace's unique qualities and lack of interest in sports and music they realized they might have to save money to pay for Trace to attend college.

They searched for scholarships to charm schools, which to their dismay, turned out to be offered mainly to girls. Trace, being the precocious child he is, thought a scholarship to charm school would be perfect. William and Kate disagreed, and are now on a mission to find ways to pay for each of their children to attend 4 years of college at State University, beginning at age 18.

They completed the FAFSA on-line and found some scholarship funds to offset more than half of the cost of tuition and fees, but the scholarship does not pay for books, room and board, transportation or meals while living away from home. The Windsor's need help identifying how to pay for Kylie's current college expenses while also planning for Tyler's and Trace's future college expenses.

They are willing to make changes to their finances to pay for Tyler and Trace to attend college, but also need your help determining how much they should save and where they should invest the money until the boys are ready to attend college.

Goals (in order of priority)
1. College education of children for 4 years, each beginning at age 18, at the state university.
2. Retirement at age 64 with 60% of preretirement income including Social Security. Life expectancy is age 96 for both.
3. Appropriate risk management portfolio, investment portfolio, and estate planning portfolio.
4. Pay off their debt before retirement.

External Information

Economic Information

- General inflation (CPI) is expected to be 3% annually.
- Education inflation is expected to be 6% annually.
- They live in a common law state that has no state income tax.

Bank Lending Rates

- Mortgage 30 years - conforming rate = 4.0%.
- Mortgage 15 years - conforming rate = 3.5%.
- Prime rate is 3.25%.
- They plan to stay in their home through retirement and are more concerned about paying for their children's college education than refinancing their home.

Investment Returns Expected

- General market is expected to return 8.0%.
- The Windsor's required and expected rate of return is 8.0%.
- Fixed income investments are expected to yield 6%.
- T-Bills are expected to yield 3% per year and are expected to be the proxy for the risk-free rate of return.
- William and Kate scored a 22 on the Global Portfolio Allocation Scoring System (PASS) for Individual Investors.

Education

- The Windsor's estimate that college costs at State University currently total $15,000 per child, per year in today's dollars for tuition, fees, room and board.
- State University is within commuting distance of William and Kate's home. If the children do not qualify for financial aid, and their parents cannot afford to pay the full cost of attending college and living on campus, the children can enroll in classes while living at home, or enroll in classes at the local community college to reduce the cost of admission.
- Kylie wants to live on campus and does not want to attend community college.
- William and Kate have been told that their state offers a 529 College Savings Plan as well as a unit-type prepaid tuition program.
- Each unit of pre-paid tuition purchased is redeemable for one percent of the resident undergraduate tuition at the highest-priced public university in their state.
- Their State's pre-paid tuition program is not backed by the full faith and credit of the State, but the units may also be used for eligible educational institutions across the country.

Assumption

Education assumptions include four years of college at $15,000 per year in today's dollars. The education inflation rate is 6%. Financial Aid may be possible, but do not assume outside funding assistance from the children's grandparents or any other person.

SUGGESTED SOLUTION

DETERMINING THE EDUCATION COST USING THE TRADITIONAL APPROACH

Use the traditional, three-step approach to determine the lump sum needed to fund all four years of education expense for each child. Combining the education inflation rate of 6% with an expected investment rate of return of 8%, yields a 1.8868% inflation-adjusted rate of return that is used in the first two steps of the three-step approach.

Step 1

Calculate the inflation-adjusted, four-year cost of each child's college education.

PMT_{AD}	=	$15,000
N	=	4 years
i	=	1.8868%
FV	=	0
PV_{AD}	=	$58,353.81 (this will be the same for each child)

This is also the lump-sum cost of education for Kylie, age 18, who begins college today.

The Windsor's will pay for Kylie's education as they go, or through a combination of cash flow, financial aid and tax breaks, if any are available.

Step 2

Calculate the present value of the lump-sum cost of each child's four years of college. Traditional approach to determine the cost of education for Tyler, age 12, and Trace, age 9, who will start school in 6 years and 9 years, respectively.

Tyler		
FV	=	$58,353.81
PMT	=	0
i	=	1.8868
N	=	6
PV	=	$52,162.89

Trace		
FV	=	$58,353.81
PMT	=	0
i	=	1.8868
N	=	9
PV	=	$49,318.28

Total PV for Tyler and Trace is $101,481.17 ($52,162.89 + $49,318.28).

Total PV for Kylie, Tyler and Trace is $159,834.98 ($101,481.17 + 58,353.81).

Step 3

Calculate the end of year payment needed to fund each child's college education.

Tyler		
PV	=	\$52,162.89
N	=	6
i	=	8%
FV	=	0
PMT_{OA}	=	\$11,283.64

Trace		
PV	=	\$49,318.28
N	=	9
i	=	8%
FV	=	0
PMT_{OA}	=	\$7,894.86

The total annual cost of savings to fund Tyler's and Trace's education expense = \$19,178.50.

Review the proof of education funding schedule.

USING THE UNEVEN CASH FLOW APPROACH TO CALCULATE THE NPV OF 4 YEARS OF EDUCATION EXPENSE

Present value calculation for cost of education for all three children:

10BII Keystrokes	*12C Keystrokes*
15,000 [CFj]	15,000 [g] [CF_0]
4 [ORANGE] [Nj]	4 [g] [Nj]
0 [CFj]	0 [g] [CFj]
2 [ORANGE] [Nj]	2 [g] [Nj]
15,000 [CFj]	15,000 [g] [CFj]
3 [ORANGE] [Nj]	3 [g] [Nj]
30,000 [CFj]	30,000 [g] [CFj]
15,000 [CFj]	15,000 [g] [CFj]
3 [ORANGE] [Nj]	3 [g] [Nj]
1.08 [÷] 1.06 [-] 1 [x] 100 [=] [I/YR]	1.08 [ENTER] 1.06 [÷] 1 [–] 100 [x] [i]
[ORANGE] [NPV]	[f] [NPV]
Answer: 159,835.05	**Answer: 159,835.05**

Recap

The PV of Kylie's four years of education is \$58,354.

The PV of Tyler's four years of education is \$52,163.

The PV of Trace's four years of education is \$49,318.

- The total present value of the inflated cost of education for the Windsor children is \$159,835.
- See Education Savings and Withdrawal Schedule.

The importance of financial aid for the Windsor children becomes clearer to William and Kate as they realize that whatever financial aid they receive will help them close the small annual present value deficit of funds needed to meet their education funding goal and retire at age 64.

FINDING FINANCIAL AID

The Windsors have already submitted their first FAFSA. The on-line FAFSA estimator indicated they would not be eligible to receive a Pell Grant or other federal financial aid. Their estimated Net Worth for FAFSA purposes was $41,000, and their EFC was estimated to be zero.

The Windsors linked to the State University (SU) Net Cost calculator to determine what, if any, scholarships or other funds might be available to help them pay for Kylie's college expenses. They hope to receive a formal student aid report (SAR), which will outline the financial aid they can expect. While they were trying to estimate their out of pocket expenses, they used SU's Cost Calculator (see below) and discovered that Kylie is eligible for the SU Hope Scholarship, which is funded by the Lottery for Education, and possibly the ZM Scholarship also funded by the Lottery for Education, but based on merit.

The best type of financial aid would be scholarships and grants because they do not have to be repaid.

The cost of one year of school, 15 tuition hours or more, estimated below is $10,663.

The SU Hope Scholarship is estimated to pay for 85% of Kylie's tuition for the year, but none of her books, or room and board expenses. If Kylie attends SU locally, the Windsor's will need to pay $4,258 for tuition, fees and books.

Summary of the output from State University's On-Line, Cost Calculator for one year (Fall/Spring) 2012-13 for an incoming Freshman.

	Living at Home	**Living on Campus**
Tuition (in-state)	$7,535.00	$7,535.00
Student Fees	$2,128.00	$2,128.00
Books and Supplies	$1,000.00	$1,000.00
Sub-total tuition, fees, books	**$10,663.00**	**$10,663.00**
Housing, meals, transportation	0	$8,218.00
Total cost of attendance	$10,663.00	$18,881.00
Less Scholarship	($6,404.75)	($6,404.75)
Total cost of attendance	**$4,258.25**	**$12,476.25**

If Kylie attends a state university where she must pay room, board, meals and transportation her total out of pocket expenses are estimated to be $12,476. This is slightly less than the Windsor's estimate of $15,000 but more than they can afford to pay from excess cash flow. Kylie's athletic ability and academic standing may qualify her for athletic as well as merit-based scholarships, such as the ZM Scholarship. However, the FAFSA quick check determined Kylie is not eligible for needs-based financial aid.

After finding as much 'free' financial aid as possible, the Windsor's should consider tax credits and tax deductions they can claim each year on their federal income tax return. While these credits and deductions will not help them pay Kylie's tuition bills as they come due, they will help to offset or reduce the cost of education. Plus they can estimate the impact of any tax benefits and reduce their federal income tax withholding accordingly, which will allow them to receive the projected tax benefit ratably during the year (i.e., in each pay check).

If additional funds are needed, the Windsor's should consider Federal Supplemental Education Opportunity Grants (FSEOG) and Federal Perkins Loans, which are both campus-based, student financial aid for students with low EFCs. The current rate of interest charged for Federal Perkins loans is five percent.

The Windsor's may also want to consider borrowing funds from their 401(k) plan. The rate charged is two percent above the prime rate of interest.

William and Kate should also consider whether they want their children to contribute some of the funds needed to pay for their college education. If so, the children should consider work-study options on their college campus.

Once the Windsor's have determined the type and amount of merit-based financial aid they can count on to help pay Kylie's current tuition and fees, they will need to determine whether they should require Kylie to live at home while attending college. The at-home cost of attendance is manageable and could be paid from their discretionary cash flow. The additional $8,218 for room, board, meals and transportation is more than their discretionary cash flow and would require the Windsor's to consider taking out loans in order to fund Kylie's education.

Kylie's college expenses are most urgent, but William and Kate also need to prepare to send Tyler and Trace to college. They should continue saving the maximum amount needed to qualify for their employer's matching contribution and consider contributing excess funds (those over the percentage needed to gain their employer's maximum match) into 529 Plan accounts for each son. They should also remember to begin the search for financial aid as each boy enters their senior year of high school.

Education Savings & Withdrawal

William and Kate Windsor

Year	Age of Kylie	Beginning Balance	Withdrawal (Kylie)	Withdrawal (Tyler)	Withdrawal (Trace)	Withdrawal ()	Earnings @ 8%	Contributions	Ending Balance	Tuition @ 6%	Sum of Payments
2013	18	$0	-$15,000	$0	$0	$0	-$1,200	**$0**	-$16,200	$15,000	-$15,000
2014	19	-$16,200	-$15,900	$0	$0	$0	-$2,568	$0	-$34,668	$15,900	-$15,900
2015	20	-$34,668	-$16,854	$0	$0	$0	-$4,122	$0	-$55,644	$16,854	-$16,854
2016	21	-$55,644	-$17,865	$0	$0	$0	-$5,881	$0	-$79,389	$17,865	-$17,865
2017	22	-$79,389	$0	$0	$0	$0	-$6,351	$0	-$85,741	$18,937	$0
2018	23	-$85,741	$0	$0	$0	$0	-$6,859	$0	-$92,600	$20,073	$0
2019	24	-$92,600	$0	-$21,278	$0	$0	-$9,110	$0	-$122,988	$21,278	-$21,278
2020	25	-$122,988	$0	-$22,554	$0	$0	-$11,643	$0	-$157,186	$22,554	-$22,554
2021	26	-$157,186	$0	-$23,908	$0	$0	-$14,487	$0	-$195,581	$23,908	-$23,908
2022	27	-$195,581	$0	-$25,342	-$25,342	$0	-$19,701	$0	-$265,966	$25,342	-$50,684
2023	28	-$265,966	$0	$0	-$26,863	$0	-$23,426	$0	-$316,256	$26,863	-$26,863
2024	29	-$316,256	$0	$0	-$28,474	$0	-$27,578	$0	-$372,308	$28,474	-$28,474
2025	30	-$372,308	$0	$0	-$30,183	$0	-$32,199	$0	-$434,691	$30,183	-$30,183
2026	31	-$434,691	$0	$0	$0	$0	-$34,775	$0	-$469,466	$31,994	$0
2027	32	-$469,466	$0	$0	$0	$0	-$37,557	$0	-$507,023	$33,914	$0
2028	33	-$507,023	$0	$0	$0	$0	-$40,562	$0	-$547,585	$35,948	$0
2029	34	-$547,585	$0	$0	$0	$0	-$43,807	$0	-$591,392	$38,105	$0
2030	35	-$591,392	$0	$0	$0	$0	-$47,311	$0	-$638,703	$40,392	$0
2031	36	-$638,703	$0	$0	$0	$0	-$51,096	$0	-$689,799	$42,815	$0
2032	37	-$689,799	$0	$0	$0	$0	-$55,184	$0	-$744,983	$45,384	$0
2033	38	-$744,983	$0	$0	$0	$0	-$59,599	$0	-$804,582	$48,107	$0
2034	39	-$804,582	$0	$0	$0	$0	-$64,367	$0	-$868,949	$50,993	$0
2035	40	-$868,949	$0	$0	$0	$0	-$69,516	$0	-$938,465	$54,053	$0
			$58,354	**$52,163**	**$49,318**	$159,835		PV of tuition payments today equals			**$159,835**
	Sum of payments		-$65,619	-$93,082	-$110,862						

Proof of Education funding and Withdrawals for Tyler and Trace

William and Kate Windsor

Assuming no Financial Aid

Year	Age of Kylie	Beginning Balance	Withdrawal (Kylie)	Withdrawal (Tyler)	Withdrawal (Trace)	Withdrawal ()	Earnings @ 8%	End of year 529 plan Contributions	Ending Balance	Tuition @ 6%	Sum of Payments
2013	18	$0	$0	$0	$0	$0	$0	$19,178	$19,178	$15,000	$0
2014	19	$19,178	$0	$0	$0	$0	$1,534	$19,178	$39,891	$15,900	$0
2015	20	$39,891	$0	$0	$0	$0	$3,191	$19,178	$62,261	$16,854	$0
2016	21	$62,261	$0	$0	$0	$0	$4,981	$19,178	$86,420	$17,865	$0
2017	22	$86,420	$0	$0	$0	$0	$6,914	$19,178	$112,513	$13,937	$0
2018	23	$112,513	$0	$0	$0	$0	$9,001	$19,178	$140,692	$20,073	$0
2019	24	$140,692	$0	-$21,278	$0	$0	$9,553	$7,895	$136,862	$21,278	-$21,278
2020	25	$136,862	$0	-$22,554	$0	$0	$9,145	$7,895	$131,347	$22,554	-$22,554
2021	26	$131,347	$0	-$23,908	$0	$0	$8,595	$7,895	$123,929	$23,908	-$23,908
2022	27	$123,929	$0	-$25,342	-$25,342	$0	$5,860	$0	$79,105	$25,342	-$50,684
2023	28	$79,105	$0	$0	-$26,863	$0	$4,179	$0	$56,421	$26,863	-$26,863
2024	29	$56,421	$0	$0	-$28,474	$0	$2,236	$0	$30,183	$28,474	-$28,474
2025	30	$30,183	$0	$0	-$30,183	$0	$0	$0	$0	$30,183	-$30,183
2026	31	$0	$0	$0	$0	$0	$0	$0	$0	$31,994	$0
2027	32	$0	$0	$0	$0	$0	$0	$0	$0	$33,914	$0
2028	33	$0	$0	$0	$0	$0	$0	$0	$0	$35,948	$0
2029	34	$0	$0	$0	$0	$0	$0	$0	$0	$38,105	$0
2030	35	$0	$0	$0	$0	$0	$0	$0	$0	$40,392	$0
2031	36	$0	$0	$0	$0	$0	$0	$0	-$1	$42,315	$0
2032	37	$0	$0	$0	$0	$0	$0	$0	$0	$45,384	$0
2033	38	$0	$0	$0	$0	$0	$0	$0	$0	$48,107	$0
2034	39	$0	$0	$0	$0	$0	$0	$0	$0	$50,993	$0
2035	40	$0	$0	$0	$0	$0	$0	$0	$0	$54,053	$0
			$0	**$52,163**	**$49,318**	$101,481		PV of tuition payments today equals			**$101,481**
Sum of payments			$0	-$93,082	-$110,862						

MINI CASE

Retirement Needs and Capital Needs Analysis Mini Case

4

Today is January 1, 2013

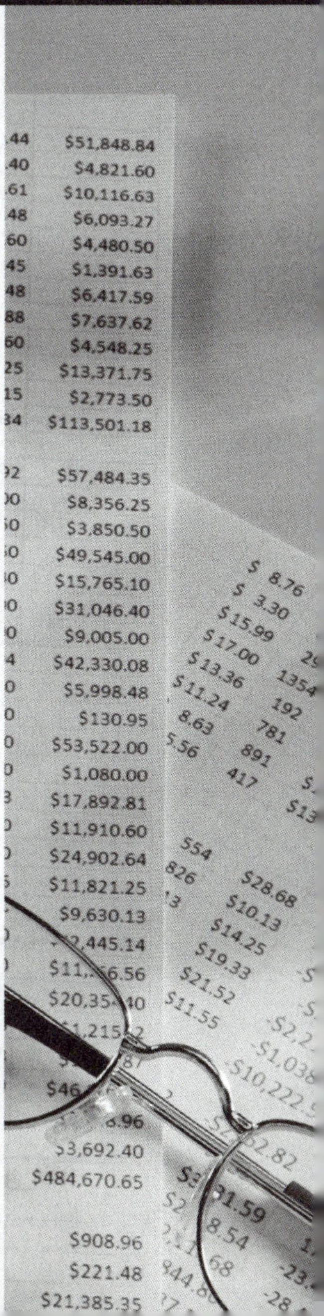

UDAY GUPTA

INTRODUCTORY DATA

Uday Gupta is 40 years old and has never married. He wants to retire at age 62 with an 80% wage replacement ratio. Uday currently earns $100,000 as an employee and has managed to save $100,000 towards his retirement goal (including investment assets and cash equivalents). He is currently saving $5,000 per year in his 401(k) plan. His employer's plan calls for a 50% match for contributions up to an employee elective deferral of 6%.

FINANCIAL GOAL

Uday's primary goal, for this example, is to retire at age 62 with an 80% wage replacement, including Social Security, projected to be $30,000 in today's dollars at normal retirement age of 67. He wants to plan for a life expectancy to age 95.

ECONOMIC AND INVESTMENT INFORMATION

- General inflation is expected to average 3.0% annually for the foreseeable future.
- Uday's expected investment portfolio rate of return is 8.5%.
- Uday's marginal income tax rate is 25%.

SUGGESTED SOLUTION

ANALYTICAL TOOL

Confirm rationality of wage replacement ratio of 80%.

Current Income	100%
Less:	
Social Security Taxes	(7.65%)
Current Savings Rate	(5.00%)
Current Consumption	87.35%

This is close enough to believe that his estimate of needs at 80% is rational.

Use the present value analysis of needs versus resources.

Step 1: Needs At Retirement (age 62)	
Current Salary	$100,000
WRR %	0.80
Total Needs	$80,000
Less: Social Security*	$21,000
Needs in Today's Dollars	$59,000

** 30,000 x 0.70 for early retirement*

Step 2		
N	=	22 (62 - 40) years
PV	=	$59,000 needs
i	=	3% inflation
FV	=	$113,050.1011

Step 3		
PMT_{AD}	=	$113,050.1011
N	=	33 (95 - 62) years
i	=	[(1.085 ÷ 1.030) - 1] x 100
$PV_{@62}$	=	$1,829,501.812

Step 4		
$FV_{@62}$	=	$1,829,501.812
N	=	22 years
i	=	8.5
PMT		0
$PV_{@40}$	=	$304,003.51

Step 5		
PV of needs	=	$304,003.51
Less: PV of resources	=	$100,000.00
Retirement Needs*	=	$204,003.51

*Set as mortgage balance

Step 6		
PV	=	$204,003.51
N	=	22 (remaining work life)
i	=	8.5
PMT_{OA}	=	$20,795.90 annual savings needed

Analytical Conclusion

He is currently saving $5,000 + $2,500 employer match which is far short of what he needs. Total annual savings to meet the goal is $20,795.90. $20,795.90 - $7,500 = $13,295.90 deficit in annual savings.

Next Step - Talk with Client

Discuss Alternatives

Alternative 1:

Save an additional $12,795.90 plus $500 employer match.

Alternative 2:

Delay retirement until normal retirement age of 67.

Analysis of Alternative 2		
Needs $80,000 - S		
PV of needs at age 67	=	$1,680,432.87
PV of needs today	=	$185,702.71
Resources today	=	$100,000.00
Retirement needs today	=	$85,702.71
Annual Savings Needed	=	$8,189.77
i	=	8.5
N	=	27

Under this alternative he must increase his total savings to $8,189.77. Current savings is $7,500, leaving a deficiency of $689.77 of which he contributes an additional $459.85 and the employer would contribute $229.92. It will cost him $459.85 x 0.75 = $344.89 in after tax costs (allows for 25% tax savings on increase contribution to 401(k) plan deferral).

Alternative 3:

Increase his savings to 13% of gross pay plus the employer match = $16,000 per year and then determine when he can retire, which turns out to be approximately age 64.

Schedule			
	Age 62	**Age 64**	**Age 67**
Current Retirement Needs	$59,000	$56,000	$50,000
Work Life Expectancy (WLE)	22	24	27
Retirement Life Expectancy (RLE)	33	31	28
Capital Needs at Retirement	$1,829,501.81	$1,797,989.94	$1,680,432.87
Net PV of Needs	$204,003.51	$153,789.42	$85,702.71
Annual Savings Required	$20,795.90	$15,220.50	$8,189.77
Annual Current Savings	$7,500.00	$7,500.00	$7,500.00
Annual Deficit	$13,295.90	$7,720.50	$689.77

It is clear from the analysis under Alternative 1 that Uday is unrealistic about retiring at age 62 unless he increases his savings rate to almost 18% (17.796% plus the 3% employer match for a total of 20.796% or $20,795.90).

It is also clear that with just a little effort he can retire at age 67. Alternative 2 only requires that he increases his savings by $459.85 ($689.77 ÷ 1.5) per year with a net after-tax cost to him of $344.89 ($459.85 x 0.75).

Alternative 3 presents the results of delaying retirement to age 64 and increasing his savings to approximately $16,000 ($13,000 plus the employer match of $3,000). If he can do this now it will become easier as he receives raises in the future.

Whichever alternative he chooses, the plan should be monitored and readjusted at least annually.

Presentation to Client

Current Goal - Retire at age 62 with an 80% wage replacement ratio including Social Security assuming an annual inflation rate of 3% and an annual retirement rate of return of 8.5% and a life expectancy to age 95.

	Alternative 1	Alternative 2	Alternative 3
Age	40	40	40
Retirement Age	62	67	64
Wage Replacement Needed	$80,000	$80,000	$80,000
Social Security Benefits	$21,000	$30,000	$24,000
Net Annual Needs (Today's $)	$59,000	$50,000	$56,000
PV of Needs (Today's $)	$304,003.51	$185,702.71	$253,789.42
Current Resources	$100,000.00	$100,000.00	$100,000.00
PV of Retirement Needs	$204,003.51	$85,702.71	$153,789.42
Annual Savings Required to Meet Needs	$20,795.90	$8,189.77	$15,220.50
Annual Current Savings	$7,500.00	$7,500.00	$7,500.00
Annual Deficit	$13,295.90	$689.77	$7,720.50

- Alternative 1: Increase savings by $13,295.90 inclusive of the $500 employer match.
- Alternative 2: Increase savings including employer match by $689.77 per year and retire at age 67.
- Alternative 3: Increase savings by $7,720.50 including employer match and retire at age 64.

Summary

Uday needs to choose. Plan 1 is unrealistic. Plan 3 is easy. He can perhaps attempt Plan 3 and it should become easier as he gets raises.

MINI CASE

Present Value Approach Mini Case

5

Today is January 1, 2013

CHARLES AND CHARLOTTE RANGLE

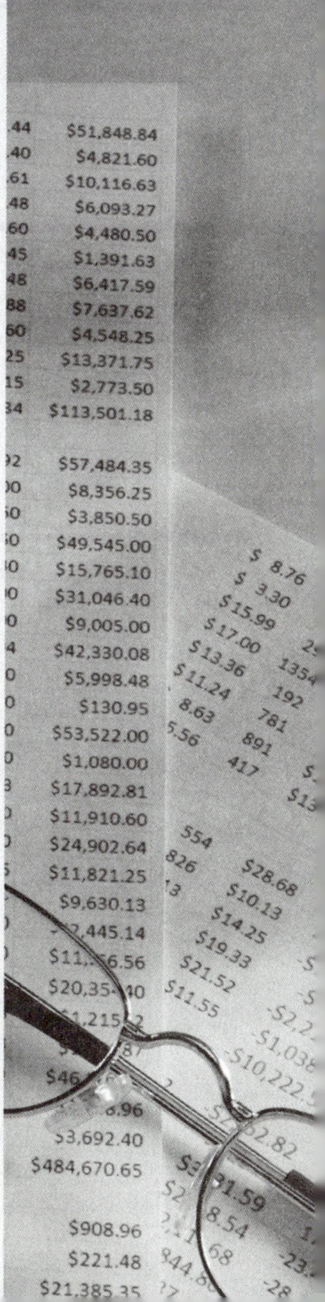

INTRODUCTORY DATA

Charles and Charlotte are both 37 years old and have two children. Charles makes $70,000 and Charlotte makes $40,000 per year.

You have gathered the following information:

1. Their expected portfolio rate of return is 8.5%.
2. They want to retire at 62 with 80% of their preretirement income. They expect to live to age 95.
3. They expect that Social Security will provide $24,000 to him and $20,000 to her at normal age retirement of 67.
4. They want to send their children to a state university. The current education inflation rate is 6%. The current cost per year is $20,000. The children are expected to attend school for 5 years. The children are ages 8 and 6 and will start college at age 18.
5. They have $150,000 in investment assets and cash and cash equivalents.
6. They have no interest in moving or refinancing.
7. At retirement, they want to buy a specialized RV. The current cost is $250,000 and is expected to increase with general inflation.
8. They are currently saving $11,000 per year (Charles: $7,000/Charlotte: $4,000) and have employer matches of $3,300 total (3% maximum match) for a total of $14,300 annually.
9. The general inflation rate (CPI) is expected to be 3%.

SUGGESTED SOLUTION

THE RV GOAL

Step 1		
N	=	25
PV	=	$250,000 needs
i	=	3% inflation
FV	=	$523,444.48

Step 2		
FV	=	$523,444.48
N	=	25
i	=	8.5
PV	=	$68.096.87

Note: This calculation can be done in one step using an inflation-adjusted discount rate.

THE EDUCATION GOAL

N	=	5
i	=	(1.085 ÷ 1.06 - 1) x 100
PV_{AD}	=	$20,000
$PV_{@18}$	=	$95,496.66926

8 Yr. Old Child		
N	=	10
i	=	(1.085 ÷ 1.06 - 1) x 100
FV	=	$95,496.66926
PV	=	$75.639.65

6 Yr. Old Child		
N	=	12
i	=	(1.085 ÷ 1.06 - 1) x 100
FV	=	$95,496.66926
PV	=	$72,194.11

THE RETIREMENT GOAL

WRR (80% of $110,000)	=	$88,000	
Less Social Security (reduced)	=	$30,800	[70% of ($24,000 + $20,000)]
Current Annual Needs	=	$57,200	

Inflate Current Needs		
N	=	25
i	=	3
PV	=	$57,200
FV	=	$119,764.0976

Calculate Capital Needs at Retirement		
N	=	33
i	=	(1.085 ÷ 1.03 - 1) x 100
PMT_{AD}	=	$119,764.0976
$PV_{@62}$	=	$1,938,155.131

Calculate the PV of Retirement Needs		
N	=	25
i	=	8.5
FV	=	$1,938,155.131
PV	=	$252,141.93

SUMMARY OF ALL LONG-TERM GOALS IN PRESENT VALUE TERMS

RV		\$68,096.87
Education		\$147,833.76
Retirement	=	\$252,141.93
Total	=	**\$468,072.56**

PRESENT VALUE OF ALL GOALS LESS CURRENT RESOURCES

Goals		\$468,072.56
Resources	=	\$150,000.00
PV Goals - Resources	=	**\$318,072.56**

The \$318,072.56 can be treated as a mortgage. Consider that hypothetically they borrow exactly this amount and then repay it over the remaining work life expectancy (WLE) at their portfolio rate of return of 8.5%. How much would they have to pay (save) annually?

PV	=	\$318,072.56
N	=	25 (the remaining WLE)
i	=	8.5 (the portfolio earnings rate)
PMT_{OA}	=	\$31,079.40 (assuming an equal annual ordinary annuity)

This amount can then be compared to their current savings amount and their capability to save to determine whether these goals are realistic. They are currently saving \$14,300 per year, including their employer match, so the deficit is \$16,779.40. Another way to look at this is the savings rate. They currently have a savings rate of 13% but they have multiple goals calling for an overall savings rate of 28.25% (\$31,079.40 ÷ \$110,000), which unlikely to be realistic.

THE ALTERNATIVES

Alternative 1

They are unlikely to reconsider the education goal, but might consider only four instead of five years of education. They might decide to forgo the RV or buy one that is less expensive. However, even if they agreed to do both of these, the results would not be sufficient to meet the retirement goal.

80% of education cost \$118,267	\$29,566.75
Reduce value of RV to \$125,000	\$34,048.44
PV of Savings	\$63,615.19
Annual Savings per Year	**\$6,215.95**

Alternative 2

They could lower the WRR to 75%, increase the overall savings rate to 18%, and delay retirement to 67.

RV reduced to:	$52,500.64
Education (stays the same)	$147,833.96
Retirement (see below)	$122,329.56
Total	**$322,664.16**

RV Analysis

PV		250,000
i	=	3
PMT	=	0
FV	=	$606,815.62
N	=	30

FV	=	$606,815.62
i	=	8.5
PMT	=	0
N	=	30
PV	=	$52,500.64

Wage Replacement Analysis

WRR is $110,000 x 0.75	$82,500
Less Social Security at age 67	$44,000
Needs	**$38,500**

Retirement Analysis

Inflate Current Needs		
PV		$38,500
N	=	30
i	=	3%
FV	=	$93,449.60514

Calculate Capital Needs at Retirement		
PMT_{AD}	=	$93,449.60514
N	=	28
i	=	(1.085 ÷ 1.03 - 1) x 100
$PV_{@62}$	=	$1,413,915.87

Calculate the PV of Retirement Needs		
FV	=	$1,413,915.87
N	=	30
i	=	8.5
PV	=	$122,329.56

Total PV of needs	$322,664.16
Current resources	$150,000.00
Net PV of needs	**$172,664.16**

Annual Savings Required

PV	$172,664.16
N	30
i	8.5
PMT_{OA}	$16,066.50

Notice that the current resources are about equal to the present value of the education needs, which they might consider simply setting aside (even hypothetically) for education. They would then need to manage the RV price and the delayed retirement.

Alternative 3 - Recommendation

	Present Value
Reduce college education to 4 years (80%)	$118,267.00
Reduce price of RV to $200,000	$46,605.76
Delay retirement until 65 and reduce WRR to 75%	$161,124.81
Total	**$325,997.57**
Less current resources	$150,000.00
PV Goals	$175,997.57
Annual savings needed	$16,656.26
Saving rate required	15.14%

Notes:

1. 80% of the education amount (5 years vs. 4 years) is not exactly the same as 4 years. However, the education has been shortened from 5 years to 4 years to reduce the cost of education.
2. The calculation of the present value of the RV needs to use 28 years.
3. The calculation of Social Security for retirement needs must include an adjustment for early retirement at age 65 – 13.333% reduction.

Alternative 3 is a compromise of delaying retirement by 3 years, reducing education to 4 years, reducing the WRR to 75%, and reducing the RV price to $200,000. The cost is to increase their savings rate to 15.14% from 13%.

Ultimately, they will have to choose.

RV Analysis

N	=	28
i	=	3
PMT	=	0
PV	=	$200,000
FV	=	$457,585.54

FV	=	$457,585.54
i	=	8.5
PMT	=	0
N	=	28
PV	=	$46,605.76

Wage Replacement Analysis

WRR is $110,000 x 0.75	$82,500
Less Social Security at age 65	$38,133
Today's Needs	**$44,367**

Retirement Analysis

Inflate Current Needs		
PV		$44,367
N	=	28
i	=	3%
FV	=	$101,508.4872

Calculate Capital Needs at Retirement		
PMT_{AD}	=	$101,508.4872
N	=	30
i	=	(1.085 ÷ 1.03 - 1) x 100
$PV_{@65}$	=	$1,581,958.504

Calculate the PV of Retirement Needs		
FV	=	$1,581,958.504
N	=	28
i	=	8.5
PV	=	$161,124.81

Tax Analysis Mini Case 6

Today is January 2, 2013

LARRY AND KAY MULLEN

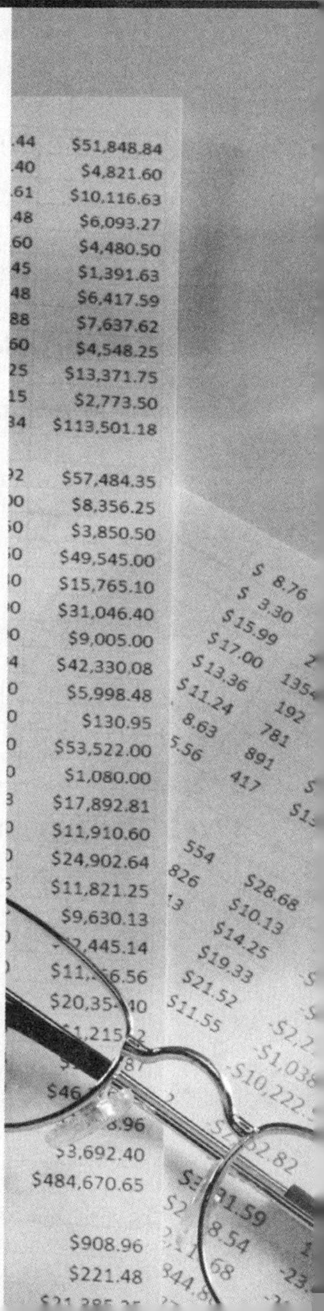

Introductory Data

Larry and Kay Mullen came to you because they need help determining how to pay for education expenses for their three children. They want to get as much financial aid from the federal and state government as they can and believe they will benefit from meeting with a CERTIFIED FINANCIAL PLANNER™ practitioner. They arrived with the following information for you to assist them in creating a plan to meet their education funding goals.

The Family

Larry Mullen, age 36, is a Master Welder who works full-time at the Oklahoma Welding Company, a large publicly owned firm with state and federal military contracts for welding services. Larry was hired for his current job three years ago after completing his Master Welder program in Tulsa, Oklahoma. The Master Welding Program cost $15,000 and Larry completed this program while he was unemployed. Though Larry's wife, Kay, also age 36, had a job during this time, Larry's unemployment strained the family's finances. They stayed current on their mortgage but ran up the balance on their credit card, which they have been aggressively paying down over the past three years.

Larry qualified for $9,000 of federal financial aid that did not need to be repaid. The federal financial aid, a combination of Pell Grant and Federal Supplemental Educational Opportunity Grant (FSEOG) funds, did not cover the total cost of the Master Welder Program. Larry and Kay paid the remaining cost of his program with a $6,000 subsidized Stafford loan. The loan charges interest at a rate of 6.0% and carries a 10 year repayment term, repaid on a monthly basis.

Larry and Kay attended high school together and married right after graduation. Their first child was born during their first year of marriage. The two younger children soon followed giving them three children during the first 6 years of their marriage. Kay stayed home with the kids until their youngest child started school, after which she took graphic design classes at the local community college. She obtained an Associate's Degree in Graphic Design and accepted a job with the local oil company, Sooner Oil, where she has been employed for the past 5 years.

The Children

Larry and Kay have three children: Matt (age 17), Megan (age 14) and Heather (age 12). The children all attend public school and are good students though none of the children exhibit extraordinary athletic ability. Larry and Kay do not want to rely on the children's ability to obtain athletic or merit-based scholarships to attend college. They want to find enough needs-based financial aid to provide each child the opportunity to attend 4 years of college at State University, or a technical school, beginning at age 18.

FINANCIAL GOALS & CONCERNS

Their primary goal, for this example, is to examine their tax withholdings and prepare a tax analysis. Their other goals and concerns are as follows:

1. College at State University for each child for 4 years, each beginning at age 18, or an equivalent amount for Technical School.
2. Retire at age 65 with 85% of pre-retirement income including Social Security. Life expectancy is age 96 for both.
3. Appropriate risk management portfolio, investment portfolio, and estate planning portfolio.
4. Pay off credit card debt as soon as possible and their mortgage debt before retirement.

EXTERNAL INFORMATION

Economic Information

- General inflation (CPI) is expected to be 3% annually.
- Education inflation is expected to be 6% annually.
- They live in the state of Oklahoma which has a state income tax.
- The economy is in a slow growth recovery from a recession with moderate to high unemployment.

Bank Lending Rates:

- Mortgage 30 years - conforming rate = 4.0%
- Mortgage 15 years - conforming rate = 3.5%
- They plan to stay in their home through retirement and are more concerned about paying for their children's education and saving for retirement than refinancing their home.

INVESTMENT INFORMATION

- General market is expected to return 8.0%.
- The Mullens' required rate of return is 7.5%.
- Fixed income investments are expected to yield 6%.
- T-Bills are expected to yield 3% per year and are expected to be the proxy for the risk-free rate of return.
- Larry and Kay scored a 15 on the Global Portfolio Allocation Scoring System (PASS) for Individual Investors.

PERSONAL RESIDENCE

Larry and Kay purchased their home approximately 5 years ago at a cost of $120,000. The home has decreased in value over the past few years. They put $20,000 down and financed $100,000 at 4.5% over 30 years.

ASSUMPTIONS

1. Larry and Kay expect to live to age 96.
2. They want you to ignore State Income Taxes.
3. They have a moderate risk tolerance and a required rate of return of 7.5%.
4. The youngest child attends an after-school child care program but does not expect to continue doing so beyond age 13.

STATEMENT OF FINANCIAL POSITION (BEGINNING OF YEAR)

Statement of Financial Position
Larry and Kay Mullen
Balance Sheet as of 1/1/2013

ASSETS[1]				LIABILITIES AND NET WORTH[2]			
Current Assets				**Current Liabilities**			
JT	Cash & Checking	$12,000		W	Credit Cards	$7,630	
JT	Savings	$0		**Total Current Liabilities**			$7,630
Total Current Assets			$12,000				
Investment Assets				**Long-Term Liabilities**			
H	401(k) Plan (Larry)	$50,000		JT	Principal Residence	$91,158	
W	401(k) Plan (Kay)	$20,000		H	Stafford Loan	$3,641	
Total Investment Assets			$70,000	**Total Long-Term Liabilities**			$94,799
Personal Use Assets							
JT	Principal Residence[3]	$100,000		**Total Liabilities**			$102,429
JT	Automobiles	$20,000					
JT	Furniture and Fixtures	$5,000					
W	Jewelry	$2,500		**Total Net Worth**			$112,071
JT	Clothing, Other	$5,000					
Total Personal Use Assets			$132,500				
Total Assets			**$214,500**	**Total Liabilities & Net Worth**			**$214,500**

1. Assets are stated at fair market value.
2. Liabilities are stated at principal only as of January 1, 2013 before January payments. Credit card charges 18% interest rate on the unpaid balance.
3. Home purchased for $120,000 60 months ago. Original 30-year mortgage of $100,000 at 4.5%. Land valued at $20,000.

Income Statement

Statement of Income and Expenses Larry and Kay Mullen Statement of Income and Expenses for 2012, 2013 (and Projected for 2014)					
Cash Inflows	2012		2013		Totals
Oklahoma Welding Company	$40,000		$42,000		
Sooner Oil	$20,000		$21,000		
Total Cash Inflows		**$60,000**			**$63,000**
Cash Outflows					
401(k) Plan – Larry	$4,000		$4,200		
401(k) Plan – Kay	$2,000		$2,100		
Total Savings		**$6,000**			**$6,300**
Taxes					
Federal Income Taxes Withheld	$1,200		$1,200		
Social Security Taxes	$3,060		$3,213		
Social Security Taxes	$1,530		$1,607		
Property Tax Principal Residence	$1,200		$1,200	ND	
Total Taxes		**$6,990**			**$7,220**
Debt Payments (Principal & Interest)					
Principal Residence	$6,080		$6,080	ND	
Stafford Loan	$799		$799	ND	
Credit Cards	$4,571		$4,571	ND	
Total Debt Payments		**$11,450**			**$11,450**
Living Expenses					
Utilities Principal Residence	$3,600		$4,000	ND	
Child Care	$2,400		$2,400	ND	
Auto Maintenance and Gasoline	$1,200		$1,200	ND	
Entertainment and Vacations	$600		$1,200		
Church Donations	$3,680		$3,920		
Food	$6,000		$6,000	ND	
Children's expenses	$1,000		$1,000	ND	
Education savings/expense	$0		$0		
Clothing	$600		$1,500	ND	
Miscellaneous	$750		$1,200	ND	
Total Living Expenses		**$19,830**			**$22,420**
Insurance Payments					
HO Insurance Principal Residence	$1,150		$1,150	ND	
Life Insurance	$610		$610	ND	
Health Insurance	$4,080		$4,080	ND	
Disability Insurance	$544		$544	ND	
Auto Insurance	$2,400		$2,400	ND	
Total Insurance Payments		**$8,784**			**$8,784**
Total Cash Outflows		**$53,054**			**$56,174**
Net Discretionary Cash Flows		**$6,946**			**$6,826**

ND - Non-discretionary cash flow per mutual understanding between financial planner and client.

SUGGESTED SOLUTION

The tax analysis is an approximation using 2012 numbers for personal and dependency exemptions and tax rates. These could easily be adjusted by an assumed inflation rate to project 2013. However, the results would not vary significantly. The primary purpose of a tax analysis is to determine whether the client is significantly under or over-withheld. It is also useful to review 3-5 years of previously filed tax returns to make such determinations.

Often, clients consider a refund from over-withholding a windfall and squander rather than save the refund. On the other hand, under-withholding will cause potential decreases in available funds that could be used for savings and investments. The importance of a tax analysis and review cannot be over-emphasized because in practice planners often encounter cases of extreme over and under-withholding, either of which could significantly affect a client's comprehensive financial plan. Withholding can be adjusted on Form W-4 and should be managed to help the client achieve proper withholding and maximize their savings.

Tax Analysis
Larry and Kay Mullen

	Tax 2 **2012** **Amount**	Tax 1 **2013** **Amount**
Salary 1	$40,000	$42,000
Salary 2	$20,000	$21,000
401(k) deferrals	($4,000)	($4,200)
401(k) deferrals	($2,000)	($2,100)
Total Income	**$54,000**	**$56,700**
Adjustments:		
Less Student Loan Interest	($237)	($202)
AGI	**$53,763**	**$56,498**
Less Personal Exemptions		
Larry	($3,800)	($3,800)
Kay	($3,800)	($3,800)
Kids	($11,400)	($11,400)
Less Itemized Deductions or Std. Deduction	($11,900)	($11,900)
Taxable Income	**$22,863**	**$25,598**
Income Tax (2012 MFJ bracket)	$2,559	$2,970
Self Employment tax	$0	$0
Total	**$2,559**	**$2,970**
Dependent Care Credit (non-refundable) (20%)	$480	$480
Child Tax Credit (children under age 17)	$2,000	$2,000
Tax Less Credits	**$79**	**$490**
Withholding	**$1,200**	**$1,200**
Refund	**$1,121**	**$710**

Summary of Itemized Deductions

	Prior Year 2012	Current Year 2013
Property Taxes	$1,200.00	$1,200.00
Mortgage Interest	$4,149.49	$4,060.79
Church Donations	$3,680.00	$3,920.00
Itemized deductions	**$9,029.49**	**$9,180.79**
Standard Deduction for MFJ	**$11,900.00**	**$11,900.00**

Notes:

- 2012 Federal Tax Rate Schedule was used for 2012 and projected 2013.
- In 2012, Matt is 17 years old so he is too old to qualify for the child tax credit.
- In 2012 and 2013, they are over withheld.

MINI CASE

Risk Tolerance & Investments Mini Case 7

Today is January 1, 2013

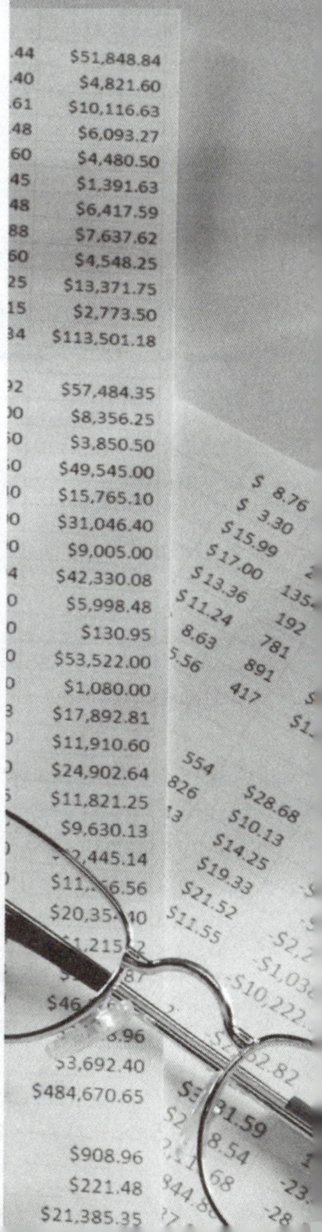

TOMMY AND KRISTINE KRAFT

INTRODUCTORY DATA

Tommy and Kristine Kraft want to begin saving for college education for their twins, Morgan and McKenna, who are having their first birthday today. The first payment will be made today, and they will begin college on their eighteenth birthday. Tommy and Kristine expect that each child will attend private college for five years with the annual payment due at the beginning of each school year. The current cost of private college education is $50,000 per year per child. It is expected that the cost of college education will increase at an average inflation rate of six percent per year. The CPI is expected to remain at three percent during this period.

The Krafts currently have $50,000 invested in a mutual fund that invests in corporate bonds and they have $50,000 invested in an index fund. The $100,000 of investments is dedicated towards education.

Tommy and Kristine have answered the following questions regarding their risk tolerance.

Investment Information

Risk Tolerance Questionnaire

Global Portfolio Allocation Scoring System (PASS) for Individual Investors[1]

Questions	Strongly Agree	Agree	Neutral	Disagree	Strongly Disagree
1. Earning a high long-term total return that will allow my capital to grow faster than the inflation rate is one of my most important investment objectives.		T, K			
2. I would like an investment that provides me with an opportunity to defer taxation of capital gains to future years.		T, K			
3. I do not require a high level of current income from my investments.		T, K			
4. I am willing to tolerate some sharp down swings in the return on my investments in order to seek a potentially higher return than would normally be expected from more stable investments.			T, K		
5. I am willing to risk a short-term loss in return for a potentially higher long-run rate of return.			T, K		
6. I am financially able to accept a low level of liquidity in my investment portfolio.		T, K			

T = Tommy, K = Kristine

Exhibit 1 below presents the expected rates of returns for various asset classes along with the expected standard deviation for each asset class.

Exhibit 1

	Expected Rates of Return	Standard Deviation of Returns
Cash and Money Market Fund	2.5%	2.0%
Treasury Bonds/ Bond Funds	4.0%	4.0%
Corporate Bonds/ Bond Funds	6.0%	5.0%
International Bond Funds	7.0%	6.0%
Index Fund	9.0%	14.0%
Large Cap Funds/Stocks	10.0%	16.0%
Mid/Small Funds/Stocks	12.0%	18.0%
International Stock Funds	13.0%	22.0%
Real Estate Funds	8.0%	12.0%

1. Global Portfolio Allocation Scoring System (PASS) for Individual Investors - developed by Dr. William Droms (Georgetown University) and Steven N. Strauss, (DromsStrauss Advisors Inc.) - model used with permission.

SUGGESTED SOLUTION

Exhibit 2 presents calculation and comparison of the expected returns for the Kraft's current portfolio and the PASS recommended portfolio, which can be found in the appendix of this book. The PASS portfolio is based on the answers to the risk tolerance questions above, which total to 22 and their long-term time horizon of 17 years.

EXHIBIT 2

	Current Porfolio (Dollars)	Current Portfolio Percentage	PASS Recommended Portfolio	Difference	Expected Rates of Return	Current Expected Return	PASS Expected Return
Cash and Money Market Fund	$0	0.0%	3%	-3.0%	2.5%	$0	$75
Treasury Bonds/ Bond Funds	$0	0.0%	12%	-12.0%	4.0%	$0	$480
Corporate Bonds/ Bond Funds	$50,000	50.0%	10%	40.0%	6.0%	$3,000	$600
International Bond Funds	$0	0.0%	5%	-5.0%	7.0%	$0	$350
Index Fund	$50,000	50.0%	20%	30.0%	9.0%	$4,500	$1,800
Large Cap Funds/Stocks	$0	0.0%	15%	-15.0%	10.0%	$0	$1,500
Mid/Small Funds/Stocks	$0	0.0%	10%	-10.0%	12.0%	$0	$1,200
International Stock Funds	$0	0.0%	10%	-10.0%	13.0%	$0	$1,300
Real Estate Funds	$0	0.0%	15%	-15.0%	8.0%	$0	$1,200
	$100,000	**100.0%**	**100%**			**$7,500**	**$8,505**
					Expected Return	7.50%	8.51%

In this case, it appears that the expected return can be increased by adjusting the Krafts' portfolio to the PASS portfolio, which should better reflect the risk level that the Krafts are both willing and able to accept. Assume that the financial planner has already assessed the Krafts ability to accept risk.

MINI CASE

Estate Planning Mini Case

8

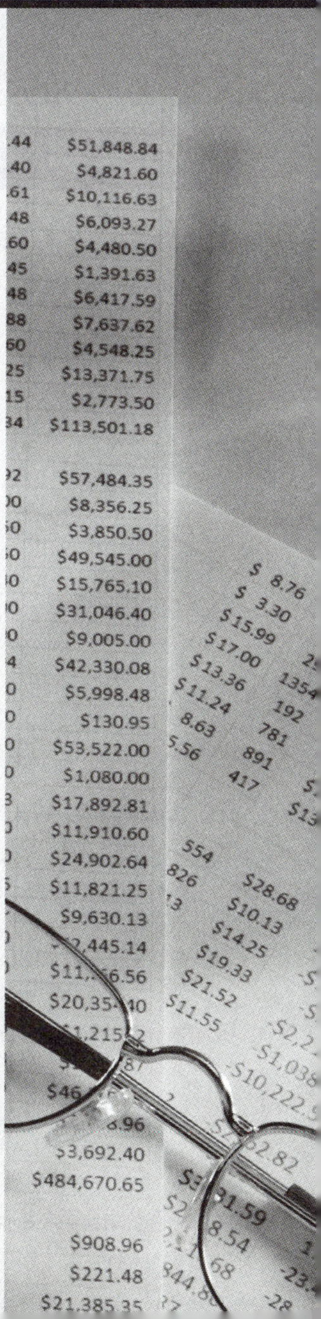

CHASE AND JANET FISHER

INTRODUCTORY DATA

Chase Fisher (age 54) is a small business owner. He and his wife, Janet, (age 53) have the following assets:

His		Hers	
Cash and Cash Equivalents	$500,000	Cash and Cash Equivalents	$200,000
Residence	$2,000,000	Retirement Plans	$1,000,000
Brokerage Account	$2,500,000	Brokerage Account	$1,000,000
Life Insurance (death benefit)	$4,000,000	Family Farm	$3,000,000
Retirement Account	$2,000,000	Miscellaneous Assets	$1,000,000
Business (90% Value)	$2,250,000	Business 10% Value	$250,000

The Fishers have determined that because of the uncertainty of Congress, they would like to freeze assets at $5.12 million x 2 = $10,240,000 and are concerned that lifetime estate and gift exemptions will be lowered.

The Fishers have three children (ages 34, 32, and 30) and nine grandchildren, 3 from each child varying in ages from 1 to 6 years old. The children are educated, healthy, happily married and are of moderate economic means.

The Fishers have done no estate planning and do not have any estate planning documents.

FINANCIAL GOALS

Their primary goal, for this example, is to prepare a basic, but adequate estate plan. Their other goals and concerns are as follows:

- Retire at age 63 and maintain control of the company until retirement.
- Protect assets from future creditors.
- Avoid probate.
- Stretch retirement distributions.

- Minimize estate tax.
- Avoid costly involvement of courts.
- Provide for the education of all grandchildren.
- Benefit children.
- Freeze their estate at $10.24 million.

Assets

- The residence is titled fee simple.
- One brokerage account is in his name only. The other is in her name only.
- The life insurance is owned by Chase and is a permanent policy with a cash value of zero. He just purchased the policy and the beneficiary is his estate.
- His retirement account (IRA) has no named beneficiary.
- His business is an LLC and he is the manager, member with a 90% interest. Janet has a 10% interest.
- Chase is the named beneficiary for Janet's retirement plan.
- The family farm is owned fee simple by Janet.
- Her miscellaneous assets include art valued at $150,000.

SUGGESTED SOLUTION

Analysis of Current Situation

If Chase dies, his current probate assets are:

Cash and Cash Equivalents	$500,000
Residence	$2,000,000
Brokerage Account	$2,500,000
Life Insurance	$4,000,000
Retirement Account	$2,000,000
Business (Full Value)	$2,250,000
	$13,250,000

If he were to die now, he would die intestate, and his assets would be distributed according to the state intestacy law. His gross estate would also equal $13,250,000. It is unclear at this time what the estate taxes would be because any marital deduction would be dependent on the state intestacy laws and any disclaimers by any statutory heirs, including Janet.

Recommendations

- Prepare wills that include survivorship clauses.
- Prepare durable powers of attorney for healthcare and make them immediately effective to each other and to each child who is competent.
- Prepare durable powers of attorney for property arrangements for Chase, for his business and for Janet for both the business and the farm. Powerholders should be each of them first, and then competent children.
- Prepare advance medical directives for each of them.

To Avoid Probate

- Establish and fund a revocable living trust to hold property - transfer to this trust all assets, except the life insurance and the retirement accounts. The spouses will be the joint trustees and beneficiaries.
- Trust provisions should include the creation of a bypass trust upon the first death of either of them.
- Assign the life insurance to an irrevocable life insurance trust with Janet as the income beneficiary for life and the children the equal remainder beneficiaries. Include a power to invade for an ascertainable standard HEMS for "all" beneficiaries. Use an independent trustee.
- Name Janet as the beneficiary of his retirement account (IRA) with the children as successor beneficiaries.

Results:

- No probate assets.
- Retirement accounts are exempt from creditors.
- Protects assets from future creditors to the extent state law permits.
- Reduces gross estate by $4 million if Chase lives 3 years from transferring the life insurance policy.

To Educate the Grandchildren

- Transfer $1,170,000 by gift ($65,000 per donor/per donee) from the revocable living trust to nine 529 Plans ($130,000 each). Chase and Janet would be the joint and survivor owners, then the blood parent of the grandchild would be the survivor owner of each account.

Result:

- Reduces the gross estate by $1,170,000.

To Reduce the Gross Estate Using a Family Limited Partnership for the Business

- Establish a family limited partnership (FLP) and fund it by transferring the business to the FLP. The value of the FLP should be split with 99% consisting of a limited partnership interest and the remaining 1% as a general partnership interest.
- It is appropriate to discount the value of the business for purposes of valuation by 35% for lack of control and lack of marketability.
- The 99% limited partnership interest can be split into units equal to $20,000, or the annual exclusion amount of $13,000 adjusted for the 35% discount. Thus, $2.5 million x 99% divided by $20,000 equals 123.75 units.
- Transfer 2 units to each child making use of the annual exclusion for the next five years, which will total 30 units (3 children x 5 years x 2 exclusions = 30).
- In the 6th year, donate 2 units to each child and grandchild for a total of 24 units each year (12 x 2 = 24). After nine years, the entire 99% interest will have been transferred without any transfer tax and without relinquishing control over the business. He would then retire and sell or donate his general partnership interest.

Results:

- $2.475 million reduction of gross estate, no transfer taxes.
- The general partnership interest can then be valued and donated to the limited partners.
- Note: Due to the 529 Plan contributions, the annual exclusion is not available for the grandchildren until year 6.

Transfer of Shares

Year 1	6.00	shares
Year 2	6.00	shares
Year 3	6.00	shares
Year 4	6.00	shares
Year 5	6.00	shares
Year 6	24.00	shares
Year 7	24.00	shares
Year 8	24.00	shares
Year 9	21.75	shares
Total	**123.75**	**shares**

Note: Even without increases in the dollar value of the annual exclusion.

At the end of the nine years, Chase has assets worth $6,415,000 and Janet has assets worth $5,615,000.

The value of their assets at the end of nine years is close to the value at which they were attempting to freeze their estate. If they wanted to accelerate this process, they could each make use of their life time exemptions. This is not recommended due to their young ages (only 54 and 53) and need for assets to live on.

Presuming that the estate and gift tax laws do not change, Chase, at his death, would make use of the maximum bypass trust (currently $5,120,000) with the trust arrangement the same as the ILIT. The balance would go outright to his wife in a qualifying way. The trust provisions in the revocable living trust could so provide and she were to die first the same. They could also sell their interest in the family farm. They could also use a tangible personal property trust for the art.

TOTAL RESULT

Asset	Chase's Assets	Comments	Asset	Janet's Assets
Cash and cash equivalents	$500,000	Transfer to Living Trust	Cash and cash equivalents	$200,000
Residence	$2,000,000	Transfer to Living Trust	Retirement Account	$1,000,000
Brokerage Account	$2,500,000	Transfer to Living Trust	Brokerage Account	$1,000,000
Life Insurance	$4,000,000	Transfer to ILIT	Family Farm	$3,000,000
Retirement Account	$2,000,000	Transfer to Living Trust	Miscellaneous	$1,000,000
Business	$2,250,000	Create FLP	Business	$250,000
Total Assets	$13,250,000		Total Assets	$6,450,000
Less transfers of FLP interests	$2,250,000		Less transfers of FLP interests	$250,000
Less donations to 529 Plans	$585,000		Less donations to 529 Plans	$585,000
Less transfer of life insurance	$4,000,000			
Transfers	$6,835,000		Transfers	$835,000
Assets after transfers*	$6,415,000		Assets after transfers	$5,615,000

* This assumes that the general partnership interest was sold to the limited partners and that all other assets remained frozen in value.

At this point, they are only 63 and 62 years old, respectively, and still have their lifetime exemption of $5,120,000 and between 12 and 15 beneficiaries (donees) (the 15 would include the spouses of children) and many years to make use of the annual exclusion and other gifts.

Mr. & Mrs. Young
Mini Case & Mini Case Exercises

Today is January 1, 2013

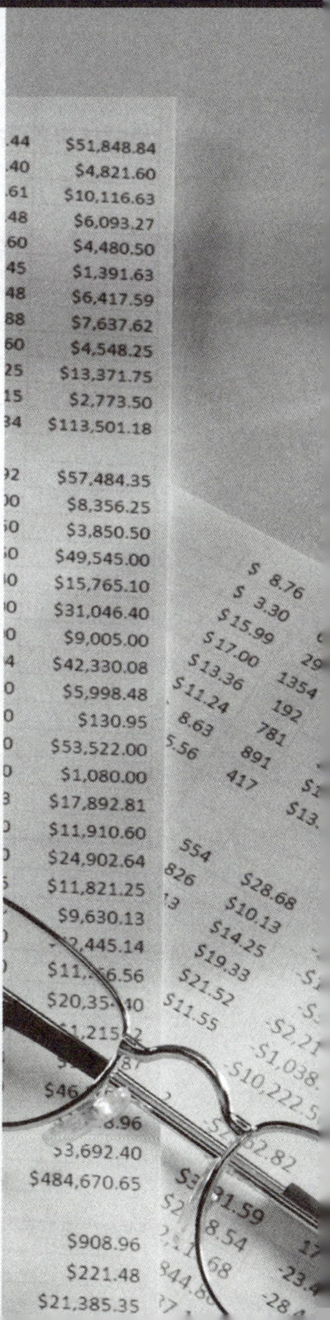

MR. & MRS. YOUNG

THE FAMILY

Mr. & Mrs. Young are both 34 years old and are currently unemployed. He was employed with a consulting firm, but did not find that the culture matched his personality, and she is a stay-at-home mom. The Youngs have two children (ages 4 and 2), a dog, and a Maine Coon cat.

Mr. Young has gone back to school for two years to get an MBA, as his first degree was in Austrian Art History and his second was in law. He has one year left to finish his MBA. Mrs. Young is also highly educated in literature and law from prestigious universities. She is also a licensed lawyer. The Youngs have been married for eight years.

Mr. Young is on a full scholarship for tuition, fees, and books for his MBA program.

The Extended Family

Mr. Young has a mother in her 60s, who is living far away and is modestly self-sufficient. He also has two siblings who are both married and self sufficient. Mr. Young inherited $1,333,000 from his late Uncle Fred, who was 100 years old when he died and had worked everyday of his life.

Mrs. Young has one brother who is married to a wealthy entrepreneur and they have two children. Mrs. Young's mother is a pharmaceutical distributor and lives in another state. She is 60 years old and modestly self sufficient. Mrs. Young's father lives in the same town as the Youngs and her brother. He is self sufficient, healthy, and has the utmost faith that the Youngs will become productive members of society.

Mrs. Young's Father (Trust #1)

Mrs. Young's father set up a trust for the benefit of Mrs. Young. Her brother is the trustee, but the trust is really controlled by her father. The trust regularly distributes $30,000 per year to Mrs. Young and from time to time, invades the corpus to buy her a new car or give her money for nonessentials. The balance in the trust is $700,000 and it has an average earnings rate of about 8.5% per year for the last ten years.

EXTERNAL INFORMATION

Economic Information

- General inflation has averaged 3.0% annually for the last 20 years and is expected to continue at 3%.
- They live in a community property state.

Bank Lending Rates

- 15-year conforming annual rate mortgages are 3.25%.
- 30-year conforming rate mortgages are 3.75%.
- Any closing costs associated with mortgage refinance are an additional 3% of the amount mortgaged and will be included in the mortgage.

Investment Information

They expect to have an 8.5% rate of return for education and 8% for retirement.

INTERNAL INFORMATION

The Residence

The current value of the residence is $550,000. The balance of the 30-year mortgage at 5.5% is $260,514. The land value is $75,000. The monthly payment is $1,703.37 and they have owned it for 8 years.

Insurance Information

Life Insurance

Neither Mr. nor Mrs. Young have life insurance.

Health Insurance

They are covered under the bar association health plan, which is an excellent plan. However, it costs $1,500 per month because the premature birth of their first child. While healthy, she has frequently been in and out of hospitals. The lifetime benefit per person is $3,000,000.

Disability Insurance

Neither Mr. nor Mrs. Young have disability insurance.

Homeowners Insurance

They have an HO3 policy with endorsements for open perils and replacement value. They have a $250 deductible. The dwelling is covered for $300,000 and they have an 80/20 coinsurance clause. The premium is $2,400 per year.

Auto Insurance

They have a personal automobile policy (PAP) covering both cars with a $250 deductible for comprehensive and collision. They do not have uninsured motorist as they do not drive much and both have safe vehicles. The liability coverage is $100,000/$300,000/$50,000. The annual premium is $1,800 for the two cars.

FINANCIAL STATEMENTS

Statement of Financial Position (Beginning of Year)

Statement of Financial Position
Mr. & Mrs. Young
Balance Sheet as of 1/1/2013

ASSETS[1/3]			LIABILITIES AND NET WORTH		
Current Assets			**Current Liabilities[2]**		
Cash & Cash Equivalents			None		
CP Banking Account	$28,000		**Total Current Liabilities**		
Total Current Assets		$28,000			
Investment Assets			**Long-Term Liabilities**		
H Portfolio	$1,333,000		CP Principal Residence	$260,514	
W Brokerage Account	$67,000				
CP 401(k) Plan	$32,000				
Total Investment Assets		$1,432,000	**Total Long-Term Liabilities**		$260,514
Personal Use Assets			**Total Liabilities**		$260,514
CP Principal Residence	$550,000				
W Automobile # 1	$40,000				
CP Automobile # 2	$25,000				
CP Furniture and Household	$150,000				
Total Personal Use Assets		$765,000	**Total Net Worth**		$1,964,486
Total Assets		$2,225,000	**Total Liabilities & Net Worth**		$2,225,000

1. Assets are stated at fair market value.
2. Liabilities are stated at principal only as of January 1, 2013 before January payments.
3. The trust assets are not included on the balance sheet.

Title Designations:

H = Husband (Sole Owner)
W = Wife (Sole Owner)
CP = Community Property

Income Statement

Statement of Income and Expenses Mr. & Mrs. Young Statement of Income and Expenses for Past Year (2012) and Expected (Approximate) For This Year (2013)			
Cash Inflows			**Totals**
Dividends and Capital Gains	$93,000		
Trust Income	$30,000		
Total Cash Inflows			$123,000
Cash Outflows			
Savings			
None	$0		
Total Savings			$0
Taxes			
Federal Estimated Payment	$18,450		
State Estimated Payment	$9,780		
Property Tax Residence	$3,000	ND	
Payroll (FICA)	$0		
Total Taxes			$31,230
Debt Payments (Principal & Interest)			
Principal Residence (P & I)	$20,440	ND	
Auto Loan	$0	ND	
Credit Cards	$0	ND	
Total Debt Payments			$20,440
Living Expenses			
Tuition to Little Darling School for the two children	$22,000	ND	
Utilities for Residence	$2,400	ND	
Entertainment/Vacation	$7,500		
Cable	$1,200	ND	
Clothing	$2,000	ND	
Auto Maintenance/Gas - Both Cars	$3,000	ND	
Food	$9,600	ND	
Total Living Expenses			$47,700
Insurance Payments			
HO Insurance Residence	$2,400	ND	
Health	$18,000	ND	
Auto Premiums	$1,800	ND	
Total Insurance Payments			$22,200
Total Cash Outflows			$121,570
Net Discretionary Cash Flows			$1,430

ND = Non-Discretionary cash flows per mutual understanding between financial planner and client.

* Federal Income Taxes and Social Security are presumed to be discretionary as opposed to nondiscretionary because job loss is the greatest risk to the emergency fund and these expenses are not incurred in the event of a job loss.

Investment Information

The Investment Portfolio

The $1,333,000 investment portfolio produces variable income from -10% to +15%, depending on the year. It was originally $2,000,000 but with poor investment returns and expenditures, it has been reduced to $1,333,000 at this time. Last year's income, which consisted mostly of dividends, was also $93,000.

Other Investment Assets

The assets in the brokerage account are from gifts from Mrs. Young's father. These assets are invested in a money market account, but are currently earning 0%.

Mr. Young's 401(k) assets, which are from when he worked at the consulting firm, are invested in an equity index fund.

Risk Tolerance

Their portfolio consists of a few energy stocks that generated dividends and capital gains of approximately seven percent. They recognize that they need to modify their asset allocation, but are not sure what to do.

They have answered the risk tolerance questionnaire below as follows:

Global Portfolio Allocation Scoring System (PASS) for Individual Investors[1]

Questions	Strongly Agree	Agree	Neutral	Disagree	Strongly Disagree
1. Earning a high long-term total return that will allow my capital to grow faster than the inflation rate is one of my most important investment objectives.	Mr., Mrs.				
2. I would like an investment that provides me with an opportunity to defer taxation of capital gains to future years.	Mr., Mrs.				
3. I do not require a high level of current income from my investments.		Mr., Mrs.			
4. I am willing to tolerate some sharp down swings in the return on my investments in order to seek a potentially higher return than would normally be expected from more stable investments.			Mr., Mrs.		
5. I am willing to risk a short-term loss in return for a potentially higher long-run rate of return.	Mr., Mrs.				
6. I am financially able to accept a low level of liquidity in my investment portfolio.		Mr., Mrs.			

1. Global Portfolio Allocation Scoring System (PASS) for Individual Investors - developed by Dr. William Droms (Georgetown University) and Steven N. Strauss, (DromsStrauss Advisors Inc.) - model used with permission.

Below are the expected rates of returns for various asset classes along with the expected standard deviation for each asset class.

PASS Score	RT1 Target 6 - 12	RT2 Target 13 - 18	RT3 Target 19 - 24	RT4 Target 25 - 30	Expected Return	Standard Deviation
Cash and Money Market Fund	5%	5%	3%	2%	2.5%	2.0%
Treasury Bonds/ Bond Funds	30%	20%	12%	0%	4.0%	4.0%
Corporate Bonds/ Bond Funds	15%	10%	10%	4%	6.0%	5.0%
International Bond Funds	0%	5%	5%	4%	7.0%	6.0%
Index Fund	20%	20%	20%	25%	9.0%	14.0%
Large Cap Funds/Stocks	25%	20%	15%	10%	10.0%	16.0%
Mid/Small Funds/Stocks	0%	5%	10%	20%	12.0%	18.0%
International Stock Funds	0%	5%	10%	15%	13.0%	22.0%
Real Estate Funds	5%	10%	15%	20%	8.0%	12.0%
	100%	100%	100%	100%		
Fixed Income	50%	40%	30%	10%		
Equities	45%	50%	55%	70%		
Real Estate	5%	10%	15%	20%		
Expected Return	6.93%	7.73%	8.51%	9.77%		
Expected Standard Deviation (est)	7.75%	8.94%	10.12%	12.20%		

Tax Information

They are low income tax payers.

Estate Information

They have not prepared any estate planning documents.

GOALS AND CONCERNS

1. Mr. Young wants to finish the MBA.
2. They want to have a proper insurance, investment, and estates portfolio.
3. They want their taxes analyzed.
4. They want to know the cost of college education for the two children so that they can approach Mrs. Young's father about fully funding 529 Plans. The current cost of education is $35,000 per year in today's dollars and the inflation rate is expected to be 5%. They expect the children to be in school for 6 years each, and while they don't know, they expect the 529 Plan's investment rate of return to be 8.5%.
5. They want to plan for an early retirement (100% wage replacement ratio) at age 55, as they want to spend the autumn of their lives together traveling and visiting friends and family. They believe that in one year Mr. Young will have finished the MBA program and will have a job with a salary of $150,000. He expects to be able to save $17,000 per year in a 401(k) plan starting in one year and to have an employer match of $6,000. They expect to live to age 90.
6. As neither of the Youngs currently have 40 quarters of Social Security earnings and because they are planning to retire at age 55, they do not want to include any Social Security retirement benefits in their planning.
7. They want to be debt free at retirement.

MINI EXERCISES

Exercise 1 - Risk Management

Prepare an analysis of the Young's current risk management situation and portfolio.

	Metric	Actual	Recommendations	Annual Cost/Savings
Life Insurance - His				
Life Insurance - Hers				
Disability Insurance - His				
Disability Insurance - Hers				
Health Insurance				
Long-Term Care				
Property Insurance - Homeowners				
Property Insurance - Auto				
Property Insurance - Other				
Liability Insurance				

Comments:

EXERCISE 2 - DEBT MANAGEMENT AND SHORT-TERM OBLIGATIONS

Calculate the Following:

15-Year Mortgage Refinanced	Monthly Payment	
	Monthly Savings	
The Emergency Fund Ratio		
The Current Ratio		
Housing Ratio 1		
Housing Ratio 2		

Comment on each of the above:

____

____

____

Calculations:

EXERCISE 3 - EDUCATION AND EDUCATION FUNDING

Calculate the present value of each child's college education. Hint: Use a real rather than a nominal approach.

Education Analysis

N	=
PMT_{AD}	=
i	=
FV	=
$PV_{@18}$	=

For the 4 Year Old

FV	=
i	=
N	=
PMT	=
PV	=

For the 2 Year Old

FV	=
i	=
N	=
PMT	=
PV	=

Calculations:

Exercise 4 - Retirement Analysis

Calculate the present value of the Young's retirement needs at age 55. These are nominal dollars. [ ]

Calculate the present value of the Young's retirement needs now at age 34. These are real dollars in today's dollars. [ ]

Retirement Analysis

PV	=
i	=
N	=
FV	=

$PV_{@55}$	=
i	=
N	=
PMT_{AD}	=

$FV_{@55}$	=
i	=
PMT	=
N	=

EXERCISE 5 - PV APPROACH FOR ALL LONG-TERM GOALS

Ignoring the fact that Mrs. Young's father may fund the 529 Plans, what is the total present value of both education and retirement?

Calculate the present value of education today.

Calculate the present value of retirement today.

Add the education and retirement together.

Compare current resources.

Calculate the net of PV goals minus current resources.

Calculations:

EXERCISE 6 - TAX ANALYSIS

Prepare an abbreviated tax analysis using the worksheet below:

Tax Analysis - MFJ with 2 Children	
Income	
Income from Investments	$
Income from Trust	$
Total Income	$
Personal & Dependency Exemptions	$
Itemized Deductions	
Mortgage Interest	$
Property Taxes	$
State Income Tax	$
Total Itemized Deductions	$
Taxable Income	$
Tax Liability (at 15% due to dividends)	$
Credits (child credit)	$
Tax Liability	$
Estimated Payments	$
Refund or (Due)	$

*** Use the table provided at www.money-education.com**

EXERCISE 7 - RISK TOLERANCE AND INVESTMENT RETURNS

Analyze the risk tolerance and asset allocation for the Young's utilizing the Pass Scoring System.

Comments:

EXERCISE 8 - ESTATE PLANNING

Describe the estate planning documents that the Youngs need immediately and what are the important provisions of each. If you recommend powers, who is the power holder?

Comments:

SUGGESTED SOLUTIONS

Solution for Exercise 1 - Risk Management

Prepare an analysis of the Young's current risk management situation and portfolio.

	Metric	Actual	Recommendations	Comments
Life Insurance - His	12-16 x GP	None	Need $2M[1] 30-yr term due to assets and income	$1,440 $0.72 per $1,000
Life Insurance - Hers	12-16 x GP	None	Need $1M 30-yr term due to assets	$360 $0.36 per $1,000
Disability Insurance - His	60-70% GP	None	Not available without employment	There may be a group minimum coverage through the Bar Assoc.
Disability Insurance - Hers	60-70% GP	None	Not available without employment	There may be a group minimum coverage through the Bar Assoc.
Health Insurance	$1M Lifetime Benefit	$3M Lifetime Benefit	No action	Could shop for high deductible, catastrophic plan
Long-Term Care	36-60 months	None	No action at this time	Not needed at this time
Property Insurance - Homeowners	HO-3 plus endorsement to FMV of dwelling	HO3 $300,000	Raise dwelling coverage to $475,000	Raise deductible to $2,000. Likely no net additional premium
Property Insurance - Auto	$100k/$300k	$100k/$300k	No action	Raise deductible to $2,000
Property Insurance - Other	N/A	N/A	No action	N/A
Liability Insurance	$1M or more	None	Buy $1M	$250

1. $2M is about 14x expected salary. Plus, he has $1.33M in assets.

SOLUTION FOR EXERCISE 2 - DEBT MANAGEMENT AND SHORT-TERM OBLIGATIONS

Calculate the Following:

15-Year Mortgage Refinance	Monthly Payment	$1,885.47
	Monthly Savings	($182.00)
The Emergency Fund Ratio		3.91426 x
The Current Ratio		Not Relevant
Housing Ratio 1		21%
Housing Ratio 2		21%

Comment on each of the above: All of the ratios are very good.

The 15-Year Mortgage Repayment

The interest rate for mortgages is ideal to refinance at 3.25% for 15 years presuming they are going to stay in the house.

Current P & I = $1,703.39
Refinance = $260,514 x 1.03 = $268,329.42
i = 3.25 ÷ 12
N = 180
PMT = $1,885.47

By adding $182 per month, they will retire the debt in 15 years rather than the current expected 22 years although either one is consistent with their retirement goal. They may not be able to refinance due to a lack of employment.

The Emergency Fund Ratio

85,840 ÷ 12 = $7,153.33
Cash and Cash Equivalents = $28,000
Emergency Fund Ratio = 3.91426 times

The Current Ratio

The current ratio is not relevant in this case because there are no current liabilities unless you count the current portion of the mortgage to give the current years payments as a current liability then the ratio is about 1.4 to 1.

Housing Ratio 1

($20,440 + $2,400 = $3,000) ÷ $123,000 = **21% (very respectable)**

Housing Ratio 2

The same at **21% (very good)**

SOLUTION FOR EXERCISE 3 - EDUCATION AND EDUCATION FUNDING

Education

The present value of education is calculated using the investment rate of return of 8.5%.

Education Analysis

N	=	6 years of education
PMT_{AD}	=	$35,000
i	=	(1.085 ÷ 1.05 - 1) x 100
FV	=	0
$PV_{@18}$	=	193,775.5276

For the 4 Year Old

FV	=	$193,775.5276
i	=	(1.085 ÷ 1.05 - 1) x 100
N	=	14
PMT	=	0
PV	=	$122,442.67

For the 2 Year Old

FV	=	$193,775.5276
i	=	(1.085 ÷ 1.05 - 1) x 100
N	=	16
PMT	=	0
PV	=	$114,670.55

The current education costs in present value terms is $237,113.22 ($122,442.67 + $114,670.55).

Unless the father is married, he can only contribute $65,000 to each child's 529 Plan for a total of $130,000. If he only contributes the $65,000 for each, the parents will have to save the additional amount.

Education		$237,113.22	
PV of 529s		$130,000.00	
PV	=	$107,113.22	
i	=	8.5	(Their earnings rate)
N	=	16	Years until 2 year old is 18
PMT_{OA}	=	$12,490.85	Savings per year at year end

If Mrs. Young's father is married, there is no problem contributing $130,000 to each 529 Plan. If he will only contribute $65,000 to each, then the parents are going to have to contribute the rest out of investments or save for it ($12,490.85 per year).

SOLUTION FOR EXERCISE 4 - RETIREMENT ANALYSIS

Calculate the present value of the Young's retirement needs at age 55. These are nominal dollars	$4,880,262.69
Calculate the present value of the Young's retirement needs now at age 34. These are real dollars in today's dollars.	$969,492.23

Retirement Analysis

PV	=	$150,000
i	=	3
N	=	21
FV	=	$279,044.1858

$PV_{@55}$	=	$4,880,262.69
i	=	[1.08 ÷ 1.03)-1] x 100
N	=	35 (90-55)
PMT_{AD}	=	279,044.1858

$FV_{@55}$	=	$4,880,262.69
i	=	8
PMT	=	0
N	=	21

SOLUTION FOR EXERCISE 5 - PV APPROACH

Ignoring the fact that Mrs. Young's father may fund the 529 Plans, what is the present value of education and the present value of retirement?

Calculate the present value of education today.	$237,113.22
Calculate the present value of retirement today.	$969,492.23
Add the education and retirement together.	$1,206,605.45
Compare current resources.	$1,333,000.00
Calculate the net of PV goals and current resources	+ $126,394.55

Retirement

They have $1,333,000 and plan to add $23,000 per year out of $150,000 salary for a savings ratio of 15.3 (good) assuming he gets a job.

Education

The present value of education is calculated using the investment rate of return of 8.5%.

Education Analysis

N	=	6 years of education
PMT_{AD}	=	$35,000
i	=	(1.085 ÷ 1.05 - 1) x 100
$PV_{@18}$	=	$193,775.5276

For the 4 Year Old

FV	=	$193,775.5276
i	=	(1.085 ÷ 1.05 - 1) x 100
N	=	14
PMT	=	0
PV	=	$122,442.67

For the 2 Year Old

FV	=	$193,775.5276
i	=	(1.085 ÷ 1.05 - 1) x 100
N	=	16
PMT	=	0
PV	=	$114,670.55

The current education costs in present value terms is $237,113.22 ($122,442.67 + $114,670.55).

Unless the father is married, he can only contribute $65,000 to each child's 529 Plan for a total of $130,000. If he only contributes the $65,000 for each, the parents will have to save the additional amount.

Education		$237,113.22	
PV of 529s		$130,000.00	
PV	=	$107,113.22	
i	=	8.5	(Their earnings rate)
N	=	16	Years until 2 year old is 18
PMT_{OA}	=	$12,490.85	Savings per year at year end

If Mrs. Young's father is married, there is no problem contributing $130,000 to each 529 Plan. If he will only contribute $65,000 to each, then the parents are going to have to contribute the rest out of investments or save for it ($12,490.85 per year).

SOLUTION FOR EXERCISE 6 - TAX ANALYSIS

Prepare an abbreviated tax analysis using the worksheet below:

Tax Analysis - MFJ with 2 Children	
Income	
Income from Investments	$93,000
Income from Trust	$30,000
Total Income	$123,000
Personal & Dependency Exemptions (3,800 x 4)	$15,200
Itemized Deductions	
Mortgage Interest	$14,506
Property Taxes	$3,000
State Income Tax	$9,780
Total Itemized Deductions	$27,286
Taxable Income	$80,515
Tax Liability (at 15% due to dividends)	$12,077
Credits (child credit)*	$700
Tax Liability	$11,377
Estimated Payments	$18,450
Refund or (Due)	$7,073

* The credit is limited by $50 for each $1,000. MAGI (line 37 on Form 1040) exceeds $110,000 for MFJ.

$123,000	$1,000
($110,000)	($650)
$13,000	$350
÷ $1,000	x 2
13	$700
x $50	
$650	

SOLUTION FOR EXERCISE 7 - RISK TOLERANCE AND INVESTMENT RETURNS

Analyze the risk tolerance and asset allocation for the Young's utilizing the Pass Scoring System.

Mr. and Mrs. Young's assets are not invested with an overall asset allocation plan. The current estimated expected return is 9.63%, based on the information provided in the case. However, the case also indicates that the expected return for the investment assets is approximately seven percent for dividends. This difference could be due to the concentration of the portfolio in energy stocks.

Below is the calculation and comparison of the expected returns for the Young's current portfolio and the PASS recommended portfolio, which can be found in the appendix of this book. The PASS portfolio is based on the answers to the risk tolerance questions in the case. Scoring their answers results in a score of 26, which corresponds to the most aggressive PASS portfolio.

	Current Porfolio (Dollars)	Current Portfolio Percentage	PASS Recommended Portfolio	Difference	Expected Rates of Return	Current Expected Return	PASS Expected Return
Cash and Money Market Fund	$67,000	4.7%	2%	2.7%	2.5%	$1,675	$716
Treasury Bonds/ Bond Funds	$0	0.0%	0%	0.0%	4.0%	$0	$0
Corporate Bonds/ Bond Funds	$0	0.0%	4%	-4.0%	6.0%	$0	$3,437
International Bond Funds	$0	0.0%	4%	-4.0%	7.0%	$0	$4,010
Index Fund	$32,000	2.2%	25%	-22.8%	9.0%	$2,880	$32,220
Large Cap Funds/Stocks	$1,333,000	93.1%	10%	83.1%	10.0%	$133,300	$14,320
Mid/Small Funds/Stocks	$0	0.0%	20%	-20.0%	12.0%	$0	$34,368
International Stock Funds	$0	0.0%	15%	-15.0%	13.0%	$0	$27,924
Real Estate Funds	$0	0.0%	20%	-20.0%	8.0%	$0	$22,912
	$1,432,000	**100.0%**				**$137,855**	**$139,906**
					Expected Return	9.63%	9.77%

It should be obvious that the Young's portfolio is not very well diversified and subject to the changes in the value of large cap stocks, especially energy stocks, as indicated in the case. The PASS portfolio recommendation provides an expected return that is actually greater than the required return in the case. In addition, the expected standard deviation of the PASS portfolio at 12.20% appears to be much less than that of the current portfolio, which would be assumed to be close to 16% (the same as large cap stocks).

SOLUTION FOR EXERCISE 8 - ESTATE PLANNING

Describe the estate planning documents that the Youngs need immediately and what are the important provisions of each. If you recommend powers, who is the power holder?

The Young's each need a will, a durable power of attorney for healthcare, and an advanced medical directive. The initial power holder should be the spouse. They should specify guardianship for their children and their property. They may want to include a transfer on death (TOD) designation for the investment portfolio and brokerage accounts.

Part 3

Comprehensive Case Example Analysis & Presentation

Case Example

John & Mary Burke Case

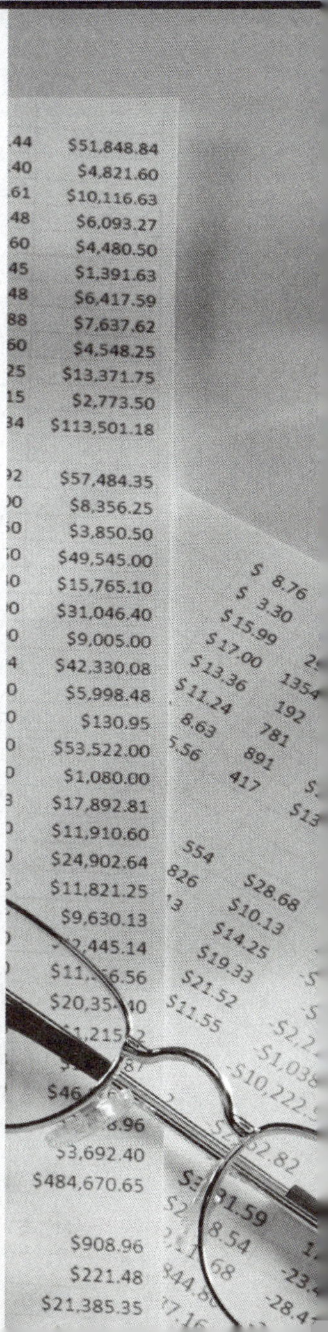

INTRODUCTORY DATA

FINANCIAL PLANNING OFFICES OF MITCHELL AND MITCHELL
MICHAEL A. MITCHELL, CFP®
ROBIN DELLE, EXECUTIVE ASSISTANT

Dialog of Phone Conversation to 850-555-9876 December 15, 2012, 10:00 a.m.	
Robin:	Good morning, Mitchell and Mitchell Financial Planners.
Caller:	Is Mr. Michael Mitchell available?
Robin:	He is currently in a meeting. May I have him return your call?
Caller:	Yes, please. This is John Burke. I am calling about financial planning for myself and my wife, Mary. My phone number is 850-555-4321.
Robin:	I can have Mr. Mitchell call you back between 1:00 and 1:30pm. Is that a good time for you?
Mr. Burke:	Yes, thank you. By the way, please tell him I was referred to him by Sally Robbins.
Robin:	I will. Thank you. Goodbye.

Dialog of Phone Conversation December 15, 2012, 1:00 p.m.	
Mike Mitchell:	Hello Mr. Burke (formal, show respect). This is Mike Mitchell returning your call from this morning. I understand you are interested in developing a financial plan for your family. Is that correct (questioning)?
John Burke:	Yes, thank you for returning my call. You come highly recommended from my good friend and mentor, Sally Robbins, who I believe is one of your financial planning clients.
Mike Mitchell:	Well thank you. Yes, Sally has been a client for some time now. I appreciate you letting me know that Sally recommended our services.
John Burke:	You're welcome.
Mike Mitchell:	I expect you want to set up an appointment? How about you and your wife meeting with me at 9:00 a.m. on January 4th at my office? Would that work for you? The meeting would last about two hours, giving us time to get to know each other. There is no charge for the initial meeting.
John Burke:	January 4th is fine and I know where your office is located. Do I need to bring anything?
Mike Mitchell:	Well, I would like to send you an email with a list of items to bring. I'll mention them now (internal data collection): your recent bank statements, investment account statements, all insurance policies, 5 years of tax returns (if you have them), employer benefits brochures, and a set of financial statements (if you have them). No need to write all of this down, I will email you a detailed list. What is your email address?
John Burke:	jburke@hotmail.com
Mike Mitchell:	Ok, great. Please do not worry if you do not have all these things; just bring what you can. The whole process takes time. By the way, would you mind if I asked you a few brief questions to help me form a picture of you and your family (life cycle information)?
John Burke:	No, go ahead.
Mike Mitchell:	Your wife's name is Mary, correct?
John Burke:	Yes.
Mike Mitchell:	How old are each of you?
John Burke:	We are both 30 years old and have been married for 3 years. I was previously married and have a 4 year old son, Patrick, but we are estranged. He lives out of state.
Mike Mitchell:	Fine. Do you plan on having additional children in the near future?
John Burke:	Yes, we would like to adopt 2 newborns in the next few years and are already approved by the adoption agency.
Mike Mitchell:	What is your approximate income and does Mary work?

John Burke:	Mary works as an administrative assistant at an accounting firm making $26,000 per year. I am an assistant marketing manager with Atlanta Gas. My annual income is $36,000 or $3,000 per month. I pay $350 a month to my ex wife for child support.
Mike Mitchell:	Good, I have a good picture now. Do you happen to know what your net worth is? And, do you own your home?
John Burke:	I am guessing our net worth is about $10,000 or so. We are just getting started and we currently rent and are saving to buy a home. We hope you can help us get on the right track.
Mike Mitchell:	That's great. It has been very nice talking with you. Do you have any questions for me at this time?
John Burke:	No, thank you.
Mike Mitchell:	I will send the email to you by tomorrow and I will see you and Mary at my office January 4th at 9:00 a.m. Please do not hesitate to call me if anything comes up during the interim.
John Burke:	Thanks, I am looking forward to meeting you in person. Goodbye.
Mike Mitchell:	Thank you. Goodbye.

Mike Mitchell's Email to John Burke
December 16, 2012

Dear Mr. Burke:

Thank you for calling me. It was a pleasure to talk with you yesterday and I look forward to our meeting on January 4th.

Please bring with you as many of the following items as you can but do not worry if you do not have everything. (You can bring originals and we can copy them or you can bring copies for us to keep.)

Insurance:

- All life insurance policies - the type - the death benefit, the annual premium(s), who pays the premium(s), who owns the policy, the insured, the beneficiary;
- Any Disability policies - who is insured, amount of premium, who pays the premium(s);
- Health insurance policies - who is covered, deductibles, co-pays, etc.
- Automobile insurance policies - who is covered, amount of premium(s);
- Homeowner's policies - what is covered, deductibles, etc.;
- Any liability policies - amount of premium(s); and
- Any long-term care policies.

Banking and Investments:

- All recent statements for checking and savings accounts;
- All recent statements and year-end statements if available for all brokerage and investment accounts; and
- All 401(k) Plan, 403(b) Plan statements.

Tax Returns:

- Five years of Federal income tax returns if you have them.

Wills, Trust:

- All copies of wills, durable powers of attorney for health care, advance medical directives; and
- Any trust documents for which you are either grantor or beneficiary if you have them.

Employee Benefits:

- Any employer brochures describing employee fringe benefits that you receive or can receive for both you and Mary.
- Summary plan description for employer-sponsored plans.

Financial Statements:

- Any prepared personal financial statements, balance sheet, and income statement.
- If you do not have financial statements, we can create them for you. Bring a list of assets and debts with interest rates, balances, and terms.
- If you can, prepare an annual or monthly statement of your income and expenses.

Call me if you have any questions. I look forward to seeing you and Mary at 9:00 a.m. on the 4th at my office.

Regards,

Mike Mitchell, CFP®
Partner
Mitchell and Mitchell
850-555-9876

At the first meeting - January 4, 9:00 a.m. - Mike Mitchell Notes

I met with John and Mary Burke and we had a good initial meeting. I described that our services involve comprehensive financial planning. They identified several financial goals. I inquired about additional savings opportunities at their place of employment. I discovered that at this time they have no plans for college education of Patrick (age 4). They did a great job of bringing in their information that I had requested in my email and I will be putting that together in a case file. While they did not have financial statements prepared, they were able to list for me their assets and liabilities. I told them that in the case file I would send them, there would be financial statements that we prepared, a prepared pie chart graphic, and some ratios for their review. I mentioned that if we were missing any data we would contact John by email.

I informed them that for this engagement we would bill $3,000 for the initial plan. Any additional services are billed per diem at the rate of $200 per hour for myself and $125 per hour for any assistant time. John informed me that his father would be paying for the comprehensive financial plan. I also explained that it would take us about twelve weeks to complete the process if we met once a week for about an hour. We discussed implementation and they indicated that where they could, they would handle the implementation.

We set the next meeting for January 18th to allow time for us to build the case file and prepare the financial statements.

Engagement Letter

Financial Planning Offices of Mitchell and Mitchell

January 4, 2013

John and Mary Burke
1420 Elm Street
Pensacola, FL 32501

RE: Financial Planning Engagement Letter

Dear Mr. and Mrs. Burke:

This letter will confirm the terms of our recent conversation regarding the financial planning services we will provide for you. The primary objective of our engagement is to prepare a review of your personal financial situation. This review will identify your personal financial goals and objectives, and will include possible strategies to achieve them. Our analysis and recommendations are based on information provided by you that will be relied upon.

The initial phase involves accumulating and organizing facts about your current financial status, identifying specific goals and objectives, and agreeing upon planning assumptions. After your financial information has been received, the data will be analyzed and projections will be made. Subsequent meetings will be held to verify the accuracy of the data and will allow you to validate the assumptions used. Alternative courses of action to meet goals and alleviate any issues will be comprehensively discussed. We will meet over a period of approximately twelve weeks (based on weekly meetings).

The methods that you choose to follow for the implementation of the financial planning recommendations are at your discretion. As you have indicated, you will be responsible for all decisions regarding implementation of the recommendations.

The fee for your comprehensive financial plan has been determined by our mutual agreement and is $3,000 which is due and payable upon return of this Engagement Letter and will be paid by John Burke's father. Please note that this fee is for the written financial plan alone and the plan shall contain all of our recommendations to you through the date of its delivery. In addition, please be advised that this fee does not include preparation of any legal documents or tax returns.

We anticipate beginning the engagement immediately. If this letter meets with your approval, please sign the enclosed copy in the space provided and return it to us. You are free to terminate this agreement at any time and we will bill you for the portion of work that is complete.

We thank you for the opportunity to be of service, and we welcome you as a valued client.

Sincerely,
Michael A. Mitchell, CFP®

I/We agree to the above terms & conditions:

Client Signature: ______________________________ Date: ________________________
John Burke

Client Signature: ______________________________ Date: ________________________
Mary Burke

PERSONAL BACKGROUND AND INFORMATION COLLECTED

THE FAMILY

John Burke, age 30, is an assistant manager in the marketing department of Florida Gas. His annual salary is $36,000. His wife, Mary, is an administrative assistant with an accounting firm. Mary is also 30 years old and has an annual salary of $26,000.

John and Mary have been married for three years and have no children from their marriage. They hope to have two to three children in the next five years. However, John has one child, Patrick (age 4), from a former marriage. Patrick lives with his mother, Kathy, out of state and as a result, John has not seen Patrick for three years.

John pays $350 per month in child support to Kathy for Patrick until he reaches age 18. John also pays for a term life insurance policy on himself for Kathy (beneficiary) as a result of the divorce. The contingent beneficiary on the policy is Patrick. Patrick's education is fully funded by a 529 Plan established by Kathy's father.

EXTERNAL INFORMATION

ECONOMIC INFORMATION

- Inflation is expected to be 3.0% annually.
- The Burke's salaries should increase 4.0% for the next five to ten years.
- There is no state income tax.
- It is expected that there will be a slow growth economy; stocks are expected to return an average of 9.0% annually.

BANK LENDING RATES

- 15-year mortgage rate is 5.0%.
- 30-year mortgage rate is 5.5%.
- Secured personal loan rate is 8.0%.
- Credit card rates are 18%.
- Prime rate is 3.0%.

EXPECTED INVESTMENT RETURNS

- Their expected rate of return is 8.5%.

	Return	Standard Deviation
Cash and Money Market Fund	2.5%	2.5%
Guaranteed Income Fund	2.5%	2.5%
Treasury Bonds/ Bond Funds	4.0%	4.0%
Corporate Bonds/ Bond Funds	6.0%	5.0%
Municipal Bonds/ Bond Funds	5.0%	4.0%
International Bond Funds	7.0%	6.0%
Index Fund	9.0%	14.0%
Large Cap Funds/Stocks	10.0%	16.0%
Mid/Small Funds/Stocks	12.0%	18.0%
International Stock Funds	13.0%	22.0%
Real Estate Funds	8.0%	12.0%

INTERNAL INFORMATION

Insurance Information

Life Insurance

	Policy A*	Policy B	Policy C
Insured	John	John	Mary
Face Amount	$500,000	$50,000	$26,000
Type	Term	Group Term	Group Term
Cash Value	$0	$0	$0
Annual Premium	$600	$178	$50
Who pays premium	John	Employer	Employer
Beneficiary	Kathy then Patrick	Kathy	John
Policy Owner	Kathy	John	Mary
Settlement options clause selected	None	None	None

** John is required, as a result of the divorce, to maintain a term life insurance policy (Policy A) of $500,000. The premiums are $50 per month.*

Health Insurance

John and Mary are both covered under John's employer health plan. The policy is an indemnity plan with a $300 deductible per person per year and an 80/20 major medical coinsurance clause with a family annual stop loss of $2,000 and lifetime benefits of $1,000,000 each person. Patrick's health insurance is provided by his mother.

Long-Term Disability Insurance

- John is covered by an "own occupation" policy with premiums paid by his employer. The benefits equal 60 percent of his gross pay after an elimination period of 90 days. The policy covers both sickness and accidents and is guaranteed renewable. The term of benefits is to age 66.
- Mary is not covered by disability insurance.

Long-Term Care Insurance

- Neither John nor Mary have long-term care insurance.

Renters Insurance

- The Burkes have an HO4 renters policy (a Contents Broad Form policy that covers contents and liability) without endorsements. The annual premium is $600.
- Content coverage is $25,000 and liability coverage is $100,000.

Automobile Insurance

- Both their car and truck are covered.
- They do not have any separate insurance on John's motor scooter.

Type	PAP
Bodily Injury	$50,000/$100,000
Property Damage	$10,000
Medical Payments	$5,000 per person
Physical Damage	Actual Cash Value
Uninsured Motorist	$25,000/$50,000
Comprehensive Deductible	$200
Collision Deductible	$500
Premium (annual)	$3,600

Personal Liability Insurance

- Neither John nor Mary have PLUP coverage.

INVESTMENT INFORMATION

John owns 1,000 shares of Crossroads Inc. stock that was inherited by him. Its current value is $8,000 and it pays a dividend of 34 cents per share for a total of $340 per year which is included in investment income.

John also owns 100 shares of Gladwell, Inc. stock that was received by him as a gift. The adjusted taxable basis is $4,000 and the fair market value is $4,000. Both the Gladwell and Crossroads stocks are large cap stocks.

Five years ago, John invested in a balanced mutual fund that was initially started with $8,000 he received as a gift. He has reinvested all dividends and capital gains each year. The gains and dividends together reported on their tax returns from the balanced mutual fund were as follows:

	Dividends & Interest	Capital Gains	Total
5 Years Ago	$160	$140	$300
4 Years Ago	$170	$580	$750
3 Years Ago	$180	$1,020	$1,200
2 Years Ago	$190	$600	$790
Last Year	$200	$760	$960

The 401(k) plan portfolio is invested in a balanced mutual fund expected to earn 8.5%. Their overall expected investment rate of return is 8.5%.

Risk Tolerance Questionnaire

Global Portfolio Allocation Scoring System (PASS) for Individual Investors[1]

Questions	Strongly Agree	Agree	Neutral	Disagree	Strongly Disagree
1. Earning a high long-term total return that will allow my capital to grow faster than the inflation rate is one of my most important investment objectives.	J	M			
2. I would like an investment that provides me with an opportunity to defer taxation of capital gains to future years.		M	J		
3. I do not require a high level of current income from my investments.		J, M			
4. I am willing to tolerate some sharp down swings in the return on my investments in order to seek a potentially higher return than would normally be expected from more stable investments.	J	M			
5. I am willing to risk a short-term loss in return for a potentially higher long-run rate of return.		J	M		
6. I am financially able to accept a low level of liquidity in my investment portfolio.		J	M		

J = John, M = Mary

1. Global Portfolio Allocation Scoring System (PASS) for Individual Investors - developed by Dr. William Droms (Georgetown University) and Steven N. Strauss, (DromsStrauss Advisors Inc.) - model used with permission.

FINANCIAL STATEMENTS: STATEMENT OF FINANCIAL POSITION 1/1/2013

Statement of Financial Position
John and Mary Burke
Balance Sheet as of 1/1/2013

ASSETS[1]			LIABILITIES AND NET WORTH		
Current Assets			**Current Liabilities[2]**		
JT Checking Account	$3,000		H Credit Card Balance Visa	$9,000	
JT Savings Account	$0		W Credit Card Balance MC	$5,000	
Total Current Assets		$3,000	**Total Current Liabilities**		$14,000
Investment Assets			**Long-Term Liabilities[2]**		
H Crossroads Inc. (1,000 Shares)[3]	$8,000		H Student Loan - John[4]	$54,298	
H Gladwell Inc. (100 Shares)	$4,000		W Auto Loan - Mary	$10,047	
H Balanced Mutual Fund	$12,000				
H 401(k) Plan Account Balance	$4,320		**Total Long-Term Liabilities**		$64,345
Total Investment Assets		$28,320			
Personal Use Assets			**Total Liabilities**		$78,345
W Auto - Mary	$18,500				
H Truck - John	$12,000		**Total Net Worth**		$10,475
H Motor scooter - John	$2,000				
JT Personal Property & Furniture	$25,000				
Total Personal Use Assets		$57,500			
Total Assets		**$88,820**	**Total Liabilities & Net Worth**		**$88,820**

1. Assets are stated at fair market value.
2. Liabilities are stated at principal only as of January 1, 2013 (prior to January payments). The current portion of long-term liabilities of the student loan and the auto loan were unknown at the time this financial statement was prepared. The current portion of these two loans should be classified as a current liability.
3. Crossroads Inc.'s current dividend is $0.34 per year per share.
4. The interest rate on the student loan is 6.9% for a 10-year term on a consolidation loan John just made.

JT = Joint Tenancy
H = Husband
W = Wife

FINANCIAL STATEMENTS: INCOME STATEMENT

Statement of Income and Expenses Mr. and Mrs. Burke Statement of Income and Expenses for Past Year and Expected (Approximate) For 2013			
CASH INFLOWS			**Totals**
Salaries			
John's Salary	$36,000		
Mary's Salary	$26,000		
Investment Income*	$1,300		
Total Cash Inflows			$63,300
CASH OUTFLOWS			
Savings			
Savings - House down payment	$2,500		
401(k) Plan Contribution	$1,080		
Total Savings			$3,580
Fixed Outflows			
Child Support	$4,200	ND	
Life Insurance Payment (Term)	$600	ND	
Rent	$8,400	ND	
HO 4 Renters Insurance	$600	ND	
Utilities	$720	ND	
Telephone	$360	ND	
Auto payment P&I	$3,600	ND	
Auto Insurance	$3,600	ND	
Gas, Oil, Maintenance for Auto	$2,400	ND	
Student Loan Payments	$7,695	ND	
Credit Card Payments	$3,000	ND	
Total Fixed Outflows			$35,175
Variable Outflows			
Taxes - John FICA	$2,754		
Taxes - Mary FICA	$1,989		
Taxes - Federal Tax Withheld	$12,660		
Food	$3,600	ND	
Clothing	$1,000	ND	
Vacations	$1,500		
Total Variable Outflows			$23,503
Total Cash Outflows			$62,258
NET DISCRETIONARY CASH FLOWS			$1,042

ND = Non-Discretionary

Income Tax Information

The filing status of the Burkes for federal income tax is married filing jointly. Patrick is claimed as a dependent on Kathy's tax return as part of John and Kathy's divorce agreement. There is no state income tax. Their average income tax rate is 17 percent and their marginal income tax rate is 25 percent.

Retirement Information

John currently contributes three percent of his salary to his 401(k) plan. The employer matches each $1 contributed with $0.50 up to a total employer contribution of three percent. Mary has a 401(k) plan that provides a match of 25 percent of her contributions up to six percent. Mary has never contributed to her 401(k) plan.

Gifts, Estates, Trusts, and Will Information

- John has a will leaving all of his probate estate to Patrick. He did not change the will after his marriage to Mary.
- Mary does not have a will.
- The Burkes live in a common law property state.

INFORMATION REGARDING ASSETS AND LIABILITIES

Automobile

The automobile was purchased January 1, 2011 for $19,993 with 20 percent down and 80 percent financed over 60 months with payments of $300 per month.

Financial Goals

- Increase savings.
- Debt reduction.
- Save enough for a down payment on a home of 20 percent of $180,000 in today's dollars for purchase in three years. Property taxes are expected to be one percent of the value of home. Homeowners insurance (HO3 endorsed - a Special Form Homeowner's policy that covers a wide variety of perils) will be one percent of the value of the home.
- For education, they plan to spend $20,000 per year for four years each for each of the two children at the child's age 18. The expected education inflation rate is five percent. Assume they have twins two years from now for the calculation of education funding.
- For retirement, they want to plan for 100% ($62,000) wage replacement at age 65, without any consideration of Social Security. If they cannot achieve that they will consider a compromise between delaying retirement and lowering the wage replacement ratio as long as the wage replacement is no less than 75% and the delayed retirement is no later than age 67. They expect to live to age 95.
- Have a good risk management portfolio and assume a rate of return of 8.5%.
- Develop a comprehensive financial plan.

John & Mary Burke Case Analysis

Based on the initial telephone communication, here is the relevant information collected.

Summary of Data Collected - Life Cycle Approach	
Ages	John 30, Mary 30
Marital Status	Married Filing Jointly filing status
Children	John has one child, age 4 (living out of state, estranged), they would like two to three within the next five years.
Grandchildren	None
Net Worth	Approximately $10,000
Income	$36,000 John, $26,000 Mary
Self-Employed	No
Other	John pays $350 per month in child support. One of their goals is to save for a home.

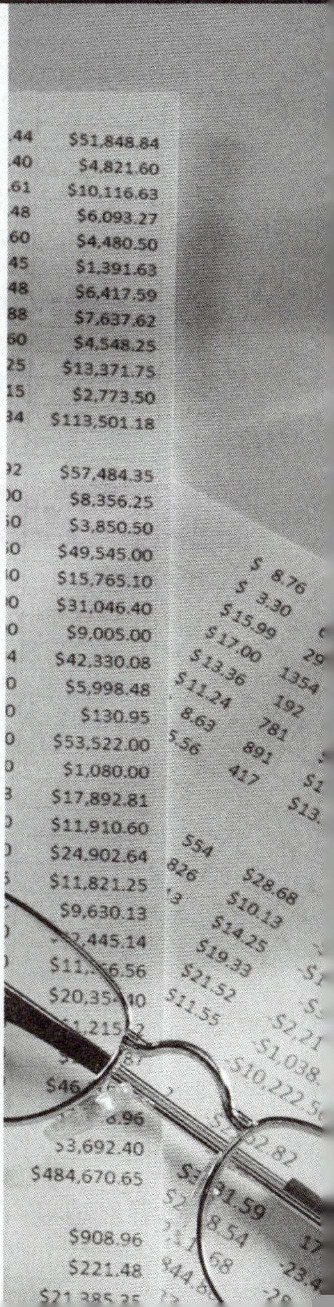

Mike Mitchell's Preliminary Conclusions Regarding the Burkes: (Using the Life Cycle Approach)

The life cycle data suggests the Burkes are in the accumulation and risk management phases. Therefore, they need a thorough risk management analysis: life needs, health, disability, property and liability. They also need to save at least 10 - 13 percent of their income for the basic goal of retirement security and probably need a savings rate greater than 10 - 13 percent to accommodate the college education of two to three children.

- Their personal risks are:
    - untimely death,
    - health problems, and
    - disability risks.

- They are probably underinsured for catastrophic risks.
- They likely have cars that need the proper liability and property insurance coverage.
- They likely need but do not have a personal liability umbrella policy.
- Their potential goals are:
    - buying a house,
    - savings for children's education, and
    - beginning to save for retirement.
- They probably do not have personal financial statements.
- They probably have a wide assortment of debt.

Applying Financial Planning Approaches

The Burke client relationship has now been established and the internal and external data has been collected. Next, the financial planner is ready to analyze and evaluate the client's financial status. The following approaches will be applied in order to form client recommendations.

- Pie Chart Approach
- Financial Statement Analysis-Ratio Analysis Approach
- The Two-Step / Three-Panel / Metrics Approach
- The Present Value of All Goals Approach
- The Cash Flow Approach
- Strategic Approach

Each approach is applied to the Burke case for practical application purposes so that the financial planner can learn how to identify weaknesses in the financial situation. In addition, the practitioner can also learn how to use the varied approaches together to analyze and evaluate the client's financial circumstances to arrive at the best recommendations for the client.

PIE CHART APPROACH

Introduction

The pie chart approach to analysis provides the financial planner and the client with a visual representation of the balance sheet and the income statement. The financial statements are prepared first and then they are depicted in pie charts. The pie charts provide a fairly high level view, rather than a detailed analysis, and are only used as a starting point for discussions with the client. They do, however, provide the planner with sufficient insight to the client's financial profile to have that high level conversation. Below each pie chart are the planner's observations, which affords the opportunity for a more in-depth discussion with the clients on each observation point.

Data for Pie Chart Approach - Balance Sheet 1/1/2013

Burke Balance Sheet

Assets = 100%		
Cash or Cash Equivalents	$3,000	3.38%
Investment Assets	$28,320	31.88%
Personal Use Assets	$57,500	64.74%
	$88,820	100.00%

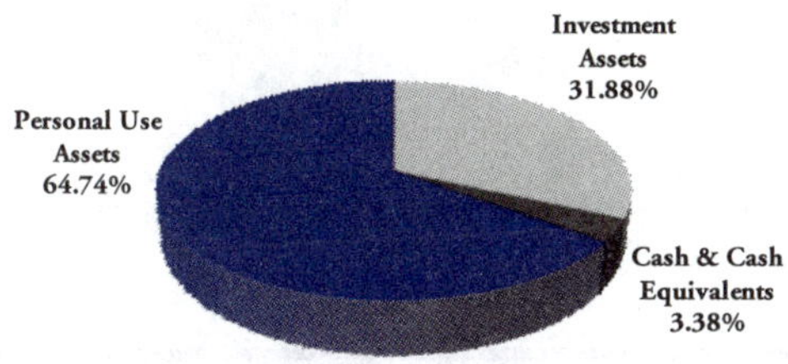

Liabilities & Net Worth = 100%		
Current Liabilities	$14,000	15.76%
Long-Term Liabilities	$64,345	72.44%
Net Worth	$10,475	11.79%
	$88,820	100.00%

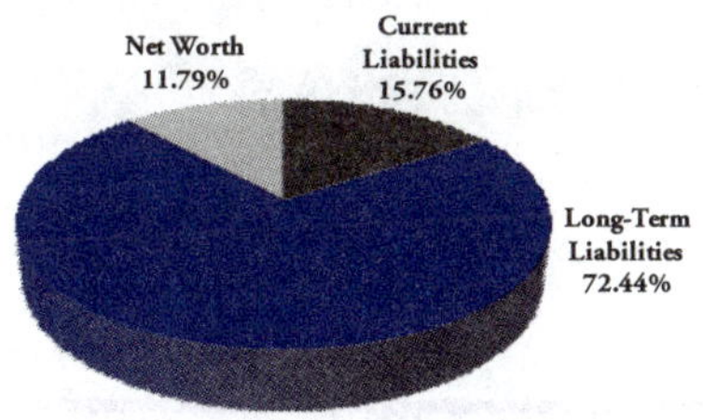

Benchmark Balance Sheet (From Fundamentals of Financial Planning)

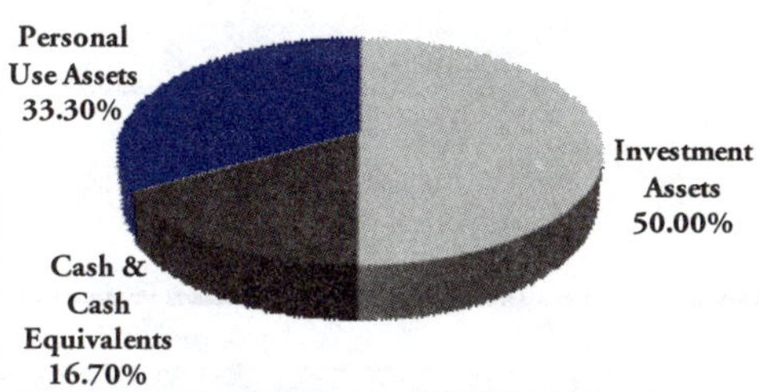

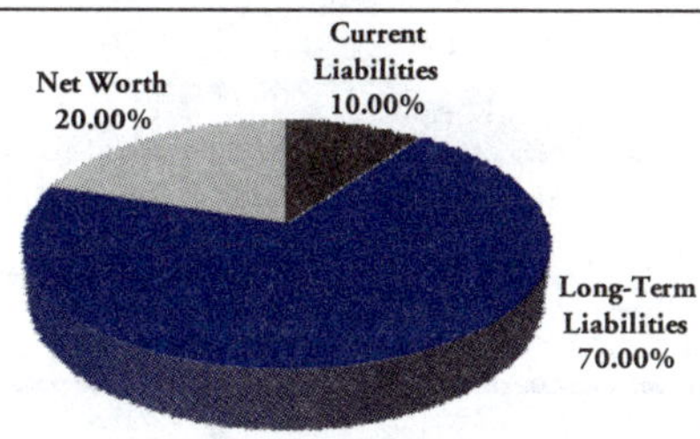

Note: The balance sheet benchmarks are never exactly precise, but it is clear that the Burkes should have a greater amount of money in an emergency fund and more investment assets for their current age. It is also clear that relative to the benchmarks, debt is high.

Observations

The balance sheet pie chart indicates the following:

- cash and cash equivalents are low (3.4%), therefore the emergency fund and current ratios are also probably low,
- the net worth is low relative to the client's age, and
- investment assets are low relative to gross pay.

These deficiencies can be overcome in a relatively short period of time by increasing the savings rate, reducing debt, and managing interest rates on debt.

Data for Pie Chart Approach - Income Statement 1/1/2013

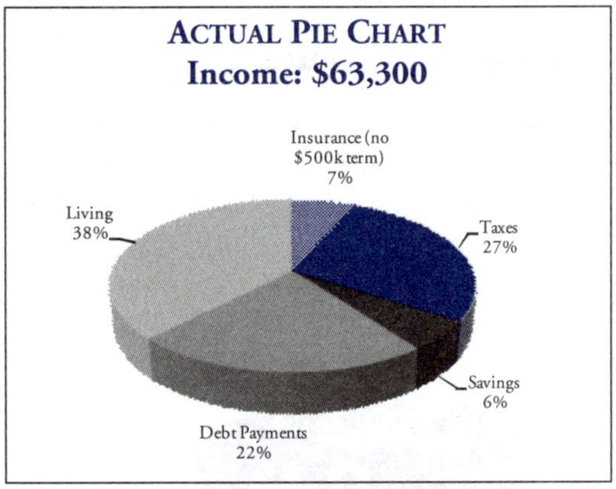

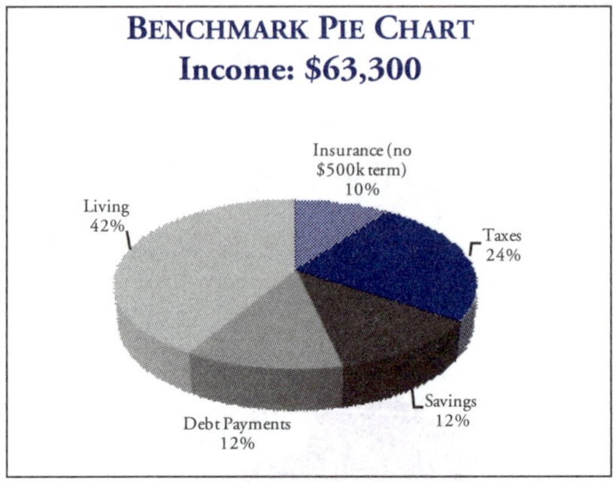

Income	100%	$63,300
Other Living Expenses	21.77%	The balance of living expenses*
Debt Payments	22.58%	($3,600 + $7,695 + $3,000)
Savings Rate	5.66%	$3,580 ÷ $63,300
Insurance	6.64%	($3,600 + $600)
Housing Costs	14.22%	($8,400 + $600)
Taxes	27.49%	($2,754 + $1,989 + $12,660)
Discretionary Cash Flows	1.64%	$1,042

** $4,200 + $720 + $360 + $2,400 + $3,600 + $1,000 + $1,500*

Note: With the employer match, the savings rate is 6.5 percent. If you consider the child support of $350 per month and life insurance payment as required by the court of $50 per month as debt, the financial picture is weaker. Keep in mind that benchmarks are averages for a group and may not apply exactly to a client's personal financial situation.

Observations

The first observation is that the expenditures for debt repayments is high (22.58%) and the savings rate (5.66%) is low. In addition, the expenditure percentage for insurance looks to be low relative to the benchmark. Each of these issues will require investigation and resolution. While it is not uncommon to have percentages like these, the Burkes are more likely to meet their goals by reducing debt, increasing savings, and making sure they are adequately protected by insurance.

The overall savings rate with the employer 401(k) plan match is 6.5 percent and can easily be increased by John increasing his elective deferral to receive the maximum match from his employer. An additional $1,080 elective deferral would generate an additional match of $540 and would change the savings rate to 9.1%.

Financial Statement Analysis - Ratio Analysis Approach

Introduction

The liquidity ratios provide insight into the client's ability to pay short-term obligations and fund an emergency. The housing ratios and total debt to asset ratios help the financial planner to assess the client's ability to manage debt. The savings rate provides the planner with a good perspective of whether the client is committed financially to all of his goals, which includes saving for retirement and other goals. In addition, the investment assets to gross pay ratios help the planner to determine the progress of the client in achieving the goal of financial security based on the client's age and income. Lastly, the performance ratios indicate how well the investment assets have performed to benchmarks. The ratios should be compared to appropriate benchmarks to be meaningful.

BURKE'S RATIO ANALYSIS

Ratio	Formula		Comment	Benchmark
LIQUIDITY RATIOS				
Emergency Fund Ratio =	$\frac{\text{Cash \& Cash Equivalents}}{\text{Monthly Non-Discretionary Cash Flows}}$	$\frac{\$3,000}{\$3,315} = 0.91 < 1$ month	Very Weak	3 - 6:1
Current Ratio =	$\frac{\text{Cash \& Cash Equivalents}}{\text{Current Liabilities}}$	$\frac{\$3,000}{\$14,000} = 0.21\%$	Very Weak	1 - 2
DEBT RATIOS				
Housing Ratio 1 (HR 1) =	$\frac{\text{Housing Costs}}{\text{Gross Pay}}$	$\frac{\$9,000}{\$63,300} = 14.22\%$	Strong	≤ 28%
Housing Ratio 2 (HR 2) =	$\frac{\text{Housing Costs + Other Debt Payments}}{\text{Gross Pay}}$	$\frac{\$23,295}{\$63,300} = 36.80\%$	Weak	≤ 36%
Debt to Total Assets =	$\frac{\text{Total Debt}}{\text{Total Assets}}$	$\frac{\$78,345}{\$88,820} = 88.21\%$	Weak	Age Dependent
Net Worth to Total Assets =	$\frac{\text{Net Worth}}{\text{Total Assets}}$	$\frac{\$10,475}{\$88,820} = 11.79\%$	Weak	Age Dependent
RATIOS FOR FINANCIAL SECURITY GOALS				
Savings Rate =	$\frac{\text{Savings + Employer Match}}{\text{Gross Pay}}$	$\frac{\$3,580 + \$540}{\$63,300} = 6.5\%$	Weak	Goal Driven At Least 10-13%
Investment Assets to Gross Pay =	$\frac{\text{Investment Assets + Cash \& Cash Equivalents}}{\text{Gross Pay}}$	$\frac{\$28,320 + \$3,000}{\$63,300} = 0.49:1$	Very Weak	1:1 Age Dependent
PERFORMANCE RATIOS				
Return on Investments =	$\frac{I_1 - (I_0 + \text{Savings})}{I_0}$	Unavailable (Need beginning and ending balance sheet)		N/A
Return on Assets =	$\frac{A_1 - (A_0 + \text{Savings})}{A_0}$	Unavailable (Need beginning and ending balance sheet)		N/A
Return on Net Worth =	$\frac{NW_1 - (NW_0 + \text{Savings})}{NW_0}$	Unavailable (Need beginning and ending balance sheet)		N/A

Comments on Calculated Ratios

Many of the Burke's ratios are currently low, but can be substantially improved over the next few years.

The Burkes are just getting started in their married life and while many of their ratios are weak today, they have a long work life expectancy. They will want to build an emergency fund, increase savings, and pay off their credit card debt. They may even want to delay the purchase of a home if the rent they are paying will be substantially less than the net after tax amount of the mortgage they will be paying. This decision will depend on market rates of rent, cost of houses, interest rates for mortgages, and marginal tax rates presuming mortgage interest remains an itemized deduction for income tax purposes. This analysis should be made in the three to five year period ahead.

THE TWO-STEP / THREE-PANEL / METRICS APPROACH

INTRODUCTION

The two-step approach (cover the risks, save and invest), looks at personal risks as potentially leading to catastrophic financial results and dependence on someone else for well being. Savings and investments are the road to financial security or independence in the long run. Generally, dependence can be caused by an event that can occur at any moment, whereas financial independence is earned over a long period of time.

A modification to the two-step approach is the three-panel approach, which provides the planner and the client with a methodology for planning. Step 1 is to evaluate each of the insurance risks and then evaluate the client's actual portfolio of insurance to determine the adequacy of the current coverage. Step 2 is to calculate the emergency fund ratio and housing ratios (or take them from the financial statement analysis approach). Step 3 focuses on the long-term savings and investments in order to meet the financial security goal (retirement with adequate income to maintain the pre-retirement lifestyle) and requires persistent savings, adequate investment performance, and a benchmark of investment assets appropriate for the age and gross pay of the client. Step 3 also considers education goals, lump-sum goals, and legacy goals. The goal of the three-panel / metrics approach is to identify specific recommendations for the client to improve the overall financial plan.

Risk Management Data

	Actual	Metric	Comment / Recommendation
Personal Insurance:			
Life Insurance[1,2]	$50,000 + $26,000	$360k - $576k $260k - $416k	They are significantly underinsured for life insurance.
Health Insurance	Indemnity 80 /20 Stop Loss $2,000 Life-Term Benefit $1,000,000/per person	Same	Okay
Disability Insurance	John - 60% of Gross Pay/ Guaranteed Renewable / 90-day Elimination/ Own Occupation Mary - None	John is fine. Mary needs disability insurance.	Mary needs disability insurance
Long-Term Care Insurance	None	None at this time	Okay
Property and Liability Insurance:			
Homeowners Insurance	HO4 without endorsements	HO4 with endorsements	Add endorsements for all risk and replacement value.
Automobile Insurance[3]	$50,000/$100,000/$10,000	$100k/$300k/$50k	Upgrade the liability per the requirements of PLUP carrier and re-quote the premium. Should be in $2,000 - $2,500 range.
Motor Scooter Insurance	None	≤ FMV + Liability	Stop driving, add insurance, or sell motor scooter.
Liability Insurance	None	Need $1M PLUP coverage.	Add PLUP coverage of $1M.

[1] Note that the owner of the $500,000 term policy is John's ex-wife, Kathy, and that is why it is not included here.

[2] They need to change Policy B beneficiary to Mary from Kathy at no cost.

[3] Note that they requested auto quotes, but due to their driving records, the premium was not lowered.

Short-Term Savings and Investments

	Actual	Metric	Comment / Recommendation
Emergency Fund	0.91 month	3 - 6 months	Deficient
Housing Ratio 1 (HR1)*	14.22%	≤ 28%	Excellent
Housing Ratio 2 (HR2)	36.8%	≤ 36%	Fair - need to improve metric for home purchase.

*Although the Burkes do not own a home, the financial planner should evaluate their housing ratios using their rent and renter's insurance in the calculation.

Debt Management Data

	Balance	Interest Rate	Payment	Balance of Term	Comment / Recommendation
Credit Cards	$14,000	18% /yr.	$250 / month	124 months	Pay off if possible.
Auto	$10,047	4.75% /yr.	$300 / month	36 months	Pay as agreed.
Student Loans	$54,298	6.9%/ yr.	$7,695 / year	10 years	Pay as agreed.

Long-Term Goals

	Actual	Metric	Comment / Recommendation
Overall Savings Rate	6.5%	At least 10 - 13%	Too Low to Meet Goals / Increase
Investment Assets / Gross Pay	0.49:1	1:1	Too Low for Age / Increase Over Time

HOME PURCHASE ANALYSIS - SCHEDULE A

Home Down Payment Calculation

The purpose of this calculation is to determine the funds required to meet a 20 percent down-payment for the Burke's home purchase goal.

PV	=	$180,000 (current price of home)
N	=	3 (periods until expected purchase)
i	=	3% inflation
PMT	=	0
FV	=	$196,690.86 (future value of house) x 20% = $39,338 down payment required

Mortgage on Home

The purpose of the following computations is to determine the projected debt ratios should the Burkes purchase a home.

PV ($196,690.86 x 0.80)	=	$157,352.69 (loan amount)
N (term in months)	=	360 months
i (interest rate)	=	5.5 ÷ 12
FV (balance in 30 yrs)	=	0
PMT_{OA} (monthly payment)	=	$893.43 (principal and interest)

	Monthly	Annually
Principal and Interest	$893.43	$10,721
Property Taxes	$163.92	$1,967
HO Insurance	$163.92	$1,967
Total House Payment	**$1,221.27**	**$14,655**

Projections for the Home Purchase (in three years)

- Projected income = $62,000 x $(1.04)^3$ = $69,742 in three years.
- Therefore, HR1 = 21.01% [Excellent ($14,655 ÷ $69,742)].
- As adjusted HR2 = 32% [Okay, qualifies ($14,655 + $7,695 ÷ $69,742)].
- The car and credit cards are paid off and the student loan is the only debt remaining.

Savings Schedule - Schedule B

The following schedule projects the savings requirement and debt retirement needed to meet the Burke's 3-year goals.

Objective	Cash Needed	Comment / Recommendation
Save	$39,338	Will need to save $12,117 at 8.5% per year for three years.
Pay off auto	$10,047	Will be paid off in three years with current payments of $3,600 per year.
Pay off credit cards	$14,000	Will be paid off immediately by using the proceeds from the sale of assets.
Total Cash Needed	**$63,385**	**Cash required in the next three years.**

Payment Schedule - Schedule C

Knowing the debt retirement issues shown in Schedule B, the practitioner can plan for debt reduction on a monthly basis. Note that for comparison purposes, if the Burkes pay $250 per month on their credit card balance, they would remain with a $5,000 balance (plus interest) in three years.

Scheduled Payments	Annual Payment	Current Balance	Balance 3 Years Future	Payments
Auto Loan	$3,600	$10,047	$0	$300 / month
Credit Cards*	$3,000	$14,000	$5,000 + interest	$250 / month

* Note that the credit cards, however, will be paid off now with the sale of the assets.

AUTO INTEREST - SCHEDULE D

Automobile Interest Rate Calculation		Calculation		
Purchase Price	$19,993.00			
20% Down	- 3,998.60	FV	=	0
Balance	$15,994.40	PV	=	$15,994.00
Payment	$300	PMT	=	($300)
Term	60	N	=	60 months
Therefore i = annual rate	4.75%	i	=	0.3957 x 12 = 4.75%

COMMENTS ON THREE-PANEL / METRICS APPROACH ANALYSIS

The Burkes need life insurance because they are dependent on each other's income to support their current lifestyle and they have told the financial planner that they want to have two to three children fairly soon.

Their health insurance is adequate although they are dependent on their employer for coverage. They would be covered under COBRA for 18 to 36 months if John was terminated.

The Burkes need disability insurance on Mary because it provides for income replacement.

The homeowners (renters) policy can be improved by endorsing the personal property coverage for all risks and for replacement value. The standard HO4 policy has coverage for 18 perils (not all) and actual cash value (not replacement value).

The Burkes should also purchase a personal liability insurance policy. The PLUP issuer will likely require that they increase their liability coverages to $100k/$300k/$50k. They need to annually shop the automobile insurance premium because it is high due to their recent driving records.

The emergency fund needs to be increased. The Burke's currently cover about one month (0.91) of non-discretionary cash flow with their cash and cash equivalents. They would be in financial difficulty if one or both of them lost their jobs.

The Burkes housing ratio 1 is excellent at 14.22 percent, but the back ratio of 36.8 percent already indicates they have too much debt. They will need to improve this ratio significantly before buying a home.

The Burkes need to pay off the credit cards and pay off the automobile loan within the 36 months remaining. Schedule D above reflects the calculation of the rate of interest on the auto loan (4.75%).

The Burkes overall savings rate, including the employer match, is only 6.5 percent of gross pay. It needs to be 10 to 13 percent of gross pay just to drive the financial security goal. If the Burke's are going to have a home purchase goal and college education goal for two to three children, they are going to need to increase the savings rate to 10 to 13 percent for retirement, save an average of 18 percent for the home purchase down payment (see Schedule A), and four to five percent for college education (total 32 to 36% (See Schedule B). This is an important task and they might consider delaying the home purchase until such time as they have saved the 20 percent down payment. They need to increase the 401(k) plan deferrals to maximize employer matches.

Schedule C illustrates that the client will have the auto paid off in three years and can at that time add the $3,600 per year to their savings rate.

The three-panel / metrics approach dictates that the recommendations are prioritized (see the cash flow approach) and that there is an estimate of the impact of each on the income statement and balance sheet (see projected financial statements later in this chapter). In the case of the Burkes, the financial planner is able to improve the insurance portfolio, increase savings and increase the employer match to the maximum in the 401(k) plan, and pay off the credit cards. The credit card debt reduction is accomplished by selling the individual stocks and the motor scooter. The individual stocks were not diversified and the scooter was not insured. The complete rearrangement provides the Burkes with a much better financial plan.

The financial planner should note that the client will need to address the large student loans balance and it will take time to save for the home they expect to purchase especially if they have two to three children relatively soon. The Burkes have been advised that they need to get their wills and other estate planning documents in order and they expect to do that in Year 2.

It is important for the financial planner to take note of where they can usually find the resources to pay for the recommendations. The places we find resources are:

- refinancing a home mortgage at a lower rate,
- reducing our withholding of income tax,
- the sale of assets from the balance sheet (usually from an inappropriate or no longer desired investment or personal use asset), and
- changing lifestyle (this is the last place we look because it requires behavioral change like cutting vacations).

Sometimes there simply are not sufficient financial resources to solve all the problems immediately. That is why in the cash flow approach recommendations are listed in order of priority. In the event there are insufficient financial resources, the financial planner and client simply solve the problems that they can today and use future resources as they become available. Whatever financial weaknesses the client has generally took some time to develop, and may also take some time to resolve.

Risk Tolerance and Asset Allocation

The chart below depicts the scoring system for the PASS risk tolerance questionnaire. Based on the Burke's answers, their PASS[1] score is 23.5, which corresponds to the RT3 target.

1. Global Portfolio Allocation Scoring System (PASS) for Individual Investors - developed by Dr. William Droms (Georgetown University) and Steven N. Strauss, (DromsStrauss Advisors Inc.) - model used with permission.

Global Portfolio Allocation Scoring System (PASS) for Individual Investors						
Questions	Strongly Agree	Agree	Neutral	Disagree	Strongly Disagree	John & Mary
1. Earning a high long-term total return that will allow my capital to grow faster than the inflation rate is one of my most important investment objectives.	5	4	3	2	1	4.5
2. I would like an investment that provides me with an opportunity to defer taxation of capital gains to future years.	5	4	3	2	1	3.5
3. I do not require a high level of current income from my investments.	5	4	3	2	1	4
4. I am willing to tolerate some sharp down swings in the return on my investments in order to seek a potentially higher return than would normally be expected from more stable investments.	5	4	3	2	1	4.5
5. I am willing to risk a short-term loss in return for a potentially higher long-run rate of return.	5	4	3	2	1	3.5
6. I am financially able to accept a low level of liquidity in my investment portfolio.	5	4	3	2	1	3.5
						23.5

Below are the recommended portfolios based on the time horizon and answers to the risk tolerance questionnaire.

	Short-Term Horizon				Intermediate-Term Horizon				Long-Term Horizon			
	RT1 Target	RT2 Target	RT3 Target	RT4 Target	RT1 Target	RT2 Target	RT3 Target	RT4 Target	RT1 Target	RT2 Target	RT3 Target	RT4 Target
PASS Score	6 - 12	13 - 18	19 - 24	25 - 30	6 - 12	13 - 18	19 - 24	25 - 30	6 - 12	13 - 18	19 - 24	25 - 30
Cash and Money Market Fund	40%	30%	20%	10%	5%	5%	5%	5%	5%	5%	3%	2%
Treasury Bonds/ Bond Funds	40%	30%	30%	20%	60%	35%	20%	10%	30%	20%	12%	0%
Corporate Bonds/ Bond Funds	20%	30%	30%	40%	15%	15%	15%	10%	15%	10%	10%	4%
Subtotal	**100%**	**90%**	**80%**	**70%**	**80%**	**55%**	**40%**	**25%**	**50%**	**35%**	**25%**	**6%**
International Bond Funds	0%	0%	0%	0%	0%	5%	5%	5%	0%	5%	5%	4%
Subtotal	**0%**	**0%**	**0%**	**0%**	**0%**	**5%**	**5%**	**5%**	**0%**	**5%**	**5%**	**4%**
Index Fund	0%	10%	10%	10%	10%	15%	20%	20%	20%	20%	20%	25%
Large Cap Value Funds/Stocks	0%	0%	5%	5%	5%	5%	10%	10%	10%	10%	5%	5%
Large Cap Growth Funds/Stocks	0%	0%	0%	0%	5%	5%	5%	10%	15%	10%	10%	5%
Mid/Small Growth Funds/Stocks	0%	0%	0%	0%	0%	0%	5%	5%	0%	0%	5%	10%
Mid/Small Value Funds/Stocks	0%	0%	0%	5%	0%	5%	5%	5%	0%	5%	5%	10%
Subtotal	**0%**	**10%**	**15%**	**20%**	**20%**	**30%**	**45%**	**50%**	**45%**	**45%**	**45%**	**55%**
International Stock Funds	0%	0%	0%	5%	0%	5%	5%	10%	0%	5%	10%	15%
Subtotal	**0%**	**0%**	**0%**	**5%**	**0%**	**5%**	**5%**	**10%**	**0%**	**5%**	**10%**	**15%**
Real Estate Funds	0%	0%	5%	5%	0%	5%	5%	10%	5%	10%	15%	20%
Subtotal	**0%**	**0%**	**5%**	**5%**	**0%**	**5%**	**5%**	**10%**	**5%**	**10%**	**15%**	**20%**
Total	**100%**	**100%**	**100%**	**100%**	**100%**	**100%**	**100%**	**100%**	**100%**	**100%**	**100%**	**100%**

This information and the risk and return information are used to determine and estimate the expected return for the current portfolio versus the recommended PASS[1] portfolio.

1. Global Portfolio Allocation Scoring System (PASS) for Individual Investors - developed by Dr. William Droms (Georgetown University) and Steven N. Strauss, (DromsStrauss Advisors Inc.) - model used with permission.

	Current Porfolio (Dollars)	Current Portfolio Percentage	PASS Recommended Portfolio	Difference	Expected Rates of Return	Current Expected Return	PASS Expected Return
Cash and Money Market Fund	$3,000	9.6%	3%	6.6%	2.5%	$75	$23
Treasury Bonds/ Bond Funds	$0	0.0%	12%	-12.0%	4.0%	$0	$150
Corporate Bonds/ Bond Funds	$8,160	26.1%	10%	16.1%	6.0%	$490	$188
International Bond Funds	$0	0.0%	5%	-5.0%	7.0%	$0	$110
Index Fund	$8,160	26.1%	20%	6.1%	9.0%	$734	$564
Large Cap Funds/Stocks	$12,000	38.3%	15%	23.3%	10.0%	$1,200	$470
Mid/Small Funds/Stocks	$0	0.0%	10%	-10.0%	12.0%	$0	$376
International Stock Funds	$0	0.0%	10%	-10.0%	13.0%	$0	$407
Real Estate Funds	$0	0.0%	15%	-15.0%	8.0%	$0	$376
	$31,320	**100.0%**				**$2,499**	**$2,664**
					Expected Return	7.98%	8.51%

As indicated above, the expected return slightly increases over the current portfolio and the return is consistent with the required return in the case. In addition, the portfolio should be better positioned to reflect the risk tolerance of the Burkes.

The Present Value of all Goals Approach

Goals:

1. Retirement - $62,000 in today's dollars, 3% inflation, at 65 to 95 without consideration of Social Security.
2. Education of 2 children - $20,000 per year in today's dollars, starting in 20 years. Inflation is expected to be 5%. The children will attend college for 4 years each. They do not plan to pay for Patrick.
3. Home down payment - $36,000 down payment in three years from now.

Calculation of Retirement Needs in PV Terms

N = 35	PMT_{AD} = \$174,459.47	FV = \$2,718,862.76
i = 3	N = 30	N = 35
PV = \$62,000	i = (1.085 ÷ 1.03 - 1) x 100	i = 8.5
FV = \$174,459.47	$PV_{@65}$ \$2,718,862.76	PV_{Today} = \$156,439.51

Calculation of Education Needs in PV Terms

PMT_{AD} = \$20,000	FV = \$152,423.22 (for 2 children)
i = (1.085 ÷ 1.05 - 1) x 100	N = 20 (children born 2 years from now)
N = 4	i = (1.085 ÷ 1.05 - 1) x 100
$PV_{@18}$ = \$76,211.60757	PV_{Today} = \$79,112.00

Calculation of Home Down Payment in PV Terms

N = 3	FV = \$39,338.17
i = 3	i = 8.5
PV = \$36,000	N = 3
FV = \$39,338.17	PV = \$30,798.17

THE SUMMARIZATION OF THE PRESENT VALUE OF GOALS

Retirement	\$156,439.51	
Education	\$79,112.00	
Home Down Payment	\$30,798.11	
Total	\$266,349.62	
Current Resources	\$31,320.00	(this is before using \$14,000 to pay off credit cards)
Net PV of Goals	\$235,029.62	
N	35	(to retirement)
i	8.5%	(portfolio rate)
PMT_{OA}	\$21,197.17	(annual savings needed)
Current Savings	- \$4,120.00	
Tax Analysis Savings	- \$7,618.00	(See Schedule D)
Shortfall	**\$9,459.17**	

The Burke's are still \$9,459.17 short on annual savings. However, by adding the additional \$1,080 + \$1,560 + \$660 (see cash flow approach), they will reduce the shortfall to \$6,159.17. Their current wage replacement ratio is 100% but if they save as above, the real needed WRR is \$62,000 - Savings (\$15,038) and - Social Security (\$4,743) or \$42,219 which is 68.095%. So, you could use 75% which would reduce the PV of retirement needs by \$39,109.88 and thus the annual savings needed by \$3,527.30, making then only approximately \$2,600 annual savings short which they could make up with raises over the 35 years.

THE CASH FLOW APPROACH

The cash flow approach essentially adjusts the cash flows on the income statement to what they would be after implementing all of the recommendations that the planner has suggested. It starts with the discretionary cash flows at the bottom of the income statement and accounts for the recommendations in the order of priority by charging the cost of the expense against the discretionary cash flows, regardless of any negative cash flow impact. The analysis is prepared carefully to differentiate between recurring cash flows and non-recurring cash flows.

BURKE CASH FLOW APPROACH WITH RECOMMENDATIONS

	Income Statement Recurring Cash Flows	Statement of Financial Position Non-Recurring Cash Flows	Comments/Explanations
Beginning Cash Flow (Income Statement)	**$1,042**		From the original income statement
Recommendations:			
Risk management:			
Term life insurance for John	($375)		Buy $500,000 term
Term life insurance for Mary	($250)		Buy $500,000 term
Disability insurance for Mary	($600)		Buy disability
Homeowners insurance	($100)		Endorse
Automobile insurance	($400)		Upgrade
Motor scooter	$0	**$2,000**	Sell motor scooter
Personal liability umbrella	($200)		$1,000,000 PLUP
Prepare proper estate documents		**($1,000)**	
Debt management:			
Pay off credit cards		**($14,000)**	Reduces expenditures by $3,000 per year
Savings from credit card payoffs	$3,000		Pay off credit cards with proceeds from asset sale
Increase John's 401(k) plan deferrals*	($1,080)		3% additional
Begin Mary's 401(k) plan deferrals*	($1,560)		6% of salary
Savings from 401(k) plan deposits	$660		From income tax reductions (25% of 401(k) plan deferrals)
Savings from Change in W=4**	$7,618		This will initially go to the emergency fund
Ending cash flow after implementation	$7,755		This is the positive recurring cash flow to add to savings
Sell assets to pay credit card (Crossroads and Gladwell stock)		**$12,000**	Sold stocks, etc. to pay off credit cards
TOTAL of Changes in Cash Flows	**$7,755**	**($1,000)**	

Note that the numbers in parenthesis are expenditures.

* The Burkes had to choose between increasing savings to the 401(k) plan and paying down on the student loans. They expect John will get a substantial raise in 4-5 years and choose to save rather than pay the student loans even though they were at 6.9% interest. There also is a possibility that their parents will help with the student loans.

** See Tax Analysis.

Assets Sold to Pay Off Credit Cards - Schedule A

Assets Sold to Pay Off Credit Cards	
Motor scooter	$2,000
Crossroads Inc.	$8,000
Gladwell Inc.	$4,000
TOTAL	**$14,000**

STRATEGIC APPROACH

Introduction

The strategic approach encompasses establishing a mission, a mission statement, a set of goals, and a set of objectives. The planner analyzes the mission, goals, and objectives given both internal client data and relevant external data and creates a plan for the long-run accomplishment of the mission with the short and intermediate accomplishment of objectives and goals.

Mission Statement (An Enduring Long-Term Statement)

- Financial security (maintaining lifestyle without the need for current employment).

Goals (Broadly Conceived Goals)

- Adequate risk management portfolio.
- Adequate savings rate for retirement and education.
- Adequate emergency fund.
- Adequate debt management.
- Adequate investment portfolio.
- Adequate estate plan.

Objectives (Narrow Measurable Objectives)

Risk Management

- Immediately buy term life insurance on both John and Mary at $500,000 each.
- Purchase disability insurance on Mary at 60% to 70% of gross pay with a 90 day elimination period.
- Add endorsement for HO4 to all risk / replacement value.
- Upgrade liability on automobile insurance to meet PLUP carrier requirements.
- Sell motor scooter.
- Add PLUP of $1,000,000.

Debt Management

- Pay off credit cards ($14,000).
- Keep credit card purchases to $1,000 per year.

Tax Management and Emergency Fund

- Use the extra $7,618 in income tax overwithholding to build an emergency fund. (See Schedule D - Tax Analysis on the following pages).

Savings and Investments

- Increase John's 401(k) plan deferral to $2,160 (increasing the employer match to $1,080).
- Have Mary defer $1,560 to her 401(k) plan (employer match is $1,560 x 0.25 = $390).
- Move all 401(k) plan investments to a balanced portfolio.

Estate Plan

Have estate planning documents prepared (will, durable power of attorney for healthcare, advance medical directive) within the second year (expected cost = $1,000).

Comments on Strategic Approach

The strategic approach takes into consideration needs versus wants. Needs are defined as necessary by law (e.g., auto liability insurance) or required to make the plan work (e.g., savings). Wants on the other hand are somewhat discretionary (e.g., home purchase, vacation).

Even if the planner started with the strategic approach, the financial planning method would probably follow with the cash flow approach and recommendations to be assured that the implementation is feasible.

PRESENTATION TO JOHN AND MARY BURKE PROJECTED FINANCIAL STATEMENTS AND RATIOS

The next step for the financial planner is to project financial statements at least one year out to be able to present to the client where they will be in a year if they follow and implement the recommendations. This is one way to help clients get and stay motivated while implementing the plan. In order to project both the balance sheet and the income statement and to prepare pro forma (projected) ratios, the planner will need to prepare schedules of savings and earnings. For the Burkes, the planner has prepared schedules A - E and the projected financial statements.

Schedule A - Analysis of John's 401(k) Plan

	Beginning Balance January 1	Employee Deferrals	Employer Match	Earning Rate 8.5%*	Ending Balance December 31
2013	$4,320	$2,160	$1,080	$505	$8,065
2014	$8,065	$2,246	$1,123	$830	$12,264
2015	$12,264	$2,336	$1,168	$1,191	$16,959
2016	$16,959	$2,429	$1,215	$1,596	$22,199

* Earnings are for 1/2 year on new deposits. Rounded.

SCHEDULE B - ANALYSIS OF MARY'S 401(k) PLAN

	Beginning Balance January 1	Employee Deferrals	Employer Match	Earning Rate 8.5%	Ending Balance December 31
2013	$0	$1,560	$390	$83	$2,033
2014	$2,033	$1,622	$406	$259	$4,320
2015	$4,320	$1,687	$422	$456	$6,885
2016	$6,885	$1,755	$439	$678	$9,757

* Earnings on the balanced mutual fund is 8.5% for 1/2 year on new deposits. Rounded to nearest $1.

SCHEDULE C - COMBINED SAVINGS RATE AFTER RECOMMENDATIONS (NOT INCLUDING TAX OVERWITHHELD)

	Savings	
House Savings	$1,200	
Reinvestment of Earnings	$1,300	
John's 401(k) Plan Deferral	$2,160	
Employer 401(k) Plan Match	$1,080	
Mary's 401(k) Plan Deferral	$1,560	
Employer 401(k) Plan Match	$390	
	$7,690	÷ $63,300 = 12.15% current savings rate

SCHEDULE D - INCOME TAX ANALYSIS

The Burkes average income tax rate is approximately 8 percent (8% x $63,300 = $5,042) and their marginal income tax rate is 15 percent. The Burkes are overwithheld by approximately $7,618 annually ($12,660 - $5,042). The Burkes should invest the $7,618 annually in the emergency fund by changing the income tax withholding form (W-4) to 1 (for self) and 1 (for spouse) and saving approximately $635 per month to the emergency fund.

Abbreviated Tax Analysis

	2012	2013**	2013 After Recommendations
Gross Income	$63,300	$63,300	$63,300
401(k) - John	($1,080)	($1,080)	($2,160)
401(k) - Mary			($1,560)
AGI	$62,220	$62,220	$59,580
Personal & Dependency Exemptions	$7,600	$7,800	$7,800
Standard or Itemized Deduction	$11,900	$12,200	$12,200
Taxable Income	$42,720	$42,720	$39,580
Tax Liability (estimated)	$5,538	$5,438	$5,042
Withholding	$12,660	$12,660	$12,660
Over Withheld Refund Expected*	$7,122	$7,212	$7,618

* This could be added to savings on an annual basis.

**Assume 3% inflation causing adjustment to exemptions, standard deduction, and brackets.

FINANCIAL STATEMENT: PROJECTED STATEMENT OF FINANCIAL POSITION

Statement of Financial Position Mr. and Mrs. Burke Projected Balance Sheet End of 2013					
ASSETS[1]			**LIABILITIES AND NET WORTH**		
Current Assets			**Current Liabilities[2]**		
Cash and Cash Equivalents[4]	$12,418		Credit Card Balance	$0	
Total Current Assets		$12,418	**Total Current Liabilities**		$0
Investment Assets			**Long-Term Liabilities[2]**		
Crossroads Inc. (1,000 Shares)	$0		Student Loan[3] - John	$50,350	
Gladwell Inc. (100 Shares)	$0		Auto Loan - Mary	$6,856	
House Down Payment	$1,200				
Balance Mutual Fund	$13,020		**Total Long-Term Liabilities**		$57,206
John's 401(k) Plan	$8,065				
Mary's 401(k) Plan	$2,033				
Total Investment Assets		$24,318			
Personal Use Assets			**Total Liabilities**		$57,206
Auto - Mary	$18,500				
Truck - John	$12,000		**Total Net Worth**		$35,030
Motor scooter - John	$0				
Personal Property & Furniture	$25,000				
Total Personal Use Assets		$55,500			
Total Assets		**$92,236**	**Total Liabilities & Net Worth**		**$92,236**

1. Assets are stated at fair market value.
2. Liabilities are stated at principal only as of December 31, 2013 before January payments.
3. The interest rate on the student loan is 6.9% for 10 years on a consolidation loan.
4. The $7,618 from tax analysis was added to cash.

SCHEDULE E - RECONCILIATION OF YEAR-END NET WORTH

Change in Projected Net Worth January 1, 2013 - December 31, 2013	
Beginning Net Worth	$10,475
Home Savings	$1,200
Emergency Fund Growth	$1,800
Debt Reduction (student loan)	$3,948
Debt Reduction (automobile loan)	$3,191
Growth of John's Mutual Fund	$1,020
Growth of John's 401(k) Plan	$3,745
Growth of Mary's 401(k) Plan	$2,033
Cash from Tax Analysis	$7,618
Total Ending Net Worth	**$35,030**

PROJECTED FINANCIAL STATEMENTS: INCOME STATEMENT

Statement of Income and Expenses Mr. and Mrs. Burke Statement of Income and Expenses for Past Year and Expected (Approximate) For 2014			
CASH INFLOWS			
Salaries			
John's Salary	$37,440		
Mary's Salary	$27,040		
Investment Income	$2,067		
Total Cash Inflows			$66,547
CASH OUTFLOWS			
Savings			
Savings - House down payment	$1,200		
Reinvestment of Investment Income*	$2,067		
401(k) Plan Contribution - John	$2,246		
401(k) Plan Contribution - Mary	$1,622		
Total Savings			$7,135
Fixed Outflows			
Child Support/Court Rqd. Insurance	$4,800	ND	
Rent	$8,400	ND	
HO 4 Renters Insurance*	$718	ND	
Utilities*	$742	ND	
Telephone	$360	ND	
Auto payment P&I	$3,600	ND	
Auto Insurance	$4,000	ND	
Gas, Oil, Maintenance for Auto*	$2,472	ND	
Student Loan Payments	$7,695	ND	
Insurance (Life, Disability, PLUP)	$1,425	ND	
Fee for Estates Documents	$1,000		
Credit Card Payments**	$1,000	ND	
Total Fixed Outflows			$36,212
Variable Outflows			
Taxes - John and Mary FICA	$4,933		
Taxes - Federal Tax Withheld	$5,042		
Food*	$3,708	ND	
Clothing	$1,000	ND	
Vacations	$1,500		
Total Variable Outflows			$16,183
Total Cash Outflows			$59,530
NET DISCRETIONARY CASH FLOWS			**$7,017**

**Subject to 3% inflation*

***They continue to incur $1,000 yearly in credit card debt for incidentals.*

PROJECTED SELECTED RATIOS

SCHEDULE F - PROJECTED RATIOS

End of Year 1 Projected Ratios December 31, 2013		
	Beginning of Year 1	**End of Year 1**
Current Ratio	0.21	N/A no C.L.
Emergency Fund Ratio	0.91 x	3.7x*
HR 1	14.22%	14.14%
HR 2	36.8%	33.21%
Net Worth / Total Assets	11.79%	32.39%
Savings Rate	6.5%	12.15%
Investment Assets / Gross Pay	0.4947 x	0.4516 x**

* Denominator is based on beginning of year totals.

** The reason the end of year 1 investment assets to gross pay ratio is down from 0.4947 x to 0.4516 x is because the client sold the two stocks to pay off the credit card debt. This was a strategic choice of the client. If the $12,000 that decision represented were added to the year-end investment assets to gross pay ratio it would be 0.6376 x, so the Burkes are making good progress.

SUMMARY

Assuming the Burkes follow and implement all of the recommendations, they will have significantly increased their emergency fund ratio, reduced both housing ratios 1 and 2, almost tripled their net worth, and increased their savings rate from 6.5 percent to 12.15 percent at the end of the first year. These are remarkable results to accomplish in one year. If the Burkes continue on the plan, they will meet their financial goals as they come due.

Closing Engagement Letter

Financial Planning Offices of Mitchell and Mitchell

April 18, 2014

John and Mary Burke
1420 Elm Street
Pensacola, FL 32501

RE: Financial Plan

Dear Mr. and Mrs. Burke:

This letter will confirm the completion of our services related to your current financial plan. At this time we have delivered your financial plan based on your goals and objectives. The financial plan was reviewed in detail with you at our April 11, 2013 meeting. As previously indicated our analysis and recommendations are based on information provided by you that were relied upon.

In addition, the methods that you choose to follow for the implementation of the financial planning recommendations are at your discretion. As you have indicated, you will be totally responsible for all decisions regarding implementation of the recommendations. The financial plan presented provides the following recommendations for your implementation:

Financial Planning Category	Specific Planning Area	Recommendation
Risk Management		
	Life Insurance	Both John and Mary need additional life insurance ($500,000 each) to protect each other and to protect any future child.
	Disability Insurance	Mary needs disability insurance in the event of loss of income due to disability.
	Homeowner's/Renters Insurance	There is a need to increase coverage on the renter's policy by endorsing the personal property coverage for all risks and for replacement value.
	Personal Liability Insurance	There is a need to purchase personal liability insurance. This may require the need to increase automobile liability coverage.
*Debt Management		
	Credit Cards, Auto and Student Loans	The credit cards need to be paid off immediately and the auto and student loans need to be paid as agreed. Note that the parents may assist with student loan debt.

Financial Planning Offices of Mitchell and Mitchell

**Savings Management		
	Emergency Fund	The emergency fund will be increased to reach a 3-6 month balance, rather than the current .91 month balance from savings from tax analysis.
	Retirement Savings	Currently the overall savings rate is 6.5% of gross pay (including employer match). For the retirement savings goal, the savings rate needs to be increased to 10-13%. John needs to increase his 401(k) plan deferral for maximum employer match and Mary needs to begin contributing to her 401(k) plan.
	Home Purchase Savings	The savings rate needs to reach 18% of gross pay for the home purchase 20% down payment ($39,338 needed in three years). Note that the parents may contribute towards down payment.
	College Savings for Children	The savings rate for college education for children should be 4-5% of gross pay per child.
Investment Management		
	Retirement Plans	All 401(k) plan investments need to be placed in a balanced portfolio.
Estate Planning Management		
	Estate Planning Documents	Have estate documents (will, durable power of attorney for healthcare, advance medical directive, etc.) prepared within two years.

*Note that the credit card debt can be paid off by funds acquired from the sale of the motor scooter and the sale of Crossroads and Gladwell stock.
**The savings rate can be increased after the automobile is paid off.

We thank you for the opportunity to be of service. Please contact us with any questions you may have regarding your current financial plan. We look forward to continuing a long term relationship with you as your financial situation requires additional planning services.

Sincerely,

Michael A. Mitchell, CFP®

Part 4

Comprehensive Cases

CASE

Grayson and Tally Alexander Case 1

Today is January 1, 2013

INTRODUCTORY DATA

Grayson and Tally Alexander have come to you, a financial planner, to help them transition into retirement. They have met most of their financial goals, including retirement, but feel they could benefit from assistance in developing a sustainable retirement income as well as a reasonable risk management and estate distribution plan. From your initial meeting together, you have gathered the following information.

THE FAMILY

Grayson Alexander, age 63, grew up with his grandparents in Texas. Grayson realized that he would have to provide his own college education so at an early age he began writing to his local congressman to secure an appointment to West Point Military Academy. By the time Grayson was ready to apply for college his grandparents were both deceased but his place at the Academy was secure. His military training, work ethic and sense of humor allowed him a unique and successful career, but he is ready to retire. Grayson is keenly aware of the challenges a life without resources could present and worries that he does not have enough to sustain the lifestyle he has created for himself and his family.

Tally Alexander, age 55, grew up in Louisiana. She has been married and divorced, raised a child by herself, and enjoyed two careers – one as a CPA and the second as a Financial Advisor. Before she met Grayson she planned to retire at age 55 to a life of part-time employment, doing something fun and creative, preferably something she had never tried before, that would allow her to paint, play golf, travel and intermittently spoil her grandchildren.

The Children and Grandchildren

Grayson has two children from two prior marriages. His oldest son, Colt, age 38, is divorced and has three children (1 boy and 2 girls) who range in age from 21 to 14. Colt's children live with their mother but visit their father often. All of the grandchildren are healthy and plan to attend college or technical school.

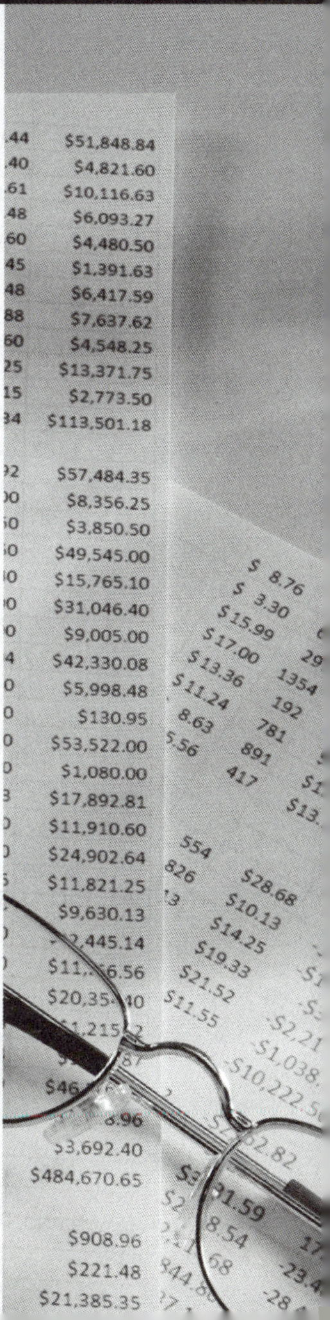

Grayson's youngest son, Sig, age 23 lives with his mother, and is in his junior year of college. Sig is majoring in math and hopes to finish college in two years or less. He's not sure what he will do with his degree when he graduates but hopes the slow economy will have picked up sufficiently that he will be able to find a job.

Tally has one child from a prior marriage. Her daughter, Melissa, is 33 years old, and just went through a divorce. Melissa has three children (1 girl and 2 boys) who range in age from 13 to 6. Melissa's children are bright, healthy (though the youngest child has special needs) and plan to attend college or technical school.

The Alexanders

Grayson and Tally met through an on-line dating service and have been happily married for 3 years. They have each been successful in their respective careers and in melding their finances into what most would consider a secure capital base upon which to retire. They feel they have already done their part to provide for their children and grandchildren, and now want to focus their financial resources on their retirement.

Grayson's parents are both deceased. Besides his children, Grayson's only living family member is a brother. Tally's father is deceased but he left her mother, Nelda (age 76), a comfortable retirement income consisting of two pensions and a social security benefit. Nelda lives about three miles from Grayson and Tally and has been through numerous medical challenges, including cancer. Nelda has long-term care (LTC) insurance. Luckily, none of these medical issues have caused Nelda to use any of her LTC coverage.

Tally manages her mother's investments and provides bill paying support for her mother so her mother can focus on enjoying life. Tally has two brothers who are distant from their mother and who rely on Tally for news on how Nelda is doing. Potentially Tally and her brothers will share equally in whatever inheritance comes their way. For planning purposes, Tally tells you she plans to disclaim her share of any inheritance. Tally explains that her mother's will provides the amount disclaimed by a child will be held in trust for the children of the disclaiming child.

Grayson and Tally have shifted their general focus to taking care of each other and planning for an active and comfortable retirement. Together they watch over Nelda and have agreed that within a few years they will relocate to a smaller city in a cooler climate than Texas. If Nelda is still living they will take her with them. They started a list of the things that are important to them so they can do the research to find a retirement home in a new state.

Grayson and Tally think alike on almost everything except investments. While they agree on how to spend their money and their goals are aligned, they have very different risk tolerances. Tally is a long-term investor with considerable investment training and experience. She is very comfortable handling her separate and their joint wealth, but has concerns about managing Grayson's separate wealth. Grayson is suspicious of the financial markets. He believes the financial markets are rigged and manipulated and does not trust anyone, except Tally, to handle his or their finances. That said, Grayson prefers to keep his 401(k) plan invested in his employer's guaranteed income option. They are both very concerned about which election Grayson should make for his pension benefit.

FINANCIAL GOALS & CONCERNS

1. Provide a secure retirement income. Grayson can either receive a $1,600,000 lump-sum payment from his pension plan this year, or a Single Life Annuity of $10,000 per month, or a Joint and 100% Survivor Annuity of $7,877 per month. They are conflicted as to which option they should choose and need you to make a detailed analysis of all of their options with the pros and cons of each option clearly provided, as well as your conclusion and your supporting argument. Include an analysis as to when Grayson should take Social Security.

2. They want a retirement income of $120,000 per year. Grayson prefers to claim his Social Security benefit as soon as he stops working but does not want to increase their marginal tax rate above 25%. He believes the government will renege on its promise to older Americans and wants to get as much out of the system as possible before the system goes bankrupt.
3. They want to purchase a retirement home on a golf course in a retirement community. The state needs to offer a low tax environment (income, property, estate and sales tax), as well as good light so Tally can paint, mild weather so they can golf, and favorable gun laws so Grayson can maintain his Concealed Handgun License (CHL).
4. They want to pay for Grayson to obtain a Master's Degree in Military History.
5. They want to pay for Tally to attend Art School.
6. They want to build a fund to cover their medical expenses in retirement.

EXTERNAL INFORMATION

Economic Information

- Inflation is expected to be 3% annually.
- Education inflation is expected to be 6% annually.
- Texas has no state income tax.
- The yield curve is slightly upward sloping, but relatively flat.
- The economy is in a slow growth recovery from a recession with moderate to high unemployment.

Bank Lending Rates

- 15 year mortgages 3.5%.
- 30 year mortgages 4.5%.
- Prime rate is 3.25%.
- Auto loans are 7%.
- 30 Year Treasury Securities Rate (TSR) is 3.11%.
- The 24 month average TSR is 4.0%.

Investment Return Expectations

	Return	Standard Deviation
Cash and Money Market Fund	2.5%	2.5%
Guaranteed Income Fund	2.5%	2.5%
Treasury Bonds/ Bond Funds	4.0%	4.0%
Corporate Bonds/ Bond Funds	6.0%	5.0%
Municipal Bonds/ Bond Funds	5.0%	4.0%
International Bond Funds	7.0%	6.0%
Index Fund	9.0%	14.0%
Large Cap Funds/Stocks	10.0%	16.0%
Mid/Small Funds/Stocks	12.0%	18.0%
International Stock Funds	13.0%	22.0%
Real Estate Funds	8.0%	12.0%

INTERNAL INFORMATION

FINANCIAL STATEMENTS

Statement of Financial Position (Beginning of Year)

Statement of Financial Position
Grayson and Tally Alexander
Balance Sheet as of 1/1/2013

ASSETS[1]				LIABILITIES AND NET WORTH			
Current Assets				**Current Liabilities[2]**			
CP	Cash & Checking	$29,607		H	Credit Card 1[3]	$2,000	
CP	Money Market	$136,000		W	Credit Card 2[4]	$400	
Total Current Assets			$165,607	JT	Current Portion of Mortgage	$10,413	
				Total Current Liabilities			$12,813
Investment Assets							
W	Cash Value of Life Insurance[5]	$6,762		**Long-Term Liabilities**			
W	Brokerage Account	$148,999		JT	Principal Residence[6]	$191,362	
JT	Commodities Account[7]	$100,000		**Total Long-Term Liabilities**			$191,362
JT	Rental Property[8]	$150,000					
H	401(k) Plan	$400,000					
W	Traditional IRA[9]	$600,000					
H	PV of Pension Benefit	$1,600,000					
Total Investment Assets			$3,005,761	**Total Liabilities**			$204,175
Personal Use Assets							
JT	Principal Residence (land $55,000)	$275,000					
W	Jewelry	$50,000					
CP	Furniture, Clothing	$22,000		**Total Net Worth**			$3,379,193
H	Chrylser 300	$15,000					
W	Lexus	$20,000					
H	Guns/Ammo	$30,000					
Total Personal Use Assets			$412,000				
Total Assets			**$3,583,368**	**Total Liabilities & Net Worth**			**$3,583,368**

1. Assets are stated at fair market value.
2. Liabilities are stated at principal only as of January 1, 2013 before January payments.
3. Credit card 1 carries interest rate of 12%. Balance paid in full each month.
4. Credit card 2 carries interest rate of 5.9%. Balance paid in full each month.
5. Tally's UL policy credits interest at the rate of 4%.
6. Home refinanced as of 12/31/11 at $201,775 at 3.5% for 15 years, and payments are $1,442 per month.
7. Commodities account recently established and has no investment performance history.
8. Rental Property has a Land Value of $10,000.
9. Balance of Traditional IRA includes a small Cash Balance Pension Plan that credits interest at a rate of 4% per year.

Statement of Income and Expenses

Statement of Income and Expenses

Grayson and Tally Alexander
Statement of Income and Expenses for 2012

Cash Inflows			
Grayson's Salary (vacation)	$250,000		
Rental Income	$9,600		
Tally's consulting	$42,000		
Total Cash Inflows			**$301,600**
Savings			
Money Market	$1,200		
401(k) Plan - Grayson	$22,000		
401(k) Plan - Tally	$0		
Education (529 Plan)	$0		
Total Savings			**$23,200**
Taxes			
Federal Income Taxes Withheld	$55,860		
Grayson's Social Security Taxes	$8,249		
Tally's Social Security Taxes	$4,667		
Property tax Principal Residence	$8,888	ND	
Property Rental Property	$3,600	ND	
Total Taxes			**$81,264**
Debt Payments			
Principal Residence	$17,309	ND	
Mortgage on Rental Property	$0	ND	
Student loans	$0	ND	
Auto loans	$0	ND	
Credit Cards	$2,400	ND	
Total Debt Payments			**$19,709**
Living Expenses			
Utilities Principal Residence	$8,100	ND	
Lawn and cleaning service at principal residence	$4,320	ND	
Gasoline for Autos	$2,400	ND	
Rental Property expenses (HOA; Alarm; Ins)	$1,274	ND	
Entertainment	$3,600		
Vacations	$0		
Church Donations	$1,200	ND	
Rx and Medical	$1,200	ND	
Auto Maintenace	$1,200	ND	
Tally's business expenses	$3,000	ND	
Food	$4,800	ND	
Grayson's truck	$0		
Miscellaneous (includes Res HOA)	$3,260	ND	
Total Living Expenses			**$34,354**
Insurance Payments			
HO Insurance Principal Residene	$3,341	ND	
Auto Insurance Premiums	$1,200	ND	
Medical, Life and Tally's LTC Insurance Premiums	$7,605	ND	
Total Insurance Payments			**$12,146**
Total Cash Outflows			**$170,673**
Net Discretionary Cash Flows			**$130,927**

ND = Non Discretionary

Projected Statement of Income and Expenses

	Statement of Income and Expenses Grayson and Tally Alexander		
Age Beginning of Year	63/55 Updated 2013	64/56 Projected 2014	65/57 Projected 2015
Cash Inflows *			
Grayson's vacation pay	$ 21,666	$ -	$ -
Grayson's Social Security*	$ -	$ -	$ -
Tally's consulting	$ 42,000	$ 43,680	
Rental Income	$ 9,600	$ 9,600	
Portfolio Income			
Total Cash Inflows	$ 73,266	$ 53,280	$ -
Savings			
Total Savings	0	0	0
Taxes			
Federal Income Tax	$ 25,000	$ 25,000	$ 25,000
Grayson's SS	$ 1,292	$ -	$ -
Grayson's Mcare Part B prem.	$ -	$ 599	$ 1,199
Tally's SE tax	$ 5,369	$ 5,584	
Residence Prop Tax	$ 8,888	$ 9,244	$ 9,613
Rental Prop Tax	$ 3,600	$ 3,744	
Total Taxes	**$ 44,149**	**$ 44,171**	**$ 35,812**
Debt Payments			
Residence P & I	$ 17,309	$ 17,309	$ 17,309
Credit Card Payment	$ 2,400	$ 2,400	$ 2,400
Total Debt Payments	**$ 19,709**	**$ 19,709**	**$ 19,709**

	Statement of Income and Expenses Grayson and Tally Alexander		
Age Beginning of Year	63/55 Updated 2013	64/56 Projected 2014	65/57 Projected 2015
Living Expenses			
Residence Utilities	$ 8,100	$ 8,424	$ 8,761
Lawn & Cleaning Svc @ Res	$ 4,320	$ 4,493	$ 4,673
Gasoline for Autos	$ 2,400	$ 2,496	$ 2,596
Rental expenses ((HOA, Alarm	$ 1,274	$ 1,325	
Entertainment	$ 3,600	$ 3,744	$ 3,894
Travel expense	$ 10,000	$ 10,400	$ 10,816
Charity	$ 1,200	$ 1,248	$ 1,298
Rx and other medical	$ 1,200	$ 1,248	$ 1,298
Auto Maintenance	$ 1,200	$ 1,248	$ 1,298
Tally's Business expenses	$ 3,000	$ 3,120	
Food	$ 4,800	$ 4,992	$ 5,192
Miscellaneous	$ 3,260	$ 3,390	$ 3,526
Sig's books and fees	$ 2,400	$ 2,496	
Grayson's truck	$ 25,000	0	0
Grayson's tuition/fees		$ 10,600	$ 11,236
Tally's tuition/fees		$ 3,180	$ 3,307
Wills	$ 1,000		
Total Living Expenses	**$ 72,754**	**$ 62,404**	**$ 57,894**
Insurance Payments			
Tally's Univeral Life Policy	$ 180	$ 180	$ 180
Tally's Term on Melissa	$ 315	$ 315	$ 315
Group/Retiree Health & Denta	$ 4,560	$ 4,742	$ 4,932
HO3 on Primary Residence	$ 2,668	$ 2,775	$ 2,886
Residence Flood	$ 365	$ 380	$ 395
Umbrella	$ 308	$ 320	$ 333
Auto	$ 1,200	$ 1,248	$ 1,298
Tally's LTC	$ 1,040	$ 1,040	$ 1,040
Grayson's LTC	$ 3,760	$ 3,760	$ 3,760
Total Insurance Payments	**$ 14,396**	**$ 14,760**	**$ 15,139**
Total Cash Outflows	$ 151,008	$ 141,044	$ 128,553
Net surplus (deficit)	**$ (77,742)**	**$ (87,764)**	**$ (128,553)**

Notes:

- Grayson's pension and social security excluded because they have not decided how to take them.
- Assumes ½ a year of Medicare part B premiums in 2014, then full year in 2015.
- Assumes Rental Property sold in 2015 and Rental Expenses stop in 2015.
- Assumes Tally quits working in 2015.
- General inflation of 4%.
- No step-down in expenses.

Insurance Information

Life Insurance

	Policy 1	Policy 2	Policy 3
Insured	Grayson Alexander	Tally Alexander	Tally Alexander
Face Amount	$450,000	$250,000	$50,000
Type	Group Term	Group Term Spousal	Universal Life A
Cash Value	None	None	$6,762
Annual Premium	$1,090	$420	$180
Premium Paid By	Grayson Alexander	Grayson Alexander	Tally Alexander
Beneficiary	Tally Alexander	Grayson Alexander	Melissa Castle
Owner	Grayson Alexander	Grayson Alexander	Tally Alexander
Settlement Options	None	None	None
Portable / Convertible	No	No	No

Tally also owns a $250,000, 20-year term policy on Melissa's life. Tally is the beneficiary. She took out the policy 7 years ago as a way to provide extra financial support to her grandchildren should Melissa die prematurely. The funds would provide a way for Tally to fund 'perpetual gifts from Melissa' to her grandchildren. Tally pays a premium of $315 per year for this coverage.

Grayson and Tally are insurable and could obtain life insurance but have stated they do not wish to purchase additional life insurance coverage.

Health Insurance

Grayson and Tally are currently covered under Grayson's Group Health Insurance Plan indemnity plan. Grayson's employer will provide retiree health insurance coverage for both of them at a cost of $150 per person, per month until Tally reaches age 65, qualifies for Medicare coverage, or current efforts to reform health care cause Grayson's employer to drop retiree health insurance coverage. This coverage includes a $500 annual individual deductible with a $1,000 annual family deductible, 80/20 coverage, with a $5,000 annual stop-loss and out-of-pocket limit and a $3 million lifetime cap on benefits.

Grayson and Tally are concerned they will be left without health insurance coverage before Tally reaches age 65. They want to fund a health and welfare account that can be available to pay for medical, dental and other needs as they age. They would like to build this fund over time in a tax-advantaged way, if possible. They would like to hold in reserve $300,000 for anticipated retiree medical expenses.

Long-Term Care Insurance

Grayson does not have coverage.

Tally has an indemnity policy she purchased 7 years ago that costs $1,040 per year. It is a joint policy with Nelda (taken out when Nelda lived with Tally), and offers a daily benefit of $250 with a 90 day elimination period and a 3 year benefit period for a total benefit amount payable of $273,750. The policy offers a $250 daily benefit for both Facility Services (in a Nursing Facility or Assisted Living Facility) as well as a Daily Benefit for Home and Community Based Services. It also offers a $100 monthly prescription drug benefit, Respite Care benefit, as well as coverage outside the United States, or its territories, or Canada for a period of up to 30 days per calendar year.

Grayson has longevity on his side of the family but Tally does not. Grayson estimates that he will live until age 95. Tally estimates she will live until age 90, and will need long-term care the last three years of her life. Given these concerns she wants to pursue a joint long-term care policy with Grayson as long as Nelda can keep her portion of their existing joint policy in force, with a minor adjustment to price and no need to undergo medical underwriting again. Their joint life expectancy is 37 years.

Property and Liability Insurance

Homeowners Insurance

Personal Residence	
Type	HO3 without endorsements
Dwelling	$314,400
Other Structures	$110,000
Personal Property	$150,000
Personal Liability	$500,000
Medical Payments	$25,000
Deductible	1% and 3% (wind)
Co-Insurance %	80/20
Annual Premium	$2,668 (annual)

The Alexander's carry an HO-3 policy without endorsements for replacement value and open perils for personal property. The current dwelling coverage of $314,400 is 100% replacement value with an inflation rider. Their HO-3 policy has a 1% deductible ($3,144) for losses with a separate 3% deductible ($9,432) for Wind and Hailstorm coverage, due to their proximity to the Gulf of Mexico. This policy also offers $500,000 of Personal Liability coverage and costs $2,668 per year.

While their home is not in a flood zone, they carry Flood Insurance coverage of $250,000 on the dwelling and $100,000 for contents. Their flood insurance policy has a $1,000 deductible for each type of coverage and a total cost of $365.00 per year.

The Alexander's have a Renter's Insurance policy on the rental home they own and lease to Melissa. The home is covered at $167,000 with a 2% deductible ($3,340) with Business Liability coverage of $300,000 for each occurrence and $600,000 annual aggregate. The policy costs $579 per year.

Automobile Insurance

Grayson and Tally carry Part A and Part C coverage of $250,000/$500,000/$100,000 on both of their vehicles with $1,000 deductible for D1 (other than collision) and D2 (collision).

Grayson's vehicle was recently caught in rising water while parked at his office. The vehicle was towed and repaired for a total cost of $3,000.

Personal Liability Umbrella Policy

Grayson and Tally have a $1,000,000 personal liability policy taken out years ago by Tally. Grayson and his vehicle, along with their joint rental property were added to this policy. They have a self-insured retention of $1,000, and pay $308 a year for this coverage but wonder if it will be sufficient after Grayson retires.

Investment Information

Grayson does not trust the market and does not like to involve himself in discussions about risk tolerances, asset allocations or portfolio holdings. He trusts Tally to handle their day-to-day financial management and their investments. When asked, he expresses a preference for cash over stocks and bonds, and wants to maintain a substantial emergency reserve. Grayson believes their checking account balance should not fall below $30,000 and prefers to hold three years of expenses in cash – just in case the market trades lower.

Two years ago Tally convinced Grayson to invest a portion of his 401(k) plan contributions in a balanced mutual fund. The funds grew at a respectable pace, but a market adjustment caused Grayson to transfer the invested funds back into the guaranteed income option (paying 4%) offered by his employer's plan. Since the transfer, the guaranteed income option has dropped to an annual rate of 2.5%, a 3-year return of 3.6%, and a five-year return of 4.15%. Grayson has expressed interest in taking the lump-sum from his pension plan and investing it in the guaranteed income option in his 401(k) plan. Tally believes they should only take the lump-sum pension benefit if Grayson agrees that it must be invested in a diversified retirement income portfolio yielding a rate of return equal to or greater than the inflation rate they expect over their planning horizon.

Tally manages her brokerage account and retirement funds. She enjoys doing research on stocks, mutual funds, ETFs and commodities, and has built a diversified portfolio, heavy on equities. She is interested in discussing the link she's observed between gold and global liquidity. She feels that the current market environment might be a good time to hold commodities like gold, silver, palladium, cocoa, natural gas, sugar, even oil – though she and Grayson have avoided oil investments until now, due to his access to confidential information at work.

Tally's portfolio closely mirrors the S&P 500 Index sectors with exceptions for Financial Services and Energy due to her previous employment and Grayson's current employment in those fields. Tally is an active trader and her returns have exceeded Index returns as follows:

	YTD	1 year	3 years	5 years	10 years
Brokerage	3.5%*	7.5%	22.5%	4.2%	6.2%
IRAs	6.6%	10.0%	22.9%	3.0%	5.6%
S&P 500 Index	4.2%	4.5%	19.2%	0.33%	3.52%

*Tally withdrew funds from this account and from their joint checking account to purchase a rental home for Melissa to lease post-divorce.

Grayson appreciates Tally handling her separate and their joint investments. He believes she will do a good job handling his separate wealth too, but Tally thinks Grayson's separate wealth should be handled by an investment professional. She wants someone to handle the day-to-day management of Grayson's portfolio so she can enjoy her retirement. She also wants a backup in case something happens to her. Her goal is to establish a relationship with you so that you will manage Grayson's separate investments, upon retirement, and her investments, if she becomes incapacitated.

Grayson and Tally think an expected return of 4% on Grayson's separate retirement investments will allow them to live comfortably in retirement. Tally has asked you to ignore their short-term needs, as she agrees with Grayson, and wants to hold 3 years of cash as their emergency fund.

Risk Tolerance Questionnaire

Global Portfolio Allocation Scoring System (PASS) for Individual Investors[1]

Questions	Strongly Agree	Agree	Neutral	Disagree	Strongly Disagree
1. Earning a high long-term total return that will allow my capital to grow faster than the inflation rate is one of my most important investment objectives.	T				G
2. I would like an investment that provides me with an opportunity to defer taxation of capital gains to future years.	G,T				
3. I do not require a high level of current income from my investments.	G,T				
4. I am willing to tolerate some sharp down swings in the return on my investments in order to seek a potentially higher return than would normally be expected from more stable investments.		T			G
5. I am willing to risk a short-term loss in return for a potentially higher long-run rate of return.	T				G
6. I am financially able to accept a low level of liquidity in my investment portfolio.		T			G

G = Grayson, T = Tally

Pension Plans

Grayson's defined benefit plan offers a 2.4% credit for each year of service up to a maximum of 25 years of service. The monthly benefit is determined based on the average of the highest 3 years of income. This pension plan offers a lump sum payment option calculated using a 24 month average of the 30-year TSR rate less 2%, with a floor of 2%.

Grayson's employer is an international oil company with substantial overseas ties. Many employees take the lump-sum option when they retire. He provided his latest plan statement which included the following information about his alternatives:

- A monthly single life annuity - $10,000 per month
- A monthly joint & 100% survivor annuity - $7,877 per month
- A lump-sum option, using 2% average 30-year TSR - $1,600,000

Tally has two small pensions – a Qualified Domestic Relations Order (QDRO) from her previous divorce settlement and a small cash balance plan from a previous employer. The two benefits combined offer her a $400 monthly single life annuity beginning at age 65.

1. Global Portfolio Allocation Scoring System (PASS) for Individual Investors - developed by Dr. William Droms (Georgetown University) and Steven N. Strauss, (DromsStrauss Advisors Inc.) - model used with permission.

Portfolio Information

Tally's actively manages the holdings in her brokerage and IRA account. She estimated that she currently owns 30 stocks, 5 ETFs and 15 different mutual funds. She fully invested her account during the market downturn. Tally maintains a wish list of stocks she would like to own and has asked about investing more of their overall investment assets into Real Estate and Commodities. Grayson and Tally want you to propose a suitable asset allocation for their retirement funds (Grayson's 401k, and pension if taken as a lump-sum).

Alexander Retirement Portfolio Information 12/31/12

Total Portfolio*

Cash and Cash Equivalents Plus Investments

	Dollars	%
Cash	$2,299,407	100%
Fixed income	$0	0%
US Equities	$0	0%
Foreign Equities	$0	0%
Total	$2,299,407	100%

*Excludes Cash Value of Life Insurance

Account	Cash	Bonds	US Equities	Foreign Equities	Total
Cash & Cash Equiv	$299,407				$299,407
Brokerage account					$0
Commodities account					$0
Web Options					$0
Rental Property					$0
Education Account					$0
401(k) Plan	$400,000				$400,000
401(k) Plan					$0
Traditional IRA					$0
PV of Pension Benefit	$1,600,000				$1,600,000
					$0
Total	$2,299,407	$0	$0	$0	$2,299,407

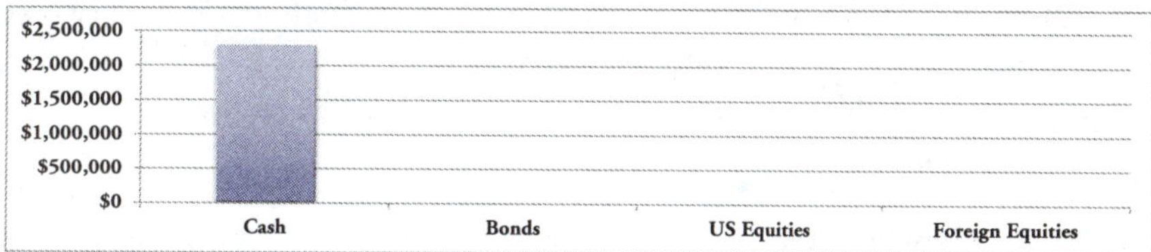

Total Portfolio - Account Types

	Dollars	%
Taxable	$299,407	13%
Education	$0	0%
Tax Deferred	$2,000,000	87%
Roth Accounts	$0	0%
Total	$2,299,407	100%

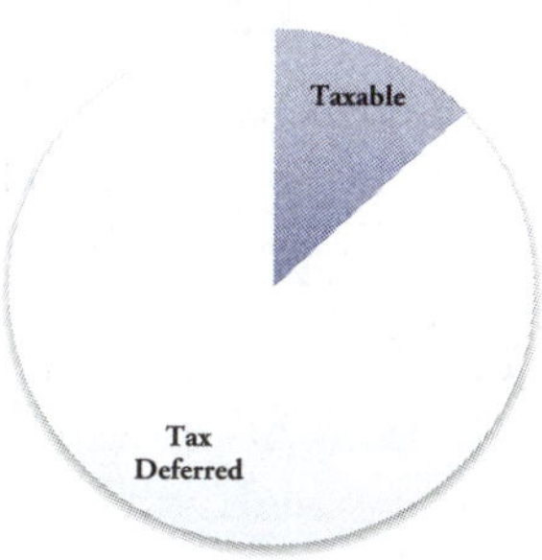

Account	Taxable	Education	Tax Deferred	Roth	Total
Cash & Cash Equiv	$299,407				$299,407
Brokerage account					$0
Commodities account					$0
Web Options					$0
Rental Property					$0
Education Account					$0
401(k) Plan			$400,000		$400,000
401(k) Plan					$0
Traditional IRA					$0
PV of Pension Benefit			$1,600,000		$1,600,000
					$0
					$0
Total	$299,407	$0	$2,000,000	$0	$2,299,407

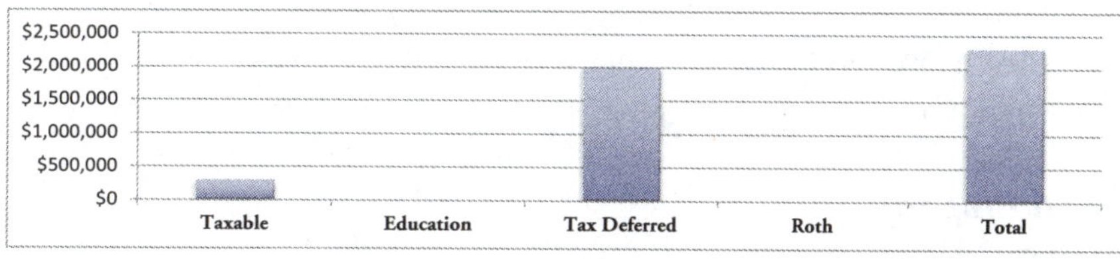

Education Information

Grayson and Tally strongly believe in education. Sig is currently finishing college through the Texas Guaranteed Tuition Plan (formerly the Texas Tomorrow fund) established by his grandfather years ago. Sig lives with his mother and uses a vehicle provided by her, but may need occasional financial support as his books and some fees are not covered by the plan.

Grayson will fund whatever expenses Sig needs out of living expenses and estimates this will cost no more than $2,400 per year over the next two years (2013 and 2014).

Grayson estimates it will take 2 years at a cost of $10,000 per year (in today's dollars) to complete a Master's in Military History from an accredited university. He plans to begin taking classes next year (2014).

Tally expects to take Art classes while Grayson is in school. She estimates that the classes will cost a total of $6,000 (in today's dollars) and will be paid for out of living expenses over 2 years (2014 and 2015).

Last year Grayson and Tally celebrated the enrollment of their oldest grandchild in the University of Oklahoma. They made gifts to Colt and Melissa to help pay for current and future education costs. The gifts were each less than the annual exclusion amount and no gift tax returns were filed.

Estate Planning Information

The Alexander's began the process of updating their legal documents two years ago. They executed Durable Powers of Attorney for Healthcare and Property as well as Advanced Medical Directives, but their Wills were never completed. The Wills are still in Draft form and need to be revisited in light of tax law changes, their marriage and their blended family.

Grayson and Tally have kept gifts to their children below the annual exclusion amount and have not made any prior taxable gifts. They would like to leave a legacy for their children (and grandchildren) but are unsure they have sufficient resources to provide for their retirement and healthcare needs.

Grayson has expressed a desire to leave his brother a small bequest at his death as long as Tally has sufficient assets to sustain her through the end of her life.

Other Information Regarding Assets and Liabilities

Home and Furnishings

Tally purchased a new home 9 years ago for $295,900. She put down 20% and financed the balance at 5.5% over 30 years. Three years ago she refinanced to a 15 year loan at 4.375% interest. Falling interest rates allowed Tally and Grayson to refinance the remaining balance of $201,775 down to 3.5% over 15 years. Their monthly payment is $1,442.45. Property taxes associated with this home total $8,888 per year, homeowner's insurance coverage costs $2,668 annually, flood insurance totals $365 per year, their umbrella policy costs $308 per year, and their HOA fee is $860 per year.

Rental Property

Grayson and Tally purchased this property for $135,000 last year. They paid cash for the property and signed a one year lease with Melissa to pay $800 per month. They are reluctant landlords and do not intend to hold this property long-term. As soon as Melissa can afford a place of her own, she will either buy this home or move so her mother and step-father can sell the property. Grayson and Tally think they will be able to sell the rental property (to Melissa or a third-party) in 2015.

The most recent tax statement valued the home at $150,000, but this valuation has been appealed. Property taxes are estimated to be $3,600 per year, and property insurance coverage costs $579 per year.

Grayson and Tally established an operating account for the Rental property. Melissa's rent is automatically transferred from her checking account into this account, and any expenses or property improvements are paid out of this account.

Automobiles

Chrysler 300 and Lexus LS460 are both paid for and at least 6 years old. When Grayson retires they plan to trade-in his Chrysler 300 for a truck. They expect to use $25,000 in cash to purchase a 2013 vehicle.

Collectibles

Grayson collects firearms and estimates he owns approximately $30,000 in guns and ammunition. Tally does not collect jewelry but her family has gifted her around $50,000 in jewelry. All of these items are stored in a large safe in their home.

CASE ASSUMPTIONS

1. The Alexander's are conservative and want to use 4% inflation for planning purposes.
2. They are in the 33% marginal income tax bracket.
3. Retirement income will be provided by Grayson's 401k and Pension plan assets. Grayson prefers to leave Tally's assets out of the retirement funding solution.
4. Grayson is expected to live to age 95, Tally to age 90. Their joint life expectancy is 37 years.
5. Tally will need custodial care the last three years of her life.
6. Unless otherwise stated, all interest, dividends and capital gains are accumulated in cash and will be used for lifestyle expenses.
7. Assume that the discretionary cash flow from 2012 was included in the Cash and Money Market account balances as of 1/1/2013.
8. Tally's potential inheritance is to be left out of any retirement planning and health care funding solutions.
9. When they relocate to a new community for retirement, they will sell their existing home and pay cash for a new home of equal value.
10. Tally will continue to work part-time for the next two years with 4% increases in her income.
11. Tally will take Social Security at age 62 and begin Required Minimum Distributions at age 70.

CASE

George and Laura Freeman Case 2

Today is January 1, 2013

INTRODUCTORY DATA

THE FAMILY

George Freeman (age 46) is the owner of a tool and die company, GMED Manufacturing Inc., (GMED) and is married to Laura Freeman (age 46) who is a self-employed graphic designer. They have four children: Jordan (age 7), Colin (age 5), Cate (age 3), and Caroline (age 1). George and Laura have been married for 11 years.

George's salary is $235,000. Their net worth is approximately $1.9 million at this time; of which $1.0 million is the value of his business, GMED. Laura has an office, but primarily works from home so that she can also take care of the children. She has no employees and has Schedule C net income of $100,000 per year.

FINANCIAL GOALS & CONCERNS

1. They want to provide for their children's college education (4 years each) expected to cost $25,000 per year in today's dollars.
2. They want to save for weddings for each of their three daughters. They expect the weddings will cost $40,000 each in today's dollars and want to plan that each child will marry at age 23. They believe wedding costs are subject to general inflation.
3. They want to retire debt free when they are age 62 (when they both plan to retire).
4. They initially define adequate retirement income as 80% of preretirement income.
5. They want to have adequate risk management coverage.
6. In case of his death, George is primarily concerned with providing income for Laura for the duration of her life and secondarily, leaving the remainder of his estate to their children.
7. George and Laura have mutually agreed to buy Colin a Porsche or give him the equivalent amount of money as they pay for the girl's weddings at his age 23. They have not yet told Colin.
8. To have an appropriate investment portfolio.
9. To have an appropriate estate plan.

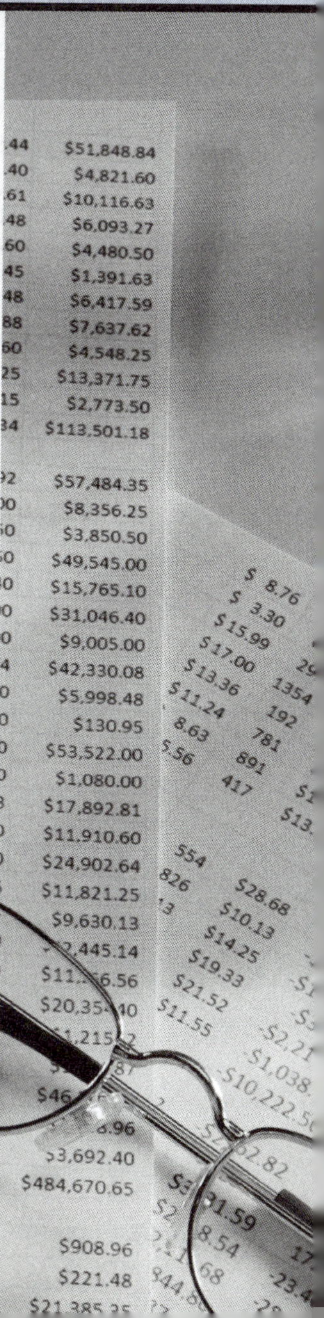

EXTERNAL INFORMATION

ECONOMIC INFORMATION

- General inflation is expected to average 3.0% annually for the foreseeable future.
- Education inflation is expected to be 6% annually.
- Real GDP has been 2.75% and is expected to continue to be 2.75% for the next several years.
- It is expected that the S&P 500 will return approximately 9% this year and for the foreseeable future.
- T-bills are considered the appropriate proxy for the risk-free rate of return and are currently earning 2.5%.

BANK LENDING RATES

- 15-year conforming annual rate mortgages are 3.75%.
- 30-year conforming rate mortgages are 4.0%.
- Any closing costs associated with mortgage refinance are an additional 3% of the amount mortgaged and will be included in the mortgage or paid directly.
- The secured personal loan rate is 8.0%.
- Credit card rates are 18%.
- Prime rate is 3.25%.

INVESTMENT RETURN EXPECTATIONS

	Return	Standard Deviation
Cash and Money Market Fund	2.5%	2.0%
Treasury Bonds/ Bond Funds	4.0%	4.0%
Corporate Bonds/ Bond Funds	6.0%	5.0%
International Bond Funds	7.0%	6.0%
Index Fund	9.0%	14.0%
Large Cap Funds/Stocks	10.0%	16.0%
Mid/Small Funds/Stocks	12.0%	18.0%
International Stock Funds	13.0%	22.0%
Real Estate Funds	8.0%	12.0%

INTERNAL INFORMATION

Financial Statements

Statement of Financial Position (Beginning of Year)

Statement of Financial Position
George and Laura Freeman
Balance Sheet as of 1/1/2012

Assets[1]				Liabilities and Net Worth		
Current Assets				**Current Liabilities[2]**		
JT	Cash & Checking[2]	$30,000		W Credit Cards	$30,000	
JT	Money Market	$100,000		**Total Current Liabilities**		$30,000
Total Current Assets			$130,000			
Investment Assets				**Long-Term Liabilities[2]**		
H	GMED Manufacturing, Inc[3]	$1,000,000		JT Principal Residence[5]	$749,726	
H	Investment Portfolio	$350,000		H Mountain Condo	$107,582	
H	Education Account[4](529) Plan	$46,000		**Total Long-Term Liabilities**		$857,308
H	Cash Value of Life Insurance	$60,000				
H	401(k) Plan w/ Roth	$25,748				
W	Traditional IRA	$14,252				
W	Roth IRA	$19,000				
Total Investment Assets			$1,515,000	**Total Liabilities**		$887,308
Personal Use Assets						
JT	Principal Residence[5]	$600,000				
H	Mountain Condo	$220,000				
JT	Furniture, Clothing	$100,000		**Total Net Worth**		$1,762,692
H	Car # 1	$25,000				
W	Car # 2	$35,000				
H	Snowmobiles	$25,000				
Total Personal Use Assets			$1,005,000			
Total Assets			$2,650,000	**Total Liabilities & Net Worth**		$2,650,000

1. Assets are stated at fair market value.
2. Liabilities are stated at principal only as of January 1, 2012 before January payments.
3. This is George's 100% interest and the value is based on his estimate.
4. The 529 Plan is for the children. George currently saves $6,000 per year into this account (see portfolio).
5. Land value is $50,000.

Title Designations:
H = Husband (Sole Owner)
W = Wife (Sole Owner)
JT = Joint Tenancy with Survivorship Rights

Statement of Financial Position (End of Year)

Statement of Financial Position
George and Laura Freeman
Balance Sheet as of 12/31/12 (and 1/1/2013)

ASSETS[1]				LIABILITIES AND NET WORTH			
Current Assets				**Current Liabilities[2]**			
JT	Cash & Checking	$25,000		W	Credit Cards	$30,000	
JT	Money Market	$100,000		**Total Current Liabilities**			$30,000
Total Current Assets			$125,000				
Investment Assets				**Long-Term Liabilities[2]**			
H	GMED Manufacturing, Inc[3]	$1,000,000		JT	Principal Residence[5]	$736,802	
H	Investment Portfolio	$500,000		H	Mountain Condo	$100,848	
H	Cash Value of Life Insurance	$60,000					
H	Education Account[4](529)	$46,000		**Total Long-Term Liabilities**			$837,650
H	401(k) Plan w/ Roth	$50,000					
W	Traditional IRA	$15,000					
W	Roth IRA	$20,000					
Total Investment Assets			$1,691,000	**Total Liabilities**			$867,650
Personal Use Assets							
JT	Principal Residence[5]	$600,000					
H	Mountain Condo	$220,000					
JT	Furniture, Clothing	$100,000		**Total Net Worth**			$1,953,350
H	Car # 1	$25,000					
W	Car # 2	$35,000					
H	Snowmobiles	$25,000					
Total Personal Use Assets			$1,005,000				
Total Assets			$2,821,000	**Total Liabilities & Net Worth**			$2,821,000

1. Assets are stated at fair market value.
2. Liabilities are stated at principal only as of December 31, 2012 before January payments.
3. This is George's 100% interest and the value is based on his estimate.
4. This is for the children. George currently saves $6,000 per year into this account (see portfolio).
5. Land value is $50,000.

Title Designations:
H = Husband (Sole Owner)
W = Wife (Sole Owner)
JT = Joint Tenancy with Survivorship Rights

Income Statement

Statement of Income and Expenses George and Laura Freeman Statement of Income and Expenses for Past Year (2012) and Expected (Approximate) For This Year (2013)			
Cash Inflows			**Totals**
George's Salary	$235,000		
Laura's Salary	$100,000		
Total Cash Inflows			$335,000
Cash Outflows			
Savings			
Money Market	$6,500		
401(k) Plan	$17,000		
Education (529 Plan)	$6,000		
Total Savings			$29,500
Taxes			
Federal Income Taxes Withheld	$51,435		
George's Social Security Taxes	$10,029		
Laura's Social Security Taxes	$15,300		
Property Tax Principal Residence	$8,000	ND	
Property Tax Mountain Condo	$4,000	ND	
Total Taxes			$88,764
Debt Payments (Principal & Interest)			
Principal Residence	$57,557	ND	
Mountain Condo	$14,051	ND	
Association Fees for Mountain Condo	$2,000	ND	
Credit Cards	$5,000	ND	
Total Debt Payments			$78,608
Living Expenses			
Utilities Principal Residence	$5,000	ND	
Mountain Condo Expenses (net of rental income of $5,000)	$15,000	ND	
Gasoline for Autos	$5,000	ND	
Lawn Service	$2,000	ND	
Entertainment	$15,000		
Vacations	$25,000		
Church Donations	$10,000	ND	
Clothing	$18,000	ND	
Auto Maintenance	$2,000	ND	
Satellite TV	$1,800	ND	
Food	$8,000	ND	
Miscellaneous	$10,000	ND	
Total Living Expenses			$116,800
Insurance Payments			
HO Insurance Principal Residence	$4,200	ND	
HO Insurance Mountain Condo	$3,500	ND	
Auto Premiums	$2,100	ND	
Life Insurance #1	$8,000	ND	
Life Insurance #3	$1,000	ND	
Total Insurance Payments			$18,800
Total Cash Outflows			$332,472
Net Discretionary Cash Flows			$2,528

ND = Non-Discretionary cash flows per mutual understanding between financial planner and client.

* Federal Income Taxes and Social Security are presumed to be discretionary as opposed to nondiscretionary because job loss is the greatest risk to the emergency fund and these expenses are not incurred in the event of a job loss.

INSURANCE INFORMATION

Life Insurance

	Policy 1	Policy 2	Policy 3
Insured	George Freeman	George Freeman	Laura Freeman
Face Amount	$1,500,000	2 x Salary = $470,000	$400,000
Type	Whole Life Policy	Group Term - Employer Provided	Individual Term Policy 10-Year Level Term issued 5 years ago
Cash Value	$60,000	$0	$0
Annual Premium	$8,000	$700	$1,000
Beneficiary	Laura Freeman	Laura Freeman	George Freeman
Owner	George Freeman	George Freeman	Laura Freeman

Health Insurance

George currently has an indemnity group health and major medical hospitalization plan through his company. Laura, George, and their children are all currently covered by his health insurance plan. GMED pays the entire premium for the health insurance policy, which has the following characteristics:

- $500 per individual deductible per year
- $1,000 total family deductible per year
- 80% / 20% co-insurance clause for major medical
- $1M lifetime benefit limit per person
- $3,000 annual family stop loss limit

Long-Term Disability Insurance

Long-Term Disability Policy - George	
Type	Own Occupation
Insured	George
Guaranteed Renewable	Yes
Benefit	60% of Gross Pay
Premium Paid By	Employer
Residual Benefits Clause	Yes
Elimination Period	90 Days
Annual Premium	$2,000

Laura is not covered by a long-term disability insurance policy.

Long-Term Care Insurance

Neither George nor Laura have long-term care insurance.

Property and Liability Insurance

Homeowners Insurance

	Personal Residence	Mountain Condo
Type	HO3 without endorsements	HO3 without endorsements
Dwelling	$1,000,000	$200,000
Other Structures	$150,000	$20,000
Personal Property	$333,333	$100,000
Personal Liability	$100,000	$100,000
Medical Payments	$10,000	$10,000
Deductible	$1,000	$1,000
Co-Insurance %	80 / 20	80 / 20
Annual Premium	$4,200	$3,500

There is no flood insurance on the personal residence or the mountain condo.

Auto Insurance

	Auto #1 George's Car	Auto # 2 Laura's Car
Type	Personal Automobile Policy (PAP)	Personal Automobile Policy (PAP)
Liability (Bodily Injury)	$100,000/$300,000/$50,000	$100,000/$300,000/$50,000
Medical Payments	$10,000	$10,000
Uninsured Motorist	$100,000/$300,000	$100,000/$300,000
Collision Deductible	$1,000	$500
Comprehensive Deductible	$500	$250
Annual Premium	$900	$1,200

Other Property Insurance

There is no insurance on the snowmobiles (property or liability).

Liability Insurance

The Freeman's do not have a personal liability umbrella policy (PLUP).

Investment Information

- The Freemans have a required rate of return on investments of eight percent (8%) on their overall investment portfolio.
- The Freeman's believe they have a moderate risk tolerance; answered the following Risk Tolerance Questionnaire as indicated.
- George expects to be able to sell his interest in GMED to other employees to partially fund his retirement.
- Their money market fund is primarily invested in a taxable money market account earning 2.5 percent.

Risk Tolerance Questionnaire

Global Portfolio Allocation Scoring System (PASS) for Individual Investors[1]

Questions	Strongly Agree	Agree	Neutral	Disagree	Strongly Disagree
1. Earning a high long-term total return that will allow my capital to grow faster than the inflation rate is one of my most important investment objectives.		G	L		
2. I would like an investment that provides me with an opportunity to defer taxation of capital gains to future years.	G, L				
3. I do not require a high level of current income from my investments.	G, L				
4. I am willing to tolerate some sharp down swings in the return on my investments in order to seek a potentially higher return than would normally be expected from more stable investments.				G, L	
5. I am willing to risk a short-term loss in return for a potentially higher long-run rate of return.		G		L	
6. I am financially able to accept a low level of liquidity in my investment portfolio.			G, L		

G = George, L = Laura

1. Global Portfolio Allocation Scoring System (PASS) for Individual Investors - developed by Dr. William Droms (Georgetown University) and Steven N. Strauss, (DromsStrauss Advisors Inc.) - model used with permission.

Description of Investment Assets

GMED Manufacturing, Inc.

When George attempted to value his business, his accountant advised him to use a multiple of revenue approach. George's accountant suggested using a multiple of five times net cash flows to value the business. George estimated the value of the business based on net cash flows of $200,000 for 2012.

Brokerage Account

The brokerage account consists of the mutual funds described below. Any interest and dividends earned on the investments is reflected in the account balance and is not counted or separately stated on the income statement.

INVESTMENT PORTFOLIO

Mutual Funds as of 12/31/2012

Mutual Funds									
Name	**Shares**	**Cost per Share**	**NAV**	**Beta**	**R^2 to S&P 500**	**Yield**	**One Year Return**	**Standard Deviation**	**Total FMV**
A	2,526	$50	$75	1.1	0.76	0.9%	6%	0.16	$189,450
B	1,468	$25	$20	0.98	0.95	1.2%*	12%	0.15	$29,360
C	2,570	$22	$87	1.24	0.88	0.5%	146%	0.14	$223,590
D	1,200	$45	$48	0.78	0.50	1.4%	4%	0.13	$57,600
								Totals	**$500,000**

* The dividend for mutual fund B is expected to grow at 3% per year.

George has been considering replacing Mutual Fund A with Mutual Fund Z. Both mutual funds have a similar investment objective.

Mutual Fund									
Name	**Shares**	**Cost per Share**	**NAV**	**Beta**	**R^2 to S&P 500**	**Yield**	**One Year Return**	**Standard Deviation**	**Total FMV**
Z	-	-	$89	1.35	0.89	0.75%	7.5%	0.17	-

Education Account (529)

The contributions to and balances of this account are invested in a diversified portfolio of mutual funds based on the age of the youngest beneficiary. George selected an overall investment strategy that resulted in "moderate risk" investments.

George & Laura Freeman Portfolio Information 01/01/13

Total Portfolio*		
Cash and Cash Equivalents Plus Investments		
	Dollars	%
Cash	$175,000	23%
Fixed income	$58,000	8%
US Equities	$523,000	69%
Foreign Equities	$0	0%
Total	**$756,000**	**100%**

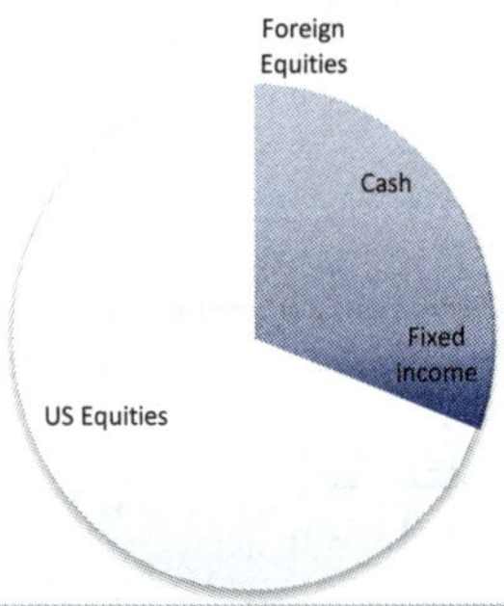

Excludes Cash Value of Life Insurance

Account	Cash	Bonds	US Equities	Foreign Equities	Total
Cash	$125,000				$125,000
Investment Portfolio			$500,000		$500,000
Education Account (529)		$23,000	$23,000		$46,000
401(k) Plan with Roth	$50,000				$50,000
Traditional IRA		$15,000			$15,000
Roth IRA		$20,000			$20,000
Total	$175,000	$58,000	$523,000	$0	$756,000

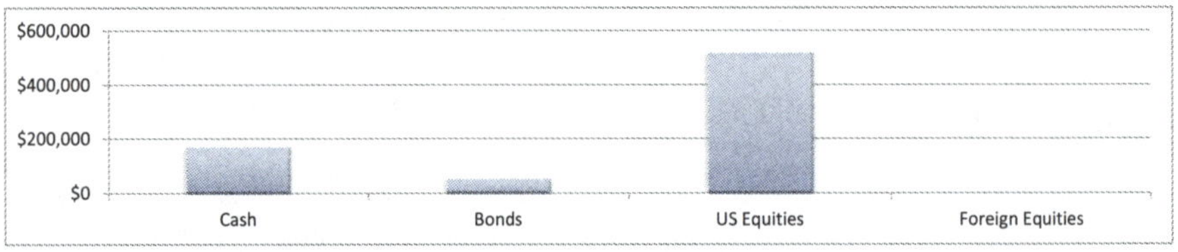

Total Portfolio - Account Types		
	Dollars	%
Taxable	$625,000	83%
Education	$46,000	6%
Tax Deferred	$40,000	5%
Roth Accounts	$45,000	6%
Total	**$756,000**	**100%**

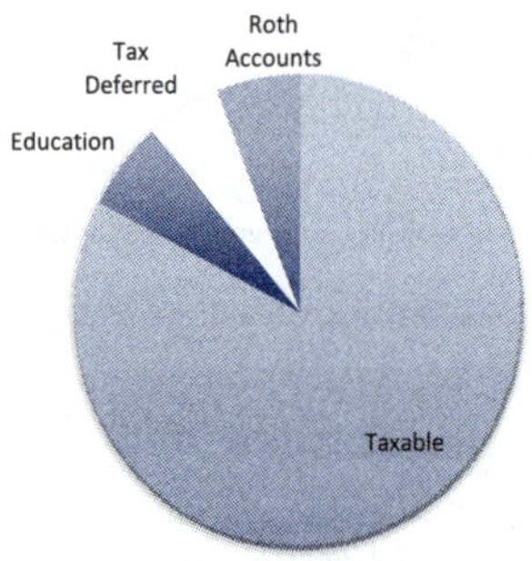

Account	Taxable	Education	Tax Deferred	Roth	Total
Cash	$125,000				$125,000
Investment Portfolio	$500,000				$500,000
Education Account (529)		$46,000			$46,000
401(k) Plan with Roth			$25,000	$25,000	$50,000
Traditional IRA			$15,000		$15,000
Roth IRA				$20,000	$20,000
Total	$625,000	$46,000	$40,000	$45,000	$756,000

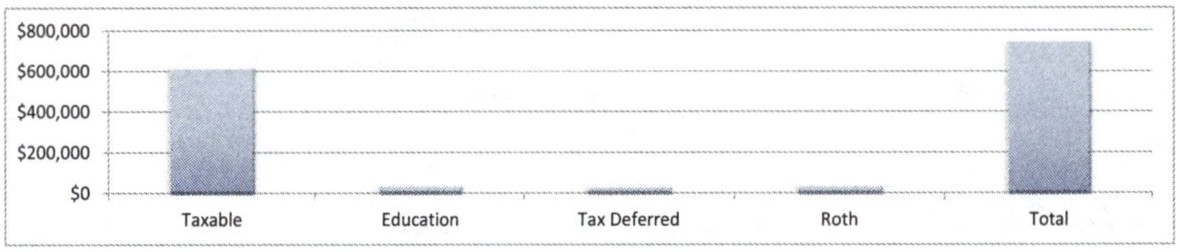

Traditional IRA

The Traditional IRA is invested in a series of zero coupon bonds. The investment returns in this account over the past five years have been:

Year	Returns
1	6.50%
2	4.75%
3	- 3.25%
4	- 2.50%
5	5.25%

George is uncertain what his compounded investment rate of return has been and whether the investments and returns are appropriate for his goals.

Roth IRA

The Roth IRA is currently invested in a bond mutual fund. The income is reinvested and not reflected on the income statement.

INCOME TAX INFORMATION

The Freemans are in the 35 percent marginal income tax bracket for federal income tax purposes and there is no state income tax. Capital gains are taxed at 15 percent at the federal level.

RETIREMENT INFORMATION

George has a safe harbor 401(k) plan, which was recently adopted through his company (GMED). He contributes $17,000 from his salary each year. His company matches dollar for dollar on the first three percent of salary and then $0.50 on the dollar on the next two percent of salary to a maximum contribution of four percent of covered compensation. George also has an integrated profit sharing plan through his company (GMED). The company adds the amount necessary to the profit sharing plan so that the total contribution to the plan is $50,000 and has done so since January 1, 2011. Laura is self-employed and does not currently have any retirement plan. George's total savings, including the employer match, is $50,000 per year.

GMED 401(k) Plan with Roth Account

George experienced serious losses in his 401(k) plan during this past year and has moved all funds to cash. He had invested in a single highly speculative mutual fund that had the worst year in its history. George made his first contribution to this account in 2011.

Social Security Information

George and Laura each estimate they will receive $25,000 in today's dollars at normal age retirement, age 67. The Freemans initially define adequate retirement income as 80 percent of pre-retirement income. They both plan to live until age 95 after retiring when age 62.

ESTATE PLANNING INFORMATION

George has not arranged for any estate planning. Laura has a will leaving all of her assets outright to her mother, Madelyn. Other than Laura's will, she has not arranged for any other estate planning.

Other Information Regarding Assets and Liabilities

Personal Residence

The Freemans purchased their personal residence for $1,000,000 (67 months ago). They borrowed $800,000 for 30 years at six percent. They were considering refinancing the house but decided not to when the appraised value came in at only $600,000 due to market conditions. The housing market has been devastated. They pay their homeowner's insurance premiums and property taxes separately from their mortgage. Their property taxes are $8,000 yearly. They intend to continue living in this house through their retirement.

Mountain Condo

George purchased the mountain condo 20 years ago for $220,000, and had a mortgage of $176,000 at seven percent for 30 years. The mountain condo is rented for 14 days a year to one of George's key customers for $5,000. The $5,000 is used against expenses and is included in the income statement. The property taxes are $4,000 a year and the homeowners insurance is $3,500 per year. Both taxes and insurance are paid separately from the mortgage payment. They don't want to refinance the property today because they are considering selling it and purchasing a different condo in the mountains.

Snowmobile

The Freeman's purchased four snowmobiles (two adult and two kid-sized) for a total of $25,000 four years ago in January 2009. There is no debt on the snowmobiles. The Freeman's do not have a separate property or liability insurance policy on the snowmobiles.

GMED Manufacturing, Inc. (GMED)

George started GMED Manufacturing, Inc. over 20 years ago. Today, it is one of the larger tool and die manufacturers in the area. GMED Manufacturing, Inc. has traditionally offered employees health insurance, group-term life insurance, a 401(k) plan with a Roth component and an integrated profit sharing plan. The profit sharing plan requires age 21 and one year of service for participation. George usually receives the maximum allowed for the combination of the profit sharing plan and 401(k) plan deferrals, including matching and catch-up contributions.

Emergency Fund

The Freemans have an untapped line of credit for up to $100,000. The line is unsecured and carries an interest rate of prime plus one percent.

CASE ASSUMPTIONS

1. Required return – use the required return as long as it is less than expected return based on the asset allocation. If the required return is greater than the expected return, then you should use the expected return based on the asset allocation.
2. Unless the income statement indicates otherwise, all interest, dividends and capital gains are included in the overall investment rate of return and are therefore are not reflected on the income statement. If these items were included on the income statement they would overstate the savings rate and understate the investment return.
3. For retirement and other long-term goals, assume cash and cash equivalents are added to investment accounts for purposes of projections and asset allocation decisions.

CASE 3

Trevor and Linda Gates Case

Today is January 1, 2013

INTRODUCTORY DATA

Trevor and Linda Gates have come to you, a financial planner, for help in developing a plan to accomplish their financial goals. From your initial meeting together, you have gathered the following information.

THE FAMILY

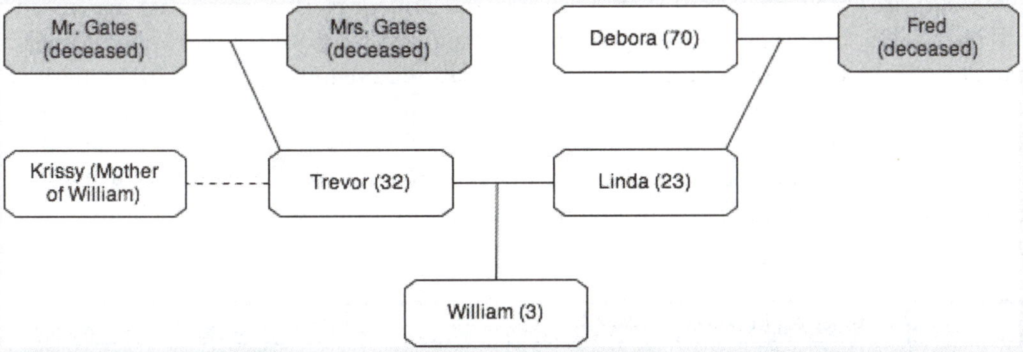

Trevor Gates (Age 32)

Trevor grew up with video games and computers. After graduating from college with a degree in computer science, Trevor joined a small internet service company, Web Ideas, Inc. (Web). Trevor has been employed with Web for the last seven years. His salary is $75,000 and he regularly receives Web stock options. In addition, Trevor generates approximately $40,000 in self-employment income from consulting work outside of Web. Trevor is also interested in starting his own internet service business three years from now.

Linda Gates (Age 23)

Linda is an assistant manager and the benefits officer for Clothes Are Us, Inc. a medium sized retail store in local shopping malls (they have several locations within the city). Clothes Are Us, Inc. operates as a C corporation. Linda began working there in high school and continued to work there throughout college and after. She currently earns $40,000, but is able to buy clothes at a substantial discount.

The Children

Trevor and Linda have been married for approximately one year and have no children together. Trevor has a son, William, from a former marriage who lives with them. William is three years old and has already begun playing on the computer, the internet, and with his dad's iPad2.

The Gates

Trevor and Linda have really enjoyed their first year of marriage and anticipate having additional children. The only sore spot in the marriage is that Trevor is required to pay $500 in alimony each month to his former wife Krissy until her death or remarriage. As per the divorce agreement, Krissy does not have to pay child support to Trevor. All of the support she provides for William is discretionary and in the form of clothes, toys, and other items she pays for out of her current budget.

Krissy does not have custody of William, but is allowed visitation on a regular basis. Krissy is a self-employed interior decorator. During 2012, she had several large jobs that lost money and for the year she ended up with expenses equaling her revenues. Fortunately, Krissy has investment portfolio income of $5,000 annually, in addition to the alimony she receives from Trevor.

Debora Trebora

Debora, who will be seventy-one years old in December of this year, is the mother of five children, including her baby, Linda. Linda was a big surprise to Debora and Fred. Fred, her late husband, died five years ago in an earthquake in Los Angeles. Fred's will created a testamentary charitable remainder unitrust (CRUT) that initially provided income to Debora of approximately $30,000 per year. The trust calls for a required unitrust payment of 8 percent to be paid each year. However, with the economic downturn, the value of the CRUT assets was devastated. Unfortunately, the assets were in no way insured and there is no possibility of recovering the losses. Today, the value of the CRUT assets is only $85,000. As a result of the enormous loss in the value of the CRUT assets, the trustee has selected new asset managers and the funds have been invested in a balanced fund expected to earn a consistent 5 percent rate of return. Debora has the following other assets:

	Value as of January 1, 2013	Notes
Cash	$250,000	Held at her local bank
Investments	$80,000	Held in her brokerage account
Fred's IRA	$134,000	
Debora's IRA*	$100,000	
Debora's Qualified Plan	$54,000	Includes a life insurance policy
Home and Furnishings	$215,000	The home is worth $150,000

Debora needs approximately $60,000 to live on each year and she receives $10,000 of that from Social Security. However, her needs have been increasing at about five percent per year. Therefore, she has been withdrawing from her asset accounts listed above to provide for her remaining financial needs. The average rate of return on her assets has been and is expected to continue to be 4 percent, excluding furnishings.

Based on her parents' ages at their death, Deborah expects to live until age 95. She is open to selling her home and moving in with one of her children to save money.

*Debora has named William as the beneficiary of her IRA, at the recommendation of her late husband Fred. Linda and her four siblings are named contingent beneficiaries of the IRA to share equally in the event that something should happen to William.

Mr. & Mrs. Gates

Unfortunately, Mr. & Mrs. Gates died in a plane crash while traveling outside the United States. While they had assets, they also had a significant amount of debt and what was left for Trevor was very minimal. Trevor is most upset that William and any other children they may have will grow up without knowing their grandparents.

Financial Goals & Concerns

1. Provide for retirement. They would like to retire when Trevor is age 62. Because of his age, he wants to plan on $155,000 in today's dollars, which is a wage replacement ratio of approximately 100%. He does not want to plan for Social Security benefits. They would like to plan on funding potential retirement expenditures until Linda turns age 95 and would like to maintain the same level of spending, even if Trevor is deceased.
2. Provide for the cost of William's college education, as well as any additional children the Gates have.
3. Provide the necessary support for Linda's mother. However, at this point, they have not needed to provide her with any financial support. When she runs out of money, they will have to support her and her expenditures will continue to increase at 5%. Deborah has a life expectancy of age 95.
4. Save enough to start an Internet company in three years. Trevor expects that he will need $300,000 at that time in today's dollars.

EXTERNAL INFORMATION

Economic Information

- Inflation is expected to be 3.0% annually.
- Salaries should increase 4.0% for the next 5 to 10 years.
- The Gates are in the 25% marginal income tax bracket.
- There is no state income tax.
- The yield curve is slightly upward sloping, but relatively flat.
- The historic and expected correlation between the equity markets in the modernized countries is relatively high. The correlation between these markets increase especially during economic crisis.
- They have a required rate of return of 10%.
- The economy is in a steady slow growth expansion phase with moderate unemployment.

Bank Lending Rates

- 15 year mortgages: 5%.
- 30 year mortgages: 6%.
- Secured personal loans: 10.0%.
- Credit cards: 18%.

Investment Return Expectations

	Return	Standard Deviation
Cash and Money Market Fund	2.5%	2.0%
Treasury Bonds/ Bond Funds	4.0%	4.0%
Corporate Bonds/ Bond Funds	6.0%	5.0%
International Bond Funds	7.0%	6.0%
Index Fund	9.0%	14.0%
Large Cap Funds/Stocks	10.0%	16.0%
Mid/Small Funds/Stocks	12.0%	18.0%
International Stock Funds	13.0%	22.0%
Real Estate Funds	8.0%	12.0%

INTERNAL INFORMATION

FINANCIAL STATEMENTS

Statement of Financial Position (Beginning of Year)

Statement of Financial Position
Trevor and Linda Gates
Balance Sheet as of 1/1/2013

ASSETS[1]				LIABILITIES AND NET WORTH			
Current Assets				**Current Liabilities[2]**			
JT	Cash & Checking	$7,194		JT	Credit Card 1	$30,000	
JT	Money Market	$25,500		H	Credit Card 2	$20,000	
Total Current Assets			$32,694	**Total Current Liabilities**			$50,000
Investment Assets				**Long-Term Liabilities**			
H	Cash Value of Life Insurance	$2,000		JT	Principal Residence	$153,735	
H	Brokerage Account[3]	$70,000		JT	Mortgage on Vacant Lot	$136,883	
H	Municipal Bonds[4]	$45,000		H	Student Loan[5]	$30,909	
H	Web Options	$475,000		H	Auto Loan	$37,211	
H	IBM Stock	$40,000		H	Brokerage Loan	$20,000	
H	Education Account	$10,000		**Total Long-Term Liabilities**			$378,738
H	401(k) Plan [6]	$96,000					
W	401(k) Plan	$20,000					
W	Traditional IRA	$20,000					
W	ESOP	$20,000					
Total Investment Assets			$798,000	**Total Liabilities**			$428,738
Personal Use Assets							
JT	Principal Residence (land $50,000)	$200,000					
H	Residential Lot	$225,000					
JT	Furniture, Clothing	$80,000		**Total Net Worth**			$980,956
H	Audi	$18,000					
H	Porsche Boxster	$55,000					
H	Kayak	$1,000					
Total Personal Use Assets			$579,000				
Total Assets			**$1,409,694**	**Total Liabilities & Net Worth**			**$1,409,694**

1. Assets are stated at fair market value.
2. Liabilities are stated at principal only as of January 1, 2013 before January payments.
3. Trevor has an outstanding margin loan – interest is 1.5% above prime.
4. The municipal bond portfolio has a modified duration of 5 and a current YTM of 7%.
5. Trevor had to take out student loans to pay for part of his college tuition.
6. Trevor's 401(k) plan has borrowing provision at 3% per year.

Title Designations:
H = Husband (Sole Owner)/W = Wife (Sole Owner)/JT = Joint Tenancy with Survivorship Rights

Statement of Income and Expenses

Statement of Income and Expenses

Trevor and Linda Gates

Statement of Income and Expenses for 2012 & Expected for 2013

Cash Inflows			
Trevor's Salary	$75,000		
Linda's Salary	$40,000		
Trevor consulting	$40,000		
Total Cash Inflows			**$155,000**
Savings			
Money Market	$1,000		
401(k) Plan - Trevor	$10,000		
401(k) Plan - Linda	$4,000		
Education (529 Plan)	$500		
Total Savings			**$15,500**
Taxes			
Federal Income Taxes Withheld	$30,000		
Trevor's Social Security Taxes	$5,738		
Linda's Social Security Taxes	$3,060		
Property tax Principal Residence	$4,000	ND	
Property tax vacant lot	$4,000	ND	
Total Taxes			**$46,798**
Debt Payments			
Principal Residence	$11,511	ND	
Mortgage on vacant lot	$15,189	ND	
Student loans	$4,015	ND	
Auto loans	$10,693	ND	
Credit Cards	$5,000	ND	
Total Debt Payments			**$46,408**
Living Expenses			
Utilities Principal Residence	$3,900	ND	
Lawn service at principal residence	$1,400	ND	
Gasoline for Autos	$4,500	ND	
Lawn Service for VACANT LOT	$900	ND	
Entertainment	$2,000		
Vacations	$2,000		
Church Donations	$500	ND	
Clothing	$3,000	ND	
Auto Maintenace	$2,000	ND	
Satelite TV	$2,000	ND	
Food	$6,000	ND	
Alimony	$6,000	ND	
Miscellaneous	$1,500	ND	
Total Living Expenses			**$35,700**
Insurance Payments			
HO Insurance Principal Residene	$3,000	ND	
Auto Insurance Premiums	$3,300	ND	
Life Insurance Policy A Premium	$2,100	ND	
Total Insurance Payments			**$8,400**
Total Cash Outflows			**$152,806**
Net Discretionary Cash Flows			**$2,194**

ND = Nondiscretionary expense

Note: Federal Income Taxes and Social Security are presumed to be discretionary as opposed to nondiscretionary because job loss is the greatest risk to the emergency fund and these expenses are not incurred in the event of a job loss.

Education Information

Trevor and Linda strongly believe in education. They want William to attend an Ivy League school for undergraduate studies and attend a very good law school. They also would like to pay for his entire seven years of school so that William can focus on his studies and not be burdened by a part-time job. The current cost of college is $55,000 per year for undergraduate and approximately $70,000 per year for a high quality law school. Tuition has been increasing annually at seven percent, which is expected to continue indefinitely.

The Gates' would like to establish an investment portfolio to be exclusively used for funding William's college tuition. Based on discussions with his broker, Trevor expects to earn an average return on investments of ten percent per year. The Gates' have $10,000 set aside for education and anticipate contributing to the fund each year until William goes to college. The funds are currently invested in a large cap mutual fund and are held at the broker's firm.

Insurance Information

Life Insurance

	Policy A	Policy B	Policy C
Insured	Trevor	Trevor	Linda
Face Amount	$250,000	$150,000	$40,000
Type	Whole Life	Group Term	Group Term
Cash Value	$2,000	$0	$0
Annual Premium	$2,100	$156	$50
Who pays premium	Trevor	Employer	Employer
Beneficiary	Trevor's Estate	Krissy	Trevor
Policy Owner	Trevor	Trevor	Linda
Settlement options clause selected	None	None	None

Health Insurance

Trevor and Linda are covered under Trevor's employer plan which is an indemnity plan with a $200 deductible per person per year and an 80/20 major medical co-insurance clause with a family annual stop loss of $1,500. The lifetime limit for major medical is $1.5 million per family member.

Long-Term Disability Insurance

Trevor is covered by an "own occupation" policy with premiums paid by his employer. The benefits equal 60% of his gross pay after a 90-day elimination period. The policy covers both sickness and accidents and is guaranteed renewable.

Linda is not covered by any disability insurance.

Homeowners Insurance

The Gates have a HO3 policy with endorsements for replacement value and open perils for personal property. The current dwelling coverage is 100% replacement value with an inflation rider.

Automobile Insurance

Both cars.

Type	PAP
Bodily Injury	$100,000/$300,000
Property Damage	$50,000
Medical Payments	$5,000 per person
Physical Damage	Actual Cash Value
Uninsured Motorist Bodily Injury	$100,000/$300,000
Uninsured Motorist Property Damage	$50,000
Comprehensive Deductible	$1,000
Collision Deductible	$1,000
Premium (annual)	$3,300

The Gates do not have a personal liability policy.

Investment Information

The Gates think that they need six months of cash flow, net of all taxes, savings, vacation, and discretionary cash flow, in an emergency fund. They are willing to include in the emergency fund the savings account and Trevor's 401(k) plan balance because it has borrowing provisions (3% per year). The Gates are not well educated in the area of investments, but like to dabble with stocks and mutual funds. They are willing to accept enough risk to accomplish their goals, but not excessive risk.

As part of a financial planning engagement, you go through the process of assessing the Gates' risk tolerance. Trevor and Linda answered the following six questions as follows. The answers below are given at the beginning of the engagement.

Risk Tolerance Questionnaire

Global Portfolio Allocation Scoring System (PASS) for Individual Investors[1]

Questions	Strongly Agree	Agree	Neutral	Disagree	Strongly Disagree
1. Earning a high long-term total return that will allow my capital to grow faster than the inflation rate is one of my most important investment objectives.	T, L				
2. I would like an investment that provides me with an opportunity to defer taxation of capital gains to future years.	T, L				
3. I do not require a high level of current income from my investments.	T, L				
4. I am willing to tolerate some sharp down swings in the return on my investments in order to seek a potentially higher return than would normally be expected from more stable investments.		T, L			
5. I am willing to risk a short-term loss in return for a potentially higher long-run rate of return.	T	L			
6. I am financially able to accept a low level of liquidity in my investment portfolio.		T, L			

T = Trevor, L = Linda

1. Global Portfolio Allocation Scoring System (PASS) for Individual Investors - developed by Dr. William Droms (Georgetown University) and Steven N. Strauss, (DromsStrauss Advisors Inc.) - model used with permission.

Portfolio Information

Gates Portfolio Information 12/31/12

Total Portfolio*		
Cash and Cash Equivalents Plus Investments		
	Dollars	**%**
Cash	$52,694	6%
Fixed income	$113,000	14%
US Equities	$663,000	80%
Foreign Equities	$0	0%
Total	**$828,694**	**100%**

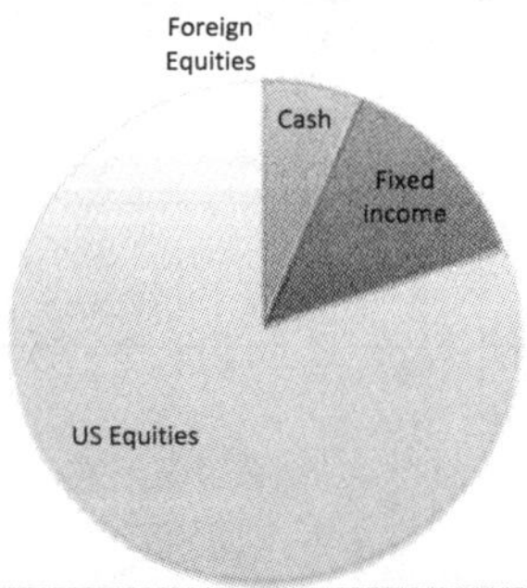

Excludes Cash Value of Life Insurance

Account	Cash	Bonds	US Equities	Foreign Equities	Total
Cash	$32,694				$32,694
Brokerage account			$70,000		$70,000
Municipal bonds		$45,000			$45,000
Web Options			$475,000		$475,000
IBM Stock			$40,000		$40,000
Education Account			$10,000		$10,000
401(k) Plan		$48,000	$48,000		$96,000
401(k) Plan	$20,000				$20,000
Traditional IRA		$20,000			$20,000
ESOP			$20,000		$20,000
					$0
Total	$52,694	$113,000	$663,000	$0	$828,694

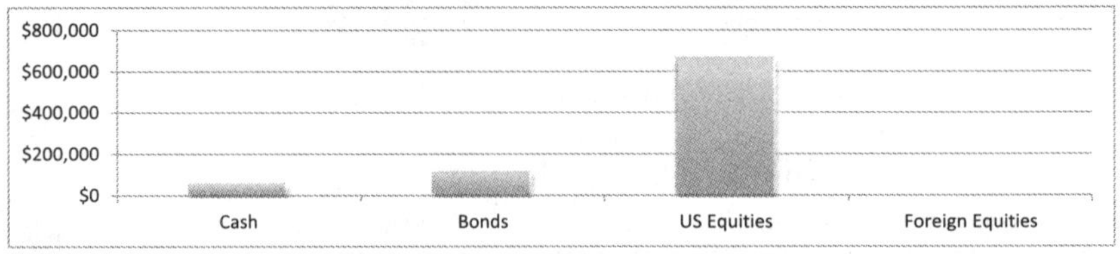

Total Portfolio - Account Types		
	Dollars	**%**
Taxable	$662,694	80%
Education	$10,000	1%
Tax Deferred	$156,000	19%
Roth Accounts	$0	0%
Total	**$828,694**	**100%**

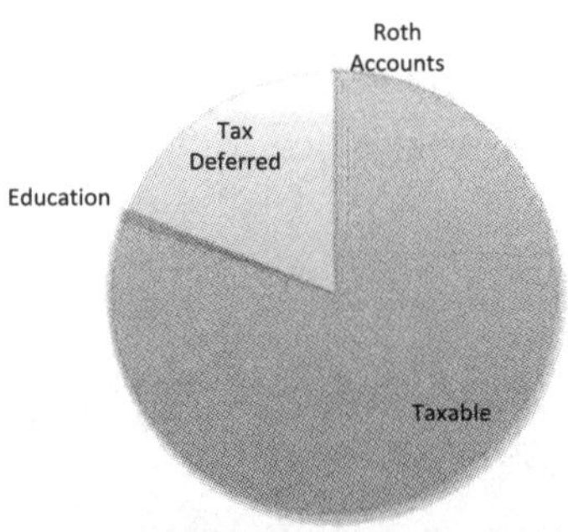

Excludes Cash Value of Life Insurance

Account	Taxable	Education	Tax Deferred	Roth	Total
Cash	$32,694				$32,694
Brokerage account	$70,000				$70,000
Municipal bonds	$45,000				$45,000
Web Options	$475,000				$475,000
IBM Stock	$40,000				$40,000
Education Account		$10,000			$10,000
401(k) Plan			$96,000		$96,000
401(k) Plan			$20,000		$20,000
Traditional IRA			$20,000		$20,000
ESOP			$20,000		$20,000
					$0
					$0
Total	$662,694	$10,000	$156,000	$0	$828,694

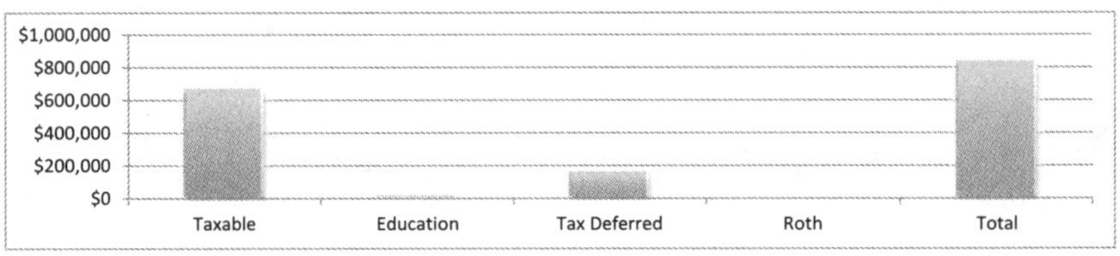

Trevor's Internet Company

Trevor is in the information-gathering phase of owning his own web-based company. He expects the company to have losses for the first several years due to the cost of capital that will be required and the necessary marketing and advertising expenses to establish brand recognition. In addition, he believes that he may need the assistance of a venture capital firm to provide some of the funding necessary for the company after it is up and running. However, he is unsure about this at this stage.

IBM Stock

Trevor believes that IBM is strategically positioned to prosper. IBM currently retains 80 percent of their profits for the purpose of growing the business. This policy has allowed them to grow their dividend every year at about seven percent. Trevor thinks that this is one of his best investments. Trevor acquired the 200 shares of IBM stock when his Uncle Steve died three months ago. The stock price on the date of death opened at 180, closed at 190, had a high of 196 and a low of 178. Uncle Steve had acquired the stock 4 weeks before his death for $195 per share, including commissions.

Other Information Regarding Assets and Liabilities

Home and Furnishings

They purchased their home 36 months ago for $200,000 and financed 80 percent of the sale price at six percent for 30 years. They considered refinancing, but their FICO score is 530 due to recent late payments on credit cards recently. They plan to sell or lease this property once their dream home is built.

Their home furnishings are relatively normal. However, Trevor inherited his great grandfather's grandfather clock, which has great sentimental value to Trevor. Trevor believes the value of the clock to be about $5,000.

Automobile

Linda's Audi is several years old and is fully paid off. Trevor has just purchased a 2012 Black Porsche Boxster S with a six-speed manual transmission one year ago. He purchased the car for $60,000, made a deposit of $15,000 and financed the remaining balance over five years at seven percent. They both love the Porsche and how they look in it.

Residential Lot

Trevor and Linda have been dreaming of building a large house and so they decided to purchase a vacant lot for $225,000. Not having sufficient cash to purchase it outright, they made a down payment of $75,000 and financed the remainder over fifteen years at 6 percent with a balloon after five years. Their first payment was 24 months ago. They have no time table for building at this time. However, under no conditions will they consider selling the lot as it took them years to find it.

Student Loans

Trevor had to take out loans to pay for college. He borrowed a total of $40,000 to be repaid over 20 years at eight percent.

Web Options

Trevor has a variety of incentive stock options (ISOs) and non-qualified stock options (NQSOs) that he has received as part of his compensation at Web. The following table below lists each of the option grants including the exercise price and grant date.

Year	Grant	Grant Date	Options Granted	Exercise Price	Vesting
2008	1	09/01/08	5,000	$35	5 years
2009	2	10/15/09	10,000	$25	5 years
2010	3	09/02/10	10,000	$15	5 years
2011	4	09/01/11	15,000	$25	5 years
2012	5	09/01/12	10,000	$28	5 years

The company grants the maximum number of ISOs to Trevor every year and the exercise price is always equal to the FMV of the stock on the date of grant. The current price of Web stock is $34 per share. The options vest over five years with 20 percent vesting each year.

Trevor is generally optimistic about the company's future. However, he is concerned about some of Web's competitors and a new technology that is emerging. Web is responding, but it is unclear how it could impact the company. Web has never issued any cash dividends, stock dividends or had any stock splits.

Clothes Are Us

Linda is the benefits administrator for her company's retirement plans. The company sponsors a 401(k) plan and an ESOP. Following is a list of employees with census information:

Name	Position	Ownership	Prior Year Salary	401(k) Deferral Percentage
Amy Gomez[1]	Founder	51%	$0	0%
Jenny Camile[2]	Co-founder & Manager	15%	$65,000	10%
Linda Gates	Asst. Manager	2.6%	$40,000	10%
Russ Ricardo	Sales Associate	2.3%	$92,000	7%
Henrietta Hynes	Sales Associate	3.0%	$88,000	8%
Ingred Iberson	Sales Associate	5.0%	$48,000	8%
Brad Larson	Sales Associate	1.5%	$37,000	6%
Allison Ulysses	Sales Associate	0.9%	$50,000	4%
David Gomez[3]	Clerk	0.2%	$25,000	0%
Nancy Miller	Clerk	0.5%	$18,000	0%

1. Amy Gomez is not an employee and has not been one for ten years.
2. Jenny Camile runs the business, with assistance from Linda.
3. David is the grandson of Amy Gomez.

The 401(k) plan permits elective deferral contributions up to 80% of an employee's compensation. There is no matching contribution. However, the company does contribute to the ESOP in profitable years, although no contribution was made during 2012 to the ESOP. The remaining ownership of the company is held by the trustee of the ESOP. The ownership in the above table reflects the total stock owned by each person, including stock owned via the ESOP. The business is valued annually for ESOP purposes by an outside appraiser, however, there was no change in value from last year to this year.

CASE ASSUMPTIONS

1. Required return – use the required return as stated in the case.
2. Unless the income statement indicates otherwise, all interest, dividends and capital gains are reinvested and included in the overall investment rate of return and, are therefore, not reflected on the income statement. If these items were included on the income statement they would overstate the savings rate and understate the investment return.
3. Trevor and Linda have included the full value of the options on the balance sheet without regard to the vesting of the options.
4. For retirement and other long-term goals, assume cash and cash equivalents are added to investment accounts for purposes of projections and asset allocation decisions.
5. Assume that the discretionary income (deficit) adds to (subtracts from) the annual savings amount.
6. Debt – assume that the equity in their current home would be used for any purchase of a new house and that there would not be any additional savings from paying off their residence prior to retirement age. In addition, assume there is no savings of the auto loan since they would likely purchase additional new cars over time.
7. After Debora exhausts her assets, then Trevor will pay for her annual expenses to age 95 and they are expected to increase at 5%.
8. They will not consider selling the lot.

CASE

Alvin and Fran Jackson Case 4

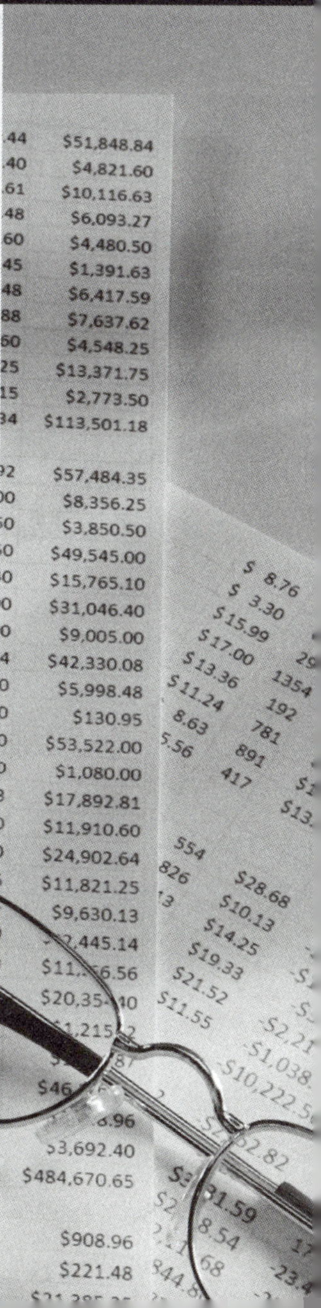

Today is January 2, 2013

INTRODUCTORY DATA

Alvin and Fran came to you, a financial planner, as a referral from the CFP Board's Make A Plan marketing outreach program. They are in the asset accumulation and risk management phases of life and need help determining how much to save so they can send their three boys to college while also securing their own retirement. They have learned that you need to be flexible when you have three children because things change, sometimes frequently and often unexpectedly. They want their financial plan to be flexible enough to meet their goals. They believe they will benefit from meeting with a CERTIFIED FINANCIAL PLANNER ™ practitioner and arrived with the following information for you to assist them in creating a plan to meet their financial goals.

THE FAMILY

Alvin Jackson, age 43, works at Mach Speed Company, a family owned firm that supplies the aerospace industry. Alvin has been with the company for 16 years. He plans to retire with 35 years of service at age 62. Alvin grew up in Idaho but moved to Seattle to attend college which is where he met and married Fran 20 years ago. They lived and worked in Seattle until Alvin was offered a higher paying job at Mach Speed which is located south of Seattle in Laplace, Washington.

Fran Jackson, age 43, grew up in Wisconsin and loves the outdoors. She moved to Seattle after high school to be close to the Pacific Ocean and milder weather. Fran learned to surf and spent a great deal of time in, on and around the water. She enjoyed the water so much that she became interested in fluid dynamics and decided to attend college. College is where she met Alvin, who also enjoyed the natural beauty and outdoor activities of the Pacific Northwest. Fran has been in and out of the work force due to having three children, but has been with her current employer, Water Striders, for five years. She expects to work until age 62.

Alvin and Fran have three children: Curly (age 12), Larry (age 8) and Moe (age 6). The boys attend public school. They are intelligent and athletic with college prospects. However, Alvin and Fran do not want to rely on the boys' ability to obtain athletic or merit-based scholarships to attend college. They want to save enough money to provide each boy with 5 years of college at State University, beginning at age 18.

Financial Goals & Concerns (in order of priority)

1. Retirement at age 62 with 80% of preretirement income including Social Security. Life expectancy is 96 for both.
2. College education of children for 5 years, each beginning at age 18, at the state university.
3. Appropriate risk management portfolio, investment portfolio, and estate planning portfolio.
4. They plan on buying a vacation home in 19 years in Colorado at a price of $350,000 in today's dollars.
5. They will not sell the movie collection and may add to it.

EXTERNAL INFORMATION

Economic Information

- General inflation is expected to average 3.0% annually for the foreseeable future.
- Education inflation is expected to be 6.0% annually.
- They live in the state of Washington which has no state income tax.
- Raises are uncertain but in the long-run are expected to be equal to general inflation (CPI).
- The economy is in a slow growth recovery from a recession with moderate to high unemployment.

Bank Lending Rates

- 15-year conforming rate mortgage is 3.75%.
- 30-year conforming rate mortgage is 4.00%.
- Any closing costs associated with any mortgage refinance are an additional 3% of any amount mortgaged and will be paid directly (i.e., not included in the new mortgage).
- They plan to stay in their home through retirement and are more concerned about cash flow and possible monthly savings than the term of debt associated with the home.

Investment Return Expectations

- General market for stocks is expected to return 9.5%.
- The Jackson's required rate of return is 8%.
- Fixed income investments are expected to earn 6%.
- T-Bills are expected to yield 3% per year and are the proxy for the risk-free rate of return.

INTERNAL INFORMATION

FINANCIAL STATEMENTS

Statement of Financial Position (Beginning of Year)

Statement of Financial Position
Alvin and Fran Jackson
Balance Sheet as of 1/1/2013

ASSETS[1]				LIABILITIES AND NET WORTH			
Current Assets				**Current Liabilities[2]**			
JT	Cash & Checking	$22,000		W	Credit Cards	$20,116	
Total Current Assets			$22,000	**Total Current Liabilities**			$20,116
Investment Assets				**Long-Term Liabilities[2]**			
JT	Stock Portfolio	$200,000		JT	Principal Residence[3]	$279,884	
H	401(k) Mach Speed	$250,000		JT	Autos	$40,000	
W	IRA Rollover Account	$28,000					
Total Investment Assets			$478,000	**Total Long-Term Liabilities**			$319,884
Personal Use Assets							
JT	Principal Residence [3]	$300,000		**Total Liabilities**			$340,000
JT	Autos	$40,000					
H	Old movie collection of 3 Stooges original Soundtrack	$100,000					
JT	Furniture and Fixtures	$100,000		**Total Net Worth**			$800,000
W	Jewelry	$50,000					
JT	Other, Clothing	$50,000					
Total Personal Use Assets			$640,000				
Total Assets			$1,140,000	**Total Liabilities & Net Worth**			$1,140,000

1. Assets are stated at fair market value.
2. Liabilities are stated at principal only as of January 1, 2013 before January payments.
3. Bought 12 years ago at $400,000 with 10% down and 30 year mortgage at 5.5%. They have 216 payments remaining. Unfortunately, the value of the residence has fallen to $300,000. Land value is $50,000.

* Federal income tax refund or liability for 2012 has not been determined and is not included.

Statement of Income and Expenses Alvin and Fran Jackson Statement of Income and Expenses for 2012 and Projected for 2013			
Cash Inflows			**Totals**
Alvin's Salary	$75,000		
Fran's Salary	$50,000		
Total Cash Inflows			$125,000
Cash Outflows			
Savings			
401(k) Plan - Alvin	$7,500		
Total Savings			$7,500
Taxes			
Federal Income Taxes Withheld	$17,625		
Alvin's Social Security Taxes	$5,738		
Fran's Social Security Taxes	$3,825		
Property Tax Principal Residence	$4,300	ND	
Total Taxes			$31,488
Debt Payments (Principal & Interest)			
Principal Residence	$24,528	ND	
Auto	$13,333	ND	
Credit Cards	$12,000	ND	
Total Debt Payments			$49,861
Living Expenses			
Utilities Principal Residence	$5,000	ND	
Child Care	$3,600	ND	
Auto Maintenance and Gasoline	$6,000	ND	
Entertainment and Vacations	$3,000		
Church Donations	$600		
Food	$10,000	ND	
Children's Field Trips, Lunches, Allowances	$800	ND	
Lawn and Cleaning Services	$1,400		
Clothing	$3,000	ND	
Miscellaneous	$0	ND	
Total Living Expenses			$33,400
Insurance Payments			
HO Insurance Principal Residence	$3,600	ND	
Life Insurance	$3,000	ND	
Health Insurance	$5,000	ND	
Disability Insurance	$1,200	ND	
Auto Insurance	$2,400	ND	
Total Insurance Payments			$15,200
Total Cash Outflows			$137,449
Net Discretionary Cash Flows			($12,449)

**All numbers rounded to nearest $.*
ND - Non-discretionary cash flow per mutual understanding between financial planner and client.

Insurance Information

Life Insurance

Policy	A	B	C	D
Insured	Fran	Alvin	Fran	Alvin
Life	$50,000	$50,000	$100,000	$225,000
Employer Provided	Yes	Yes	Owned Fran	Owned Alvin
Type	Group Term	Group Term	Term	Term
Beneficiary	Alvin	Fran	Alvin	Fran
Contingent Beneficiary	Children	Children	Children	Children
Premium (Annual)	$500	$750	$1,000	$2,000

Health Insurance

Group Major Medical	
Alvin's Group Major Medical $500,000 Life Time Benefit $3,000 Stop Loss (annual) $300 Deductible per Person 80/20 Co-insurance for Major Medical Premium-Employer provided for Alvin only. Alvin pays for the rest of the family $5,000 year after tax.	If he wants to purchase supplemental first dollar coverage and increase his lifetime benefits to $1,000,000 per person, he can do it for $1,200 per year.

Disability Insurance

Alvin's disability policy has an option to increase the elimination period to 180 days which would reduce the current annual premium from $1,200 to $800.

	Alvin	Fran
Coverage (sickness and accident); Hybrid (own and any EET)	5 yr / to age 65	None
Personally Owned	Yes	
Residual Disability Provision	Yes	
Benefit	60% of gross pay	
Benefit Term	to age 65	
Elimination Period (can be changed)	90	
Premium	$1,200 per year	

Own = own occupation, EET = experienced, educated, and trained

Long-Term Care Insurance

Neither Alvin nor Fran have long-term care insurance.

Property and Liability Insurance

Alvin and Fran met with their insurance professional who recommended that they could increase the deductibles on their homeowners insurance (savings of $1,200 per year) and auto insurance policies (savings of $300 per year) and add a rider to insure their collectibles (cost of $300 per year). Net total savings, if implemented, is estimated to be $1,200 per year.

Homeowners Insurance

Personal Residence	
Type	HO3 with endorsements
Dwelling	$250,000
Other Structures	$100,000
Personal Property	$150,000
Loss of Use (20% of dwelling)	$50,000
Deductible	$200
Premium (annually)	$3,600

Auto Insurance

Auto	
Type	Personal Automobile Policy (PAP) with $250 deductible for comprehensive and collision
Liability (Bodily Injury)	$100,000/$300,000/$50,000
Medical Payments	$25,000
Uninsured Motorist	$100,000/$50,000
Collision Deductible	$250
Other than Collision	$250
Towing and Labor	None
Annual Premium	$2,400

Liability Insurance (Personal Liability Umbrella)

Neither Alvin nor Fran have liability insurance. Coverage of this type is estimated to cost $240.00 per year for $1,000,000.

Education Information

- College costs at State University are currently $18,000 per child, per year in today's dollars or $72,000 for a four year degree.
- Alvin and Fran have been told that Washington State does not offer a 529 college savings plan, but it does operate a unit-type prepaid tuition program (GET). Each unit purchased through GET is redeemable for one percent of the resident undergraduate tuition at the highest-priced public university in Washington. The units may also be used for eligible educational institutions across the country. Washington State's GET program is backed by the full faith and credit of the State, which is unlike other states' 529 guarantees. However, they are concerned about the payout period since Curly is only six years away from entering college. They also want the flexibility to use any excess funds saved for their retirement should any of the boys get scholarships or decide not to attend college.
- If Alvin and Fran do not purchase the GET pre-paid tuition program in Washington State they might want to invest in another state's 529 savings plan.
- They tell you they have been discussing the idea of purchasing a second home in College City where they expect the boys to attend State University. They explain they would like to use proceeds from the 529 Savings Plan to purchase a home for the boys, or if necessary, purchase the home themselves and charge the boys' 529 Plan accounts rent to reflect room and board. If this is possible, they would sell the College City home when Moe finishes college and use the proceeds from the sale to purchase a Colorado vacation home for the entire family.
- They plan to pay the fall costs of college education so the children will have no debt and will not have to work during college so they can concentrate on their studies.

Investment Information

Risk Tolerance Questionnaire

Global Portfolio Allocation Scoring System (PASS) for Individual Investors[1]

Questions	Strongly Agree	Agree	Neutral	Disagree	Strongly Disagree
1. Earning a high long-term total return that will allow my capital to grow faster than the inflation rate is one of my most important investment objectives.	A,F				
2. I would like an investment that provides me with an opportunity to defer taxation of capital gains to future years.	A,F				
3. I do not require a high level of current income from my investments.	A,F				
4. I am willing to tolerate some sharp down swings in the return on my investments in order to seek a potentially higher return than would normally be expected from more stable investments.	F		A		
5. I am willing to risk a short-term loss in return for a potentially higher long-run rate of return.		F		A	
6. I am financially able to accept a low level of liquidity in my investment portfolio.			A,F		

A = Alvin, F = Fran

Stock Portfolio

The Jackson Stock Portfolio						Recent Returns (Total)				
Stock	Quantity Shares	FMV	Annual Dividend	Beta	Tax Basis	2008	2009	2010	2011	2012
A	100	$30,000	$1.00	1.20	$19,150	8	10	10	11	8
B	300	$75,000	$0.30	1.40	$52,452	9	5	(3)	12	15
C	400	$60,000	$0.70	0.90	$43,187	6	7	7	8	6
D	250	$35,000	$0	1.15	$23,389	7	8	8	9	10
		$200,000								

The coefficient of correlation between the market and the stock portfolio is 0.7% over the past 5 years. The market has yielded a geometric return of 6.8%.

1. Global Portfolio Allocation Scoring System (PASS) for Individual Investors - developed by Dr. William Droms (Georgetown University) and Steven N. Strauss, (DromsStrauss Advisors Inc.) - model used with permission.

Alvin and Fran tell you that they have owned these stocks since January of 2008 and believe they are all good stocks. They provided the tax basis for each stock (above) and want to know which stock or stocks should be sold to fund whatever they decide to do with regard to the 529 Plans or additional IRA contributions they are contemplating.

Portfolio Information

Alvin and Fran Jackson Portfolio Information 12/31/12

Total Portfolio

Cash and Cash Equivalents Plus Investments

	Dollars	%
Cash	$22,000	4%
Fixed income	$160,000	32%
US Equities	$318,000	64%
Foreign Equities	$0	0%
Total	**$500,000**	**100%**

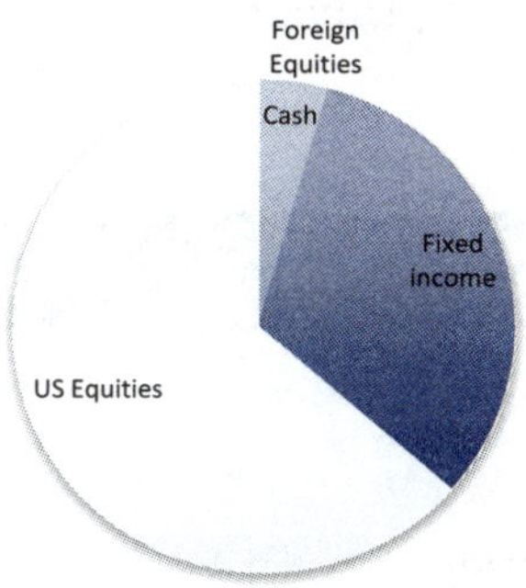

Account	Cash	Bonds	US Equities	Foreign Equities	Total
Cash	$22,000				$22,000
Brokerage account			$200,000		$200,000
401(k) Plan		$160,000	$90,000		$250,000
IRA Rollover			$28,000		$28,000
Total	$22,000	$160,000	$318,000	$0	$500,000

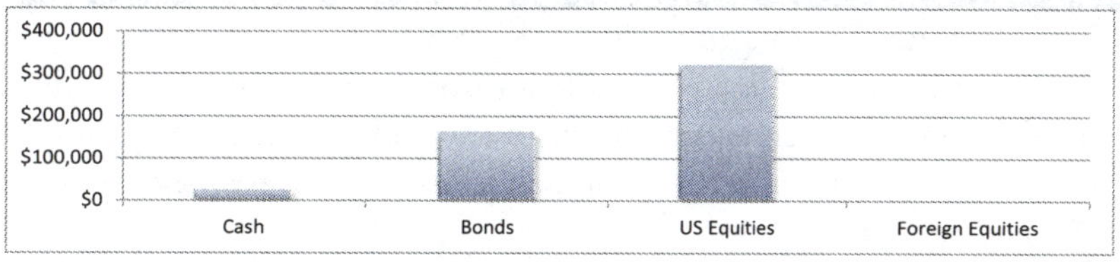

Total Portfolio - Account Types

	Dollars	%
Taxable	$222,000	44%
Education	$0	0%
Tax Deferred	$278,000	56%
Roth Accounts	$0	0%
Total	**$500,000**	**100%**

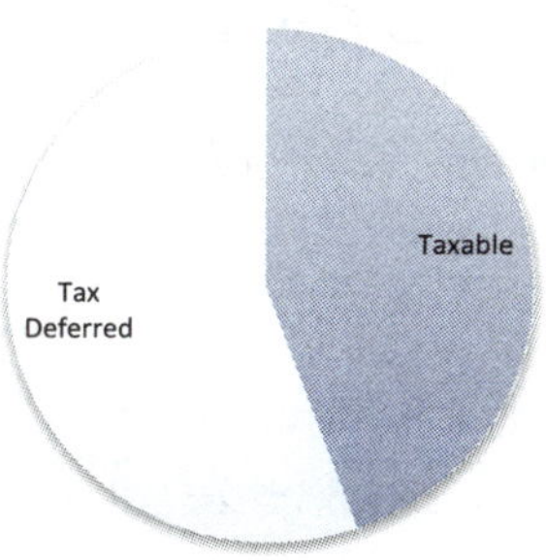

Account	Taxable	Education	Tax Deferred	Roth	Total
Cash	$22,000				$22,000
Brokerage account	$200,000				$200,000
401(k) Plan			$250,000		$250,000
IRA Rollover			$28,000		$28,000
Total	$222,000	$0	$278,000	$0	$500,000

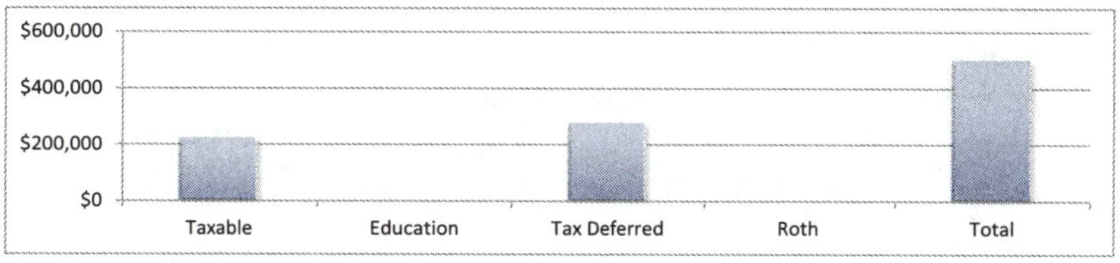

Retirement Information

- Both Alvin and Fran have similar 401(k) profit sharing plans at their respective employers. The plans are safe harbor plans with an employer match of 1% for the first 3% contributed and ½% for any contribution greater than 3% up to 5%. The total possible employer match is 4% of each salary.
- Alvin participates in his employer's plan contributing 10% of his annual salary. They would like for Fran to participate in her employer's plan but she has not signed up yet.
- Alvin and Fran are also interested in contributing to traditional IRA accounts for the tax deduction and want to know your thoughts on such a contribution.

Estate Planning Information

Alvin and Fran have no legal or estate planning documents. While they do not expect to take care of their parents they also do not expect to receive any inheritances from their parents or grandparents.

They want to take care of each other and leave any remaining assets in trust for their boys. They tell you that they dislike paying taxes and remind you that they like flexibility. They ask if their estate planning documents can be drafted to reflect these preferences.

CASE ASSUMPTIONS

1. Alvin and Fran expect to live to age 96.
2. They have a moderate risk tolerance and a required rate of return of 8%.
3. The children's child care expenses are paid to a child care center.
4. They will refinance their home, if possible, and use the additional cash flow to fund savings for retirement, college or both.
5. They will pay any expected expenses from refinancing from their investment account.
6. They want to buy a vacation home in Colorado for $350,000 in today's dollars in 19 years (2032), but would accelerate the purchase of a second home if they could use proceeds from 529 accounts to purchase a home for the boys to live in while in college. They would sell the College City property after Moe completes his degree and use the proceeds to purchase a vacation home for the entire family in Colorado.
7. Alvin's parents are retired and live on their savings and Social Security. They have told Alvin and his brothers, Theodore and Simon, that they have purchased long-term care insurance so they would not be a burden to anyone.
8. Fran's parents are also retired with a pension and social security. They have not purchased long-term care insurance. Fran tells you there is no history of Alzheimer's on either side of her family and that all of her grandparents are still alive and well, living in retirement communities in Arizona and Florida.
9. Alvin's Social Security retirement benefit at normal retirement age of 67 is $2,250 per month in today's dollars. Fran's Social Security retirement benefit at normal retirement age of 67 is $1,800 per month in today's dollars.
10. Alvin and Fran want to retire at age 62.
11. They purchased a luxury SUV at the beginning of last year and financed $53,333 for 48 months at 0% interest. They pay $1,111.10 per month ($13,333 per year).

Unit Prices Over Time

The GET unit price is established through a complex actuarial formula which accommodates projected tuition increases, projected investment returns, a stabilization reserve and administrative costs. It has increased annually since the program began.

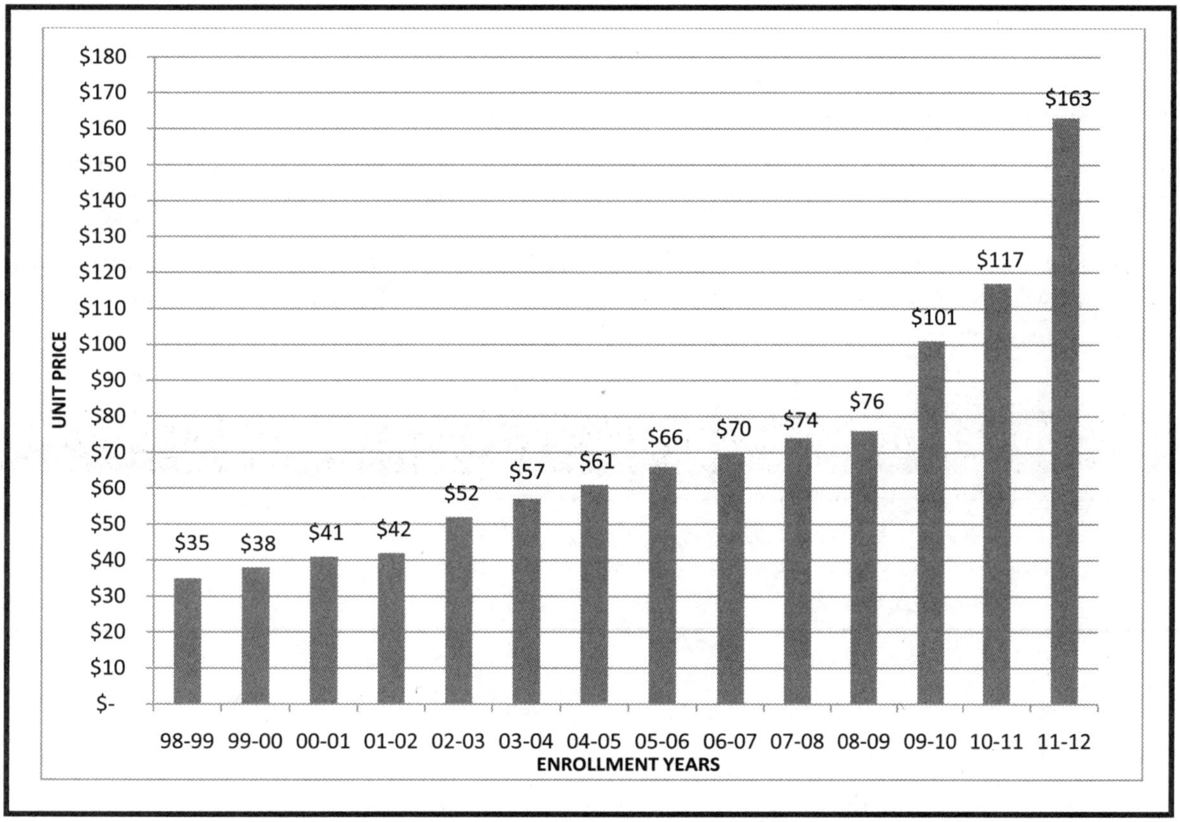

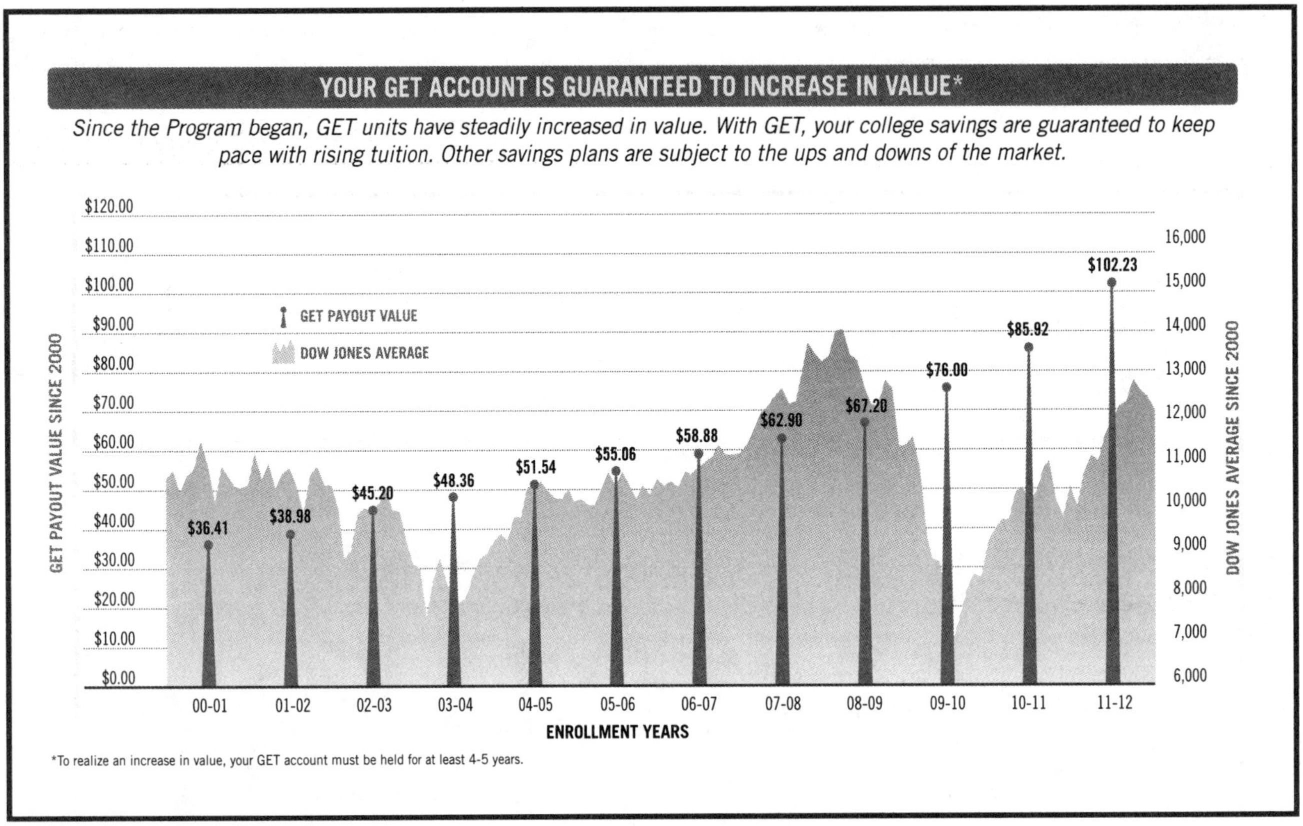
YOUR GET ACCOUNT IS GUARANTEED TO INCREASE IN VALUE*
Since the Program began, GET units have steadily increased in value. With GET, your college savings are guaranteed to keep pace with rising tuition. Other savings plans are subject to the ups and downs of the market.
GET PAYOUT VALUE
DOW JONES AVERAGE
GET PAYOUT VALUE SINCE 2000
DOW JONES AVERAGE SINCE 2000
ENROLLMENT YEARS
$120.00
$110.00
$100.00
$90.00
$80.00
$70.00
$60.00
$50.00
$40.00
$30.00
$20.00
$10.00
$0.00
16,000
15,000
14,000
13,000
12,000
11,000
10,000
9,000
8,000
7,000
6,000
00-01
01-02
02-03
03-04
04-05
05-06
06-07
07-08
08-09
09-10
10-11
11-12
$36.41
$38.98
$45.20
$48.36
$51.54
$55.06
$58.88
$62.90
$67.20
$76.00
$85.92
$102.23
*To realize an increase in value, your GET account must be held for at least 4-5 years.

CASE

Sharon Laynee Case 5

Today is January 1, 2013

INTRODUCTORY DATA

Sharon Laynee came to you, a financial planner, as a referral from one of your other clients. Sharon and her long-time husband, Dick, were divorced about two years ago. The divorce was costly to Sharon and negatively impacted her financial condition. As a result of the property settlement, Sharon was ordered to transfer assets to Dick and to pay him alimony. The alimony payments are a component of Sharon's deficit spending. Sharon also has a daughter, son-in-law and granddaughter living with her as well as a mother who may need financial help in the next ten years. She wants to help her mother and Amy, her daughter, but needs your assistance in getting her own finances under control before she can help the rest of her family. From your initial meeting together, you have gathered the following information.

THE FAMILY

Sharon Laynee (Age 50)

Sharon met her ex-husband Dick in college and they married after Sharon graduated. While in college, Sharon made connections with two other students that allowed the three of them to start their own business, Petro King, a C-corporation. The business prospered such that years later Sharon's income and Sharon and Dick's assets are the result of this early and lucrative investment. Sharon and Dick had one child, Amy. Dick was a stay-at-home dad. After Amy started school, Dick was used to staying home and did not pursue outside employment. As a result of the divorce, Sharon was ordered to pay $8,000 a month in alimony to Dick (age 58) until he is 65 years old. She is in excellent health.

Lucy (Age 75, Dependent)

Lucy, a wonderful mother and good judge of character, never liked Dick. She was unhappy with Sharon's marriage to Dick but was thrilled when their first and only child, her first grandchild, Amy, was born. Lucy's husband, Argus, died a few years ago. Argus never liked insurance companies and did not anticipate a need for long-term care insurance. He left

Lucy a modest investment portfolio that would have sustained Lucy through her life expectancy, had she not developed Alzheimer's. Unfortunately, she has no memory and Sharon found it was in Lucy's best interest to live in a facility for patients with Alzheimer's. Doctors tell Sharon her mother has a 20 year life expectancy and Sharon wants to ensure that when Lucy's resources run out, which is projected to be in 10 years, Lucy can stay in the Alzheimer's facility until her death.

Amy (Age 28, Daughter) and Her Family

Sharon has one child, Amy, age 28, who is married to John also age 28. Amy and John have one child, Allison, age 3. Amy and her family moved in with Sharon at the beginning of last year. John was recently discharged (honorably) from the Army and has found a part-time job to provide income while he uses his veteran's benefits to return to school. He needs two years to earn an undergraduate degree in engineering. Amy and John want to live with Sharon while John is in school, and Sharon is happy to have her daughter and granddaughter in close proximity. Sharon is concerned that her deficit spending will increase as she continues to provide a home for Amy, John and Allison.

Allison, age 3, is a beautiful and intelligent child. Amy plans to stay home with Allison while John is working part-time and in school. Allison's art work is extraordinary for a child her age. Sharon and Allison's parents believe Allison's talent is a predictor of a multi-faceted and talented adult. They want to ensure that Allison is given every chance to develop her many talents and attend a quality college. Sharon has decided to create a college fund for Allison. Current annual tuition is $30,000 and is expected to increase at 6%.

FINANCIAL GOALS & CONCERNS

1. Determine Sharon's tax filing status. Whatever her filing status, Sharon has informed you that she will spend any refund she gets.
2. Determine how she can increase her monthly cash flow and/or reduce her monthly expenses.
3. Retire at age 65 with annual income of $200,000 in today's dollars including Social Security estimated to be $25,000 per year at full retirement age (in today's dollars).
4. Provide for her mother, Lucy, who has a life expectancy of approximately 20 years.
5. Provide a quality college education for Allison.
6. Review and update her risk management plan and investment portfolio.
7. Create an estate plan.
8. Sharon is unwilling to sell her antiques or her car. She says they make her the new Sharon.

EXTERNAL INFORMATION

ECONOMIC INFORMATION

- Inflation is expected to be 3% annually.
- Salary increases are expected to be 7% for 1-2 years, then at the inflation rate.
- Education inflation is expected to be 6% annually.
- They all live in Nevada which has no state income tax.
- The economy is in a slow growth recovery from a recession with moderate to high unemployment.
- Real GDP has been 2.75% and is expected to continue to be 2.75% for the next several years.
- It is expected that the S&P 500 will return approximately 9% this year and for the foreseeable future.
- T-bills are considered the appropriate proxy for the risk-free rate of return and are currently earning 2.5%.

Bank Lending Rates

- 15 year mortgages 3.75%.
- 30 year mortgages 4.0%.
- The prime rate is 3.25%.
- The secured personal loan rate is 8.0%.
- Credit card rates are 18%.

Investment Return Expectations

	Return	Standard Deviation
Cash and Money Market Fund	2.5%	2.0%
Treasury Bonds/ Bond Funds	4.0%	4.0%
Corporate Bonds/ Bond Funds	6.0%	5.0%
International Bond Funds	7.0%	6.0%
Index Fund	9.0%	14.0%
Large Cap Funds/Stocks	10.0%	16.0%
Mid/Small Funds/Stocks	12.0%	18.0%
International Stock Funds	13.0%	22.0%
Real Estate Funds	8.0%	12.0%

INTERNAL INFORMATION

FINANCIAL STATEMENTS

Statement of Financial Position (Beginning of Year)

Statement of Financial Position Sharon Laynee Balance Sheet as of 1/1/2013					
ASSETS[1]			**LIABILITIES[2] AND NET WORTH**		
Current Assets			**Current Liabilities**		
Cash & Checking	$30,000		Credit Cards	$0	
Money Market	$25,000				
Total Current Assets		$55,000	**Total Current Liabilities**		$0
Investment Assets			**Long-Term Liabilities**		
Petro King Interest[3]	$1,000,000		Principal Residence[4]	$600,000	
Investment Portfolio A	$400,000		Auto Loan[5]	$100,000	
401(k) Plan[6]	$0				
Total Investment Assets		$1,400,000	**Total Long-Term Liabilities**		$700,000
Personal Use Assets					
Principal Residence	$800,000		**Total Liabilities[7]**		$700,000
Furniture, Clothing	$150,000				
Car	$100,000				
Antique Collection	$100,000		**Total Net Worth**		$1,955,000
Miscellaneous	$50,000				
Total Personal Use Assets		$1,200,000			
Total Assets[7]		**$2,655,000**	**Total Liabilities & Net Worth**		**$2,655,000**

1. Assets are stated at fair market value.
2. Liabilities are stated at principal only as of January 1, 2013 before January payments.
3. This is Sharon's 30% interest in Petro King and the value is based on appraisal. The value of the Petro King C-Corporation is based on an appraisal and the fact that she has a put option to sell (based on the appraisal price) anytime she wants to up to age 65, when she is required to sell. The company is valued annually and there are no minority or liquidity discounts considered. The growth rate for the company is 3% per year.
4. Home loan original balance of $883,662 financed at 5% for 30 years. Payments are $56,937 per year.
5. Vehicle was purchased post divorce for $133,334 and financed at 0% for 8 years. Payments are $16,667 per year.
6. Sharon transferred her entire 401(k) plan balance to her husband as part of the divorce. They only settled the property agreement as of 1/1/2013. That is why the 2012 401(k) plan contribution is not on the balance sheet.
7. This schedule does not include any projected federal income tax refund or federal income tax liability for the prior year.

Statement of Income and Expenses Sharon Laynee Statement of Income and Expenses for 2012			
CASH INFLOWS			**Totals**
Sharon's Salary	$350,000		
Total Cash Inflows			$350,000
CASH OUTFLOWS			
Savings			
401(k) Plan Contributions	$22,500		
Total Savings			$22,500
Taxes			
Federal Income Taxes Withheld	$75,000		
Sharon's Social Security Taxes	$11,896		
Property Tax Principal Residence	$15,000	ND	
Total Fixed Outflows			$101,896
Debt Payments (Principal & Interest)			
Principal Residence	$56,937	ND	
Auto Loan	$16,667	ND	
Alimony	$96,000	ND	
Credit Cards	$4,000	ND	
Total Debt Payments			$173,604
Living Expenses			
Utilities Principal Residence	$5,000	ND	
Gasoline for Auto	$5,000	ND	
Lawn Service	$2,000	ND	
Entertainment	$0		
Vacations	$0		
Auto Maintenance	$15,000	ND	
Clothing	$18,000	ND	
Satellite TV	$1,800	ND	
Food	$8,000	ND	
Miscellaneous	$10,000	ND	
Total Living Expenses			$64,800
Insurance Payments			
HO Insurance Principal Residence	$6,000	ND	
Auto Premiums	$1,200	ND	
Total Insurance Payments			$7,200
Total Cash Outflows			$370,000
NET DISCRETIONARY CASH FLOWS			($20,000)

ND = Non-Discretionary cash flows per mutual understanding between financial planner and client.

Insurance Information

Life Insurance

Sharon does not have life insurance at this time.

Health Insurance

Sharon currently has an indemnity group health and major medical hospitalization plan through her company. Dick is covered under this plan as well due to COBRA, and pays his own premium. The company pays the entire premium for Sharon's health insurance policy, which has the following characteristics:

- $500 per individual deductible per year
- $1,000 total family deductible per year
- 80% / 20% co-insurance clause for major medical
- $1M lifetime benefit limit per person
- $3,000 annual family stop loss limit

Long-Term Disability Insurance

Long-Term Disability Policy – Sharon	
Type	Own Occupation
Insured	Sharon
Guaranteed Renewable	Yes
Benefit	60% of Gross Pay to age 65
Premium Paid By	Employer
Residual Benefits Clause	Yes
Elimination Period	180 Days
Annual Premium	$2,000

Long-Term Care Insurance

Sharon is not covered by a long-term care insurance policy.

Property and Liability Insurance

Homeowner's Insurance

Homeowner's Insurance is without endorsements and has a $2,500 limit on collectibles.

Personal Residence	
Type	HO3 without endorsements
Dwelling	$800,000
Other Structures	$150,000
Personal Property	$400,000
Personal Liability	$100,000
Medical Payments	$10,000
Deductible	$1,000
Co-Insurance %	80 / 20
Annual Premium	$6,000

Auto Insurance

Auto #1 Sharon's Car	
Type	Personal Automobile Policy (PAP)
Liability (Bodily Injury)	$100,000/$300,000/$50,000
Medical Payments	$10,000
Uninsured Motorist	$100,000/$300,000
Collision Deductible	$1,000
Comprehensive Deductible	$1,000
Annual Premium	$1,200

Liability Insurance

Sharon does not have a personal liability umbrella policy (PLUP).

Debt

		Monthly Payment
Mortgage	Original balance of $883,862 (15 years left; 5% payment)	$4,744.76
Property Taxes	$15,000 annually	$1,250.00
Homeowner's Insurance	$6,000 annually	$500.00
	P+I+T+I	$6,494.76
Auto Loan	Original balance of $133,334 for 8 years. (72 months left with no interest)	$1,388.89

Education Information

Sharon, Amy and John believe in education and would like to ensure Allison can attend a private college. Sharon wants to create a college fund so Allison can spend four years in school at an annual cost of $30,000 per year (in today's dollars).

Divorce

In the divorce Dick was awarded alimony of $8,000 per month until he is age 65. He is now 58 years old. As part of the divorce settlement, Sharon was required to transfer her entire 401(k) plan balance to Dick. She did not have to share her ownership of Petro King with Dick, and she was awarded their family home and corresponding mortgage. Dick asked for Sharon to be required to secure her alimony obligation with life insurance. However, language for this requirement did not make it into the final divorce decree.

Investment Information

Sharon would like to earn 8.5% or better on her investment assets. Petro King is growing at 3% per year which is better than the general economy but too slow for Sharon. She plans to discuss growth and expansion plans with her partners and design a marketing campaign to increase sales.

Sharon is willing to reallocate this portfolio for her long-term needs.

Risk Tolerance Questionnaire

Global Portfolio Allocation Scoring System (PASS) for Individual Investors[1]

Questions	Strongly Agree	Agree	Neutral	Disagree	Strongly Disagree
1. Earning a high long-term total return that will allow my capital to grow faster than the inflation rate is one of my most important investment objectives.		S			
2. I would like an investment that provides me with an opportunity to defer taxation of capital gains to future years.	S				
3. I do not require a high level of current income from my investments.	S				
4. I am willing to tolerate some sharp down swings in the return on my investments in order to seek a potentially higher return than would normally be expected from more stable investments.			S		
5. I am willing to risk a short-term loss in return for a potentially higher long-run rate of return.		S			
6. I am financially able to accept a low level of liquidity in my investment portfolio.			S		

S = Sharon

Portfolio information

Sharon tells you that her investment holdings were not actively managed last year. The account did not increase in value so she transferred the entire remaining balance into the S & P Index fund at year end. She hopes that you will help her do a better job of investing these funds so that next year's performance will be positive, if not impressive.

Sharon contributes $22,500 to her 401(k) plan and the company matches her contributions, dollar-for-dollar up to a maximum match of 4.2% of her covered compensation. Sharon plans to continue these contributions (with no increases) until she retires.

1. Global Portfolio Allocation Scoring System (PASS) for Individual Investors - developed by Dr. William Droms (Georgetown University) and Steven N. Strauss, (DromsStrauss Advisors Inc.) - model used with permission.

Laynee Portfolio Information 12/31/12

Total Portfolio

Cash and Cash Equivalents Plus Investments

	Dollars	%
Cash	$55,000	4%
Fixed income	$0	0%
US Equities	$1,400,000	96%
Foreign Equities	$0	0%
Total	**$1,455,000**	**100%**

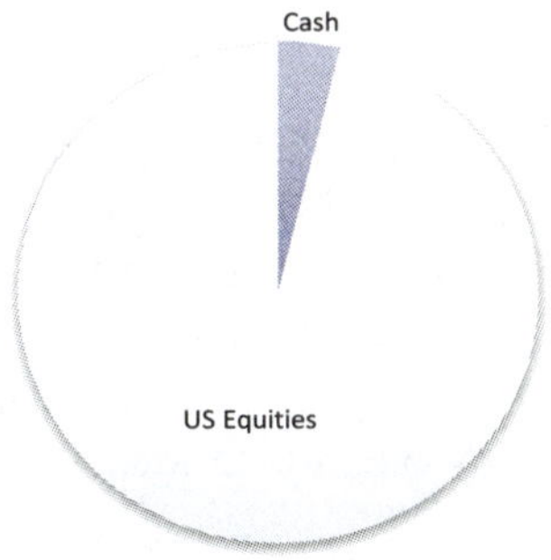

Account	Cash	Bonds	US Equities	Foreign Equities	Total
Cash	$55,000				$55,000
Brokerage account			$400,000		$400,000
Municipal bonds					$0
Web Options					$0
IBM Stock					$0
Education Account					$0
401(k) Plan					$0
401(k) Plan					$0
Traditional IRA					$0
ESOP					$0
Petro King Interest			$1,000,000		$1,000,000
Total	$55,000	$0	$1,400,000	$0	$1,455,000

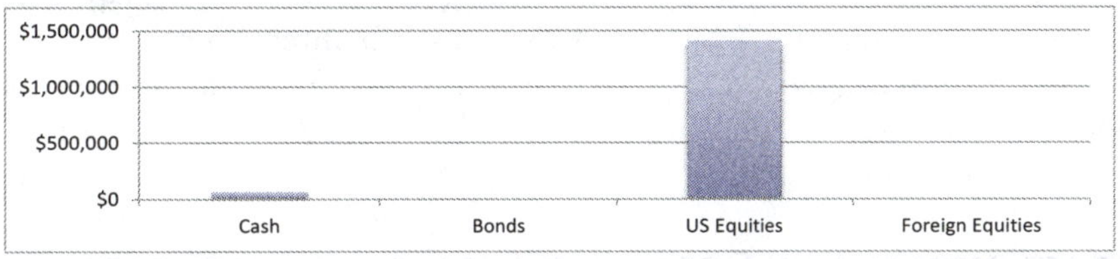

Total Portfolio - Account Types

	Dollars	%
Taxable	$1,455,000	100%
Education	$0	0%
Tax Deferred	$0	0%
Roth Accounts	$0	0%
Total	**$1,455,000**	**100%**

Account	Taxable	Education	Tax Deferred	Roth	Total
Cash	$55,000				$55,000
Brokerage account	$400,000				$400,000
Municipal bonds					$0
Web Options					$0
IBM Stock					$0
Education Account					$0
401(k) Plan					$0
401(k) Plan					$0
Traditional IRA					$0
ESOP					$0
Petro King Interest	$1,000,000				$1,000,000
					$0
Total	$1,455,000	$0	$0	$0	$1,455,000

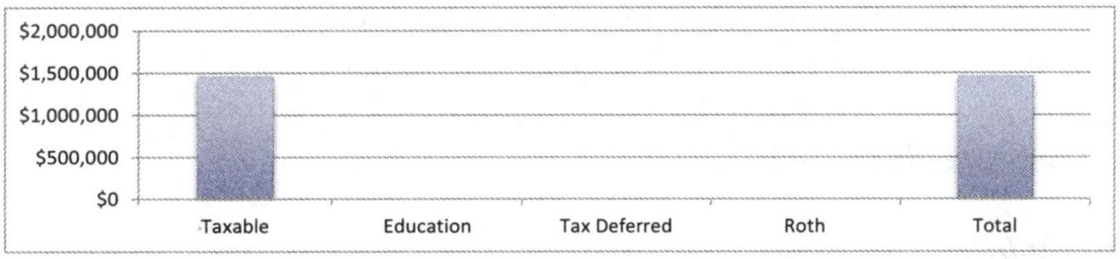

Estate Documents

Sharon and Dick executed legal documents 20 years ago when Amy was a minor. Their Wills left everything to each other, including Sharon's business. The put option described below was agreed to by Sharon and the other business owners after Sharon and Dick's original estate planning documents were executed. Durable Powers of Attorney for Healthcare and Property as well as Advanced Medical Directives were completed.

Sharon knows she needs to update her estate planning documents to reflect the divorce from Dick as well as her wishes with respect to Amy, John and Allison. Sharon would like to leave whatever assets remain at her death in trust for Amy and Allison.

Sharon has a put option to sell her 30 percent interest in Petro King at any time up to age 65, when she is required to sell. The value of Petro King is based on appraisal without minority or liquidity discounts. The growth rate for the company is three percent per year. Sharon has a holding requirement which makes her employment contingent upon her continued ownership interest. The holding requirement lapses at age 65 when she is required to sell her interest in the company. If Sharon waits to sell her interest until age 65, the remaining owner's may offer her a consulting contract that would allow her to continue receiving a salary for up to two years post-sale. Sharon has indicated that once she sells her interest in the company, she will retire. The company has not funded the put option.

Other Information Regarding Assets and Liabilities

Home and Furnishings

Sharon and Dick purchased the home Sharon was awarded in the divorce about 15 years ago for approximately $1,104,827 with 20% down and a mortgage of $883,862 at 5% for 30 years. The economic downturn reduced the value of the home to $900,000 as of 1/1/2012. Within a year, Sharon's home decreased by another $100,000 so that by 1/1/2013 the home was valued at $800,000. Sharon likes the home but is concerned the falling value will erode her equity in the home. She is willing to refinance her existing home to reduce her expenses, but is concerned that the home will not appraise and/or she will not qualify for a new mortgage, even at reduced interest rates.

Sharon has a buyer interested in purchasing her current home for $800,000. She is considered selling and has found a home she would be willing to purchase that is the close to the same size but further out, making it more economical to own. The new home would cost $450,000. Closing costs to sell the old home and to purchase the new home are estimated at 7% for each transaction. Sharon has indicated she would use existing funds or any federal income tax refund she might qualify for to pay the closing costs to purchase the new home. The new home is located in a neighborhood that is acceptable to Amy and John. They have told Sharon they are willing to pay rent of $15,000 in the new home.

Automobiles

Sharon was awarded her vehicle in the divorce, but decided to trade it in for a new Mercedes. The new vehicle cost $133,333 (after trade-in) and was financed over eight years with zero percent interest. Sharon loves this vehicle and plans to keep it as long as she can.

Collectibles

Sharon has a collection of antique clocks, which she would never part with, that she values at $100,000.

CASE ASSUMPTIONS

1. Any closing costs associated with a mortgage refinance are an additional 3% of the amount mortgaged and will be paid directly (i.e., not included in the amount of the mortgage).
2. Estimated cost to sell or purchase a home are 7% and will be paid directly.
3. Sharon is in the 33% marginal federal income tax bracket.
4. Sharon is expected to live to age 95.
5. Lucy's care costs $60,000 per year today and her assets are sufficient to pay for the next ten years of her care. Inflation for Lucy's care is expected to be 3%.
6. Unless otherwise stated, all interest, dividends and capital gains are reinvested.
7. Assume that the discretionary cash flow deficit from 2012 was included in the Cash and Money Market account balances as of 1/1/2013.
8. Sharon does not expect to receive an inheritance of any type. She expects Lucy to spend all of her money.
9. Sharon is willing to refinance or sell the existing home if doing so will help her achieve her goals. She has found a home that is the same size but further out and less expensive than her current home. She has discussed the purchase and new neighborhood with Amy and John. They are willing to move with Sharon and pay rent of $15,000 in the new home. They plan to live with Sharon for two or more years. Sharon has indicated that when Amy and John move out, she will modify her spending based on the decline in rental income and possible change in tax filing status.
10. Sharon can sell her business at any age up to age 65. In order for her to continue her employment, she must own the stock (i.e., she has a holding requirement until age 65).
11. At age 65, Sharon must sell her interest in Petro King. At age 65, she may be offered a consulting contract allowing her to continue her employment for two years after the sale of Petro King, at a salary to be negotiated at the time of sale.
12. Sharon intends to sell her interest in Petro King and retire at age 65.
13. Sharon will never consider selling her antiques or her car.
14. Sharon thinks that a comprehensive income tax analysis is a good idea. She tells you she has no idea if she is over, under, or properly withheld.

CASE

Argo and Marie Merritt Case 6

Today is January 1, 2013

INTRODUCTORY DATA

THE FAMILY

Argo Merritt (age 60) is a self employed contractor and is married to Marie Merritt (age 56), who is an employee of ATI Inc. They have been married for 16 years. Argo has 2 adult married children from a former marriage. He has five grandchildren ages 10, 8, 6, 4, and 2 who are all close to Argo and Marie. Argo and Marie do not reside in a community property state.

Argo's makes $50,000 as Schedule C income. Marie's salary is $50,000 per year. Their net worth is $500,000.

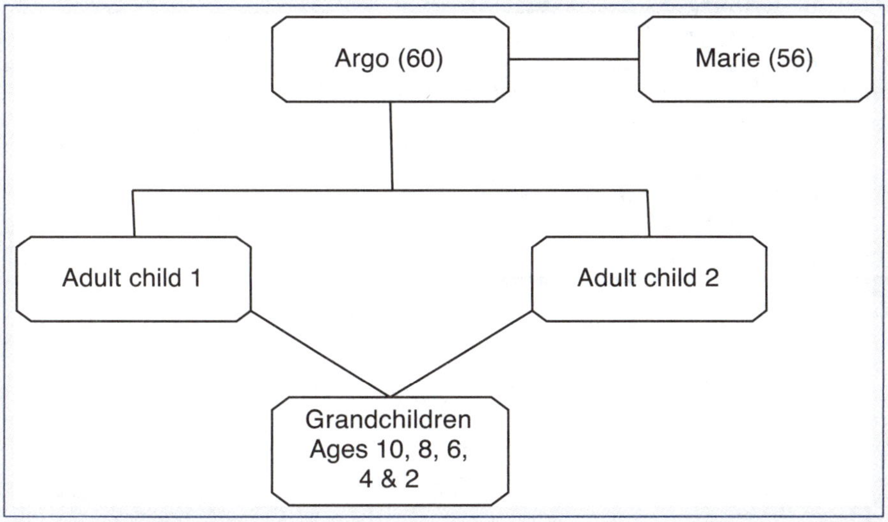

Financial Goals & Concerns

1. They want to plan for retirement at Argo's age 66 with 80% of preretirement income. They expect to live until Argo is 95 years old and they will include Social Security benefits in any retirement needs analysis.
2. They want to carefully review and improve their insurance and investment portfolios.
3. They want to be debt free at retirement except for their mortgage.
4. They want to start 529 Plans for each of the grandchildren.
5. They want to have a properly prepared estate plan (expected to cost $1,000).

EXTERNAL INFORMATION

Economic Information

- General inflation is expected to average 3.0% annually for the foreseeable future.
- Education inflation is expected to be 5.5% annually.
- They expect Treasury Bills to yield 1.5%, notes 2.5%, and bonds 4.0%.

Bank Lending Rates

- 15-year conforming rate mortgage is 4.00%.
- 30-year conforming rate mortgage is 4.50%.
- Any closing costs associated with any mortgage refinance are an additional 3% of any amount mortgaged.
- There is a lender 80% loan to value requirement to refinance, ignoring closing costs which may be added to any new mortgage.

Investment Return Expectations

	Return	Standard Deviation
Cash and Money Market Fund	2.5%	2.0%
Treasury Bonds/ Bond Funds	4.0%	4.0%
Corporate Bonds/ Bond Funds	6.0%	5.0%
International Bond Funds	7.0%	6.0%
Index Fund	9.0%	14.0%
Large Cap Funds/Stocks	10.0%	16.0%
Mid/Small Funds/Stocks	12.0%	18.0%
International Stock Funds	13.0%	22.0%
Real Estate Funds	8.0%	12.0%

INTERNAL INFORMATION

FINANCIAL STATEMENTS

Statement of Financial Position

Statement of Financial Position Argo and Marie Merritt Balance Sheet as of 1/1/2013								
ASSETS[1]				**LIABILITIES AND NET WORTH**				
Current Assets				**Current Liabilities[2]**				
JT	Cash & Cash Equivalents	$15,840		W	Credit Cards	$6,910		
				Total Current Liabilities			$6,910	
Total Current Assets			$15,840					
Investment Assets				**Long-Term Liabilities[2]**				
W	401(k) Plan and Profit Sharing	$186,968		JT	Mortgage Principal Residence	$238,335		
H	Roth IRA	$20,000		H	Vehicle Loans	$26,495		
H	SEP	$27,192		**Total Long-Term Liabilities**			$264,830	
H	Taxable Mutual Funds	$50,000						
H	Cash Value of Life Insurance	$50,000						
Total Investment Assets			$334,160	**Total Liabilities**			$271,740	
Personal Use Assets								
JT	Principal Residence[4]	$238,335						
JT	Vehicles	$33,119						
H	Sports Memorabilia Collection	$25,000		**Total Net Worth**			$500,000	
W	Jewelry	$25,286						
JT	Clothing, Furniture, Fixtures	$100,000						
Total Personal Use Assets			$421,740					
Total Assets			$771,740	**Total Liabilities & Net Worth**			$771,740	

1. Assets are stated at fair market value.
2. Liabilities are stated at principal only as of January 1, 2013 before January payments are made.
3. Credit card debt is at low annual interest rate of 6% from credit union.
4. Lot value is $38,335.

Title Designations:
H = Husband (Sole Owner)
W = Wife (Sole Owner)
JT = Joint Tenancy with Survivorship Rights

Income Statement

Statement of Income and Expenses
Argo and Marie Merritt
Statement of Income and Expenses Projected for Current Year (2013)

			Totals
Cash Inflows			
Argo (Schedule C)	$50,000		
Marie's Salary	$50,000		
Total Cash Inflows			$100,000
Cash Outflows			
Savings			
Argo	$0		
Marie's 401(k) Plan	$5,000		
Total Savings			$5,000
Taxes			
Federal Income Taxes Withheld	$6,000		
Argo's Estimated Payments[1]	$13,650		
Marie's Social Security Taxes	$3,825		
Property Tax Principal Residence	$5,000	ND	
State Income Tax	$0		
Total Taxes			$28,475
Debt Payments (Principal & Interest)			
Principal Residence	$22,151	ND	
Vehicle Payments	$6,000	ND	
Credit Cards	$2,000	ND	
Total Debt Payments			$30,151
Living Expenses			
Utilities Principal Residence	$3,960	ND	
Gasoline for Autos	$6,000	ND	
Auto Repair and Maintenance	$1,000	ND	
Church Donations	$1,300		
Food	$6,000	ND	
Entertainment, Travel, and Gifts	$5,000		
Total Living Expenses			$23,260
Insurance Payments			
HO Insurance Principal Residence	$2,800	ND	
Disability Insurance for Marie	$1,200	ND	
Auto Premiums	$2,400	ND	
Health Insurance	$4,800	ND	
Total Insurance Payments			$11,200
Total Cash Outflows			$98,086
Net Discretionary Cash Flows			$1,914

ND = Non-Discretionary cash flow per mutual understanding between financial planner and client.

1. Estimated payments are for federal income tax and self-employment tax.

INSURANCE INFORMATION

Life Insurance

Policy 1	
Insured	Marie Merritt
Face Amount	$50,000
Type	Group Term
Cash Value	$0
Annual Premium	Paid by employer
Date Purchased	Group Term
Current Coverage	$50,000
Beneficiary	Argo Merritt
Owner	Marie Merritt

Policy 2	
Insured	Argo Merritt
Face Amount	$100,000
Type	Modified Premium Whole Life
Cash Value	$50,000
Annual Premium	Not currently paying premiums
Date Purchased	1990
Current Coverage	$100,000
Beneficiary	Marie Merritt
Owner	Argo Merritt
Interest Crediting Rate	5% reduced by mortality costs

Health Insurance

Argo and Marie are covered under the ATI Company health plan. The Merritt's currently pay $400 per month for the employer-provided indemnity health and major medical plan. The deductible is $500 per person up to a maximum of three persons. There is a stop loss of $3,000 per year and an 80/20 coinsurance provision. The plan provides COBRA benefits. When Argo is 66 Marie will be 62. When Argo retires, Marie can receive COBRA benefits for 36 months (3 years) to age 65 at which time she will be eligible for Medicare.

Disability Insurance

Marie has a private provided disability insurance policy that covers accident and sickness and has an own occupation definition with a 180-day elimination period. The policy pays benefits of 60 percent of Marie's current gross income until she reaches age 65. Argo has no disability insurance.

Property and Liability Insurance

Homeowners Insurance

Personal Residence	
Type	HO3 without endorsements
Dwelling	$330,000
Other Structures	$33,000
Personal Property	$165,000
Loss of Use (20% of dwelling)	$66,000

**There is no rider for replacement value on personal property. There is a rider for furs and jewelry (premium $30 annually included in the $2,800 annual premium).*

Auto Insurance

	Auto #1 Argo's Car	Auto # 2 Marie's Car	Semiannual Premium
Type	Personal Automobile Policy (PAP)	Personal Automobile Policy (PAP)	
Liability (Bodily Injury)	$100,000/$300,000/$50,000	$100,000/$300,000/$50,000	$500
Medical Payments	$10,000	$10,000	$100
Uninsured Motorist	$100,000/$300,000	$100,000/$300,000	$200
Collision Deductible	$500	$500	$250
Other than Collision	$250	$250	$150
Towing and Labor	$100 maximum	$100 maximum	$0
Semiannual Premium	$600	$600	$1,200

Liability Insurance (Personal Liability Umbrella)

The Merritts do not have any liability insurance at this time.

Investment Information

Portfolio Expected Rate of Return = 7.5%

Risk Tolerance Questionnaire

Global Portfolio Allocation Scoring System (PASS) for Individual Investors[1]

Questions	Strongly Agree	Agree	Neutral	Disagree	Strongly Disagree
1. Earning a high long-term total return that will allow my capital to grow faster than the inflation rate is one of my most important investment objectives.		A, M			
2. I would like an investment that provides me with an opportunity to defer taxation of capital gains to future years.			A, M		
3. I do not require a high level of current income from my investments.			A	M	
4. I am willing to tolerate some sharp down swings in the return on my investments in order to seek a potentially higher return than would normally be expected from more stable investments.				A, M	
5. I am willing to risk a short-term loss in return for a potentially higher long-run rate of return.			A, M		
6. I am financially able to accept a low level of liquidity in my investment portfolio.			A, M		

A = Argo, M = Marie

1. Global Portfolio Allocation Scoring System (PASS) for Individual Investors - developed by Dr. William Droms (Georgetown University) and Steven N. Strauss, (DromsStrauss Advisors Inc.) - model used with permission.

Portfolio Information

Merritt Portfolio Information 12/31/12

Total Portfolio*

Cash and Cash Equivalents Plus Investments

	Dollars	%
Cash	$15,840	5%
Fixed income	$190,676	54%
US Equities	$93,484	27%
Foreign Equities	$50,000	14%
Total	**$350,000**	**100%**

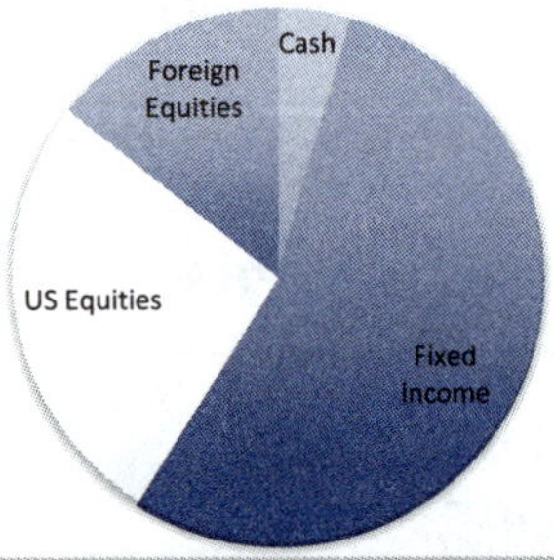

*Includes Cash Value of Life Insurance

Account	Cash	Bonds	US Equities	Foreign Equities	Total
Cash	$15,840				$15,840
401(k) & PS Plan		$93,484	$93,484		$186,968
Roth IRA		$20,000			$20,000
SEP		$27,192			$27,192
Taxable Mutual Funds				$50,000	$50,000
Cash Value of Life Insurance		$50,000			$50,000
Total	$15,840	$190,676	$93,484	$50,000	$350,000

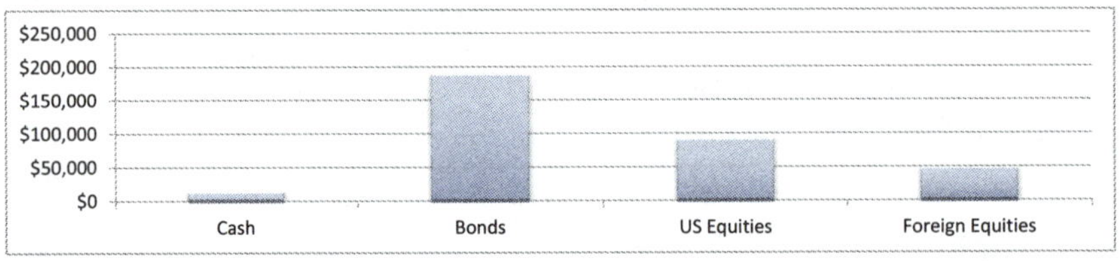

Total Portfolio - Account Types

	Dollars	%
Taxable	$65,840	19%
Education	$0	0%
Tax Deferred	$264,160	75%
Roth Accounts	$20,000	6%
Total	**$350,000**	**100%**

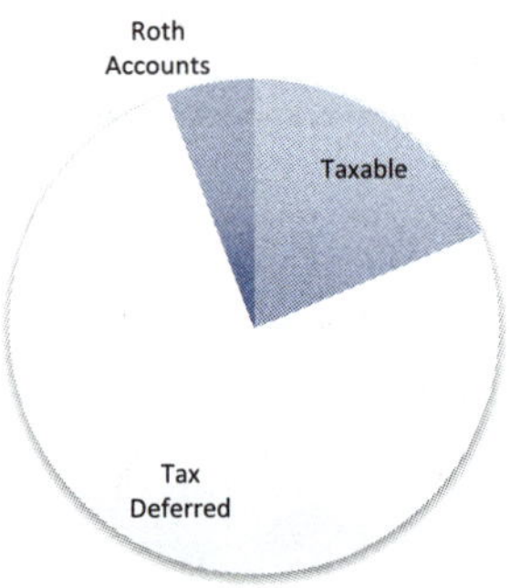

Account	Taxable	Education	Tax Deferred	Roth	Total
Cash	$15,840				$15,840
401(k) & PS Plan			$186,968		$186,968
Roth IRA				$20,000	$20,000
SEP			$27,192		$27,192
Taxable Mutual Funds	$50,000				$50,000
Cash Value of Life Insurance			$50,000		$50,000
Total	$65,840	$0	$264,160	$20,000	$350,000

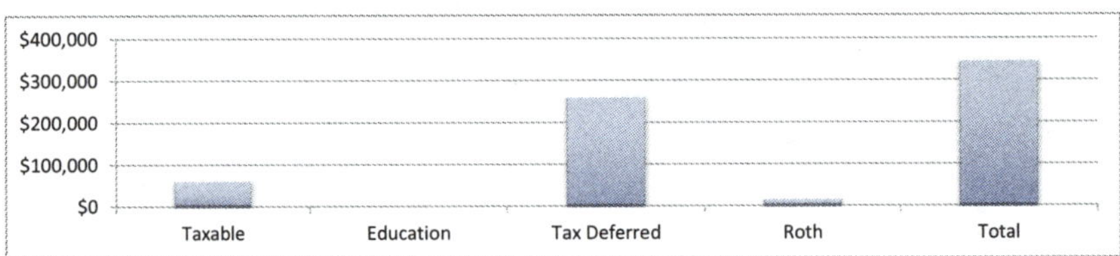

Note: The funds in the mutual funds are invested in foreign equities.

Other Information Regarding Assets and Liabilities

Personal Residence

The Merritt's purchased their personal residence for $330,000 eight years ago with a down payment of 20 percent and the balance mortgaged over 30 years at 7.5 percent. Unfortunately even though they have excellent credit, they think they cannot refinance due to loan to value issues. The value of the principal residence today is $238,335 or equal to the mortgage. They like the house and plan to remain in it through retirement.

Their property tax for their home is at a milage rate of 0.0151515 of actual value. Lowering the dwelling coverage to $200,000 will save them $800 annually. An endorsement for replacement value and open perils will cost approximately $400 annually.

Automobiles

Just today they purchased two new vehicles, a car for Marie and a truck for Argo. The total price was $33,119 with 20 percent down and payments of $500 a month for 60 months.

Income Tax Information

The Merritt's are in the 15 percent marginal income tax bracket for federal income tax purposes and there is no state income tax. Some 19 years ago, Argo inherited quite a bit of money and invested it in a beach high-rise construction project at the suggestion of his realtor friend. Unfortunately, the project was a disaster and he lost his entire investment. At the time, he elected the 20-year carryforward for his net operating loss and his current remaining NOL is $160,000. He is very concerned about Congress raising the income tax rates in the future.

Retirement Information

Marie has a 401(k) plan in which she defers $5,000 per year. Her employer, ATI, has historically matched her contributions with four percent of salary and from time to time made profit sharing contributions. Argo is not currently saving anything. They expect to retire at Argo age 66, Marie age 62. They expect to have a life expectancy of 29 years post retirement. Social Security retirement benefits for Argo will be $20,000 in today's dollars at full retirement age (FRA) of age 66. For Marie, Social Security retirement benefits will be $20,000 at FRA (66) in today's dollars (75% of FRA benefits at age 62).

The company has made the following profit-sharing contributions to the retirement plan for Marie for each of the related years. However, the company has indicated they can no longer continue any level of funding for 2013 and beyond.

Marie	
2012	$5,000
2011	$4,800
2010	$3,900
2009	$0
2008	$3,300
2007	$2,500
2006	$2,400
Balance 1/1/06	$0

* *Contributions are made on 12/31 for each year.*

The 401(k) plan has a Roth account available, although Marie has always deferred her compensation into the traditional 401(k). In addition to her deferrals, Marie rolled over funds from a prior 401(k) plan when she joined ATI. The value of the rollover funds is currently $130,000.

The funds in her 401(k) plan are invested half in an index fund and half in a bond mutual fund, with a duration of 5 and a yield to maturity of 6%.

Roth IRA

The funds in the Roth IRA are invested in Treasury STRIPS with an average yield of 7% and a duration of 10.

SEP

The funds in the SEP are invested in Treasury STRIPS with an average yield of 8% and a duration of 13.

Estate Planning Information

They do not have any estate planning documents or estate plan at this time.

Case

The Berry Case 7

Today is January 1, 2013

INTRODUCTORY DATA

THE FAMILY

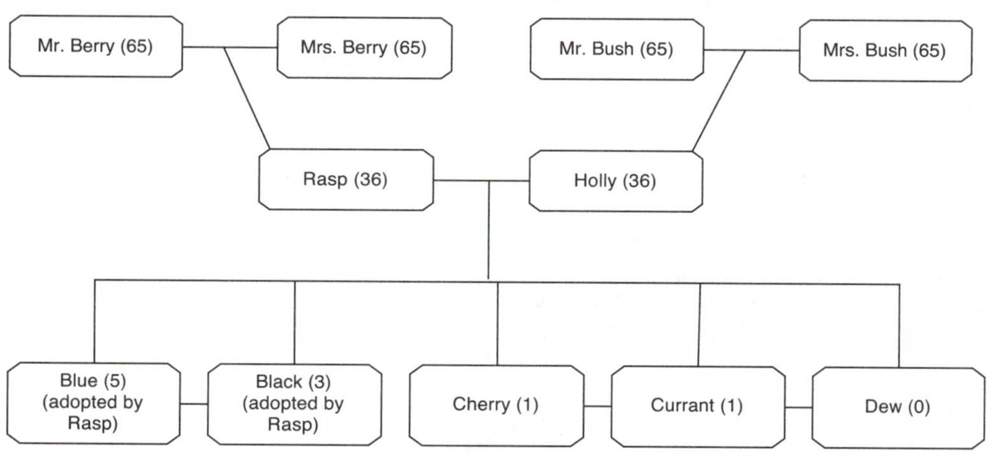

Rasp and Holly Berry are both 36 years old. They married in 2011 and he adopted her two children, Blue and Black. They have three additional children of their own, Cherry, Currant, and Dew.

Four of the five children are happy and healthy. Blue is 5 years old, Black is 3 years old, Cherry and Currant are one-year old twins and Dew was just born. Blue has a significant learning disability, but he is still expected to attend and complete college.

Both Rasp and Holly's parents are living and 65 years old. Rasp and Holly have no expectations of any inheritance from either couple. Fortunately, it looks like each set of parents is self-sufficient.

Rasp is a regional manager with a hotel chain and makes an annual salary of $180,000 with a bonus of $20,000. Holly is a drug counselor, who makes $50,000 annually.

Financial Goals & Concerns

- To retire at age 62 with $200,000 in income in today's dollars.
- To decide what to do with their condo. They are horrified that it will bankrupt them.
- To make sure they have an adequate insurance portfolio.
- To make sure they have an appropriate investment portfolio for their financial situation.
- To provide college education at the state university for each child for 4 years.
- They want you to make a detailed cash flow analysis to determine where they are relative to bankruptcy.

EXTERNAL INFORMATION

Economic Information

- CPI inflation is expected to be 3%.
- Education inflation is expected to be 5%.
- The economy is expanding slowly.

Bank Lending Rates

- 15-year conforming annual rate mortgages are 3.50%.
- 30-year conforming rate mortgages are 4.0%.
- Any closing costs associated with mortgage refinance are an additional 3% of the amount mortgaged and will be included in the mortgage or paid directly.

Investment Return Expectations

The Berry's expected / required rate of return on all investments is 8.5%.

	Return	Standard Deviation
Cash and Money Market Fund	2.5%	2.0%
Treasury Bonds / Bond Funds	4.0%	4.0%
Corporate Bonds / Bond Funds	6.0%	5.0%
International Bond Funds	7.0%	6.0%
Index Fund	9.0%	14.0%
Large Cap Funds/Stocks	10.0%	16.0%
Mid/Small Funds/Stocks	12.0%	18.0%
International Stock Funds	13.0%	22.0%
Real Estate Funds	8.0%	12.0%

FINANCIAL STATEMENTS

Statement of Financial Position

Statement of Financial Position
Rasp and Holly Berry
Balance Sheet as of 12/31/12 (and 1/1/2013)

ASSETS[1]				LIABILITIES AND NET WORTH		
Current Assets				**Current Liabilities[2]**		
JT	Cash & Checking	$15,000		W Credit Cards	$10,000	
JT	Money Market	$25,000		**Total Current Liabilities**		$10,000
Total Current Assets			$40,000			
Investment Assets				**Long-Term Liabilities[2]**		
H	Retirement	$0		JT Principal Residence	$540,000	
H	Non-retirement	$0		JT Condo Mortgage	$400,000	
JT	Condo	$900,000		JT Automobiles	$38,000	
			$900,000	**Total Long-Term Liabilities**		$978,000
Total Investment Assets				**Total Liabilities**		$988,000
Personal Use Assets						
JT	Principal Residence	$500,000				
JT	Furniture, Clothing	$100,000		**Total Net Worth**		$592,000
H	Car # 1	$20,000				
W	Car # 2	$20,000				
Total Personal Use Assets			$640,000			
Total Assets			$1,580,000	**Total Liabilities & Net Worth**		$1,580,000

1. Assets are stated at fair market value.
2. Liabilities are stated at principal only as of December 31, 2012 before January 2013 payments.

H = Husband
W = Wife
JT = Joint

Income Statement

Rasp and Holly Berry Statement of Income and Expenses Expected For This Year (2013)			
Cash Inflows			**Totals**
Rasp's Salary	$180,000		
Rasp's Bonuses	$20,000		
Holly's Salary	$50,000		
Total Cash Inflows			$250,000
Cash Outflows			
Savings			
Rasp's 401(k)	$17,000		
Holly's 401(k)	$17,000		
Outside of retirement plan savings	$0		
Total Savings			$34,000
Taxes			
Rasp's Federal Income Taxes Withheld	$36,000		
Holly's Federal Income Taxes Withheld	$9,000		
Rasp's Social Security Taxes	$9,720		
Holly's Social Security Taxes	$3,825		
Property Tax - Residence	$10,000	ND	
Property Tax - Condo	$10,800	ND	
Total Taxes			$79,345
Debt Payments (Principal & Interest)			
Principal Residence Mortgage	$38,851	ND	
Condo Mortgage Payment	$44,949	ND	
Credit Cards	$3,500	ND	
Auto Payment	$6,500	ND	
Total Debt Payments			$93,800
Living Expenses			
Utilities Principal Residence	$6,000	ND	
Gasoline for Autos	$2,400	ND	
Lawn Service	$1,800	ND	
Entertainment	$10,000		
Vacations	$10,000		
Church Donations	$1,800	ND	
Clothing	$5,000	ND	
Auto Maintenance	$2,000	ND	
Satellite TV	$1,200	ND	
Food	$8,000	ND	
Utilities - Condo	$3,600	ND	
Private School Education Family Rate	$15,000	ND	
Total Living Expenses			$66,800
Insurance Payments			
Health Insurance	$9,600	ND	
HO Insurance Principal Residence	$10,000	ND	
HO Insurance - Condo	$12,000	ND	
Auto Insurance Premiums	$5,000	ND	
Condo Association Fees	$12,000	ND	
Total Insurance Payments			$48,600
Total Cash Outflows			$322,545
Net Discretionary Cash Flows (Annual)			($72,545)

ND = Non-Discretionary cash flows per mutual understanding between financial planner and client.

Insurance Information

Life Insurance

Rasp has $50,000 of employer provided group-term life insurance policy. Holly is the beneficiary. Holly has $50,000 of employer-provided group term life insurance; Rasp is the beneficiary.

Health Insurance

They are all covered under Rasp's employer plan, which is a POS plan with co-pays of $25, no deductible in network and a maximum out-of-pocket annual limit of $2,500. The maximum lifetime benefit per person is unlimited. The monthly premium is $800.

Disability Insurance

Both, Rasp, and Holly have disability policies provided by their respective employers that provide 65% of gross pay with an elimination period of 90 days. The policies are guaranteed renewable and define disability for any occupation for which they are educated, trained, or experienced. The policies cover both sickness and accidents.

Long-Term Care Insurance

The Berrys do not have long-term care insurance at this time.

Homeowners Insurance

Personal Residence - HO 3 plus endorsements
A very high quality policy
Condo - HO 6 plus endorsements
A very high quality policy

Automobile Insurance

They have 2 cars, both covered by XYZ Auto Insurance for 100/300/50 and uninsured motorist, cash value for property, and $1,000 deductible each. The annual premium is $5,000.

PLUP

They have no personal liability umbrella policy.

Special Needs ILIT Trust

They want to set up a special needs trust funded with a second-to-die life insurance policy. The beneficiary of the trust will be Blue. They will fund the trust with $12,000 per year until they retire to fund a $1,000,000 permanent insurance policy.

Investment Information

Risk Tolerance Questionnaire

Global Portfolio Allocation Scoring System (PASS) for Individual Investors[1]

Questions	Strongly Agree	Agree	Neutral	Disagree	Strongly Disagree
1. Earning a high long-term total return that will allow my capital to grow faster than the inflation rate is one of my most important investment objectives.		R, H			
2. I would like an investment that provides me with an opportunity to defer taxation of capital gains to future years.		R, H			
3. I do not require a high level of current income from my investments.			R, H		
4. I am willing to tolerate some sharp down swings in the return on my investments in order to seek a potentially higher return than would normally be expected from more stable investments.		R	H		
5. I am willing to risk a short-term loss in return for a potentially higher long-run rate of return.		R	H		
6. I am financially able to accept a low level of liquidity in my investment portfolio.		R, H			

R = Rasp, H = Holly

Other Information Regarding Assets and Liabilities

Automobiles

- They purchased new cars at $20,000 each plus $625 of taxes.
- They pay $6,500 per year with zero interest.
- They will pay for approximately 6.25 years.

Personal Residence

They bought the house in Slidell, Louisiana in July 2011 for $600,000 with a 30 year mortgage for $540,000 at 6% with no principal payment until 2013 when they start 30-year payments of $3,237.57 (P & I) monthly. The value of the house in Slidell has fallen to $500,000 due to market conditions.

Condo

Rasp inherited a French Quarter condo in New Orleans from his Uncle BJ after Hurricane Katrina, in January 2006. The fair market value at Uncle BJ's death was $600,000. Rasp lived there by himself until 2011 when he

1. Global Portfolio Allocation Scoring System (PASS) for Individual Investors - developed by Dr. William Droms (Georgetown University) and Steven N. Strauss, (DromsStrauss Advisors Inc.) - model used with permission.

married Holly. After they married, they decided to renovate the condo and borrowed $400,000 at 9% for 20 years to do a first-class job of upgrading the condo. The terms of the loan included interest only for the first two years then amortized over 18 years. They were thinking that they could sell it for over $1,000,000, but they have little knowledge of accounting, finance, or real estate.

In January 2011, Rasp transferred a ½ interest in the condo to Holly as a gift. They moved to Slidell, Louisiana in July 2011.

Annual Cash Flows and Valuation Information for French Quarter Condo

Year	FMV Value	Mortgage Pmt.	Taxes	Insurance	Condo Fee	Renovation
2006	$150,000	0	$1,800	$2,000	$6,000	
2007	$600,000	0	$3,000	$3,000	$7,000	
2008	$500,000	0	$4,000	$3,000	$8,000	
2009	$400,000	0	$5,000	$5,000	$9,000	
2010	$450,000	0	$8,000	$8,000	$10,000	
2011	$800,000	0	$10,000	$10,000	$11,000	$400,000
2012	$900,000	**	$10,800	$12,000	$12,000	

*** To be calculated*

Rasp and Holly provided you with the following information about the condo:

1. They believe the appraisal they have for the condo of $900,000 is correct even though nothing is selling. The market has not moved in more than two years.
2. They have a firm cash offer of $600,000 to sell the condo now.
3. On a sale they would pay 6% commission.
4. They can rent the property for two weeks at Christmas, Sugar Bowl, and New Years for $20,000 gross less a 25% rental fee.
5. They could rent by the week and the realtor told them they could get about 100 rental days a year at $500 per day less a rental fee of 25%. Alternatively, they think they could rent it themselves for $400 per day for 80 days. If they did this, they would plan to use the property about 60 days a year personally.
6. They could rent it out on a years lease for $4,000 a month less a 10% rental fee.
7. If they rent it out less than a year, they would pay all of the utilities.

Other Information on the Condo

- Mortgage - $400,000 at 9% for 18 years beginning January 1, 2013
- Taxes - $10,800 annually
- Insurance - $12,000 annually (stays the same if rented)
- Condo Association Fees - $12,000 annually
- Utilities - $300 per month
- Any depreciation is over 20 years (special go zone rate) on the adjusted taxable basis of $550,000 (land value is zero).

The family moved to Slidell, Louisiana, an hour away from the French Quarter, for Rasp's work in July 2011. They continued to use the condo as a vacation home and go there about 20 weekends a year for various festivals and shopping. The condo is up for sale, but the market is soft and it has not sold.

Condo Concerns

They have heard there are various tax benefits to renting and selling their condo property but are not certain that they know enough to make a decision. They want you to explain all of the cash flow and tax implications of each of their alternatives and help them make a decision as to what they should do with the condo in the French Quarter. They also want to include any refinance alternatives. They are very concerned at the prospect of negative cash flows, thinking that if they do not do something they may be forced into foreclosure or bankruptcy.

Mortgage Market Conditions

Current interest rates are 3.5% for 15 years conforming rate mortgages and 4.0% for 30 years conforming rate mortgages. However, borrowers must meet strict 80% loan to value requirements and must meet housing ratios of 28% and all debt ratios of 36% of gross income.

Education

The cost of in state college education is $17,000 per year in today's dollars. The Berry's have the five-year old and the three-year old in private school and pay $15,000 per year for the family rate no matter how many children in excess of 2 go to school. Therefore they expect this cost to be with them for the next 17 - 18 years. The Berry's want you to include Blue in any education analysis because he may use resources equal to or even greater than the other children for his education.

Retirement Information

They would like to retire at age 62 with annual income of $200,000 in today's dollars. Their life expectancy is assumed to be to age 95. They expect to earn 8.5% on investments and they expect $50,000 (total for both of them) in today's dollars for Social Security at normal retirement age at age 67. While they have made no contributions to date, they each expect to contribute $17,000 in this next year to their respective 401(k) plans. He has no employer match but her employer match is 4%.

CASE

John and Jackie Griffin Case

8

Today is January 2, 2013

INTRODUCTORY DATA

John and Jackie Griffin came to you because they are overspending their income each month and have significant debt. They bought a home, then started their family and have been taking on more debt each year. The Griffin's believe they will benefit from meeting with a CERTIFIED FINANCIAL PLANNER™ practitioner. They arrived with the following information for you to assist them in creating a plan to help their get their debt under control.

THE FAMILY

John and Jackie Griffin are both 37 years old and have been married for 10 years. John Griffin is a Geologist who works full-time for a small, privately held Oil Exploration and Production Company. John and Jackie met in their last year of college. They dated while John was in graduate school and married a few years after he graduated.

Jackie worked as an Office Manager in a small firm until their first child was born, then she became a stay-at-home mom. She is willing to return to work but is very concerned about the quality of available child day care and the potential cost of that care. She believes her skill-set has eroded while she has been at home and does not believe she will make enough money to justify going back to work. They need your help to identify the pros and cons of their options to get out of and stay out of debt. John and Jackie have three children:

The Children

Jack, age 6, just started first grade. Jill, age 3, is not in school or day-care, and Jane, age 1, is not in day-care. The children have all been at home with Jackie since their birth. Jackie spent a good deal of time working with Jack to ensure he could read and write before he entered school. As a result of her efforts, Jack is ahead of his classmates and doing very well in school. Jackie has already begun working will Jill and hopes to do the same with Jane in another year or so.

John and Jackie believe in education, but they have not saved any money to send the children to college. The burden of their debt load and concerns about how to repay it make them realize they might not be able to afford to send their children to college. They want to find a way to begin saving for their children's college education and are willing to make changes to their finances to do so. However, they need your help determining how to manage their growing debt burden so they can save money for their children's college education and where they should invest the money until the children begin college.

Financial Goals & Concerns

John and Jackie provided the following goals (in order of priority):

1. College education of children for 4 years, each beginning at age 18, at the state university.
2. Reduce debt.
3. Retirement at age 62 with 70% of preretirement income including Social Security, which they expect to total $2,500 per month (for both of them) in today's dollars. Life expectancy is age 91 for both.
4. Appropriate risk management portfolio, investment portfolio, and estate planning portfolio.

EXTERNAL INFORMATION

Economic Information

- General inflation (CPI) is expected to be 3% annually.
- Education inflation is expected to be 5% annually.
- They live in a common law state that has no state income tax.

Bank Lending Rates

- Mortgage 30 years – conforming rate = 4.0%.
- Mortgage 15 years – conforming rate = 3.75%.
- Prime rate is 3.25%.

Investment Returns Expected

- General market is expected to return 8.5% in the short run.
- The Griffin's required and expected long-term rate of return is 8.5%.
- Fixed income investments are expected to yield 6%.
- T-Bills are expected to yield 3% per year and are expected to be the proxy for the risk-free rate of return.
- John and Jackie scored a 19 on the Global Portfolio Allocation Scoring System (PASS) for Individual Investors.

Investment Return Expectations

	Return	Standard Deviation
Cash and Money Market Fund	2.5%	2.5%
Guaranteed Income Fund	2.5%	2.5%
Treasury Bonds/ Bond Funds	4.0%	4.0%
Corporate Bonds/ Bond Funds	6.0%	5.0%
Municipal Bonds/ Bond Funds	5.0%	4.0%
International Bond Funds	7.0%	6.0%
Index Fund	9.0%	14.0%
Large Cap Funds/Stocks	10.0%	16.0%
Mid/Small Funds/Stocks	12.0%	18.0%
International Stock Funds	13.0%	22.0%
Real Estate Funds	8.0%	12.0%

INTERNAL INFORMATION

FINANCIAL STATEMENTS

Statement of Financial Position (Beginning of Year)

Statement of Financial Position John and Jackie Griffin Balance Sheet as of 1/1/2013					
ASSETS[1, 3]			**LIABILITIES AND NET WORTH[2 3]**		
Current Assets			**Current Liabilities**		
JT Cash & Checking	$3,500		W Credit Card 1	$16,000	
JT Money Market	$7,000		**Total Current Liabilities**		**$16,000**
Total Current Assets		**$10,500**			
Investment Assets			**Long-Term Liabilities**		
W Brokerage - Stocks	$67,647		JT Principal Residence[4]	$279,780	
H 401(k) Plan	$13,190		JT Autos	$15,748	
W 401(k) Plan	$0		H Student Loan	$24,879	
H Education Savings Account	$0		JT Bank Loan	$8,000	
Total Investment Assets		**$80,837**	**Total Long-Term Liabilities**		**$328,407**
Personal Use Assets					
JT Principal Residence	$360,000				
JT Autos	$30,000		**Total Liabilities**		**$344,407**
H ATV	$7,070				
JT Furniture and Fixtures	$71,000				
W Jewelry	$20,000		**Total Net Worth**		**$245,000**
JT Other, Clothing	$10,000				
Total Personal Use Assets		**$498,070**			
Total Assets		**$589,407**	**Total Liabilities & Net Worth**		**$589,407**

1. Assets are stated at fair market value.
2. Liabilities are stated at principal only as of January 1, 2013 before January payments.
3. Federal income tax refund or liability for 2012 has not been determined and is not included.
4. Home purchased approximately 8 years ago at $400,000 with 20% down and 30-year mortgage at 6.25%. They have 259 payments remaining. Unfortunately, the value of the residence has fallen to $360,000. Land is valued at $100,000.

Statement of Income and Expenses

Statement of Income and Expenses John and Jackie Griffin Statement of Income and Expenses for 2012 and Projected for 2013			
Cash Inflows			**Totals**
John's Salary	$85,000		
Jackie's Salary	$0		
Total Cash Inflows			**$85,000**
Savings			
401(k) Plan – H	$5,882		
401(k) Plan – W	$0		
Total Savings			**$5,882**
Taxes			
Federal Income Taxes Withheld	$15,000		
Social Security Taxes - H	$6,503		
Social Security Taxes - W	$0		
Property Tax Principal Residence	$3,250	ND	
Total Taxes			**$24,753**
Debt Payments (Principal & Interest)			
Principal Residence	$23,644	ND	
Auto Loan	$8,291	ND	
Student Loan	$6,343	ND	
Bank Loan	$8,451	ND	
Credit Cards	$3,600	ND	
Total Debt Payments			**$50,328**
Living Expenses			
Utilities Principal Residence	$1,800	ND	
Child Care	$0	ND	
Auto Maintenance and Gasoline	$1,200	ND	
Entertainment and Vacations	$3,600		
Church Donations	$0		
Food	$4,800	ND	
Children's lessons, lunches, allowances	$0	ND	
Lawn and cleaning services	$0		
Clothing	$1,200	ND	
Miscellaneous	$710	ND	
Total Living Expenses			**$13,310**
Insurance Payments			
HO Insurance Principal Residence	$1,625	ND	
Life Insurance	$0	ND	
Health Insurance	$1,200	ND	
Disability Insurance	$900	ND	
Auto Insurance	$1,200	ND	
Total Insurance Payments			**$4,925**
Total Cash Outflows			**$99,197**
Net Discretionary Cash Flows			**($14,197)**

ND - Non-discretionary cash flow per mutual understanding between financial planner and client.

Insurance Information

Life Insurance

Insured	John
Life	$25,000
Employer Provided	Yes
Type	Group Term
Beneficiary	Jackie
Contingent Beneficiary	Children
Premium (Annual)	Employer Paid

Health Insurance

(John's) Group Major Medical
• $2,000,000 Lifetime benefits per person. • $5,000 Stop loss (annual). • $200 Deductible per person. • 80/20 Co-insurance for major medical. • Premium employer provided for John. • Additionally, John pays $1,200 per yr. for family coverage.

Disability Insurance

John's personal disability policy has an option to increase the elimination period to 90 or 180 days.

	John	Jackie
Coverage is for accidental disability own occupation	Own Occupation	None
Personally Owned	Yes Guaranteed Renewable	
Residual Disability Provision	Yes	
Benefit	$3,700 per month	
Benefit Term	to age 65	
Elimination Period	30 Days	
Premium	$900 per year	

Own = own occupation, EET = experienced, educated, and trained

Long-Term Care Insurance

The Griffins do not have long-term care insurance at this time.

Property – Home and Automobile Insurance

John and Jackie met with their insurance professional who indicated the premiums they pay for their Homeowner's coverage are very competitive and cannot be reduced without changing their coverage. However, their auto policy can be improved and should be changed to higher limits and possibly higher deductibles.

Homeowner	• HO3 with endorsements, open perils and replacement value. • 3% deductible, coverage of $240,000 for the home. • Annual premium $1,625.
Auto	• 10/20/10 • State-mandated minimum coverage, $200 deductible for comprehensive and collision. • Annual premium $1,200.

Liability Insurance

They do not have a Personal Liability Umbrella Policy (PLUP). Their insurance professional suggested a $1,000,000 policy that will cost $250.00 per year.

INVESTMENT INFORMATION

Brokerage Account

John and Jackie tell you that Jackie was gifted two stocks by Jackie's spinster Great-Aunt, Pam, many years ago. The FMV of the two stocks when Aunt Pam gifted them was $60,000 ($38,000 for Stock A and $22,000 for Stock B). They have information from Aunt Pam's CPA that indicates Pam's adjusted tax basis in the stocks at the date of gifting was $70,000 ($50,000 for Stock A and $20,000 for Stock B).

John is willing to sell both stocks, but Jackie is only willing to sell one of the two stocks. She wants your help determining which stock to sell based on the following information:

Equity Portfolio											
Asset	**# of shares**	**Current FMV**	**Aunt Pam's Basis**	**Date Acquired**	**Risk Beta**	**Dividend Yield**	**Annual Returns**				
							2008	**2009**	**2010**	**2011**	**2012**
Stock A	800	$43,541	$50,000	1/1/08	0.9	-	-10	-3	4	6	4.76
Stock B	500	$24,106	$20,000	1/1/08	1.15	-	-15	-5	6.7	10	8.77
		$67,647	**$70,000**								

Risk Tolerance Questionnaire

Global Portfolio Allocation Scoring System (PASS) for Individual Investors[1]

Questions	Strongly Agree	Agree	Neutral	Disagree	Strongly Disagree
1. Earning a high long-term total return that will allow my capital to grow faster than the inflation rate is one of my most important investment objectives.		Jo, Ja			
2. I would like an investment that provides me with an opportunity to defer taxation of capital gains to future years.			Jo, Ja		
3. I do not require a high level of current income from my investments.			Jo, Ja		
4. I am willing to tolerate some sharp down swings in the return on my investments in order to seek a potentially higher return than would normally be expected from more stable investments.			Jo, Ja		
5. I am willing to risk a short-term loss in return for a potentially higher long-run rate of return.			Jo, Ja		
6. I am financially able to accept a low level of liquidity in my investment portfolio.			Jo, Ja		

Jo = John, Ja = Jackie

1. Global Portfolio Allocation Scoring System (PASS) for Individual Investors - developed by Dr. William Droms (Georgetown University) and Steven N. Strauss, (DromsStrauss Advisors Inc.) - model used with permission.

John and Jackie Griffin Portfolio Information 12/31/12

Total Portfolio

Cash and Cash Equivalents Plus Investments

	Dollars	%
Cash	$10,500	11%
Fixed income	$0	0%
US Equities	$80,837	89%
Foreign Equities	$0	0%
Total	**$91,337**	**100%**

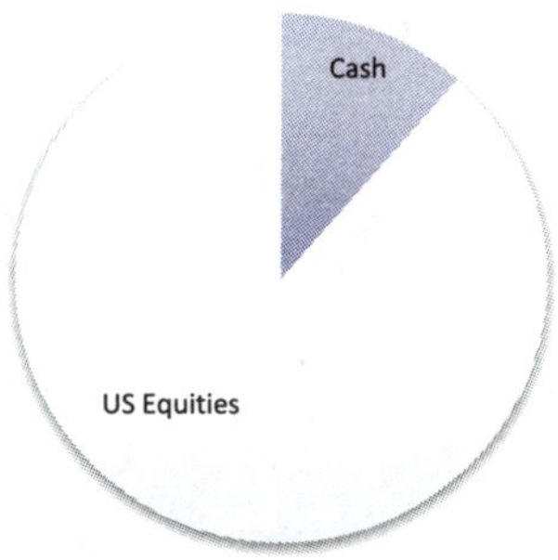

Account	Cash	Bonds	US Equities	Foreign Equities	Total
Cash	$10,500				$10,500
Brokerage account			$67,647		$67,647
401(k) Plan	$0	$0	$13,190		$13,190
401(k) Plan		$0	$0		$0
Education Svgs		$0	$0		$0
Education Svgs		$0	$0		$0
Education Svgs		$0	$0		$0
Total	$10,500	$0	$80,837	$0	$91,337

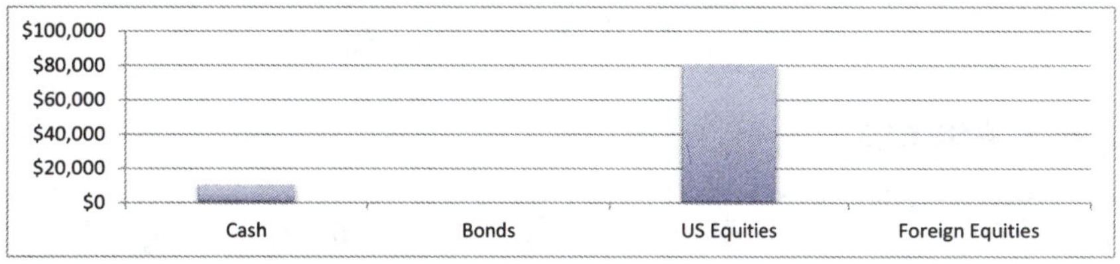

Total Portfolio - Account Types

	Dollars	%
Taxable	$78,147	86%
Education	$0	0%
Tax Deferred	$13,190	14%
Roth Accounts	$0	0%
Total	**$91,337**	**100%**

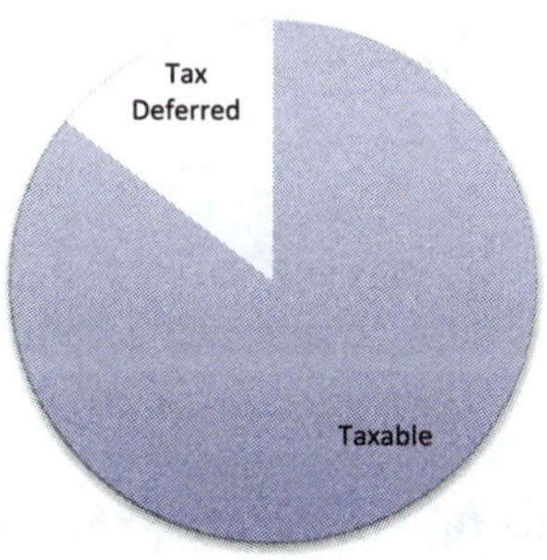

Account	Taxable	Education	Tax Deferred	Roth	Total
Cash	$10,500				$10,500
Brokerage account	$67,647				$67,647
401(k) Plan	$0		$13,190		$13,190
Total	$78,147	$0	$13,190	$0	$91,337

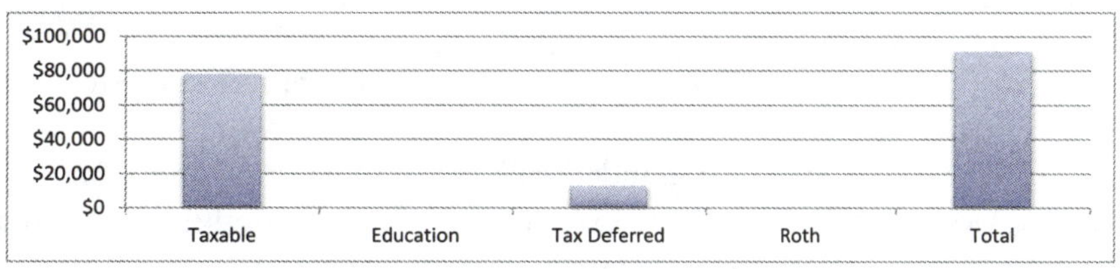

Education Information

- The Griffin's estimate that college costs at State University currently total $17,000 per child, per year, in today's dollars for tuition, fees, room and board (all in).
- The Griffin's enjoyed college and John enjoyed graduate school. They want their children to have the same opportunity to live away from home as they did. If they cannot save enough money to send their children 'away' to school, they will consider letting them attend the local community college or state college while living at home. A state university and community college are both within commuting distance of John and Jackie's home.

- The Griffin's do not think they will qualify for financial aid to send their children to college.
- John and Jackie have been told that their state offers a 529 college savings plan as well as a unit-type pre-paid tuition program and that each unit of pre-paid tuition purchased is redeemable for one percent of the resident undergraduate tuition at the highest-priced public university in their state.
- Their State's pre-paid tuition program is not backed by the full faith and credit of the State, but the units may also be used for eligible educational institutions across the country.

HOME

The Griffin's purchased their dream home approximately eight years ago and used all of their excess cash to make the down payment and to pay the closing costs to purchase the home. They plan to stay in this home through retirement.

Several years ago the Griffin's qualified for a 15 year, secured but unused Home Equity Line of Credit (HELOC), for $50,000 with a 4% variable interest rate. The HELOC is still in existence and they want to know if they should use it to pay off some or all of their non-mortgage debt.

OTHER ASSETS

John purchased an ATV (80 horse power) and various accessories for it several years ago at a cost of $7,070. He enjoys using it, but Jackie thinks it is too dangerous for John to be riding and wants John to sell it. Jackie has seen similar vehicles listed for sale for $4,000 and would like to get the vehicle out of their garage. They both agree that if they keep it, they should insure it, but thus far they have been unable to agree on selling it, so it remains uninsured.

RETIREMENT INFORMATION

- John started contributing to his employer's 401(k) plan last year. He currently contributes 6.92% of his annual salary. John's employer plan matches his contribution dollar-for-dollar up to 3% of John's salary.
- John chose a moderate asset allocation in his retirement account.
- John's 401(k) plan has a loan feature that charges 3% above the prime rate.
- John does not know the return on his plan balance, but he considers this account to be a long-term investment and is not concerned about short-term returns.

ESTATE PLANNING INFORMATION

John and Jackie do not have any estate planning documents. They know who they want to name as a guardian for their children, but have not taken the time to put their wishes in writing.

John and Jackie's parents (the grandparents) are still working and looking forward to retirement. They have told John and Jackie not to expect to receive any inheritances from them, but that they would be happy to contribute to the grandchildren's education while they are still working.

John and Jackie want to take care of each other and leave any remaining assets in trust for their children.

Debt

John and Jackie have accumulated a significant amount of debt. They are spending more than John's salary each month. They took out a bank loan last year to help pay for living expenses. They made a few extra payments of principal on the bank loan which reduced the outstanding balance to $8,000 before realizing the need for a structured approach to paying down their debt.

They would like to refinance the mortgage on their home, but do not believe they can qualify to do so until they deal with their debt problem. Their goal is to get their non-mortgage debt under control then refinance the existing mortgage on their home while interest rates are low.

Liabilities	Rates and Terms	Original Balance	Additional Info	Monthly Payment
Credit Card	Variable @ 18%	Outstanding Balance $16,000		$300.00
Student Loan	10 years @ 10%	Orig. $40,000	60 months remaining	$528.60
Auto Loan	4 years @ 5%	Orig. $30,000	24 months remaining	$690.88
Bank Loan	18 months @ 7%	Orig. $12,000	12 months remaining	$704.21
Mortgage Loan	30 years @ 6.25%	Orig. $320,000	101 payments made; 259 to go	$1,970.30
Total				**$4,193.99**

CASE ASSUMPTIONS

1. John and Jackie expect to live to age 91 (i.e., through age 90).
2. They have a moderate risk tolerance and a required rate of return of 8.5%.
3. Jackie is a stay-at-home mom and will stay home for another 5 years.
4. She is willing to go back to work in 5 years, if necessary. She believes if she returns to work in five years she will be able earn $26,000, but estimates before and after school child care for children along with Summer Camp programs will cost $1,200 per month. She also expects to see an increase of $550 per month for other expenses such as food, gasoline, auto maintenance, clothing, lawn and housekeeping services. She estimates a total increase of $1,750 per month in expenses before federal income taxes and payroll taxes, insurance and any type of retirement contribution.
5. John and Jackie want to retire at age 62 with 70% of their pre-retirement income (including their estimated combined Social Security benefit of $30,000 at normal retirement age).
6. They are willing to sell one of Jackie's stocks, and to discuss selling John's ATV.
7. They have decided to purchase $780,000 of 30-year term life insurance on Jackie for an annual premium of $280, but are unsure of the amount of life insurance to purchase on John's life.

CASE

Bob & Candi Sweet Case

9

Today is January 1, 2013

INTRODUCTORY DATA

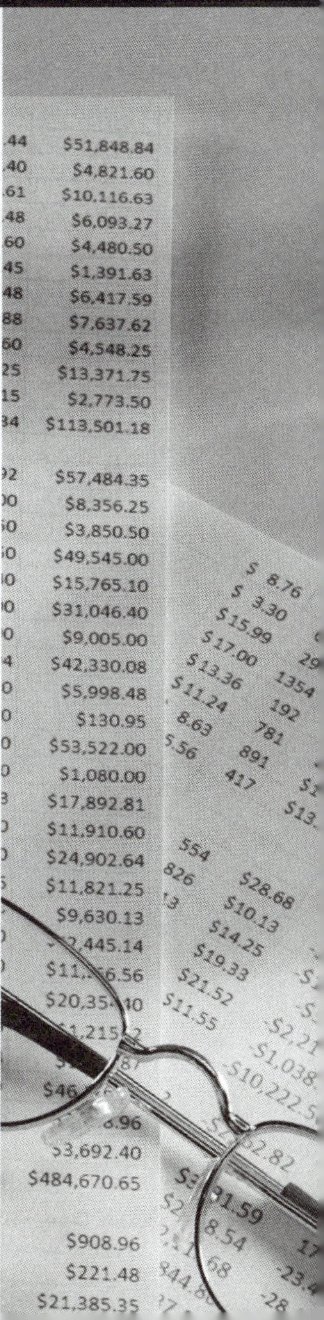

The Family

Candi and Bob Sweet own a boutique truffle shop that offers delectable treats that are enjoyed by the local residents. Like many entrepreneurs, the Sweets have been very focused on their business and have sacrificed much, including not planning for their own retirement. However, Bob's recent 55th birthday bash sparked their interest and focus on retirement and retirement planning. They have come to you to assist them with planning for their retirement and to assist them with their family business.

They want their financial plan to be flexible enough to meet their goals. They believe they will benefit from meeting with a CERTIFIED FINANCIAL PLANNER™ practitioner and arrived with the following information for you to assist them in creating a plan to meet their financial goals.

Bob Sweet

Bob is 55 years old and is currently the president of Truffle Times. He was raised in the south as a member of a large family and learned to cook from his mother, Lori, who cooked daily for the entire family. He is currently in very good health, exercises regularly and competes in local runs and sprint triathlons. Bob and Candi are hands on with both kids in school, Cinnamon and Pepper, and have high hopes for their oldest child, Sam.

Candi Sweet

Candi is 45 years old and is currently the CTO (Chief Truffle Officer), in charge of all of the candies that are created and sold. She was raised in Seattle, but moved to New Orleans to attend culinary school. She spent two years working with Emeril Lagasse at Commander's Palace as the pastry chef. She spent her childhood learning to cook from her grandmother, Betty, who owned a very popular diner. Candi is also in good health and likes to run and cycle.

Cinnamon Sweet

Cinnamon (age 16) is a junior in high school. She works part time at Truffle Times, volunteers at Children's Hospital as a candy striper, and plays on the high school volleyball team. She is also an avid runner.

Pepper Sweet

Pepper (age 17) is a senior in high school and spends most of his time practicing with the baseball and football teams as well as studying for his classes. He does not work at the family business, but he is interested in running the business someday.

Sam Sweet

Sam (age 25) is a bright young man who graduated from college with a BA in History and a MS in History. He is currently working at Truffle Times as a vice-president over supply chain management. In reality, this means that he gets supplies for the kitchen and coordinates the boxes for shipping truffles. He has never had another job but would like to run Truffle Times.

Financial Goals & Concerns

Bob and Candi have expressed the following goals:

1. They would like to retire when Bob is age 60 with $250,000 of annual income in today's dollars. They expect Social Security will reduce what they need to save. For planning purposes, they plan on living until Bob is age 100.
2. They want to pay for their children's college education and expect Cinnamon and Pepper will attend college for 5 years each and will need about $60,000 per year in today's dollars. They expect that the cost of tuition will continue to increase at 6% per year, which has been the trend lately.
3. They want to purchase a 40-foot sailboat when they retire so they can sail around the world. They expect they will purchase a boat that is about $300,000 in today's dollars. They expect that the cost of the boat will increase at the general rate of inflation. This acquisition will increase their annual operating costs, but any increase should be covered in the $250,000 of annual income needs.
4. They want to decide what to do with Truffle Times in terms of transferring it or selling it. They are certainly open to discussing other alternatives.
5. They would like to figure out how to reduce their income tax burden.

EXTERNAL INFORMATION

Economic Information

- General inflation (CPI) is expected to be 3% annually.
- Education inflation is expected to be 6% annually.
- They live in the state of Texas which has no state income tax.
- Raises are uncertain but in the long run are expected to be equal to general inflation (CPI).
- The economy is in a slow growth recovery from a recession with moderate to high unemployment.

Bank Lending Rates

- Mortgage 30 years - conforming rate = 4.0%
- Mortgage 15 years - conforming rate = 3.75%
- Any closing costs associated with mortgage refinancing are an additional 3% of the amount mortgaged.

Investment Return Expectations

The Sweet's required rate of return is 8%.

	Return	Standard Deviation
Cash and Money Market Fund	2.5%	2.0%
Treasury Bonds/ Bond Funds	4.0%	4.0%
Corporate Bonds/ Bond Funds	6.0%	5.0%
International Bond Funds	7.0%	6.0%
Index Fund	9.0%	14.0%
Large Cap Funds/Stocks	10.0%	16.0%
Mid/Small Funds/Stocks	12.0%	18.0%
International Stock Funds	13.0%	22.0%
Real Estate Funds	8.0%	12.0%

INTERNAL INFORMATION

FINANCIAL STATEMENTS

Statement of Financial Position (Beginning of Year)

Statement of Financial Position
Bob & Candi Sweet
Balance Sheet as of 1/1/2012

ASSETS				LIABILITIES AND NET WORTH			
Current Assets				**Current Liabilities**			
JT	Cash & Checking	$15,000		JT	Credit Cards	$100	
JT	Money Market	$15,500		H	Credit Cards 2	$0	
Total Current Assets			$30,500	**Total Current Liabilities**			$100
Investment Assets				**Long-Term Liabilities**			
H	Brokerage Account	$0		JT	Principal Residence	$543,053	
H	IRA Rollover	$28,000		W	Infiniti	$40,000	
W	IRA Rollover	$23,000		**Total Long-Term Liabilities**			$583,053
JT	Truffle Times (est.)	$78,643					
Total Investment Assets			$129,643				
Personal Use Assets				**Total Liabilities**			$583,153
JT	Principal Residence (land $50,000)	$600,000					
H	Porsche Cayanne	$50,000					
W	Infiniti	$45,000		**Total Net Worth**			$371,989
JT	Clothing, Furniture, Fixtures	$100,000					
Total Personal Use Assets			$795,000				
Total Assets			**$955,143**	**Total Liabilities & Net Worth**			**$955,143**

Title Designations:
H = Husband (Sole Owner)
W = Wife (Sole Owner)
JT = Joint Tenancy with Survivorship Rights

Statement of Financial Position (End of Year)

Statement of Financial Position
Bob & Candi Sweet
Balance Sheet as of 1/1/2013

ASSETS				LIABILITIES AND NET WORTH			
Current Assets				**Current Liabilities**			
JT	Cash & Checking	$5,000		JT Credit Cards		$100	
JT	Money Market	$15,500		H Credit Cards 2		$0	
Total Current Assets			$20,500	**Total Current Liabilities**			$100
Investment Assets				**Long-Term Liabilities**			
H	Brokerage Account	$0		JT Principal Residence		$533,924	
H	IRA Rollover	$30,000		W Infiniti		$27,586	
W	IRA Rollover	$25,000		**Total Long-Term Liabilities**			$561,510
JT	Truffle Times (est.)	$4,341,552					
Total Investment Assets			$4,396,552				
Personal Use Assets				**Total Liabilities**			$561,610
JT	Principal Residence (land $50,000)	$500,000					
H	Porsche Cayanne	$50,000					
W	Infiniti	$45,000		**Total Net Worth**			$4,550,443
JT	Clothing, Furniture, Fixtures	$100,000					
Total Personal Use Assets			$695,000				
Total Assets			**$5,112,052**	**Total Liabilities & Net Worth**			**$5,112,052**

Title Designations:
H = Husband (Sole Owner)
W = Wife (Sole Owner)
JT = Joint Tenancy with Survivorship Rights

Income Statement

Statement of Income and Expenses Bob and Candi Sweet Statement of Income and Expenses for 2013 (estimate)			
Cash Inflows			
Bob Salary & Bonus	$250,000		
Candi Salary	$100,000		
Total Cash Inflows			$350,000
Savings			
Bob 401(k) Plan Deferral	$0		
Candi 401(k) Plan Deferral	$0		
Total Savings			$0
Taxes			
Federal Income Taxes Withheld - Bob	$50,000		
Federal Income Taxes Withheld - Candi	$20,000		
Federal Estimated Tax payments	$125,000		
Bob Social Security Taxes	$10,451		
Candi Social Security Taxes	$7,650		
Property Tax Principal Residence	$9,000	ND	
Total Taxes			$222,101
Debt Payments			
Principal Residence	$36,074	ND	
Auto Loan (Infiniti)	$14,821	ND	
Other	$0	ND	
Total Debt Payments			$50,895
Living Expenses			
Utilities Principal Residence	$6,000	ND	
Gasoline for Autos	$2,400	ND	
Lawn Service	$1,800	ND	
Entertainment	$10,000		
Vacations	$10,000		
Church Donations	$3,000	ND	
Clothing	$6,000	ND	
Auto Maintenance	$0	ND	
Satellite TV	$800	ND	
Food	$6,500	ND	
Tuition for high school (both kids)	$40,000	ND	
Total Living Expenses			$86,500
Insurance Payments			
HO Insurance Principal Residence	$4,000	ND	
Auto Insurance Premiums	$4,000	ND	
Life Insurance Premiums (Bob & Candi)	$12,400	ND	
Liability Insurance	$500	ND	
Total Insurance Payments			$20,900
Total Cash Outflows			$380,397
Net Discretionary Cash Flows[1]			**($30,397)**

1. The Sweets take distribution from Truffle Times in an amount sufficient enough to make up for cash flow deficiencies.

INSURANCE INFORMATION

Life Insurance

Bob has a whole life policy that he acquired while he worked in the corporate world. His former company paid the premiums for the policy, but now he pays the premiums. The policy has a face value of $2 million and has a monthly premium of $1,000. It currently has a cash value of $40,000. The crediting rate is 4%.

Candi has a term policy that is paid for by Truffle Times. It has a face value of $250,000 with an annual premium of $400.

Health Insurance

Bob and Candi are covered under the Truffle Times health policy. They believe the policy is satisfactory in every way regarding major medical, stop loss, etc.

Disability Insurance

Bob and Candi are covered under disability policies paid for by Truffle Times. The policies provide for a 90 day elimination period and provide benefits of 60% of gross pay up to age 65. The policies have an own occupation definition and cover both accidents and sickness. The annual premiums are $1,500 for each policy - $3,000 total.

Property – Home and Automobile Insurance

Bob and Candi have the following coverages:

Homeowner	HO3 with endorsements $250 deductible low premiums Annual premium $4,000
Auto	$100k/$300k/$50k PAP with $250 deductible for comprehensive and collision Annual premium $4,000

Liability Insurance

Bob and Candi have a personal liability umbrella policy with a face value of $1 million. The annual premium is $500.

INVESTMENT INFORMATION

The Sweets think that they need nine months of cash flow, net of all taxes, savings, vacation, and discretionary cash flow, in an emergency fund. They are willing to include in the emergency fund their savings account. The Sweets are not well educated in the area of investments. They are willing to accept enough risk to accomplish their goals, but not excessive risk.

Bob had amassed a sizable investment portfolio, both in taxable and tax deferred accounts. However, with the recent economic troubles, most of his portfolios have been devastated. In fact, his brokerage account has gone to zero. He really has to begin again. Fortunately, Truffle Times is growing. However, there are challenges and growing pains with the company.

As part of a financial planning engagement, you go through the process of assessing the Sweets risk tolerance. Bob and Candi answered the following six questions as follows. The answers below are given at the beginning of the engagement.

Risk Tolerance Questionnaire

Global Portfolio Allocation Scoring System (PASS) for Individual Investors[1]

Questions	Strongly Agree	Agree	Neutral	Disagree	Strongly Disagree
1. Earning a high long-term total return that will allow my capital to grow faster than the inflation rate is one of my most important investment objectives.		B, C			
2. I would like an investment that provides me with an opportunity to defer taxation of capital gains to future years.	B, C				
3. I do not require a high level of current income from my investments.	B, C				
4. I am willing to tolerate some sharp down swings in the return on my investments in order to seek a potentially higher return than would normally be expected from more stable investments.		B	C		
5. I am willing to risk a short-term loss in return for a potentially higher long-run rate of return.		B	C		
6. I am financially able to accept a low level of liquidity in my investment portfolio.		B, C			

B = Bob, C = Candi

1. Global Portfolio Allocation Scoring System (PASS) for Individual Investors - developed by Dr. William Droms (Georgetown University) and Steven N. Strauss, (DromsStrauss Advisors Inc.) - model used with permission.

EDUCATION INFORMATION

The Sweets are currently sending their children to The Village School, which is a college preparatory school. The annual tuition is currently $20,000 for each child. They want their children to go to a top tier private school and expect that the tuition and all the other costs will be about $60,000 per year in today's dollars. They want to plan on the children attending for five years and assume that tuition costs will continue to rise at about six percent per year.

TRUFFLE TIMES

Truffle Times (TT) started out as a small retail shop with owners who had a love for candies. However, it has grown dramatically over the last two years. Bob spent time in the corporate world and has some experience in online commerce. He has helped the company grow by selling over the Internet. Bob believes the success over the recent years is largely due to his strategic planning and decision-making.

As the company has grown, Bob has added employees. A little over a year ago, he brought in Dustin Offer and Ben Candik, who are considered experts in e-commerce and marketing. Bob sees their addition to the company as an investment in the business and his future. Bob believes that without Dustin and Ben, Truffle Times might not make it as an online company because of the complexity and competitiveness of the industry.

TT is primarily a B2C company that focuses on individual consumers. While this strategy results in a large volume of transactions, it has the benefit of generating timely cash flows since most transactions are paid with credit cards. They have considered going after the B2B market, but have not taken steps at this point to do so.

One issue that has come up recently is creating a significant amount of tension in the business. Bob's son, Sam, has expressed an interest in taking over the business. Despite Bob's experience in the corporate world, he has given Sam's interest some consideration. Dustin and Ben are extremely concerned about the possibility of Sam taking over the business, since he has absolutely no experience working anywhere other than at Truffle Times and lacks basic business training, including accounting, marketing, sales, etc. They see this possibility as a huge risk for the business and for themselves. In addition, they have considered leaving if Sam should take over as the situation stands.

Dustin and Ben have discussed their concerns with Bob, but he is uncertain what to do and would like an outside opinion of how to have his son be part of the business, but also satisfy the concerns of Dustin and Ben. Bob realizes it is critical to keep Dustin and Ben and agrees that Sam could use training and experience. However, Bob would like the business to be run by Sam at some point and does not want to work forever. He also realizes that the business is growing in value and selling it at some point might make sense.

Bob has considered several scenarios to deal with the issue of Dustin and Ben, as well as Sam:

- ***Scenario 1: Do Nothing*** - As they are both being paid a lot of money. They may not leave and even if they did, he might be able to replace one or both of them.
- ***Scenario 2: Deferred Compensation*** - Establish a deferred compensation plan for them in which 10% of the net income of the business is contributed to a fund that has a guaranteed annual rate of return of 8%. The contributions would terminate after 10 years or 10 payments or upon the termination of their employment.
- ***Scenario 3: Sales Proceeds*** - Consider giving them each 5% of the proceeds of any sale. Bob expects that the business could be sold in 5 years (when Bob turns 60) for at least 6 times net income. In addition, he expects that the business will grow at an annual rate of 20% (revenue and net income) in 2014, 2015, and

2016. He expects it to grow at an annual rate of 10% after that until sold. He has valued the business at 10 times net income on his most recent balance sheet.

- ***Scenario 4: ESOP*** - Regarding any sale, Bob has considered selling to a third party, but realizes that this might mean that Sam could not run the business. As an alternative, he has given some thought to an ESOP, but is not sure of the advantages or disadvantages.

Truffle Times is a corporation that has filed an S election and is owned jointly by Candi and Bob.

Truffle Times Inc. Sales: Summary of Units and Pricing

	Local Unit sales				Internet orders			
Products	2010	2011	2012	2013 est	2010	2011	2012	2013 est
Individual truffles	10,000	12,000	16,000	18,000	-	-	-	-
Small Boxes of truffles (12)	6,000	8,000	12,000	15,000	-	500	10,000	18,000
Large Boxes of truffles (24)	4,000	6,500	9,000	12,000	-	2,000	10,000	17,000
Other specialty items	2,000	3,500	6,000	7,000	-	-	-	-
Dark Chocolate Bars	-	1,200	7,000	8,500	-	500	5,000	12,000
Custom Chocolate Bars	-	100	500	1,500	-	200	1,500	5,000
Shipping	-	-	-	-	-	-	-	-
	22,000	**31,300**	**50,500**	**62,000**	-	**3,200**	**26,500**	**52,000**

	Prices				Sales			
Products	2010	2011	2012	2013 est	2010	2011	2012	2013 est
Individual truffles	$2.00	$2.50	$3.00	$3.00	$20,000	$30,000	$48,000	$54,000
Small Boxes of truffles (12)	$25.00	$29.00	$34.00	$35.00	$150,000	$246,500	$748,000	$1,155,000
Large Boxes of truffles (24)	$45.00	$52.00	$60.00	$60.00	$180,000	$442,000	$1,140,000	$1,740,000
Other specialty items	$4.00	$4.50	$5.00	$5.00	$8,000	$15,750	$30,000	$35,000
Dark Chocolate Bars	$5.00	$5.25	$5.50	$5.75	$0	$8,925	$66,000	$117,875
Custom Chocolate Bars		$7.50	$8.00	$9.00	$0	$2,250	$16,000	$58,500
Shipping					$0	$38,400	$344,500	$728,000
					$358,000	**$783,825**	**$2,392,500**	**$3,888,375**

Truffle Times Inc. Income Statement

	2010	2011	2012	2013 est.
Sales	$358,000	$783,825	$2,392,500	$3,888,375
COGS	$25,955	$54,868	$161,494	$252,744
Profit Margin	$332,045	$728,957	$2,231,006	$3,635,631
Rent	$30,000	$30,000	$30,000	$45,000
Salaries	$261,600	$462,000	$864,000	$1,134,400
Benefits	$31,392	$73,920	$146,880	$204,192
Marketing	$3,000	$8,000	$250,000	$350,000
Credit Card Fees	$14,400	$31,433	$95,780	$155,535
Shipping	-	$30,720	$310,050	$728,000
Computer	$5,000	$12,000	$8,000	$10,000
Internet	-	$20,000	$20,000	$20,000
Convention	-	$3,000	$5,500	$6,000
Health and Other Insurance	$20,000	$25,000	$30,000	$33,000
Cleaning	$2,000	$2,000	$2,000	$2,500
Kitchen Equipment	$8,000	$10,000	$5,000	$5,000
Office	$2,000	$4,000	$4,500	$5,000
Phone	$1,200	$1,200	$2,000	$2,300
Life and Disability	$3,400	$3,400	$3,400	$3,400
Auto Expense	-	-	$14,821	$14,821
Utilities	$4,000	$4,500	$5,000	$8,000
Total Expenses	**$385,912**	**$721,093**	**$1,796,851**	**$2,727,148**
Net Income	**$(53,867)**	**$7,864**	**$434,155**	**$908,483**

Employee Census

	Name	Age	2010	2011	2012	2013 est.	Ownership	Hours
1	Bob	55	$90,000	$125,000	$150,000	$250,000	50%	2,000
2	Candi	45	$40,000	$50,000	$60,000	$100,000	50%	2,000
3	Dustin	35	-	$50,000	$200,000	$250,000	0%	2,000
4	Ben	37	-	$50,000	$200,000	$250,000	0%	2,000
5	Sam	25	$40,000	$45,000	$50,000	$55,000	0%	2,000
6	Anthony	47	$25,000	$28,000	$30,000	$30,000	0%	2,000
7	Raaj	24	-	-	$30,000	$30,000	0%	2,000
8	Andrea	28	$25,000	$25,000	$27,000	$29,000	0%	2,000
9	Cinnamon	16	$3,600	$5,000	$6,000	$6,400	0%	400
10	KS1	24	$20,000	$20,000	$20,000	$20,000	0%	2,000
11	KS2	25	$18,000	$18,000	$18,000	$18,000	0%	2,000
12	KS3	32		$16,000	$16,000	$16,000	0%	1,500
13	KS4	19		$15,000	$15,000	$15,000	0%	1,500
14	KS5	23		$15,000	$15,000	$15,000	0%	1,550
15	KS6	26			$15,000	$15,000	0%	1,500
16	KS7	18			$12,000	$12,000	0%	1,200
17	KS8	19				$9,000	0%	950
18	KS9	20				$7,000	0%	900
19	KS10	22				$7,000	0%	900
	Salary		**$261,600**	**$462,000**	**$864,000**	**$1,134,400**		

KS - Kitchen Staff

INCOME TAX INFORMATION

Bob and Candi take distributions from Truffle Times to help pay their estimated taxes.

RETIREMENT INFORMATION

Bob has considered setting up a retirement plan at Truffle Times. Certainly, many of the employees have inquired about one. Bob is open to the idea, but wants to understand the costs and implications, in addition to understanding the options available.

Bob expects to receive $30,000 (in today's dollars) annually from Social Security when he attains full retirement age of 67. Candi expects to receive $20,000 (in today's dollars) from Social Security when she attains full retirement age of 67. Bob believes they should delay receiving payments from Social Security until they are age 70 so they can take advantage of the increase in benefits.

ESTATE PLANNING INFORMATION

Bob and Candi had wills prepared a few years ago that leave all probate assets to each other with their children as contingent beneficiaries.

Other Information Regarding Assets and Liabilities

Automobiles

Bob and Candi purchased new cars one year ago. Bob purchased a Porsche Cayenne and Candi purchased an Infiniti. They decided they would have Truffle Times pay for Bob's car since it is an SUV and can be used to pick up supplies and make deliveries. Bob probably uses the car for actual business about 30 percent of the time. Truffle Times owns another delivery van that is used for picking up supplies and is used exclusively for the business. In addition, the van is painted with the Truffle Times logo, website and phone number.

Personal Residence

The Sweets purchased a new residence three years ago for $700,000 and financed 80 percent of the purchase price at five percent for 30 years. Unfortunately, the value of the property has declined significantly due to the housing market. It is currently worth less than what they owe on the property.

CASE ASSUMPTIONS

Bob's Social Security retirement benefit at normal retirement age of 67 is $2,500 per month in today's dollars. Candi's Social Security retirement benefit at normal retirement age of 67 is $1,666.67 per month in today's dollars.

CASE

Elvis and Adele Singer Case

10

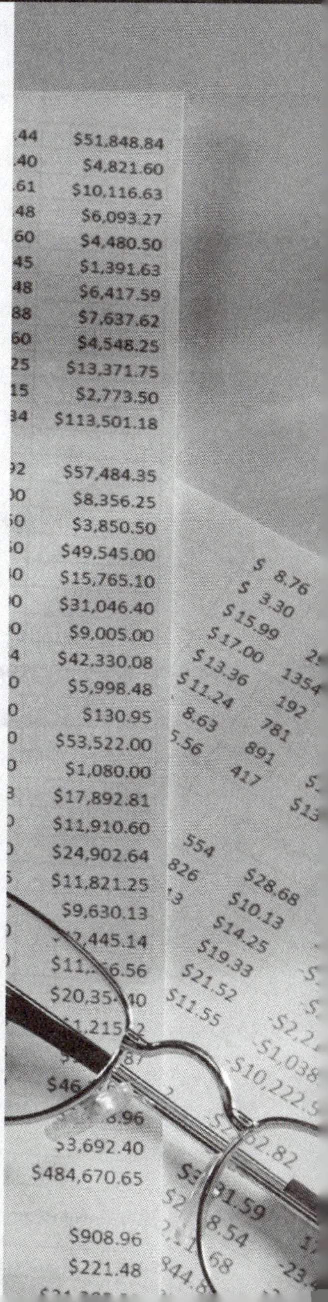

Today is January 2, 2013

INTRODUCTORY DATA

Elvis and Adele Singer came to you because their oldest child wants to attend an exclusive school for music education and they want your help to review their education savings plan and readiness for retirement. The Singer's were in serious debt 10 years ago when they sought a financial planner to help them get their spending under control. They made significant changes to their debt load, savings and discretionary cash flow and have maintained the savings goals established for them at that time. However, things have changed and the Singer's believe they will benefit from meeting with a CERTIFIED FINANCIAL PLANNER™ practitioner. They arrived with the following information for you to assist them in a comprehensive review of their overall plan.

THE FAMILY

Elvis and Adele Singer are both 47 years old and have been married for 20 years. Elvis Singer is an Artist who works full-time for a small, privately held production company. Elvis and Adele met while on a group tour of the Metropolitan Museum of Fine Art in New York. They dated while Elvis was in art school and married a few years after he graduated.

Adele worked as a self-employed vocal coach until their first child was born, then she became a stay-at-home mom. The children all attend local public schools. However, budget cuts forced their school system to cut all music, drama and choral classes from their curriculum. To offset the gap in the children's education, Adele spends a good deal of time working with each child to ensure they can sing and read music. As a result of Adele's efforts, the children are all very talented vocalists as well as good students.

The Singer's have been following the financial plan created 10 years ago, and updated every third year. At the time the plan was conceived Elvis and Adele thought they would send their children to a state university. They now believe their extraordinary children will need to attend private universities where they can receive specialized training in their areas of interest. Adele is willing to return to work to help pay for the change in education cost due to sending the children to private versus public universities.

Adele believes her vocal coaching skills to be in demand but does not know how to break into the music coaching business. If she can find work, she believes she will make enough money to help pay for the advanced training and education they hope to provide for their children. Elvis and Adele have three children.

The Children

Bing, age 16, just started his junior year of high school. Bing shows exceptional vocal talent and wants to attend Warbler University, a prestigious and expensive school of music. Celine, age 13, has exceptional vocal talent too, but she wants to attend the Old School for drama and music. Shania, age 11, has a great voice but is more interested in composing music than in singing. She is unsure of where she wants to attend school and may decide to attend the local state university.

The children's vocal and musical talent may help them qualify for merit-based aid, but the Singer's want to update their education plan to one that will provide sufficient funds to send their children to a private university. They are willing to make changes to their finances but they need your help to determine the shortfall due to the change in their education savings goal and increase in the education inflation rate to 6%.

Since their original plan, the Singer's have saved $14,925 per year toward their education savings goal and have stayed out of debt, except for the most recent car loan.

Elvis and Adele provided the following updated goals:

Financial Goals & Concerns

1. College education of children for 4 years, each beginning at age 18, at a private university costing $34,000 per year, in today's dollars with a 6% education inflation rate.
2. Pay off mortgage and HELOC before/at retirement.
3. Retirement at age 62 with 70% of preretirement income including Social Security, which they expect to total $2,500 per month in today's dollars (for both of them) at normal retirement age. Life expectancy is 91 for both.
4. Appropriate risk management portfolio, investment portfolio, and estate planning portfolio.

EXTERNAL INFORMATION

Economic Information

- General inflation (CPI) is expected to be 3% annually.
- Education inflation is expected to be 6% annually.
- They live in a common law state that has no state income tax.

Bank Lending Rates

- Mortgage 30 years - conforming rate = 4.0%
- Mortgage 15 years - conforming rate = 3.5%
- Refinancing costs are 3% of the amount refinanced and can be paid directly or included in the balance refinanced.
- The prime rate is 3.25%.

Investment Returns Expected

- General market is expected to return 8.5% in the short run but has a long-term rate of return of 10.4%.
- The Singer's required and expected long-term rate of return is 8.5%.
- Fixed income investments are expected to yield 6%.
- T-Bills are expected to yield 3% per year and are expected to be the proxy for the risk-free rate of return.
- Elvis and Adele scored a 19 on the Global Portfolio Allocation Scoring System (PASS) for Individual Investors.

Investment Return Expectations

	Return	Standard Deviation
Cash and Money Market Fund	2.5%	2.5%
Guaranteed Income Fund	2.5%	2.5%
Treasury Bonds/ Bond Funds	4.0%	4.0%
Corporate Bonds/ Bond Funds	6.0%	5.0%
Municipal Bonds/ Bond Funds	5.0%	4.0%
International Bond Funds	7.0%	6.0%
Index Fund	9.0%	14.0%
Large Cap Funds/Stocks	10.0%	16.0%
Mid/Small Funds/Stocks	12.0%	18.0%
International Stock Funds	13.0%	22.0%
Real Estate Funds	8.0%	12.0%

INTERNAL INFORMATION

FINANCIAL STATEMENTS

Statement of Financial Position (Beginning of Year)

Statement of Financial Position
Elvis and Adele Singer
Balance Sheet as of 1/1/2013

ASSETS[1,3]				LIABILITIES AND NET WORTH[2,3]		
Current Assets				**Current Liabilities**		
JT	Cash & Checking	$7,500		W Credit Cards	$0	
JT	Money Market	$25,000		**Total Current Liabilities**		**$0**
Total Current Assets			**$32,500**			
Investment Assets				**Long-Term Liabilities**		
W	Brokerage - Stocks	$24,600		JT Principal Residence[4]	$194,542	
H	401(k) Plan	$88,076		JT Autos	$15,584	
W	401(k) Plan	$0		JT HELOC	$6,716	
H	Education Savings Account	$152,235		**Total Long-Term Liabilities**		**$216,842**
Total Investment Assets			**$264,911**			
Personal Use Assets						
JT	Principal Residence[4]	$340,000		**Total Liabilities**		**$216,842**
JT	Autos	$45,000				
JT	Furniture and Fixtures	$85,000				
W	Jewelry	$30,000		**Total Net Worth**		**$605,569**
JT	Other, Clothing	$25,000				
Total Personal Use Assets			**$525,000**			
Total Assets			**$822,411**	**Total Liabilities & Net Worth**		**$822,411**

1. Assets are stated at fair market value.
2. Liabilities are stated at principal only as of January 1, 2013 before January payments.
3. Federal income tax refund or liability for 2012 has not been determined and is not included.
4. Home purchased approximately 18 years ago at $400,000 with 20% down and 30-year mortgage at 6.25%. They have 139 payments remaining. Unfortunately, the value of the residence has fallen to $340,000. Land is valued at $100,000.

Statement of Income and Expenses

Statement of Income and Expenses
Elvis and Adele Singer
Statement of Income and Expenses for 2012 and Projected for 2013

			Totals
Cash Inflows			
Elvis' Salary	$138,500		
	$0		
Total Cash Inflows			**$138,500**
Education Savings	$14,925		
401(k) Plan – H	$13,850		
	$0		
Total Savings			**$28,775**
Taxes			
Federal Income Taxes Withheld	$14,000		
Social Security Taxes - H	$8,834		
Property Tax Principal Residence	$4,000	ND	
Total Taxes			**$26,834**
Debt Payments (Principal & Interest)			
Principal Residence	$23,644	ND	
Auto Loan	$8,112	ND	
HELOC	$1,820	ND	
	$0	ND	
	$0	ND	
Total Debt Payments			**$33,576**
Living Expenses			
Utilities Principal Residence	$6,000	ND	
Auto Maintenance and Gasoline	$2,400	ND	
Entertainment and Vacations	$7,200		
Church Donations	$0		
Food	$9,600	ND	
Children's lessons, lunches, allowances	$3,600	ND	
Lawn and cleaning services	$2,400		
Clothing	$3,600	ND	
Miscellaneous	$1,800	ND	
Total Living Expenses			**$36,600**
Insurance Payments			
HO Insurance Principal Residence	$1,875	ND	
Life Insurance	$2,335	ND	
Health Insurance	$4,800	ND	
Disability Insurance	$1,200	ND	
Auto Insurance	$2,400	ND	
Total Insurance Payments			**$12,610**
Total Cash Outflows			**$138,395**
Net Discretionary Cash Flows			**$105**

ND - Non-discretionary cash flow per mutual understanding between financial planner and client.

Education Information

- The Singer's previously estimated college costs at State University totaling $17,000 per child, per year, in today's dollars for tuition, fees, room and board with a 5% inflation rate. They still want to pay for four years of schooling but have changed their goal from a State University to a Private University and have doubled their education cost estimate to $34,000 per year, per child in today's dollars. They also expect education inflation to be 6% per year rather than 5%.
- The Singer's do not think they will qualify for financial aid to send their children to college but plan to complete a Free Application for Federal Student Aid as well as the CSS Financial Aid profile for the various private universities their children may attend.
- Elvis and Adele have done some research on Warbler University and the Old School and found that both offer needs-based and merit-informed financial aid. Their understanding of merit-informed financial aid is that each potential student is required to audition for a place at the university, and that the merit-informed aid offered will depend on the results of each child's audition.
- The Singer's are positive that their children's vocal and musical talent will be rewarded and that they will qualify for some form of merit-informed financial aid.

Insurance Information

Life Insurance

A result of the financial planning done 10 years ago was the purchase of 30-year term life insurance policies on Elvis and Adele. Elvis' insurance need was estimated to be approximately 12 times his income. Coverage on Adele was designed to repay outstanding debt, fully fund the college education need, pay for a nanny for the children for 10 years and cover any final expenses.

Elvis' salary has increased over the last 10 years and his employer increased their employee benefits package a year ago which resulted in Elvis receiving a larger basic life insurance death benefit (increased from $25,000 to $50,000). They want you to review their life insurance coverage to determine if it is adequate.

	Policy A	Policy B	Policy C
Insured	Elvis	Elvis	Adele
Face Amount	$1,000,000	$50,000	$800,000
Type	Private 30-year term	Group term	Private 30-year term
Beneficiary	Adele	Adele	Elvis
Contingent Beneficiary	Children	Children	Children
Premium (annual)	$1,680	Employer Paid	$655

Health Insurance

- Group major medical
- Elvis' group major medical
- $1,000,000 lifetime benefits per person
- $5,000 stop loss (annual)
- $200 deductible per person
- 80/20 co-insurance for major medical
- Premium employer provided for Elvis. Elvis pays $4,800 per year for family coverage.

Long-Term Disability Insurance

The upgraded employee benefits package includes a basic group long-term disability income insurance policy benefit of $3,500 per month. The additional $3,500 monthly benefit is important because the monthly benefit on Elvis' private policy decreased from 70% to -43% of Elvis' gross pay due to increases in his income.

	Elvis	Elvis	Adele
Coverage is for Sickness and accidental disability	Own occupation	Any occupation	None
Personally Owned	Yes guaranteed renewable	No Group LTD	
Residual Disability Provision	Yes	Yes	
Benefit	$4,958 per month	$3,500	
Benefit Term	to age 65	to age 65	
Elimination Period	30 days	90 days	
Premium	$1,200 per year	None	

Own = own occupation, EET = experienced, educated, and trained

Long-Term Disability Insurance

Neither Elvis nor Adele have long-term disability insurance.

Homeowners Insurance

Elvis and Adele met with their insurance professional who indicated the premiums they pay for their homeowner's coverage are very competitive and cannot be reduced without changing their coverage.

HO3 with endorsements, open perils and replacement value
3% deductible, coverage of $240,000 for the home
Annual premium $1,625

Automobile Insurance

$100k/$300k/$50k
$1,000 deductible for comprehensive and collision
Annual premium $2,400

Liability Insurance

They have a $1,000,000 Personal Liability Umbrella Policy (PLUP) which costs $250.00 per year.

Investment Information

Portfolio Information

Elvis and Adele Singer Portfolio Information 12/31/12

Total Portfolio

Cash and Cash Equivalents Plus Investments

	Dollars	%
Cash	$32,500	11%
Fixed income	$20,000	7%
US Equities	$244,911	82%
Foreign Equities	$0	0%
Total	**$297,411**	**100%**

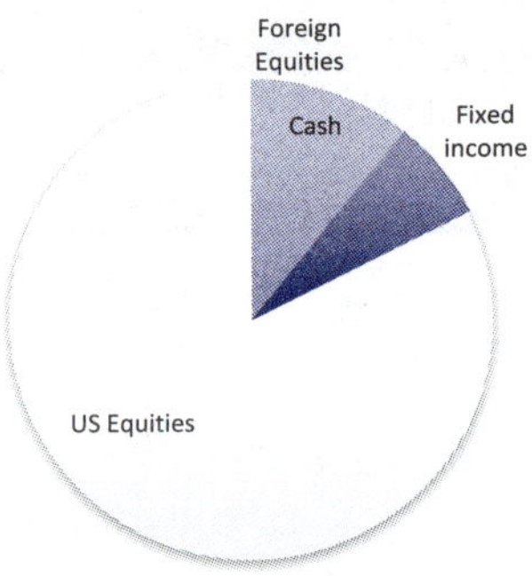

Account	Cash	Bonds	US Equities	Foreign Equities	Total
Cash	$32,500				$32,500
Brokerage account			$24,600		$24,600
401(k) Plan			$88,076		$88,076
401(k) Plan					$0
Education Svgs		$20,000	$34,595		$54,595
Education Svgs			$51,754		$51,754
Education Svgs			$45,886		$45,886
Total	$32,500	$20,000	$244,911	$0	$297,411

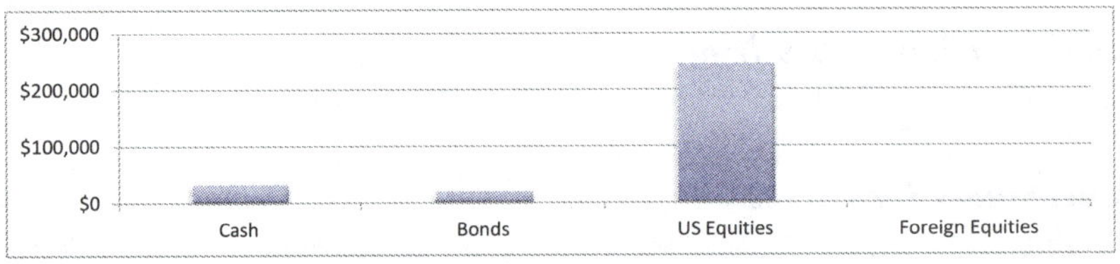

Total Portfolio - Account Types

	Dollars	%
Taxable	$57,100	19%
Education	$152,235	51%
Tax Deferred	$88,076	30%
Roth Accounts	$0	0%
Total	**$297,411**	**100%**

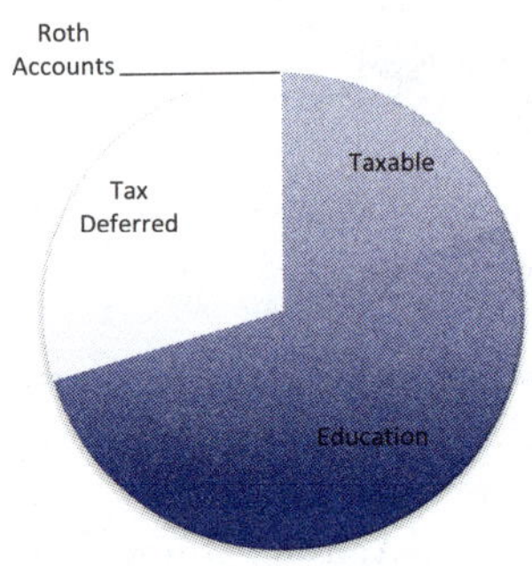

Account	Taxable	Education	Tax Deferred	Roth	Total
Cash	$32,500				$32,500
Brokerage account	$24,600				$24,600
401(k) Plan			$88,076		$88,076
401(k) Plan					$0
Education Svgs		$54,595			$54,595
Education Svgs		$51,754			$51,754
Education Svgs		$45,886			$45,886
Total	$57,100	$152,235	$88,076	$0	$297,411

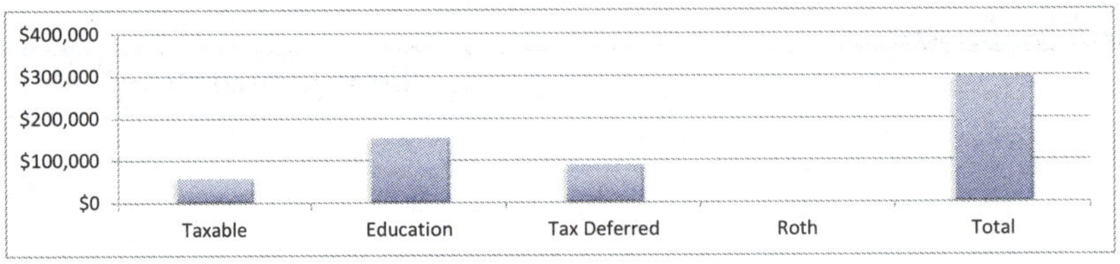

Risk Tolerance Questionnaire

Global Portfolio Allocation Scoring System (PASS) for Individual Investors[1]

Questions	Strongly Agree	Agree	Neutral	Disagree	Strongly Disagree
1. Earning a high long-term total return that will allow my capital to grow faster than the inflation rate is one of my most important investment objectives.	E, A				
2. I would like an investment that provides me with an opportunity to defer taxation of capital gains to future years.		E, A			
3. I do not require a high level of current income from my investments.			E, A		
4. I am willing to tolerate some sharp down swings in the return on my investments in order to seek a potentially higher return than would normally be expected from more stable investments.			E, A		
5. I am willing to risk a short-term loss in return for a potentially higher long-run rate of return.			E, A		
6. I am financially able to accept a low level of liquidity in my investment portfolio.			E, A		

E= Elvis, A = Adele

Brokerage Account

Elvis and Adele tell you that Adele has one stock gifted to her by Adele's spinster Great-Aunt, Pam, many years ago. The FMV of the stock when Aunt Pam gifted it was $22,000. Aunt Pam's CPA provided an adjusted tax basis for the stock at the date of gift as $20,000.

Elvis is willing to sell this stock, but Adele is not. They provided the following information:

Equity Portfolio											
Asset	# of Shares	Current FMV	Aunt Pam's Basis	Date Acquired	Risk Beta	Dividend Yield	Annual Returns				
							2008	2009	2010	2011	2012
Stock	500	$24,600	$20,000	1/1/08	1.15		-15	-5	6.7	10	8.77
		$24,600	$20,000								

1. Global Portfolio Allocation Scoring System (PASS) for Individual Investors - developed by Dr. William Droms (Georgetown University) and Steven N. Strauss, (DromsStrauss Advisors Inc.) - model used with permission.

Retirement Information

- Elvis started contributing to his employer's 401(k) plan 10 years ago. He currently contributes 10% of his annual salary. Elvis's employer plan matches his contribution dollar-for-dollar up to 3% of Elvis's salary.
- Elvis chose a moderate asset allocation in his retirement account.
- Elvis's 401(k) plan has a loan feature that charges 2% above the prime rate.
- Elvis does not know the return on his plan balance, but he considers this account to be a long-term investment and is not concerned about the short-term returns.

Estate Planning Information

Elvis and Adele have basic estate planning documents drafted 10 years ago. The documents contain the name of a primary and successor Guardian for their children as well as a primary and successor Trustee for any Trusts created under their Wills.

Elvis and Adele's parents (the grandparents) have retired and are self-sufficient. They have told the Elvis and Adele not to expect to receive any inheritances from them, and not to expect any help with their grandchildren's education now that they are retired.

Elvis and Adele have left a separate letter of instruction about their funeral arrangements. They both want their family to provide a Jazz funeral for them and intend to leave approximately $20,000 to pay for their final expenses.

Debt

Years ago Elvis and Adele accumulated a significant amount of debt. At that time they spent more than Elvis's salary each month. They met with a planner and created a plan that included paying off all non-mortgage debt by a combination of a $20,500 draw on their 15-year HELOC, the sale of one of two stocks Adele had been gifted by a relative, and some cash flow changes. The changes they made 10 years ago set up the education and retirement savings plan they have today.

They made extra payments on the HELOC balance and stayed out of debt until two years ago when they took out a $30,000 car loan for four years at 3.9%.

Interest rates are low and they want to increase their savings for education while reducing their expenses. They would like to refinance the mortgage on their home from 6.25% to a lower rate and need your help determining if they will save enough by refinancing to fund the projected increase in education expense. Interest rates on 15-year and 30-year mortgages are lower than their existing mortgage interest rate, but only the 15-year mortgage will allow them to refinance and still retire at age 62 debt free.

Liabilities	Rates and Terms	Original Balance	Additional Info.	Monthly Payment
Credit Card	Variable at 18%		Paid in full each month	$0
Auto Loan	4 yrs. @ 3.9%	$30,000	24 months remaining	$676.03
HELOC	15 yrs. @ 4.0%	$20,500	48 months remaining	$151.64
Mortgage Loan	30 yrs. @ 6.25%	$320,000	221 payments made; 139 to go	$1,970.30
Total				**$2,797.97**

Other Information Regarding Assets and Liabilities

Personal Residence

The Singer's purchased their dream home approximately 18 years ago and used all of their excess cash to make the down payment and to pay the closing costs to purchase the home. They plan to stay in this home through retirement.

The Singer's are interested in refinancing the remaining balance on their mortgage to a 15-year loan and believe the reduced interest rate for 15-year loans will help.

them save more money toward their revised education savings goal.

Over a decade ago the Singer's qualified for a 15 year, secured Home Equity Line of Credit (HELOC), for $50,000 with a 4% variable interest rate. The HELOC was still in existence when they adopted their debt reduction plan 10 years ago, so they drew $20,500 on the HELOC to help pay off their non-mortgage debt. They have a small outstanding balance on the HELOC and want to know if they should use some of the available funds on the HELOC to pay off their auto loan.

CASE ASSUMPTIONS

1. Elvis and Adele expect to live to age 91, i.e. through age 90.
2. They have a moderate risk tolerance and a required rate of return of 8.5%.
3. Elvis and Adele want to retire at age 62 with 70% of their pre-retirement income (including their estimated combined Social Security benefit of $30,000 at normal retirement age).
4. They want to refinance their existing mortgage and will roll the cost of refinancing into the amount of the loan.
5. They want to fund four years of private college for each child at a cost of $34,000 in today's dollars, and expect education inflation to be 6% per year.

Appendices

Additional resources available at www.money-education.com

Appendices

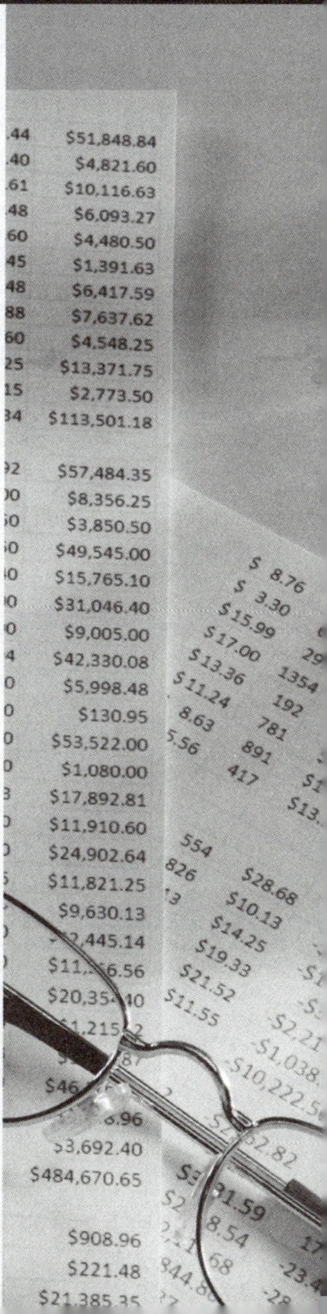

Appendix

Fundamentals

A

Fundamentals Information

Standards of Professional Conduct

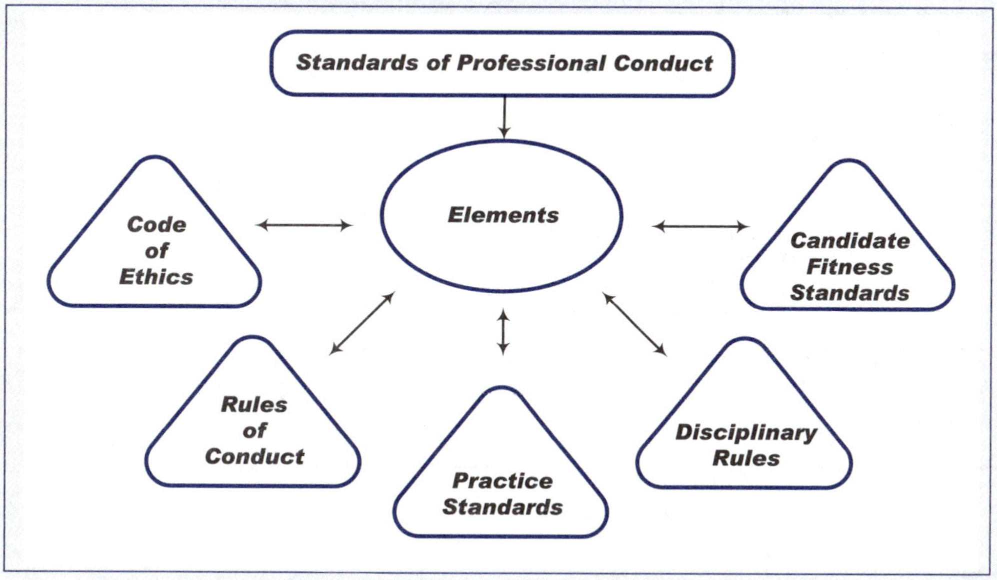

CFP Licensee Duties and Responsibilities

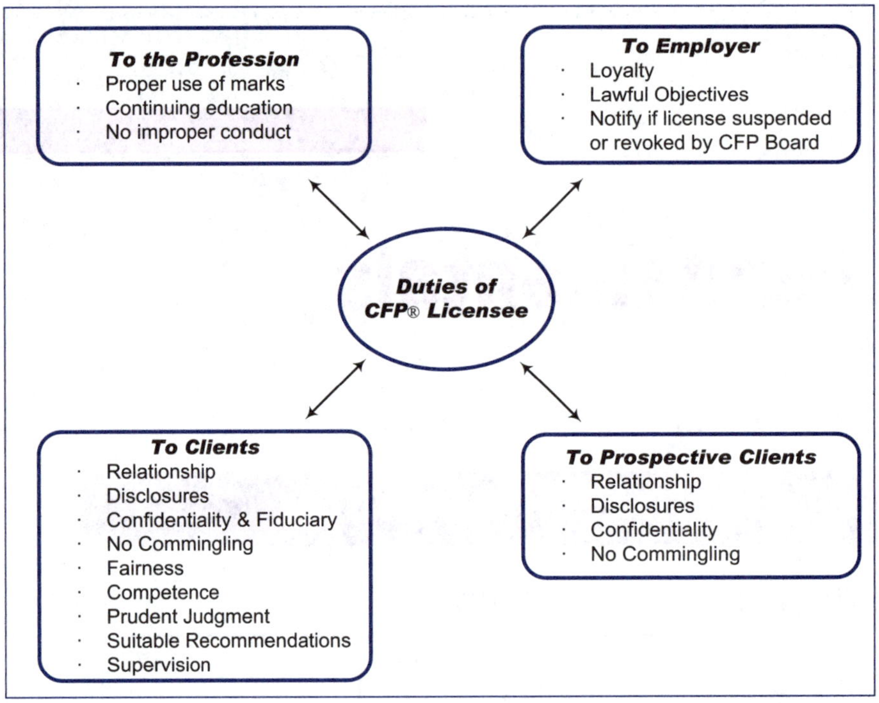

Financial Planning Process[1]

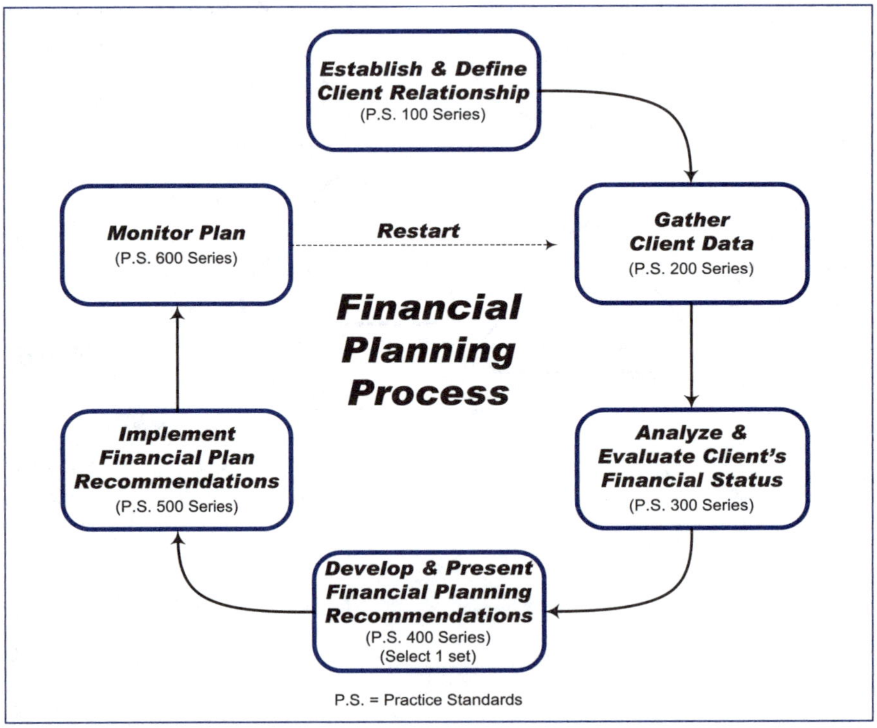

1. Abbreviated from Financial Planning Practice Standards.

Practice Standards Summary

Financial Planning Process	Related Practice Standard
1. Establishing and defining the relationship with a client	100-1 Defining the Scope of the Engagement
2. Gathering the client data	200-1 Determining a Client's Personal and Financial Goals, Needs and Priorities
	200-2 Obtaining Quantitative Information and Documents
3. Analyzing and evaluating the client's financial status	300-1 Analyzing and Evaluating the Client's Information
4. Developing and presenting financial planning recommendations	400-1 Identifying and Evaluating Financial Planning Alternative(s)
	400-2 Developing the Financial Planning Recommendation(s)
	400-3 Presenting the Financial Planning Recommendation(s)
5. Implementing the financial planning recommendations	500-1 Agreeing on Implementation Responsibilities
	500-2 Selecting Products and Services for Implementation
6. Monitoring	600-1 Defining Monitoring Responsibilities

INVESTIGATIVE AND HEARING PROCESS

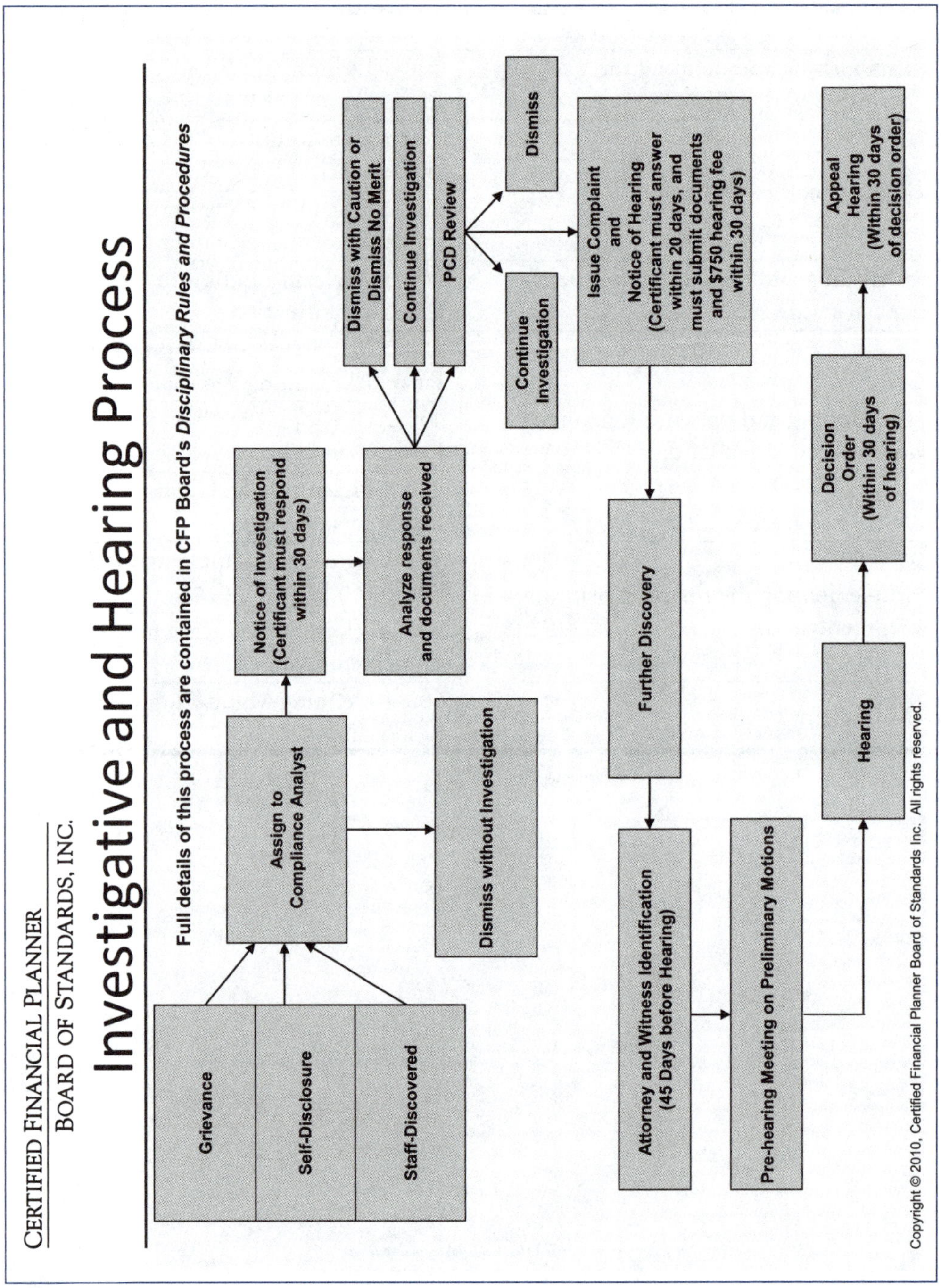

Appendix

B Insurance

Hypothetical Insurance Premiums

These hypothetical premiums are provided for use with Money Education's financial planning cases (unless otherwise stated in the case).

Life Insurance

Hypothetical life insurance premium costs comparison for term and universal per $1,000 of coverage (annual rates).

Age	Term* (10 year)	Term* (25 year)	Term* (30 year)	Universal Life
25	$0.25	$0.52	$0.60	$2.31
30	$0.25	$0.56	$0.64	$2.92
35	$0.26	$0.65	$0.72	$3.77
40	$0.31	$0.96	$1.04	$4.74
45	$0.51	$1.52	$1.68	$5.99
50	$0.83	N/A	N/A	$7.45
55	$1.40	N/A	N/A	$9.05
60	$2.39	N/A	N/A	$11.74
65	$4.08	N/A	N/A	$15.40

Price is per $1,000 of coverage ($ per 000).
For very healthy non-tobacco using male insured.
Female rates are 1/2 the male rate up to age 50 then the same rate
* Usually available to terminate at or before age 75.

Level-term insurance sample for male, age 67.

Amount	10-Year Term*	15-Year Term**
$1,000,000	$6,659	$10,454
$2,000,000	$13,249	$20,838

* MetLife Insurance
** Genworth Life Insurance

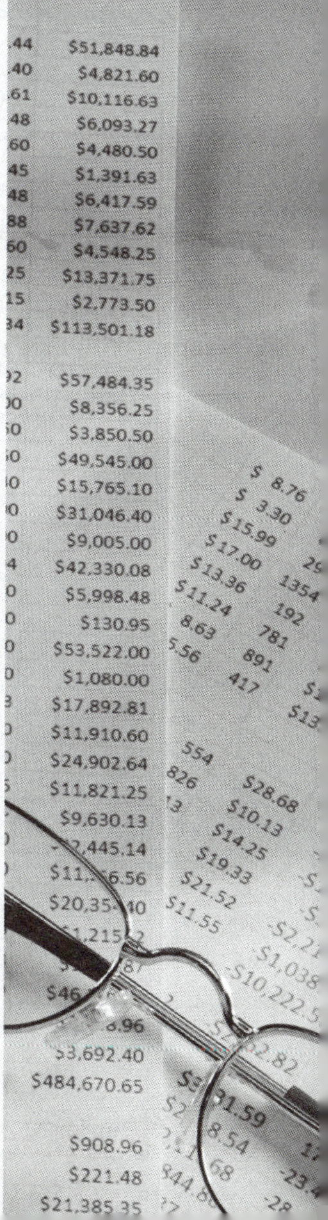

Health Insurance

Hypothetical individual health insurance monthly premiums using the following:

- Deductible: \$0 - \$10,000
- Types of Plans: PPO, POS, Network
- Office Visits: Not covered to \$50 per visit
- Co-insurance: 0 - 30%

	27 Year-Old Female	27 Year-Old Male	47 Year-Old Female	47 Year-Old Male	67 Year-Old Female	67 Year-Old Male
Premiums	\$200	\$140	\$345	\$300	\$575	\$655
Deductibles	\$0 - \$10,000	\$0 - \$10,000	\$0 - \$10,000	\$0 - \$10,000	\$0 - \$10,000	\$0 - \$10,000
Types of Plans	PPO, POS, Network*	PPO, POS, Network*	PPO, POS, Network*	PPO, POS, Network*	PPO, POS, Network*	PPO, POS, Network*
Office Visits	Not Covered to \$50/Visit	Not Covered to \$50/Visit	Not Covered to \$50/Visit	Not Covered to \$50/Visit	Not Covered to \$50/Visit	Not Covered to \$50/Visit
Co-Insurance	0 - 30%	0 - 30%	0 - 30%	0 - 30%	0 - 30%	0 - 30%

**Network plan is a variation of a PPO plan.*

www.ehealthinsurance.com

Disability Insurance

Hypothetical disability insurance monthly premiums for each \$1,000 of benefit (unisex) using G/R, own occupation for first 5 years, any occupation to age 65.

Age	Rate per \$1,000
25	\$1.00
30	\$1.02
32	\$1.10
35	\$1.20
40	\$1.37
45	\$1.55
50	\$1.83
55	\$2.18
60	\$2.58
65	\$3.08

Long-Term Care Insurance

Hypothetical long-term care insurance premiums for $150 daily benefit with a 90 day elimination period and assuming a standard health class.

Future Purchase Option

Age	3-Year Benefit Period	5-Year Benefit Period	Unlimited Benefit Period
45	$695	$825	$1,426
50	$802	$990	$1,634
55	$947	$1,257	$1,891
60	$1,183	$1,582	$2,380
65	$1,745	$2,353	$3,564

3% Compounded Inflation

Age	3-Year Benefit Period	5-Year Benefit Period	Unlimited Benefit Period
45	$1,195	$1,515	$2,454
50	$1,294	$1,710	$2,634
55	$1,451	$1,927	$2,898
60	$1,754	$2,345	$3,529
65	$2,553	$3,442	$5,213

5% Compounded Inflation

Age	3-Year Benefit Period	5-Year Benefit Period	Unlimited Benefit Period
45	$1,886	$2,485	$3,873
50	$1,989	$2,629	$4,049
55	$2,130	$2,827	$4,253
60	$2,567	$3,431	$5,163
65	$3,525	$4,754	$7,199

Homeowners Insurance

- HO2 per $100,000 dwelling use $50/month
- HO3 per $100,000 dwelling use $75/month
- HO3 endorsed for "open perils and RV" use $200 per year
- HO4 per $25,000 coverage use $20 per month
- HO6 per $25,000 coverage use $40 per month

Automobile Insurance

- For $100/$300/$50 per car use $1,200 per year

Other Property Use Insurance (Boat/RV/ATV)

- Use $100 per month for liability and property to be covered under PLUP.

Personal Liability Umbrella Policy (PLUP)

- $1,000,000 use $250 per year
- $2,000,000 use $350 per year
- $3,000,000 use $400 per year
- $4,000,000 use $450 per year

Risk Management

A planner may use a matrix to analyze each risk, such as:

Severity / Frequency	Low Frequency of Occurrence	High Frequency of Occurrence
High Severity (catastrophic financial loss) (e.g., long-term disability)	Transfer and/or Share Risk Using Insurance	Avoid Risk
Low Severity (non-catastrophic financial loss) (e.g., car gets dented in parking lot)	Retain Risk	Retain/Reduce Risk

Typical Covered Perils for Auto and Home

Personal Auto Policy (PAP)	Homeowners Insurance Policy (HO)
Fire	Fire
Storm	Lightning
Theft	Windstorm
Collision	Hail
Hail	Riot
Flood	Falling Objects
Contact with a Bird or Animal	Weight of Ice, Snow, and Sleet
Falling Objects	Smoke
Earthquake	Explosion
Windstorm	Theft

Not all risks are created equally, and not all risks are insurable. A risk that is ideally situated to be an insured risk meets the following requirements:

1. It has a large number of homogeneous exposures.
2. The insured losses must be accidental, from the insured's point of view.
3. The insured losses must be measurable and determinable.
4. The loss must not be financially catastrophic to the insurer.
5. The loss probability must be determinable.

6. The premium for such as risk coverage must be reasonable and affordable.

Rating Agency	Highest Ratings		Lowest Ratings	
A.M. Best	A++	A/A-	C/C -	D
Fitch	AAA	AA -	B+	CCC -
Moody's	Aaa	Aa2	B1	Caa
Standard and Poor's	AAA	AA-	B+	CCC
Weiss	A+	B -	F	U

METHODS TO DETERMINE LIFE INSURANCE NEEDS

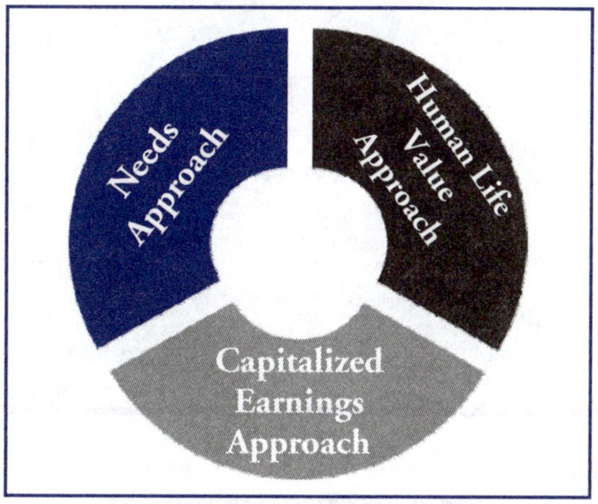

RENEWABLE TERM PREMIUM AND YEARLY RENEWABLE TERM PREMIUM (ISSUED AT AGE 25)

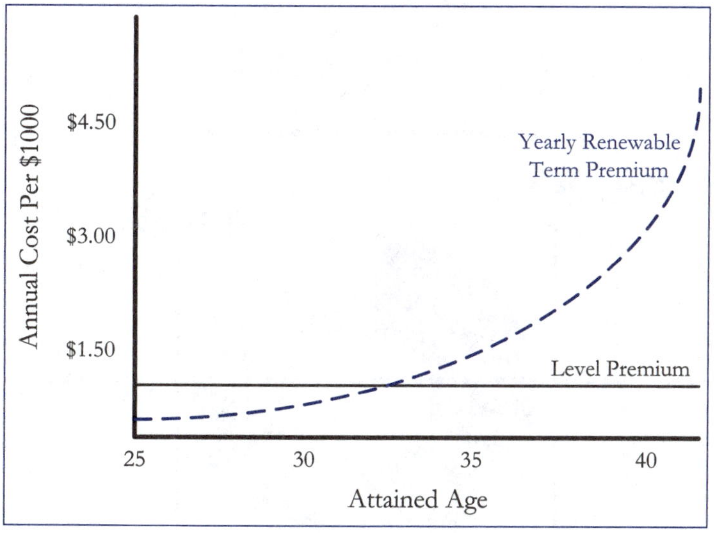

Feature Comparison of Common Life Insurance Policies

	Term Life	Whole (Ordinary) Life	Universal Life	Variable Life	Variable Universal Life
Premium $	Fixed or Variable	Fixed	Variable, subject to a required minimum	Fixed	Variable, subject to a required minimum
Death Benefit	Fixed	Fixed	May increase above initial face amount, depending on cash value accumulation	Has a guaranteed minimum, but can increase if investment experience on cash value is good	Has a guaranteed minimum, but can increase if investment experience on cash value is good
Policyowner's Control Over Investments	None	None	None	Complete	Complete
Rate of Return on Investment	None	Fixed rate	May have a minimum guaranteed rate, but can be higher depending on interest rates	No minimum guarantee, but positive investment experience can yield very high returns	No minimum guarantee, but positive investment experience can yield very high returns
Application	Large need, limited resources	Want guarantees	Flexibility without investment responsibility	Flexibility with investment responsibility, fixed premiums	Flexibility with investment responsibility, variable premiums

Likelihood of Disability

Age	Likelihood
30	4 to 1
35	3.5 to 1
40	2.7 to 1
45	2.1 to 1
50	1.8 to 1
55	1.5 to 1

Types of Disability Policies

COBRA Benefits

18 Months	• Termination of employment • Moving from full-time to part-time status
29 Months	• The employee meets the Social Security definition of disability
36 Months	• Death of a covered employee • Divorce or legal separation of a covered employee • Loss of dependent status • Eligibility for Medicare

Who Needs Long-Term Care

40% of persons receiving long-term care are between 18 and 64.
The likelihood of a disability grows as we age: Ages 44-54: 22.6% Ages 55-64: 35.7% Ages 65-69: 44.9%
At least 70 percent of people over age 65 will require some long-term care services at some point in their lives.

* *GuidetoLongTermCare.com*

Long-Term Care Premium Factors

- Age
- Benefits
- Deductible Periods
- Inflation Protection

Common Features of Long-Term Care Policies

- Renewability - Guaranteed renewability
- Nonforfeitures Benefits - Return of premium or shortened benefit period
- Waiver of premium while receiving benefits

List of Covered Perils - Property Insurance

Basic-Named Perils	
1. Fire	2. Vehicles
3. Lightning	4. Smoke
5. Windstorm	6. Vandalism or malicious mischief
7. Hail	8. Explosion
9. Riot or civil commotion	10. Theft
11. Aircraft	12. Volcanic eruption

Broad-Named Perils Includes Coverage for Basic-Named Perils (1-12) plus 13-18
13. Falling objects
14. Weight of ice, snow, sleet
15. Accidental discharge or overflow of water or steam
16. Sudden and accidental tearing apart, cracking, burning, or bulging of a steam, hot water, air conditioning, or automatic fire protective sprinkler system, or from within a household appliance
17. Freezing of a plumbing, heating, air conditioning, or automatic fire sprinkler system, or of a household appliance
18. Sudden and accidental damage from artificially generated electrical current

Open Perils (Include Coverage for Basic and Broad Perils)
Open perils means the insurance covers any risk that is not excepted in the policy.

Coverage for Different Forms of Homeowners Insurance - Section 1

	HO-2	HO-3	HO-4	HO-5	HO-6	HO-8
Coverage A Dwelling	Broad	Open	N/A	Open	Broad	Basic
Coverage B Other Structures	Broad	Open	N/A	Open	N/A	Basic
Coverage C Personal Property	Broad	Broad	Broad	Open	Broad	Basic
Coverage D Loss of Use	Broad	Broad	Broad	Open	Broad	Basic

SUMMARY OF HOMEOWNERS INSURANCE POLICIES

	HO-2 (Broad Form)	HO-3 (Special Form)	HO-5 (Comprehensive Form)	HO-8 (For Older Homes)	HO-4 (Renter's Contents Broad Form)	HO-6 (For Condominium Owners)
Perils covered	Perils 1 - 18	All perils except those specifically excluded on buildings; perils 1 - 18 on personal property	All perils except those specifically excluded	Perils 1 – 12	Perils 1 – 18	Perils 1 – 18
Section 1: Property coverages/limits						
House and any other attached buildings	Amount based on replacement cost, minimum $15,000	Amount based on replacement cost, minimum $20,000	Amount based on replacement cost, minimum $20,000	Amount based on actual cash value of the home	10% of personal property insurance on additions and alterations to the apartment	$1,000 on owner's additions and alterations to the unit
Detached buildings	10% of insurance on the home	10% of insurance on the home	10% of insurance on the home	10% of insurance on the home	Not covered	Not covered
Trees, shrubs, plants, etc.	5% of insurance on the home, $1,000 maximum per item	5% of insurance on the home, $1,000 maximum per item	5% of insurance on the home, $1,000 maximum per item	5% of insurance on the home, $1,000 maximum per item	10% of personal property insurance, $1,000 maximum per item	10% of personal property insurance, $1,000 maximum per item
Personal property (contents)	50% of insurance on the home	50% of insurance on the home	50% of insurance on the home	50% of insurance on the home	Chosen by the tenant to reflect the value of the items, minimum $6,000	Chosen by the home-owner to reflect the value of the items, minimum $6,000
Loss of use and/or add'l living expenses	30% of insurance on the home	30% of insurance on the home	30% of insurance on the home	10% of insurance on the home	30% of personal property insurance	50% of personal property insurance
Credit card, forgery, counterfeit money	$500	$500	$500	$500	$500	$500
Section 2: Liability						
Comprehensive personal liability	$100,000	$100,000	$100,000	$100,000	$100,000	$100,000
Damage to property of others	$250 - $500	$250 - $500	$250 - $500	$250 - $500	$250 - $500	$250 - $500
Medical payments	$1,000	$1,000	$1,000	$1,000	$1,000	$1,000
Special limits of liability	Special limits apply on a per-occurrence basis (e.g. per fire or theft): money, coins, bank notes, precious metals (gold, silver, etc.), $200; securities, deeds, stocks, bonds, tickets, stamps, $1,500; watercraft and trailers, including furnishings, equipment, and outboard motors, jewelry, watches, furs, $1,500; silverware, goldware, etc., $2,500; guns, $2,500.					

Appendix

Investments C

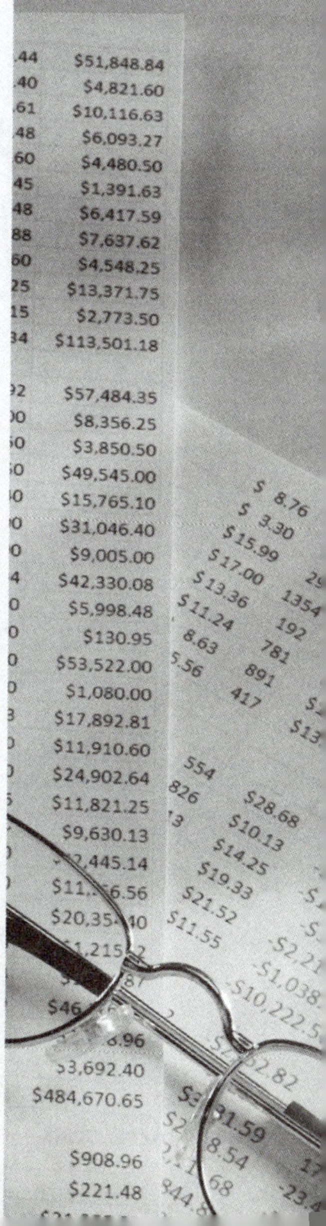

FORMULAS

Dividend Discount Model
(a.k.a. Constant Growth Model, Gordon Growth Model)

$$V = \frac{D_1}{r-g}$$

V = value
D_1 = dividend in period 1
r = required return
g = growth of dividend

This formula is used to determine the value of a stock based on a stream of dividend payments that is increasing at a constant rate of growth.

Beta

$$\beta_i = \frac{COV_{im}}{\sigma_m^2} = \frac{\rho_{im}\sigma_i}{\sigma_m}$$

β_i = beta of asset i
COV_{im} = covariance between i and the market
ρ_{im} = correlation between asset i and the market
σ_i = standard deviation of asset i
σ_m = standard deviation of the market
σ^2_m = variance of the market

Standard Deviation of Historical Returns

$$s_r = \sqrt{\frac{\sum_{t=1}^{n}(r_t - \bar{r})^2}{n-1}}$$

r_t = past returns
$\bar{r}$ = arithmetic mean of past returns
n = number of returns used
s_r = population standard deviation

Capital Asset Pricing Model
(a.k.a. the Security Market Line)

$$r_i = r_f + (r_m - r_f)\beta_i$$

r_i = required rate of return on asset i [sometimes k is substituted for r]
r_f = risk free rate
r_m = return on the market
β_i = beta of asset I [sometimes b is substituted for B]

Capital Market Line

$$r_p = r_f + \sigma_p\left(\frac{r_m - r_f}{\sigma_m}\right)$$

r_p = required portfolio return
r_f = risk free rate
r_m = return on the market
σ_p = portfolio standard deviation
σ_m = standard deviation of the market

Risk-Adjusted Measures of Portfolio Performance

Sharpe Ratio

$$S_p = \frac{r_p - r_f}{\sigma_p}$$

r_p = portfolio return
r_f = risk free rate
σ_p = portfolio standard deviation

Treynor Ratio

$$T_p = \frac{r_p - r_f}{\beta_p}$$

r_p = portfolio return
r_f = risk free rate
β_p = portfolio beta

Jensen's Alpha

$$\alpha_p = r_p - [r_f + (r_m - r_f)\beta_p]$$

α_p = portfolio alpha
r_p = portfolio return
r_f = risk free rate
r_m = return on the market portfolio
β_p = portfolio beta

Bond Duration: Macaulay

$$D = \frac{\sum_{t=1}^{n} \frac{c_t(t)}{(1+i)^t}}{\sum_{t=1}^{n} \frac{c_t}{(1+i)^t}}$$

D = Macaulay duration
C_t = the cash flow that occurs in period t
n = the total number of periods
i = yield to maturity for this bond

$$D = \frac{1+y}{y} - \frac{(1+y)+t(c-y)}{c[(1+y)^t - 1] + y}$$

c = coupon rate
y = yield to maturity
t = time to maturity
D = Macaulay duration

$$\frac{\Delta P}{P} = -D\left[\frac{\Delta y}{1+y}\right]$$

P = bond price
ΔP = the change in price
y = yield to maturity
Δy = the change in yield
D = Macaulay duration

Real Rate (Inflation Adjusted Return)

Use with education funding and retirement needs questions.

$$\text{real rate} = \left[\frac{1 + \text{nominal}}{1 + \text{inflation}} - 1\right] ¥\ 100$$

Portfolio Risk

Portfolio risk combines the individual risks of securities along with their interactive risk.

Standard deviation of a two-asset portfolio:

$$\sigma_p = \sqrt{W_i^2\sigma_i^2 + W_j^2\sigma_j^2 + 2W_iW_jCOV_{ij}}$$

Where $COV_{ij} = \sigma_i\sigma_j\rho_{ij}$

Global Portfolio Allocation Scoring System (PASS) for Individual Investors

	Short-Term Horizon				Intermediate-Term Horizon				Long-Term Horizon			
	RT1 Target	RT2 Target	RT3 Target	RT4 Target	RT1 Target	RT2 Target	RT3 Target	RT4 Target	RT1 Target	RT2 Target	RT3 Target	RT4 Target
PASS Score	6 - 12	13 - 18	19 - 24	25 - 30	6 - 12	13 - 18	19 - 24	25 - 30	6 - 12	13 - 18	19 - 24	25 - 30
Cash and Money Market Fund	40%	30%	20%	10%	5%	5%	5%	5%	5%	5%	3%	2%
Treasury Bonds/ Bond Funds	40%	30%	30%	20%	60%	35%	20%	10%	30%	20%	12%	0%
Corporate Bonds/ Bond Funds	20%	30%	30%	40%	15%	15%	15%	10%	15%	10%	10%	4%
Subtotal	**100%**	**90%**	**80%**	**70%**	**80%**	**55%**	**40%**	**25%**	**50%**	**35%**	**25%**	**6%**
International Bond Funds	0%	0%	0%	0%	0%	5%	5%	5%	0%	5%	5%	4%
Subtotal	**0%**	**0%**	**0%**	**0%**	**0%**	**5%**	**5%**	**5%**	**0%**	**5%**	**5%**	**4%**
Index Fund	0%	10%	10%	10%	10%	15%	20%	20%	20%	20%	20%	25%
Large Cap Value Funds/Stocks	0%	0%	5%	5%	5%	5%	10%	10%	10%	10%	5%	5%
Large Cap Growth Funds/Stocks	0%	0%	0%	0%	5%	5%	5%	10%	15%	10%	10%	5%
Mid/Small Growth Funds/Stocks	0%	0%	0%	0%	0%	0%	5%	5%	0%	0%	5%	10%
Mid/Small Value Funds/Stocks	0%	0%	0%	5%	0%	5%	5%	5%	0%	5%	5%	10%
Subtotal	**0%**	**10%**	**15%**	**20%**	**20%**	**30%**	**45%**	**50%**	**45%**	**45%**	**45%**	**55%**
International Stock Funds	0%		0%	5%	0%	5%	5%	10%	0%	5%	10%	15%
Subtotal	**0%**	**0%**	**0%**	**5%**	**0%**	**5%**	**5%**	**10%**	**0%**	**5%**	**10%**	**15%**
Real Estate Funds	0%		5%	5%	0%	5%	5%	10%	5%	10%	15%	20%
Subtotal	**0%**	**0%**	**5%**	**5%**	**0%**	**5%**	**5%**	**10%**	**5%**	**10%**	**15%**	**20%**
Total	**100%**	**100%**	**100%**	**100%**	**100%**	**100%**	**100%**	**100%**	**100%**	**100%**	**100%**	**100%**

Global Portfolio Allocation Scoring System (PASS) for Individual Investors – developed by Dr. William Droms (Georgetown University) and Steven N. Strauss, (DromsStrauss Advisors Inc.) – model used with permission.

PASS Scoring System[1]

Questions	Strongly Agree	Agree	Neutral	Disagree	Strongly Disagree
1. Earning a high long-term total return that will allow my capital to grow faster than the inflation rate is one of my most important investment objectives.	5	4	3	2	1
2. I would like an investment that provides me with an opportunity to defer taxation of capital gains to future years.	5	4	3	2	1
3. I do not require a high level of current income from my investments.	5	4	3	2	1
4. I am willing to tolerate some sharp down swings in the return on my investments in order to seek a potentially higher return than would normally be expected from more stable investments.	5	4	3	2	1
5. I am willing to risk a short-term loss in return for a potentially higher long-run rate of return.	5	4	3	2	1
6. I am financially able to accept a low level of liquidity in my investment portfolio.	5	4	3	2	1

1. Global Portfolio Allocation Scoring System (PASS) for Individual Investors - developed by Dr. William Droms (Georgetown University) and Steven N. Strauss, (DromsStrauss Advisors Inc.) - model used with permission.

Appendix

Income Tax D

INCOME TAX ISSUES

SOURCES OF TAX LAW

SOURCE	AUTHORITY	LAW
Statutory	Congressionally derived law through legislative power provided by the 16th Amendment to the U.S. Constitution.	Internal Revenue Code of 1986, as amended.
Administrative	• **Treasury Department:** Executive authority of law enforcement delegated to the Treasury Department. • **Internal Revenue Service:** Tax collection authority delegated by the Treasury Department to the Internal Revenue Service.	• **Treasury Regulations:** a. Proposed Regulations b. Temporary Regulations c. Final Regulations • **IRS Determinations:** a. Revenue Rulings b. Private Letter Rulings c. Determination Letters d. Revenue Procedures
Judicial	Judicial authority to determine if tax laws enacted by Congress and enforced by the President are constitutional. Also, decides whether a regulation or IRS position follows the intent of Congress.	**Case Law:** Usually a case or controversy between a taxpayer and the IRS resulting in case law expressed in the opinion of a court.

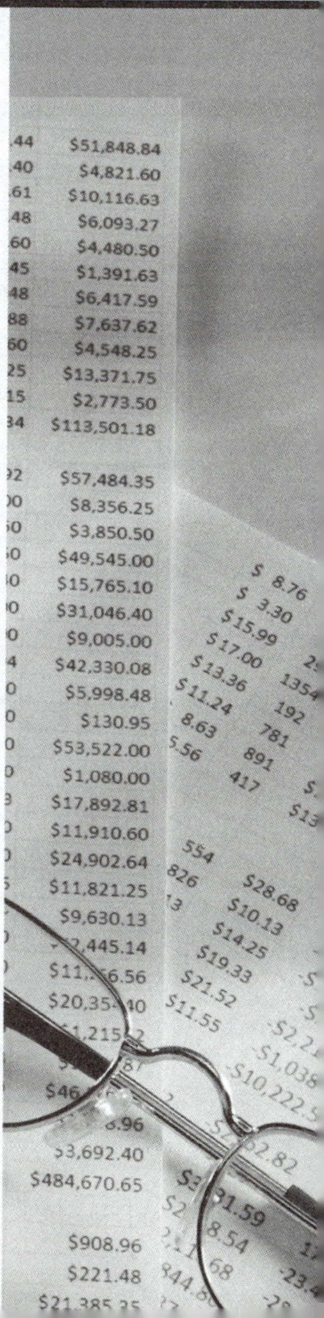

Summary of Penalties

Failure to File	5% per month or part thereof to 25% maximum
Failure to Pay	0.5% per month or part thereof to 25% maximum
Accuracy Related	20% of underpayment to 30%*
Fraud	15% per month up to 75% of underpayment

*40% if due to substantial valuation misstatement, substantial overstatement of pension liabilities, or substantial estate or gift tax valuation understatement.

Court System Summary

	Tax Court	Tax Court - Small Claims	U.S. District Court	U.S. Court of Federal Claims
What kinds of cases?	Tax Only	Tax Only	All Types	Claims Against U.S. Government
Is the taxpayer required to pay the tax?	No	No	Yes	Yes
What is the maximum amount of the claim?	N/A	$50,000	N/A	N/A
Is a jury trial available?	No	No	Yes	No
Where is court located?	Around U.S.	Around U.S.	Around U.S.	D.C. Only
To what court are appeals brought?	U.S. Court of Appeals	No Appeals	U.S. Court of Appeals	U.S. Court of Appeals - Federal Circuit

Individual Income Tax Formula

Income Broadly Defined	**$XX,XXX**
Less: Exclusions	(X,XXX)
Gross Income	**$XX,XXX**
Less: Deductions for Adjusted Gross Income (*above-the-line deductions*)	(X,XXX)
Adjusted Gross Income ("The Line")	**$XX,XXX**
Less: Deductions from Adjusted Gross Income: Greater of Standard or Itemized Deductions (*below-the-line deductions*)	(XX,XXX)
Less: Personal and Dependency Exemptions	(XX,XXX)
Taxable Income	**$XX,XXX**
Tax on Taxable Income	$X,XXX
Less: Credit for Taxes Withheld	(X,XXX)
Less: Credit for Estimated Tax Payments	(X,XXX)
Less: Other Tax Credits	(X,XXX)
Tax Due or (Refund Due)	**$XXX**

Partial List of Exclusions

- Interest income from municipal bonds
- Child support payments received from a former spouse
- Cash or property received by inheritance
- Specified employee fringe benefits
- Qualifying distributions from a Roth IRA during retirement
- Cash or property received by gift
- Deferral contributions to certain retirement plans
- Gain on the sale of a principal residence
- Scholarship or fellowship
- Life insurance proceeds received because of the death of the insured

Items Included in Gross Income

- Gains from the sale of assets
- Distributions from retirement plans
- Rental income
- Unemployment compensation benefits
- Royalty income
- Compensation (salaries and wages, etc.)
- Interest income
- Dividend income
- Alimony received
- Gross income from self-employment

Partial List of Deductions for Adjusted Gross Income

- Alimony paid
- Contributions to traditional IRAs
- Tuition for higher education
- Interest paid on student loans
- Business expenses
- Rental or royalty income expenses
- Losses from the sale of business property
- Moving expenses

Partial List of Itemized Deductions

- Miscellaneous expenses that exceed 2% of AGI
- Charitable contributions
- Tax return preparation fees
- Home mortgage interest
- Unreimbursed employee expenses
- Investment interest expense
- Medical and dental expenses in excess of 7.5% of AGI
- State and local income taxes
- Real property taxes on home
- Property taxes based on the value of a car
- Certain investment expenses
- Casualty losses in excess of 10% of AGI

Community Property States

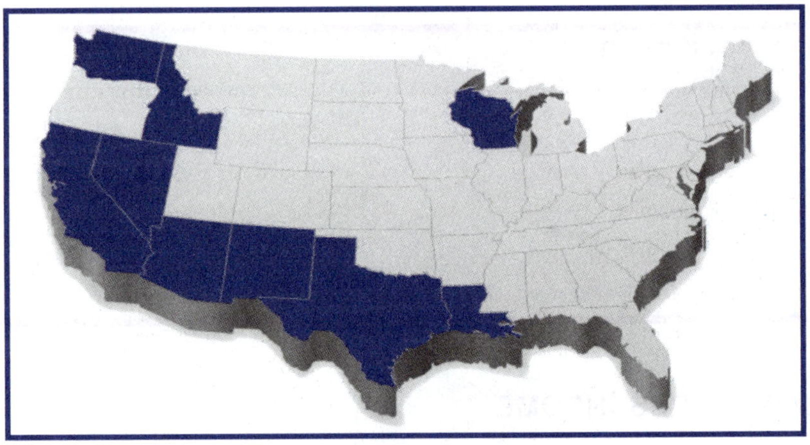

Qualified Dividend Tax Rates (2012)

Taxpayer's Regular Tax Rates	Taxpayer's Qualified Dividend Tax Rates
10% and 15%	0%
25%, 28%, 33%, and 35%	15%

Summary of Limitations on Imputed Interest

<table>
<tr><th>Loan Value</th><th>Imputed Interest</th></tr>
<tr><td>$0 ≤ $10,000</td><td>$0</td></tr>
<tr><td>$10,001 ≤ $100,000</td><td>The lesser of:<ul><li>Net investment income, or</li><li>Interest calculated using AFR less interest calculated using stated rate of the loan</li></ul>If borrower's net investment income ≤ $1,000, $0 imputed interest</td></tr>
<tr><td>> $100,000</td><td>Interest calculated using AFR less interest calculated using stated rate of the loan.</td></tr>
</table>

Inclusion/Exclusion of Compensation for Damages from Injuries

Injury Type	Compensatory Damages	Punitive Damages
Bodily injury	Excluded	Included
Personal injuries not including bodily injury	Included	Included
Lost income	Included	Included
Any other type of injury	Included	Included

Uniform Premium Table (Table 79)

Cost for Group Term Life Insurance Per $1,000 of Protection for One Month

Age	Cost
Under 25	0.05
25 through 29	0.06
30 through 34	0.08
35 through 39	0.09
40 through 44	0.10
45 through 49	0.15
50 through 54	0.23
55 through 59	0.43
60 through 64	0.66
65 through 69	1.27
70 and older	2.06

Social Security Base Amounts for Taxation

	Married Filing Jointly	All Others (Except MFJ=0)
Base Amount	$32,000	$25,000
Adjusted Base Amount	$44,000	$34,000

Deductibility of Student Loan Interest

Loan Made By	Loan Repaid By	Is it deductible?
Parent	Parent	Yes
	Student	No
Student	Parent	No
	Student	Yes

Summary of Above-The-Line Deductions for Individuals

- MSAs
- HSAs
- Trade or Business Expenses
- IRAs
- Moving Expenses
- Penalty or Early Withdrawal
- Educator Expenses
- Student Loan Interest
- Alimony Paid

Summary of Above-The-Line Business Deductions

- Ordinary
- Necessary
- Reasonable
- Fringe Benefits
- Self-Employed Retirement and Health Costs
- Social Security Costs
- Investigation of a Business
- Home Office Deduction

Summary of Deductible and Nondeductible Medical Expenses

Deductible	Nondeductible
• Prescription Drugs	• Elective Cosmetic Surgery
• Expenses Related to Diagnosis, Cure, & Treatment	• Dance Lessons
• Health Insurance Premiums	• Health Club Dues
• Capital Expenditures	• Marijuana
• Nursing Home and Special Schools	• Over-the-Counter Drugs
• Travel and Lodging	• General Health Items (e.g., vitamins)

Summary of Deductible and Nondeductible Taxes

Deductible	Nondeductible
• State and Local Income Taxes	• Fines or Fees
• State Sales Tax (Alternative Income)	• Excise Taxes
• Foreign Income Taxes	• Gift Taxes
• Property Taxes	• Estate Taxes

Summary of Deductible and Nondeductible Interest Expense as Itemized Deduction

Deductible	Nondeductible
• Qualified Residence Interest (Limit 2 houses and $1,000,000 debt)	• Personal Interest Including Credit Cards, Bank Loans, etc.
• Home Equity Line of Credit ($100,000 limit)	• Interest Used to Buy Tax-Free Municipal Bonds
• Investment Interest Expense (to extent of investment interest income)	

DEDUCTIBLE MISCELLANEOUS ITEMIZED DEDUCTIONS

FULLY DEDUCTIBLE (TIER I) (NOT SUBJECT TO 2% HURDLE)	DEDUCTIBLE (TIER II) (SUBJECT TO 2% HURDLE)
• Gambling Losses to Extent of Gains • Credit for Estate Tax on IRA Assets • Loss on Disposition of Annuity Contract • Repayment of Income	• Unreimbursed Employee Business Expenses (Travel, Journals, Uniforms, Union Dues) • Hobby Expenses to Extent of Hobby Income • Investment Expenses (e.g., Fees) • Tax Advice and Preparation • Losses on Terminated IRAs • Educational Expenses to Maintain or Improve Taxpayer Competency • Home Office Deduction

CLASSIFICATION OF RENTAL REAL ESTATE ACTIVITIES

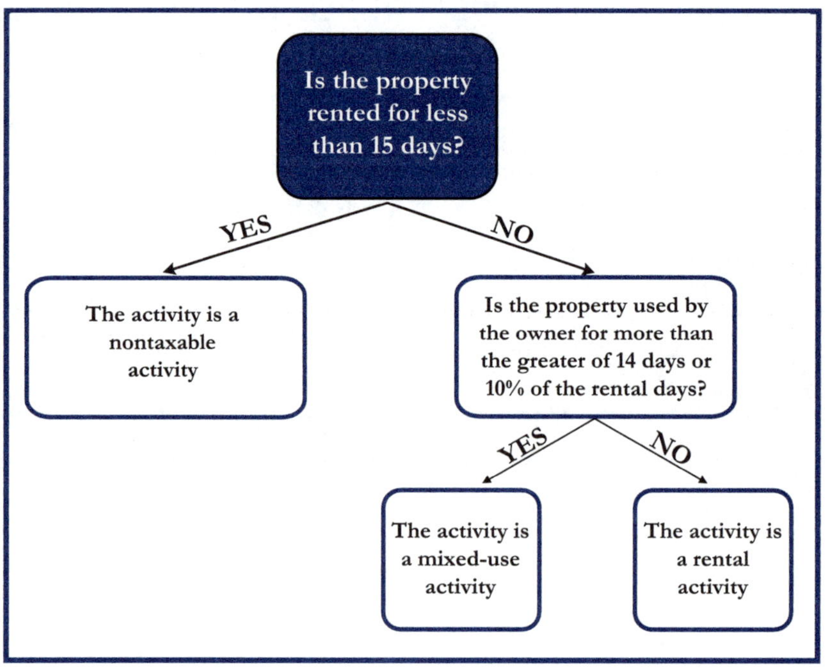

Home Ownership Classification for Income Tax Purposes

- Personal residence
- Second home
- Vacation home (rental less than 15 days)
- Mixed-use vacation home (>14 days of rental; personal use more than the greater of 14 days or 10% of rental days)
- Rental homes (>14 days of rental; personal use less than the greater of 14 days or 10% rental days)

Summary of Specific Deductions

Bad debts	If business debt and accrual method taxpayer, ordinary loss If personal, specific write off and short-term capital loss
Worthless securities	Assumed worthless at year-end of realization
Section 1244 stock	$100,000 ordinary loss for married filing jointly, excess is capital loss ($50,000 for single filers)
Losses of individuals	Not deductible except as casualty loss
Research and experimental expenditures	In year paid, amortized over 60 months, or capitalized
Net operating losses	Generally, back 2 and forward 20 years, can elect forward only (exceptions exist)
Depreciation	Ratably written off

Summary of Disallowed Losses

Temporarily Disallowed	Permanently Disallowed
• Section 1031 exchanges • Wash sales	• Related party transactions • Gifts below fair market value • Sale of personal assets at a loss

THE AMERICAN OPPORTUNITY TAX CREDIT AND LIFETIME LEARNING CREDIT COMPARED

Feature	American Opportunity Tax Credit	Lifetime Learning Credit
Base and Rate	$2,000 @ 100% plus $2,000 @ 25% (2010)	$10,000 @ 20%
Maximum Annual Credit	$2,500 per eligible student (2010)	$2,000 per tax return
General Availability	For the first four years of postsecondary education	For all years of postsecondary education and for courses to acquire or improve job skills
Years Available	Four years per student	Unlimited number of years
Degree Requirement	Student must pursue an undergraduate degree or other recognized education credential	Student does not need to pursue a degree or education credential
Half-time Requirement	Student must be enrolled at least half-time for one academic period during the year	Student must take one or more courses
Drug Conviction	No felony drug conviction on student's record	Felony drug conviction rule does not apply
Phaseout	$80,000 - $90,000 (Single) $160,000 - $180,000 (MFJ)	$52,000 - $62,000 (Single) $104,000 - $124,000 (MFJ)

Property Issues

Items Included in Basis

Purchase Price
Sales Tax
Freight
Installation and Testing Costs
"All costs to get the asset into operations"

Double Basis Rule
(Occurs when Fair Market Value < Donor's Basis at Date of Gift)

If the donee's sale price is...	less than FMV	between the original basis and FMV	greater than the original basis
Then the donee's basis used is ...	the loss basis, which is the FMV at the date of the gift	no gain or loss	the gain basis, which is the donor's original basis

Asset Categories

	Capital Assets	Ordinary Assets	1231 Assets
Sold for Gain	Capital Gain Treatment	Ordinary Income Treatment	Capital Gain Treatment (part or all gain may require recapture)
Sold for Loss	Capital Loss Treatment (current loss may be limited)	Ordinary Loss Treatment	Ordinary Loss Treatment

Holding Period Summary

Capital Gain/Loss	**Holding Period**
Long-Term Capital Gain/Loss	> 1 Year
Short-Term Capital Gain/Loss	≤ 1 Year

Summary of Holding Period Rules

Property acquired by:	Will have the following holding period / treatment:
Inheritance	Long-term holding period.
Gift	Holding period will tack to donor's holding period if the gain basis is used. If the loss basis is used, the donee's holding period begins on the date of the gift.
Related Party Transaction	The holding period starts on sale date.
Nonbusiness Bad Debts	Treated as short-term capital losses.

Long-Term Capital Gains Tax Rates Summary

0%	For individuals in the 15% or less income tax bracket through 2012
15%	For individuals in the 25% or greater income tax bracket through 2012
25%	Rate for unrecaptured gain on 1250 assets (Straight-line depreciation taken)
28%	Collectibles

Types of Income

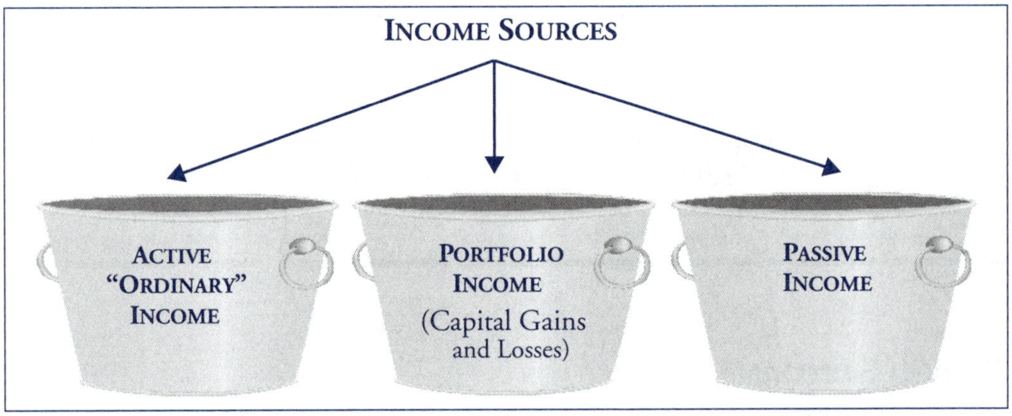

Assets that Qualify for Like-Kind Exchange Treatment

- Assets held for trade or business.
- Assets held for production of income.

Note: Personal use assets (e.g., personal residences) do NOT qualify for like-kind exchange treatment. However, personal residences are afforded special tax treatment under IRC Section 121.

Tax Consequences of a Section 1031 Exchange

1. Determine whether the taxpayer is trading up or down. Taxpayers who receive only like-kind property in the exchange will not have any current income tax consequences. The basis that they have in their investment solution is increased by any additional capital investment made in the investment solution.
2. The party trading down (receiving less like-kind property than given up) is required to recognize gain to the extent of any boot received. If the boot received exceeds the gain, the amount of the boot in excess of gain is treated as a return of capital.
3. Debt relief is treated as boot, requiring gain recognition for the party no longer responsible for the debt. The party assuming the debt will increase their basis in the replacement property by an amount equal to the debt assumed.
4. Losses realized in a like-kind exchange are not recognized until the replacement property is sold. The taxpayer's basis in the replacement property equals the fair market value of the property received in the exchange plus any disallowed loss.

Exchanging Insurance Products

This type of contract:	May be exchanged without tax recognition for:
Life Insurance	Life Insurance Modified Endowment Contract Annuity
Modified Endowment Contract	Modified Endowment Contract Annuity
Annuity	Annuity

Summary of Material Participation

1. >500 hours devoted to activity.
2. >100 hours devoted to activity and the most of any participant.
3. >100 hours devoted to several activities that add to more than 500 hours.

Alternative Minimum Tax Formula

Taxable Income (from regular tax system)
Add: Adjustments that increase AMTI
Less: Adjustments that decrease AMTI
Add: Preferences
Alternative Minimum Taxable Income (AMTI)
Less: Exemptions
AMT Tax Base
Application of Appropriate AMT Rate
Tentative Minimum Tax
Less: Foreign Tax Credit
Less: Regular Tax Liability (Form 1040)
Alternative Minimum Tax (AMT)

AMT Exemption Amounts

Filing Status	2012
Single and Head of Household	$33,750
Married Filing Jointly and Surviving Spouse	$45,000
Married Filing Separately	$22,500

AMT Phaseout Thresholds

Filing Status	2012
Single and Head of Household	$112,500 - $247,500
Married Filing Jointly and Surviving Spouse	$150,000 - $330,000
Married Filing Separately and Estates and Trusts	$75,000 - $165,000

Summary of Itemized Deductions

(Regular and Alternative Minimum Tax)

	Deductible for Regular Tax	Deductible for AMT	Differences in Deductions
Home Mortgage Interest	Regular income tax rules	Qualified mortgage interest only	Lose tax deduction for excess refinance interest. Add back interest for refinance
Medical	Excess above 7.5% AGI	Excess above 10% AGI (Add back 2.5%)	AMT costs an extra 2.5%
Taxes	Property/sales/use/ and ad valorem taxes are deductible	Taxes are not deductible, except tax on qualified motor vehicles	Lose all tax deductions under AMT (Add all back except tax on qualified motor vehicles)
Miscellaneous	Subject to 2% of AGI	Not deductible at all	Lose all miscellaneous itemized deductions (Add back with exceptions)
Charitable	Regular rules	Same as regular rules	No change
Casualty	Regular rules	Same as regular rules	No change

Deductions Lost Using AMT

- 100% of home mortgage interest on excess refinancing (current mortgage – amortized original mortgage)
- An additional 2.5% of medical and dental expenses
- 100% of state and local income, property, and sales taxes
- Almost 100% of miscellaneous itemized deductions

Appendix

Retirement & Social Security

E

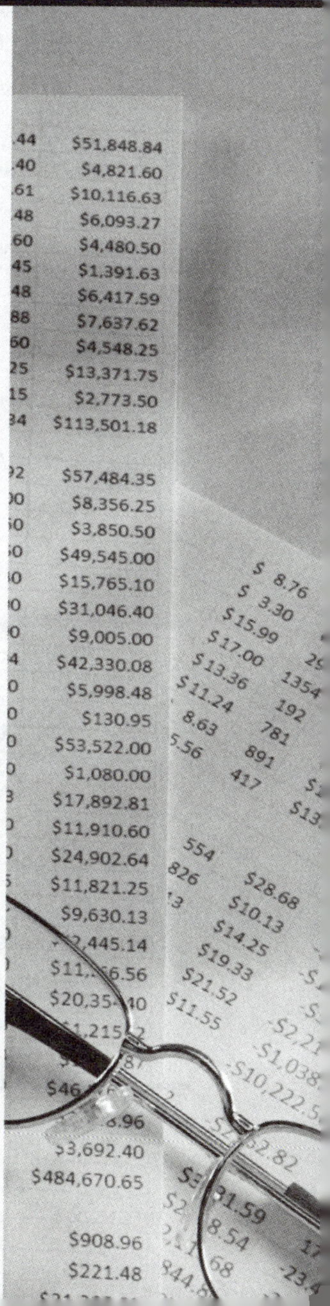

Retirement

Investment Assets / Gross Pay % Exhibit

This exhibit assumes a rate of return of 9%, inflation of 3%, and normal retirement age of 66 with and without Social Security.

Age	Investment / Gross Pay Ratio without Social Security	Investment / Gross Pay Ratio Considering Social Security
25	0.12	0.09
30	0.83	0.63
35	1.78	1.34
40	3.04	2.28
45	4.70	3.53
50	6.92	5.19
55	9.86	7.39
60	13.76	10.32
65	18.93	14.20

Investment Assets / Gross Pay % Without Social Security

Inflation	0%	WRR	80%
Annual Savings Rate	12.00%	Beginning Rate	25
Real Earnings Rate	5.8252%	Retirement Age	66
Gross Pay	$100,000	Life Expectancy	100

Age	Gross Pay	Annual Savings	BOY Investments	Earnings	Addition / Distribution	EOY Investments	Investments / Gross Pay Ratio
25	$100,000	$12,000	0	0	12,000	12,000	0.12
30	$100,000	$12,000	67,409	3,927	12,000	83,336	0.83
35	$100,000	$12,000	156,877	9,138	12,000	178,016	1.78
40	$100,000	$12,000	275,622	16,056	12,000	303,678	3.04
45	$100,000	$12,000	433,223	25,236	12,000	470,460	4.70
50	$100,000	$12,000	642,397	37,421	12,000	691,818	6.92
55	$100,000	$12,000	920,018	53,593	12,000	985,612	9.86
60	$100,000	$12,000	1,288,486	75,057	12,000	1,375,543	13.76
65	$100,000	$12,000	1,777,527	103,545	12,000	1,893,072	18.93

Investment Assets / Gross Pay % With Social Security (Example)

Inflation	0%	WRR	50%
Annual Savings Rate	9.00%	Beginning Rate	25
Real Earnings Rate	5.8252%	Retirement Age	65
Gross Pay	$100,000	Life Expectancy	100

Age	Gross Pay	Annual Savings	BOY Investments	Earnings	Addition / Distribution	EOY Investments	Investments / Gross Pay Ratio
25	$100,000	$9,000	0	0	9,000	9,000	0.09
30	$100,000	$9,000	50,557	2,945	9,000	62,502	0.63
35	$100,000	$9,000	117,658	6,854	9,000	133,512	1.34
40	$100,000	$9,000	206,717	12,042	9,000	227,758	2.28
45	$100,000	$9,000	324,918	18,927	9,000	352,845	3.53
50	$100,000	$9,000	481,798	28,066	9,000	518,864	5.19
55	$100,000	$9,000	690,014	40,195	9,000	739,209	7.39
60	$100,000	$9,000	966,364	56,293	9,000	1,031,657	10.32
65	$100,000	$9,000	1,333,145	77,659	9,000	1,419,804	14.20

Required Savings Rate for Retirement
(Assume $0 of Accumulated Savings at the Beginning Age)

Age Beginning Regular and Recurring Savings*	Savings (as percent of gross pay) Rate Required to Create Appropriate Capital*
25 - 35	10 - 13%
35 - 45	13 - 20%
45 - 55	20 - 40%**

*Assumes appropriate asset allocation for reasonable-risk investor through accumulation year; also assumes normal raises and an 80 percent wage replacement ratio at Social Security normal retirement age and includes Social Security retirement benefits.

** At age 55, the person will realistically have to delay retirement until age 70.

Benchmark for Investment Assets as a Percentage of Gross Pay
(Approximate)

Age	Investment Assets as a Ratio to Gross Pay Needed at Varying Ages
25	0.20 : 1
30	0.6 - 0.8 : 1
35	1.6 - 1.8 : 1
45	3 - 4 : 1
55	8 - 10 : 1
65	16 - 20 : 1

Required Earning Rate

Required Earning Rate			
Withdrawal Rate	Fixed Payment Required Earnings Rate	Inflation Adjusted Required Earnings Rate	Portfolio Allocation
4%	1.310%	4.349%	Conservative
5%	3.079%	6.171%	Moderate Conservative
6%	4.696%	7.837%	Moderate
7%	6.218%	9.405%	Moderate Aggressive
8%	7.678%	10.908%	Aggressive

Summary of Selected Factors Affecting Retirement Planning

Factor	Risk	Mitigator
Work Life Expectancy (WLE)	Shortened due to untimely death, disability, health, unemployment	Life insurance, disability insurance, health insurance, education, training, experience
Retirement Life Expectancy (RLE)	Lengthened	Adequate capital accumulation
Savings rate, amount, and timing	Too low and too late	Save enough; start early
Inflation	Greater than expected	Conservatively estimate inflation and needs
Retirement needs	Underestimated	Use wage replacement estimators; don't include Social Security benefits in the calculation
Investment returns	Inadequate to create necessary retirement capital	Knowledge of and investments in broad portfolio of diversified investments and proper asset allocation
Sources of retirement income	Overestimation of Social Security benefits, private pension plans, or personal income (or adverse changes in taxation of such income)	Conservatively estimate and plan for such income, as well as monitor income projections and tax policy

The Differences Between Pension Plans and Profit-Sharing Plans

Characteristic	Pension Plan	Profit-Sharing Plan
Legal promise of the plan	Paying a pension at retirement	Deferral of compensation and taxation
Are in-service withdrawals permitted?	No*	Yes (after two years) if plan document permits
Is the plan subject to mandatory funding standards?	Yes**	No
Percent of plan assets available to be invested in employer securities	10%	Up to 100%
Must the plan provide qualified joint and survivor annuity and a qualified pre-survivor annuity?	Yes	No

** Under the Pension Protection Act of 2006, defined benefit pension plans can provide for in-service distributions to participants who are age 62 or older.*
*** For plan years beginning in 2008, the funding rules under IRC §412 have been amended by the Pension Protection Act of 2006.*

Characteristics of Defined Benefit vs. Defined Contribution Plans

Characteristics	Defined Benefit	Defined Contribution
What is the Annual Contribution Limit?	The greater of (1) the sum of the plan's funding target, target normal cost, and a cushion amount over the value of the plan asset, or (2) the minimum required contribution for the plan year.*	25% of covered compensation
Who assumes the investment risk?	Employer	Employee
How are forfeitures allocated?	Reduce plan costs	Reduce plan costs or allocate to other participants
Is the plan subject to Pension Benefit Guaranty Corporation (PBGC) coverage?	Yes (except professional firms with less than 25 employees)**	No
Does the plan have separate investment accounts?	No, they are commingled	Yes, they are usually separate
Can credit be given for prior service for the purpose of benefits?	Yes	No

** This is the annual contribution limit for defined benefit plans beginning in 2008 as a result of the PPA 2006.*
*** ERISA §4021, 29 U.S.C. §1321.*

Defined Contribution Plan Vesting Schedules

Years of Service	All Employer Contributions		2-Year Eligibility Election*	Employee Contributions
	2 to 6 Year Graduated	3-Year Cliff		
1	0	0	0	100%
2	20%	0	100%	100%
3	40%	100%	100%	100%
4	60%	100%	100%	100%
5	80%	100%	100%	100%
6	100%	100%	100%	100%

** Note: The two-year vesting schedule also applies to employer contributions under a 401(k) plan that makes use of an Automatic Enrollment Feature, as outlined in PPA 2006 (effective for years after 2007).*

DEFINED BENEFIT PLAN VESTING SCHEDULE

YEARS OF SERVICE	ALL EMPLOYER CONTRIBUTIONS		2-YEAR ELIGIBILITY ELECTION	TOP-HEAVY PLAN		CASH BALANCE PLAN*
	3 TO 7 YEAR GRADUATED	5-YEAR CLIFF		2 TO 6 YEAR GRADUATED	3-YEAR CLIFF	
1	0	0	0	0	0	0
2	0	0	100%	20%	0	0
3	20%	0	100%	40%	100%	100%
4	40%	0	100%	60%	100%	100%
5	60%	100%	100%	80%	100%	100%
6	80%	100%	100%	100%	100%	100%
7	100%	100%	100%	100%	100%	100%

**Note that under IRC §411(a)(13)(B), a cash balance pension plan provides for 100% vesting of employer contributions after three years of employee service.*

COMPARISON OF ROTH IRA AND ROTH ACCOUNTS (2012)

Characteristic	Roth IRA	Roth Account
Participation	Anyone with earned income under limit	Anyone who is a participant in a 401(k), 403(b) or 457 plan that permits Roth contributions
Contribution Limits	IRA Annual limit - for 2012, $5,000 plus $1,000 catch up if age 50 or older. Subject to AGI limit: Single ($110k-$125k); MFJ ($173k-$183k)	Deferral limit - for 2012, $17,000 plus $5,500 if age 50 or older. No AGI limits.
Recharacterization Permitted	Yes - permitted[1]	No - not permitted. Once the rollover takes place, it cannot be undone.
Minimum distributions	Only after death of participant	Yes - required
Requirements for qualified distribution	5 years & on account of death, disability, age 59 ½ or first time home purchase (up to $10,000)	5 years & on account of death, disability or age 59½
Tax for nonqualified distributions (early distributions penalties may apply to part of the distribution)	Nonqualified distributions are distributed in order: contributions (basis), conversions (basis), then earnings (taxable)	Nonqualified distributions are prorated between Roth contributions (basis) and earnings (taxable)

1. The taxpayer can "reconvert" the later of: (1) the beginning of the following year after conversion, or (2) 30 days after the recharacterization.

Qualified Plan Summary of Characteristics

Qualified Plan	Who Generally Contributes	Mandatory Funding	Investment Risk	Company Stock %[1]	Permits Soc. Sec. Integration	Required Expert	Who is Generally Favored?[2]	QJSA / QOSA/ QPSA[3]
Pension Plans								
Defined Benefit Pension Plan	ER	Yes	ER	≤ 10%	Yes	Actuary and Pension Expert	Older Age Entrants	Yes
Cash Balance Pension Plan	ER	Yes	ER	≤ 10%	Yes	Actuary and Pension Expert	Younger Persons	Yes
Target Benefit Pension Plan	ER	Yes	EE	≤ 10%	Yes	Actuary once and Pension Expert	Older Age Entrants	Yes
Money Purchase Pension Plan	ER	Yes	EE	≤ 10%	Yes	None[4]	Younger Persons	Yes
Profit Sharing Plans								
Profit Sharing Plan	ER	No	EE	≤ 100%	Yes	None[2]	Highly Compensated and Younger Persons	No
Stock Bonus Plan	ER	No	EE	≤ 100%	Yes	Valuation Specialist and Pension Expert	Highly Compensated and Long Length of Service	No
ESOP	ER	No	EE	≤ 100%	No	Valuation Specialist and Pension Expert	Highly Compensated and Long Length of Service	No
401(k) Plan/ 401(k) Roth Account	EE and ER	No[5]	EE	≤ 100%	No[6]	Pension Expert	Savers and Younger Persons	No
Thrift Plan	EE	No	EE	≤ 100%	Yes	Pension Expert	Savers and Younger Persons	No
Age-Based Profit Sharing Plan	ER	No	EE	≤ 100%	Yes	Pension Expert	Older Highly Compensated	No
New Comparability Plan	ER	No	EE	≤ 100%	Yes	Pension Expert	Owners	No

EE = Employee, ER = Employer

1. Note that as a result of PPA 2006, certain defined contribution plans holding publicly traded employer securities are subject to new diversification requirements, which requires that employees be permitted to diversify 100% of their contributions and 100% of employer contributions after 3 years. See Chapter 3 for more detail.
2. Where younger persons are favored, it is because they benefit from a greater number of compounding periods. However, through cross-testing and other methods, most plans can be structured to benefit the owners and highly compensated employees.
3. Qualified Joint and Survivor Annuity/Qualified Pre-Survivor Annuity.
4. Many prototype plans are available.
5. 401(k) plans may have mandatory funding if there is a matching contribution for a safe harbor plan.
6. If a CODA feature is a part of the profit sharing plan then, the profit sharing plan can be integrated, but not the CODA portion.

401(k) NON-DISCRIMINATION TESTING

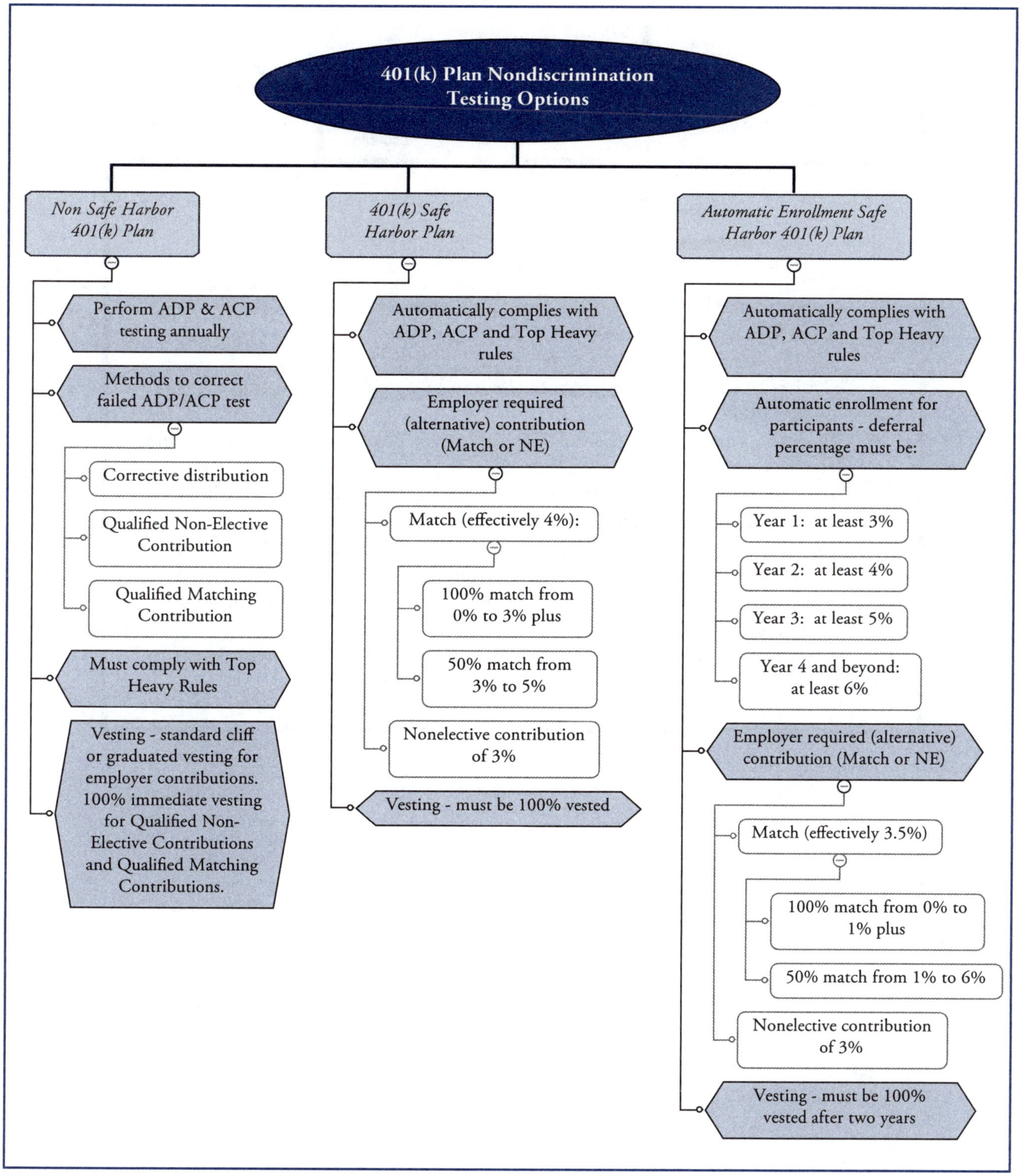

VARIOUS RELATIONSHIPS AND TRANSACTIONS IN A LEVERAGED ESOP

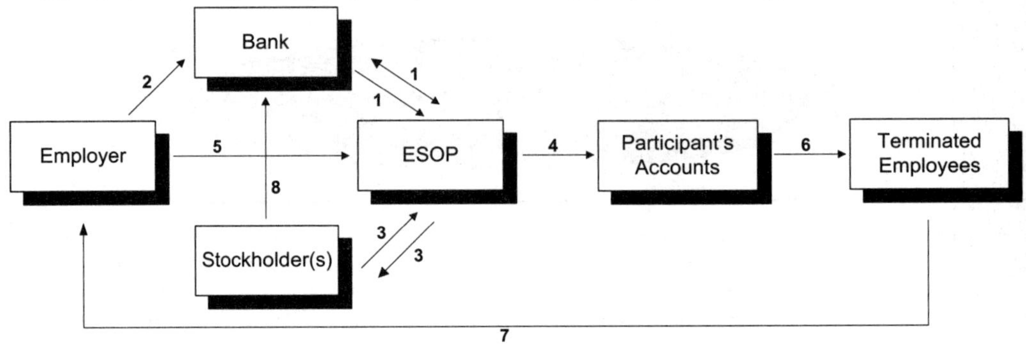

1. An ESOP obtains a loan from a bank or other outside lender. The ESOP signs a promissory note for the money.
2. The employer guarantees the loan on behalf of the ESOP.
3. The ESOP uses the money from the loan to buy stock from existing shareholder (or employer).
4. The stock purchased by the ESOP is held in an ESOP suspense account, and is released for allocation to participant accounts over time as the loan is repaid with funds contributed to the ESOP by the employer. These allocations are in lieu of a cash contribution that could have been made to a retirement plan.
5. The employer contributes funds to the ESOP so that the ESOP can make its annual debt repayment to the bank (or other lender).
6. Employees are entitled to receive distributions of employer stock in kind upon termination or retirement.
7. Employees are entitled to sell back or "put" the stock back to the employer.
8. Shareholders may also be required to guarantee the ESOP loan.

SUMMARY OF ALLOWABLE ROLLOVERS

Roll From \ Roll To	Traditional IRA	SEP-IRA	SIMPLE IRA	Roth IRA	Government 457(b)	403(b)	Qualified Plan	Designated Roth Account 401(k), 403(b), 457(b)
Traditional IRA	Yes	Yes	No	Yes, must include in income.	Yes, must have separate accounts.	Yes	Yes	No
SEP-IRA	Yes	Yes	No	Yes, must include in income.	Yes, must have separate accounts.	Yes	Yes	No
SIMPLE IRA	Yes, after 2 years.	Yes, after 2 years.	Yes	Yes, after 2 years. Must include in income.	Yes, after 2 years. Must have separate accounts.	Yes, after 2 years.	Yes, after 2 years.	No
Roth IRA	No	No	No	Yes	No	No	No	No
Government 457(b)	Yes	Yes	No	Yes. Must include in income.	Yes	Yes	Yes	Yes as in plan rollover. Must include in income.
403(b)	Yes	Yes	No	Yes. Must include in income.	Yes, must have separate accounts.	Yes	Yes	Yes as in plan rollover. Must include in income.
Qualified Plan	Yes	Yes	No	Yes. Must include in income.	Yes, must have separate accounts.	Yes	Yes	Yes as in plan rollover. Must include in income.
Designated Roth Account 401(k), 403(b), 457(b)	No	No	No	Yes	No	No	No	Yes, if a direct trustee to trustee transfer.

SUMMARY OF EXCEPTIONS FOR QUALIFIED PLANS AND IRAS

Exception to 10% Penalty	Qualified Plan	IRA	IRC §(s)
After participant/IRA owner reaches age 59	Yes	Yes	72(t)(2)(A)(i)
After death of the participant/IRA owner	Yes	Yes	72(t)(2)(A)(ii)
Total and permanent disability of the participant/IRA owner	Yes	Yes	72(t)(2)(A)(iii)
Series of substantially equal payments	Yes	Yes	72(t)(2)(A)(iv)
Separation from service during or after year employee reaches age 55 (age 50 for public safety employees)	Yes	No	72(t)(2)(A)(v) and72(t)(10)
Dividend pass through from an ESOP	Yes	N/A	72(t)(2)(A)(vi)
Because of an IRS levy of the plan	Yes	Yes	72(t)(2)(A)(vii)
Amount of your unreimbursed medical expenses (>7.5% AGI)	Yes	Yes	72(t)(2)(B)
To an alternate payee under a Qualified Domestic Relations Order	Yes	No	72(t)(2)(C)
Payment of health insurance premiums paid while unemployed	No	Yes	72(t)(2)(D)
Qualified higher education expenses	No	Yes	72(t)(2)(E)
Qualified first-time homebuyers up to $10,000	No	Yes	72(t)(2)(F)
Certain distributions to qualified military reservists called to active duty	Yes	Yes	72(t)(2)(G)
Corrective distributions	Yes	No	401(k)(8)(D), 401(m)(7), and 402(g)(2)(C)
Rollovers	Yes	Yes	402(c), 403(a)(4),403(b)(8), 408(d)(3)and 408A(d)(3)(A)
Governmental 457(b) distributions are not subject to the 10% additional tax except for distributions attributable to rollovers from another type of plan or IRA.			

Uniform Lifetime Table Used by Participants

Age of Employee	Distribution Period	Age of Employee	Distribution Period
70	27.4	93	9.6
71	26.5	94	9.1
72	25.6	95	8.6
73	24.7	96	8.1
74	23.8	97	7.6
75	22.9	98	7.1
76	22.0	99	6.7
77	21.2	100	6.3
78	20.3	101	5.9
79	19.5	102	5.5
80	18.7	103	5.2
81	17.9	104	4.9
82	17.1	105	4.5
83	16.3	106	4.2
84	15.5	107	3.9
85	14.8	108	3.7
86	14.1	109	3.4
87	13.4	110	3.1
88	12.7	111	2.9
89	12.0	112	2.6
90	11.4	113	2.4
91	10.8	114	2.1
92	10.2	115 and over	1.9

Excerpt from the Joint and Last Survivor Table

(Used by Participants with Spouses More than 10 Years Younger than the Participant)

Ages	30	31	32	33	34	35	36	37	38	39
30	60.2	59.7	59.2	58.8	58.4	58.0	57.6	57.3	57.0	56.7
31	59.7	59.2	58.7	58.2	57.8	57.4	57.0	56.6	56.3	56.0
32	59.2	58.7	58.2	57.7	57.2	56.8	56.4	56.0	55.6	55.3
33	58.8	58.2	57.7	57.2	56.7	56.2	55.8	55.4	55.0	54.7
34	58.4	57.8	57.2	56.7	56.2	55.7	55.3	54.8	54.4	54.0
35	58.0	57.4	56.8	56.2	55.7	55.2	54.7	54.3	53.8	53.4
36	57.6	57.0	56.4	55.8	55.3	54.7	54.2	53.7	53.3	52.8
37	57.3	56.6	56.0	55.4	54.8	54.3	53.7	53.2	52.7	52.3
38	57.0	56.3	55.6	55.0	54.4	53.8	53.3	52.7	52.2	51.7
39	56.7	56.0	55.3	54.7	54.0	53.4	52.8	52.3	51.7	51.2
40	56.4	55.7	55.0	54.3	53.7	53.0	52.4	51.8	51.3	50.8
41	56.1	55.4	54.7	54.0	53.3	52.7	52.0	51.4	50.9	50.3
42	55.9	55.2	54.4	53.7	53.0	52.3	51.7	51.1	50.4	49.9
43	55.7	54.9	54.2	53.4	52.7	52.0	51.3	50.7	50.1	49.5
44	55.5	54.7	53.9	53.2	52.4	51.7	51.0	50.4	49.7	49.1
45	55.3	54.5	53.7	52.9	52.2	51.5	50.7	50.0	49.4	48.7
46	55.1	54.3	53.5	52.7	52.0	51.2	50.5	49.8	49.1	48.4
47	55.0	54.1	53.3	52.5	51.7	51.0	50.2	49.5	48.8	48.1
48	54.8	54.0	53.2	52.3	51.5	50.8	50.0	49.2	48.5	47.8
49	54.7	53.8	53.0	52.2	51.4	50.6	49.8	49.0	48.2	47.5
50	54.6	53.7	52.9	52.0	51.2	50.4	49.6	48.8	48.0	47.3
51	54.5	53.6	52.7	51.9	51.0	50.2	49.4	48.6	47.8	47.0
52	54.4	53.5	52.6	51.7	50.9	50.0	49.2	48.4	47.6	46.8
53	54.3	53.4	52.5	51.6	50.8	49.9	49.1	48.2	47.4	46.6
54	54.2	53.3	52.4	51.5	50.6	49.8	48.9	48.1	47.2	46.4
55	54.1	53.2	52.3	51.4	50.5	49.7	48.8	47.9	47.1	46.3
56	54.0	53.1	52.2	51.3	50.4	49.5	48.7	47.8	47.0	46.1
57	54.0	53.0	52.1	51.2	50.3	49.4	48.6	47.7	46.8	46.0
58	53.9	53.0	52.1	51.2	50.3	49.4	48.5	47.6	46.7	45.8
59	53.8	52.9	52.0	51.1	50.2	49.3	48.4	47.5	46.6	45.7
60	53.8	52.9	51.9	51.0	50.1	49.2	48.3	47.4	46.5	45.6
61	53.8	52.8	51.9	51.0	50.0	49.1	48.2	47.3	46.4	45.5
62	53.7	52.8	51.8	50.9	50.0	49.1	48.1	47.2	46.3	45.4
63	53.7	52.7	51.8	50.9	49.9	49.0	48.1	47.2	46.3	45.3
64	53.6	52.7	51.8	50.8	49.9	48.9	48.0	47.1	46.2	45.3
65	53.6	52.7	51.7	50.8	49.8	48.9	48.0	47.0	46.1	45.2
66	53.6	52.6	51.7	50.7	49.8	48.9	47.9	47.0	46.1	45.1
67	53.6	52.6	51.7	50.7	49.8	48.8	47.9	46.9	46.0	45.1
68	53.5	52.6	51.6	50.7	49.7	48.8	47.8	46.9	46.0	45.0
69	53.5	52.6	51.6	50.6	49.7	48.7	47.8	46.9	45.9	45.0
70	53.5	52.5	51.6	50.6	49.7	48.7	47.8	46.8	45.9	44.9
71	53.5	52.5	51.6	50.6	49.6	48.7	47.7	46.8	45.9	44.9
72	53.5	52.5	51.5	50.6	49.6	48.7	47.7	46.8	45.8	44.9
73	53.4	52.5	51.5	50.6	49.6	48.6	47.7	46.7	45.8	44.8
74	53.4	52.5	51.5	50.5	49.6	48.6	47.7	46.7	45.8	44.8
75	53.4	52.5	51.5	50.5	49.6	48.6	47.7	46.7	45.7	44.8
76	53.4	52.4	51.5	50.5	49.6	48.6	47.6	46.7	45.7	44.8
77	53.4	52.4	51.5	50.5	49.5	48.6	47.6	46.7	45.7	44.8
78	53.4	52.4	51.5	50.5	49.5	48.6	47.6	46.6	45.7	44.7
79	53.4	52.4	51.5	50.5	49.5	48.6	47.6	46.6	45.7	44.7

Excerpt from the Joint and Last Survivor Table (Continued)

Ages	40	41	42	43	44	45	46	47	48	49
40	50.2	49.8	49.3	48.9	48.5	48.1	47.7	47.4	47.1	46.8
41	49.8	49.3	48.8	48.3	47.9	47.5	47.1	46.7	46.4	46.1
42	49.3	48.8	48.3	47.8	47.3	46.9	46.5	46.1	45.8	45.4
43	48.9	48.3	47.8	47.3	46.8	46.3	45.9	45.5	45.1	44.8
44	48.5	47.9	47.3	46.8	46.3	45.8	45.4	44.9	44.5	44.2
45	48.1	47.5	46.9	46.3	45.8	45.3	44.8	44.4	44.0	43.6
46	47.7	47.1	46.5	45.9	45.4	44.8	44.3	43.9	43.4	43.0
47	47.4	46.7	46.1	45.5	44.9	44.4	43.9	43.4	42.9	42.4
48	47.1	46.4	45.8	45.1	44.5	44.0	43.4	42.9	42.4	41.9
49	46.8	46.1	45.4	44.8	44.2	43.6	43.0	42.4	41.9	41.4
50	46.5	45.8	45.1	44.4	43.8	43.2	42.6	42.0	41.5	40.9
51	46.3	45.5	44.8	44.1	43.5	42.8	42.2	41.6	41.0	40.5
52	46.0	45.3	44.6	43.8	43.2	42.5	41.8	41.2	40.6	40.1
53	45.8	45.1	44.3	43.6	42.9	42.2	41.5	40.9	40.3	39.7
54	45.6	44.8	44.1	43.3	42.6	41.9	41.2	40.5	39.9	39.3
55	45.5	44.7	43.9	43.1	42.4	41.6	40.9	40.2	39.6	38.9
56	45.3	44.5	43.7	42.9	42.1	41.4	40.7	40.0	39.3	38.6
57	45.1	44.3	43.5	42.7	41.9	41.2	40.4	39.7	39.0	38.3
58	45.0	44.2	43.3	42.5	41.7	40.9	40.2	39.4	38.7	38.0
59	44.9	44.0	43.2	42.4	41.5	40.7	40.0	39.2	38.5	37.8
60	44.7	43.9	43.0	42.2	41.4	40.6	39.8	39.0	38.2	37.5
61	44.6	43.8	42.9	42.1	41.2	40.4	39.6	38.8	38.0	37.3
62	44.5	43.7	42.8	41.9	41.1	40.3	39.4	38.6	37.8	37.1
63	44.5	43.6	42.7	41.8	41.0	40.1	39.3	38.5	37.7	36.9
64	44.4	43.5	42.6	41.7	40.8	40.0	39.2	38.3	37.5	36.7
65	44.3	43.4	42.5	41.6	40.7	39.9	39.0	38.2	37.4	36.6
66	44.2	43.3	42.4	41.5	40.6	39.8	38.9	38.1	37.2	36.4
67	44.2	43.3	42.3	41.4	40.6	39.7	38.8	38.0	37.1	36.3
68	44.1	43.2	42.3	41.4	40.5	39.6	38.7	37.9	37.0	36.2
69	44.1	43.1	42.2	41.3	40.4	39.5	38.6	37.8	36.9	36.0
70	44.0	43.1	42.2	41.3	40.3	39.4	38.6	37.7	36.8	35.9
71	44.0	43.0	42.1	41.2	40.3	39.4	38.5	37.6	36.7	35.9
72	43.9	43.0	42.1	41.1	40.2	39.3	38.4	37.5	36.6	35.8
73	43.9	43.0	42.0	41.1	40.2	39.3	38.4	37.5	36.6	35.7
74	43.9	42.9	42.0	41.1	40.1	39.2	38.3	37.4	36.5	35.6
75	43.8	42.9	42.0	41.0	40.1	39.2	38.3	37.4	36.5	35.6
76	43.8	42.9	41.9	41.0	40.1	39.1	38.2	37.3	36.4	35.5
77	43.8	42.9	41.9	41.0	40.0	39.1	38.2	37.3	36.4	35.5
78	43.8	42.8	41.9	40.9	40.0	39.1	38.2	37.2	36.3	35.4
79	43.8	42.8	41.9	40.9	40.0	39.1	38.1	37.2	36.3	35.4
80	43.7	42.8	41.8	40.9	40.0	39.0	38.1	37.2	36.3	35.4
81	43.7	42.8	41.8	40.9	39.9	39.0	38.1	37.2	36.2	35.3
82	43.7	42.8	41.8	40.9	39.9	39.0	38.1	37.1	36.2	35.3
83	43.7	42.8	41.8	40.9	39.9	39.0	38.0	37.1	36.2	35.3
84	43.7	42.7	41.8	40.8	39.9	39.0	38.0	37.1	36.2	35.3
85	43.7	42.7	41.8	40.8	39.9	38.9	38.0	37.1	36.2	35.2
86	43.7	42.7	41.8	40.8	39.9	38.9	38.0	37.1	36.1	35.2
87	43.7	42.7	41.8	40.8	39.9	38.9	38.0	37.0	36.1	35.2
88	43.7	42.7	41.8	40.8	39.9	38.9	38.0	37.0	36.1	35.2
89	43.7	42.7	41.7	40.8	39.8	38.9	38.0	37.0	36.1	35.2

Single Life Expectancy Used by Beneficiaries

Age	Life Expectancy	Age	Life Expectancy	Age	Life Expectancy	Age	Life Expectancy
0	82.4	28	55.3	56	28.7	84	8.1
1	81.6	29	54.3	57	27.9	85	7.6
2	80.6	30	53.3	58	27.0	86	7.1
3	79.7	31	52.4	59	26.1	87	6.7
4	78.7	32	51.4	60	25.2	88	6.3
5	77.7	33	50.4	61	24.4	89	5.9
6	76.7	34	49.4	62	23.5	90	5.5
7	75.8	35	48.5	63	22.7	91	5.2
8	74.8	36	47.5	64	21.8	92	4.9
9	73.8	37	46.5	65	21.0	93	4.6
10	72.8	38	45.6	66	20.2	94	4.3
11	71.8	39	44.6	67	19.4	95	4.1
12	70.8	40	43.6	68	18.6	96	3.8
13	69.9	41	42.7	69	17.8	97	3.6
14	68.9	42	41.7	70	17.0	98	3.4
15	67.9	43	40.7	71	16.3	99	3.1
16	66.9	44	39.8	72	15.5	100	2.9
17	66.0	45	38.8	73	14.8	101	2.7
18	65.0	46	37.9	74	14.1	102	2.5
19	64.0	47	37.0	75	13.4	103	2.3
20	63.0	48	36.0	76	12.7	104	2.1
21	62.1	49	35.1	77	12.1	105	1.9
22	61.1	50	34.2	78	11.4	106	1.7
23	60.1	51	33.3	79	10.8	107	1.5
24	59.1	52	32.3	80	10.2	108	1.4
25	58.2	53	31.4	81	9.7	109	1.2
26	57.2	54	30.5	82	9.1	110	1.1
27	56.2	55	29.6	83	8.6	111+	1.0

DEATH OF PARTICIPANT SUMMARY

OPTIONS AFTER MINIMUM DISTRIBUTIONS BEGIN*	
Spouse Beneficiary	1. Spouse can receive distributions over the surviving spouse's remaining single life expectancy as recalculated using the single life table. 2. Rollover plan balance to an IRA in surviving spouse's name and delay distributions until spouse is 70½.
Nonspouse Beneficiary	1. Distribution period is the longer of the remaining single life expectancy (not recalculated) of the designated beneficiary (reduced by one year) or the remaining life expectancy of the participant. 2. Rollover plan balance to an IRA in nonspouse beneficiary's name and distribute over the longer of the remaining single life expectancy of the beneficiary or the remaining life expectancy of the participant (not recalculated).
No Beneficiary	1. Distributions must continue over the remaining distribution period of the deceased owner (uniform life table). The decedent's remaining distribution period is reduced by one each year.
OPTIONS BEFORE MINIMUM DISTRIBUTIONS BEGIN*	
Spouse Beneficiary	1. Distribution over surviving spouse's remaining single life expectancy as recalculated using single life expectancy table beginning when the participant would have turned 70½. 2. Distribute participant's account within 5 years. 3. Roll plan assets to an IRA in surviving spouse's name and wait until surviving spouse is 70½ to begin RMD.
Nonspouse Beneficiary	1. Distribute participant's account within 5 years. 2. Remaining single life expectancy (not recalculated) of designated beneficiary (reduced by one year). 3. Roll plan assets to an IRA in beneficiary's name and then distribute within 5 years or over the remaining single life expectancy of the beneficiary (not recalculated). (PPA 2006)
No Beneficiary	1. Distribute participant's account within 5 years.

** In all cases, the beneficiary can take more than the minimum distribution.*

Sources of Plan Information[1]

Document	Type of Information	To Whom	When
Summary Plan Description (SPD):	Primary vehicle for informing participants and beneficiaries about their plan and how it operates. Must be written for average participant and be sufficiently comprehensive to apprise covered persons of their benefits, rights, and obligations under the plan. Must accurately reflect the plan's contents as of the date not earlier than 120 days prior to the date the SPD is disclosed. See 29 CFR §§2520.102-2 and 2520.102-3 for style, format, and content requirements.	Participants and those pension plan beneficiaries receiving benefits. (Also see "Plan Documents" below for persons with the right to obtain SPD upon request). See 29 CFR §2520.102-2(c) for provisions on foreign language assistance when a certain portion of plan participants are literate only in the same non-English language.	Automatically to participants within 90 days of becoming covered by the plan and to pension plan beneficiaries within 90 days after first receiving benefits. However, a plan has 120 days after becoming subject to ERISA to distribute the SPD. Updated SPD must be furnished every 5 years if changes made to SPD information or plan is amended. Otherwise must be furnished every 10 years. See 29 CFR §2520.104b-2.
Summary of Material Modification (SMM)	Describes material modifications to a plan and changes in the information required to be in the SPD. Distribution of updated SPD satisfies this requirement. See 29 CFR §2520.104b-3.	Participants and those pension plan beneficiaries receiving benefits. (Also see "Plan Documents" below for persons with the right to obtain SMM upon request).	Automatically to participants and pension plan beneficiaries receiving benefits; not later than 210 days after the end of the plan year in which the change is adopted.
Summary Annual Report (SAR)	Narrative summary of the Form 5500. See 29 CFR §2520.104b-10(d) for prescribed format.	Participants and those pension plan beneficiaries receiving benefits. For plan years beginning after December 31, 2007, the SAR is no longer required for defined benefit pension plans, which now instead provide the annual funding notice (see below).	Automatically to participants and pension plan beneficiaries receiving benefits within 9 months after end of plan year, or 2 months after due date for filing Form 5500 (with approved extension).
Plan Documents	The plan administrator must furnish copies of certain documents upon written request and must have copies available for examination. The documents include the latest updated SPD, latest Form 5500, trust agreement, and other instruments under which the plan is established or operated.	Participants and beneficiaries. Also see 29 CFR §2520.104a-8 regarding the Department's authority to request documents.	Copies must be furnished no later than 30 days after a written request. Plan administrator must make copies available at its principal office and certain other locations as specified in 29 CFR §2520.104b-1(b).

1. Reporting and Disclosure Guide for Employee Benefit Plans, U.S. Department of Labor, October 2008.

SOURCES OF PLAN INFORMATION CONTINUED

Document	Type of Information	To Whom	When
Periodic Pension Benefit Statement	Content of statements varies depending on the type of plan. In general, all statements must indicate total benefits and total nonforfeitable pension benefits, if any, which have accrued, or earliest date on which benefits become nonforfeitable. Benefit statements for an individual account plan must also provide the value of each investment to which assets in the individual account have been allocated.	Participants and beneficiaries	In general, at least once each quarter for individual account plans that permit participants to direct their investments; at least once each year, in the case of individual account plans that do not permit participants to direct their investments; and at least once every three years in the case of defined benefit plans or, in the alternative, defined benefit plans can satisfy this requirement if at least once each year the administrator provides notice of the availability of the pension benefit statement and the ways to obtain such statement. In addition, the plan administrator must furnish a benefit statement to a participant or beneficiary upon written request, limited to one request during any 12-month period.
§404(c) Plan Disclosures	Investment-related and certain other disclosures for participant-directed individual account plans described in 29 CFR §2550.404c-1, including blackout notice for participant-directed individual account plans described in ERISA §404(c)(1)(A)(ii), as described below.	Participants or beneficiaries, as applicable.	Certain information should be furnished to participants or beneficiaries before the time when investment instructions are to be made; certain information must be furnished upon request.
Notice of Blackout Period for Individual Account Plans	Notification of any period of more than 3 consecutive business days when there is a temporary suspension, limitation or restriction under an individual account plan on directing or diversifying plan assets, obtaining loans, or obtaining distributions.	Participants and beneficiaries of individual account plans affected by such blackout periods and issuers of affected employer securities held by the plan.	Generally at least 30 days but not more than 60 days advance notice. See ERISA §101(i) and 29 CFR §2520.101-3 for further information on the notice requirement.

http://www.dol.gov/ebsa/pdf/rdguide.pdf

NQSO AND ISO SUMMARY

	NQSO	ISO
At Grant Date	No taxable income to holder if issued at the current or greater share price.	No taxable income to holder if issued at current or greater share price.
At Exercise	Executive gives options and exercise price to company. Company issues stock to executive to replace option.	Executive gives options and exercise price to company. Company issues stock to executive to replace option.
Employee Taxation	At exercise, executive recognizes W-2 income to extent of difference between current stock price and exercise price.	At exercise, executive does not recognize any regular taxable income but will have an AMT adjustment for the appreciation over the exercise price.
Employer Tax Deduction	Employer's income tax deduction equals the executive's taxable income.	The employer will not receive a tax deduction unless the stock is disposed of in a disqualifying disposition.
Adjustable Basis	Executive's adjusted basis in stock is equal to the fair market value of stock (exercise price in cash plus the recognition of W-2 income).	Executive's adjusted basis in stock is equal to the exercise price.
When Stock is Sold	Capital gain or loss treatment.	Capital gain or loss treatment.

SOCIAL SECURITY RETIREMENT BENEFIT PERCENTAGE BASED ON AGE

Age	Benefit as a Percent of PIA for FRA age of 65 (1937 or earlier)	Benefit as a Percent of PIA for FRA age of 66 (1943 and 1954)	Benefit as a Percent of PIA for FRA age of 67 (1960 or after)
62	80.00%	75.00%	70.00%
63	86.67%	80.00%	75.00%
64	93.33%	86.67%	80.00%
65	100.00%	93.33%	86.67%
66	106.50%	100.00%	93.33%
67	113.00%	108.00%	100.00%
68	119.50%	116.00%	108.00%
69	126.00%	124.00%	116.00%
70	132.50%	132.00%	124.00%

NOTES:

1. PIA - Primary Insurance Amount
2. FRA - Full Retirement Age (this age is based on the recipient's date of birth)
3. Benefits beginning prior to FRA - reduction is 5/9ths of 1% for the first 36 months prior to FRA plus 5/12ths of 1% for months beyond the first 36 months.
4. Credits for delayed benefits are equal to 8% for each year delayed if born in 1943 or later. If born in 1937 (FRA of 65), then the credit equals 6.5% for each delayed year. Between 1937 and 1943, the credit amount changes.

SUMMARY OF SOCIAL SECURITY OASDI BENEFITS (AS A PERCENTAGE OF PIA)

	Assuming Full Retirement Age of the Worker			
	Retirement	Survivorship		Disability
	Fully Insured (2)	Fully Insured (2)	Currently Insured (3)	(4)
Participant	100%	Deceased	Deceased	100%
Child Under 18 (6)	50%	75%	75%	50%
Spouse with child under 16 (7)	50%	75%	75%	50%
Spouse - Age 65 (1)	50%	100%	0%	50%
Spouse - Age 62 (1)	40%	83%	0%	40%
Spouse - Age 60 (1)	N/A	71.5%	0%	N/A
Dependent Parent (age 62)	0%	75/82.5% (5)	0%	0%

1. Includes divorced spouse if married at least 10 years (unless they have remarried). Survivorship benefits are also available to divorced spouse if remarried after age 60.
2. Fully insured is 40 quarters of coverage or one quarter for each year after age 21 but before age 62.
3. Currently insured is at least six quarters of coverage in the last 13 quarters.
4. Disability insured is based on age as follows:
   - Before age 24 - Must have 6 quarters of coverage in the last 12 quarters.
   - Age 24 through 30 - Must be covered for half of the available quarters after age 21.
   - Age 31 or older - Must be fully insured and have 20 quarters of coverage in the last 40 quarters.
5. Parent benefit is 82.5 percent for one parent and 75 percent for each parent if two parents.
6. Child under age 19 and a full-time student or of any age and disabled before age 22 also qualifies.
7. Spouse with child disabled before age 22 also qualifies.

Note: Notice that when the participant worker is alive (retirement and disability), beneficiaries who qualify for a benefit, qualify for 50% of PIA. When the participant dies, all qualified beneficiaries generally receive 75% of PIA with the exceptions being the spouse who replaces the participant at 100% and any qualified dependent parents.

Age Full Retirement Benefits Begin (Normal Age Retirement)

Full Retirement Age With Full Benefits	Year Born
65 years	Before 1938
65 years, 2 months	1938
65 years, 4 months	1939
65 years, 6 months	1940
65 years, 8 months	1941
65 years, 10 months	1942
66 years	1943-1954
66 years, 2 months	1955
66 years, 4 months	1956
66 years, 6 months	1957
66 years, 8 months	1958
66 years, 10 months	1959
67 years	1960-present

Social Security Full Retirement and Reductions* by Age

Year of Birth	Full Retirement Age	Age 62 Reduction Months	Average Monthly Percent Reduction	Total Percent Reduction
1937 or earlier	65	36	0.555	20.00
1938	65 & 2 months	38	0.548	20.83
1939	65 & 4 months	40	0.541	21.67
1940	65 & 6 months	42	0.535	22.50
1941	65 & 8 months	44	0.530	23.33
1942	65 & 10 months	46	0.525	24.17
1943-1954	66	48	0.520	25.00
1955	66 & 2 months	50	0.516	25.84
1956	66 & 4 months	52	0.512	26.66
1957	66 & 6 months	54	0.509	27.50
1958	66 & 8 months	56	0.505	28.33
1959	66 & 10 months	58	0.502	29.17
1960 and later	67	60	0.500	30.00

**Percentage monthly and total reductions are approximate due to rounding. The actual reductions are 0.555 or 5/9 of 1 percent per month for the first 36 months and.0.416 or 5/12 of 1 percent for subsequent months.*
Source: Social Security Administration (www.ssa.gov)

Appendix

Estates F

POWER OF ATTORNEY VS. POWER OF APPOINTMENT

POWER OF ATTORNEY	POWER OF APPOINTMENT
• A stand alone document that allows an agent to act for the principal and may include the power to appoint assets	• A power, usually included in a trust or power of attorney, allowing the power holder to direct assets to another
• Power to act	• Power to transfer assets
• Ends at the death of the principal	• May survive the death of the grantor
• May be general or limited	• May be general or limited
• May be revoked at any time by the principal	• May be revoked by the principal during life or at death (via last will and testament)

PROPERTY OWNERSHIP

Fee Simple Ownership Summary

Number of Owners	Only 1
Right to Transfer	Freely
Automatic Survivorship Feature	No, transfers at death via will or intestacy laws
Included in the Gross Estate	Yes, 100%
Included in the Probate Estate	Yes, 100%

Tenancy in Common Ownership Summary

Number of Owners	2 or more
Right to Transfer	Freely without the consent of other co-tenants
Automatic Survivorship Feature	No, transfers at death via will or intestacy laws
Included in the Gross Estate	Usually the FMV of ownership percentage
Included in the Probate Estate	Yes, fair market value of interest
Partitionable	Yes, with or without consent of joint owner

Joint Tenancy with Right of Survivorship Ownership Summary

Number of Owners	2 or more
Right to Transfer	Freely without consent
Automatic Survivorship Feature	Yes, transfers at death to other owners
Included in the Gross Estate	Yes, FMV times the % contributed
Included in the Probate Estate	No
Partitionable	Yes, with or without consent of joint owner

Tenancy by the Entirety Ownership Summary

Number of Owners	2 - spouses only
Right to Transfer	Need consent of other spouse
Automatic Survivorship Feature	Yes, transfers at death to other spouse
Included in the Gross Estate	Yes, always 50% of FMV
Included in the Probate Estate	No
Partitionable	Not without consent of spouse / joint owner

Community Property Ownership Summary

Number of Owners	2 - spouses only
Right to Transfer	Need consent of other spouse
Automatic Survivorship Feature	No, transfers via will or intestacy law
Included in the Gross Estate	Always 50% of community property + 100% of separate property
Included in the Probate Estate	Always 50% of community property + 100% of separate property not retitled otherwise
Partitionable	Not without consent of spouse / joint owner

Property Ownership Key Features (Summary)

Property Ownership Type	Value Included in Gross Estate	Included in Probate Estate	Automatic Survivorship Feature	Qualifies for the Unlimited Marital Deduction	Is the Property Partitionable without Consent?
Fee Simple	100%	Yes 100%	No	Yes, if spouse is the beneficiary	Not applicable
Tenancy in Common	% Owned	Yes % Owned	No	Yes, if spouse is the beneficiary	Yes
Joint Tenancy with Rights of Survivorship	Actual Contribution Rule* % Owned	No	Yes	Yes, if spouse is the beneficiary	Yes
Tenancy by the Entirety	50% Deemed Contribution Rule	No	Yes	Yes	No
Community Property	50% Deemed Contribution Rule	Yes 50% of value	No	Yes, if spouse is the beneficiary	No

*Follow the actual contribution rule except when property is jointly owned with a spouse who is always deemed to have contributed 50% of the property's purchase price.

Documents

Common Duties of Executor and Administrator

<table>
<tr><th>When the Decedent Dies Testate
(with a will)</th><th>When the Decedent Dies Intestate
(without a will)</th></tr>
<tr><td>The Executor:
• Locates and proves the will.
• Locates witnesses to the will.
• Receives letters testamentary from court.</td><td>The Administrator:
• Petitions court for his or her own appointment.
• Receives letters of administration.
• Posts the required bond.</td></tr>
<tr><th colspan="2">Duties of the Executor or Administrator</th></tr>
<tr><td colspan="2">• Locates and assembles all of the decedent's property.
• Safeguards, manages, and invests property.
• Advertises in legal newspapers that the person has died and that creditors and other interested parties are on notice of the death and opening of probate.
• Locates and communicates with potential beneficiaries of the decedent.
• Pays the expenses of the decedent.
• Pays the debts of the decedent.
• Files both federal and state income, fiduciary, gift tax, and estate tax returns (such as Forms 1040, 1041, 709, and 706 for federal tax purposes) and makes any required tax payments.
• Distributes remaining assets to beneficiaries according to the will or to the laws of intestacy.
• Closes the estate formally or informally.
• TRA 2010 permits executors or administrators of estates of decedents who died in 2010 to opt-in to the new regime and get a step-up basis or keep carryover basis and not be subject to the estate tax regime that was created in TRA 2010.
• TRA 2010 also permits executors or administrators to elect to donate the decedent's unused exemption amounts to his or her surviving spouse, thereby making the exemption portable. Note that this requires the executor/administrator to file a timely estate tax return, even if the estate is otherwise not required to file a Form 706.</td></tr>
</table>

Assets Passing Through and Around the Probate Process

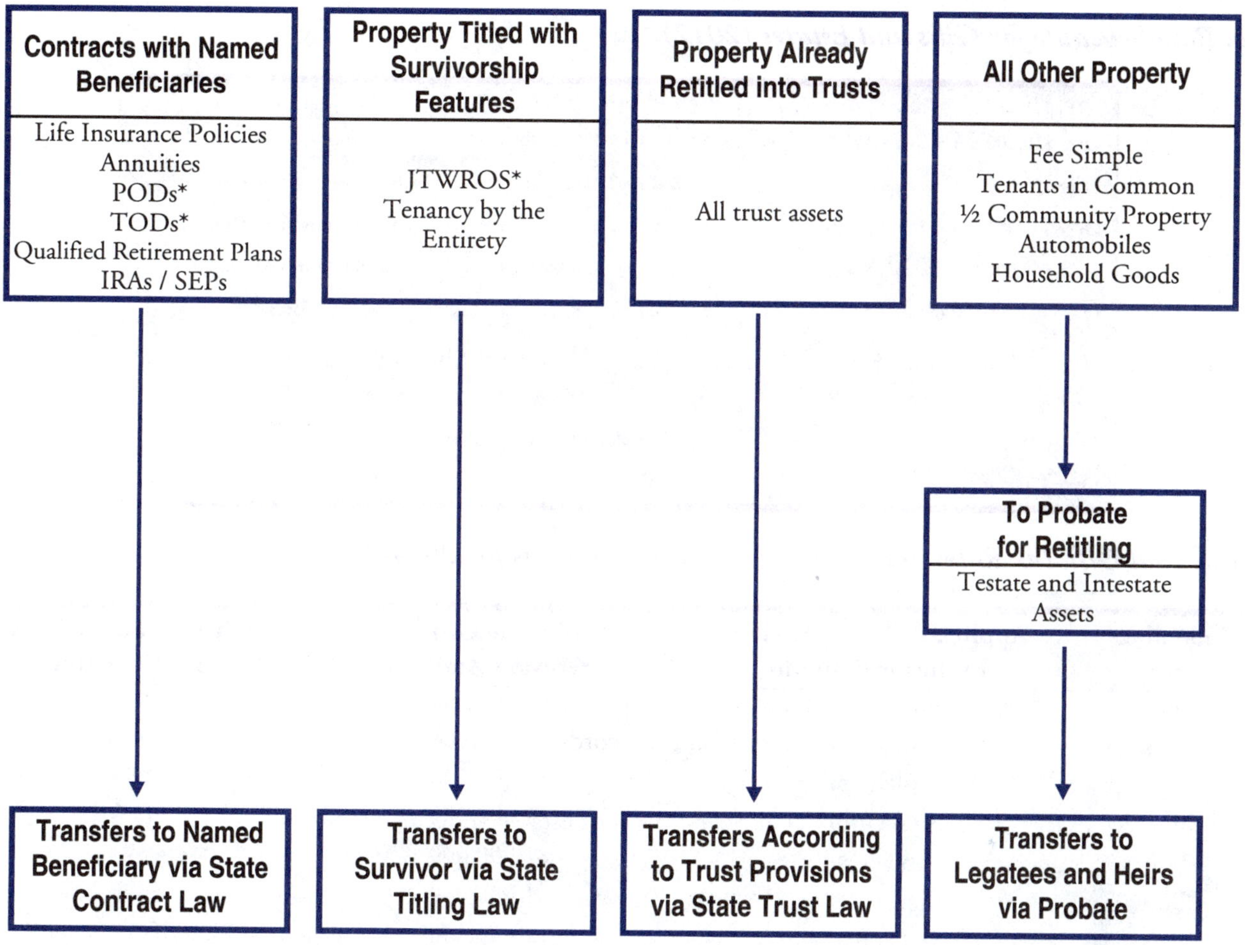

*PODs - Pay-on-death bank account with named beneficiaries.
*TODs - Transfer-on-death investment accounts with named beneficiaries.
*JTWROS - Joint tenancy with right of survivorship.

Tax Rates

Tax Rate Schedule for Gifts and Estates (2012)

Over $0 but not over $10,000	18% of such amount.
Over $10,000 but not over $20,000	$1,800 plus 20% of the excess of such amount over $10,000
Over $20,000 but not over $40,000	$3,800 plus 22% of the excess of such amount over $20,000
Over $40,000 but not over $60,000	$8,200 plus 24% of the excess of such amount over $40,000
Over $60,000 but not over $80,000	$13,000 plus 26% of the excess of such amount over $60,000
Over $80,000 but not over $100,000	$18,200 plus 28% of the excess of such amount over $80,000
Over $100,000 but not over $150,000	$23,800 plus 30% of the excess of such amount over $100,000
Over $150,000 but not over $250,000	$38,800 plus 32% of the excess of such amount over $150,000
Over $250,000 but not over $500,000	$70,800 plus 34% of the excess of such amount over $250,000
Over $500,000	$155,800 plus 35% of the excess of such amount over $500,000

Estate and Gift Tax Rates and Credit Exemption Amounts for 2004-2012

Calendar Year	Applicable Estate & GST Exclusion Amount	Applicable Gift Tax Exclusion Amount	Highest Estate, Gift & GST Tax Rates
2004	$1,500,000	$1,000,000	48%
2005	$1,500,000	$1,000,000	47%
2006	$2,000,000	$1,000,000	46%
2007	$2,000,000	$1,000,000	45%
2008	$2,000,000	$1,000,000	45%
2009	$3,500,000	$1,000,000	45%
2010	Estate Tax Repealed*	$1,000,000	35% (Gift Tax Only)*
2011	$5,000,000	$5,000,000	35%
2012	$5,120,000	$5,120,000	35%

Summary of Transfers During Life (Intra Family Transfers)

Arm's-Length Transactions for Full Consideration		
• Sale	• Installment Sale	• Exchanges
Typical Transfers to Loved Ones		
Arm's-Length	**Full-Consideration**	**Retained Interest Gifts***
• Sale • Installment Sale • Exchange	• Private Annuities • SCINs	• GRATs • GRUTs • QPRTs • TPPTs • Bargain Sale
Gifts	**Gifts With Use of Discounts**	**Transfers Resulting in No Tax**
• Outright • Gifts in Trust	• Family Limited Partnership	• Qualified Transfers • Payments for Support • Payments to Divorcing Spouses • Transfers in a Business Setting • Gifts to Spouses** • Annual Exclusion Gifts
Transfers to Charities		
• Outright Gifts • Charitable Annuities • Pooled Income Funds • Gifts in Trust	• Charitable Remainder Trusts - CRATs - CRUTs	• Charitable Lead Trusts - CLATs - CLUTs

* The four devices below (GRATs, GRUTs, QPRTs, and TPPTs) are not actually sales in the traditional sense of a sale to a transferee. Rather the grantor is exchanging an asset put in trust for a stream of dollars or use with a present value less than the value of the transferred asset. That difference being the amount of the gift in present value terms. ** Gifts to spouses are subject to gift tax, but may be nontaxable due to the marital deduction.

TRUSTS - SUMMARY OF TAX ISSUES

	Revocable Trusts	Irrevocable Trusts
Income Tax	Income is taxed to grantor.	• Income is taxed to beneficiaries if distributed. • Income is taxed to trust if retained (unless the trust is a grantor trust, in which case all income is taxed to the grantor).
Gift Tax	No gift tax consequences, since the grantor can take the property back.	• Treated as a completed gift and is subject to gift tax.
Estate Tax – Gross Estate	Full fair market value of trust assets included in the grantor's gross estate.	Not included in the gross estate of the grantor unless: • The grantor retained an interest as of the date of his death; • The grantor released an interest in the trust within 3 years of his death; or • The grantor did not retain an interest in the trust but funding the trust generated a gift tax within 3 years of the grantor's death.
Estate Tax – Adjusted Taxable Gift	No adjusted taxable gift.	• To the extent the gift to the trust exceeds the annual exclusion (if applicable), the adjusted taxable gift is added back to the tentative tax base for purposes of calculating the estate tax due.
Generation-Skipping Transfer Tax	GSTT is not an issue, since the trust assets are included in the grantor's estate.	• GSTT may be an issue, depending on the identification of the beneficiaries of the trust.

CHARITIES

Charitable Organizations

Charities that would generally qualify under this definition include:	Charities that generally do NOT qualify under this definition include:
• Churches, temples, synagogues • Public parks • Colleges and universities • United Way • Boy Scouts and Girl Scouts of America • Salvation Army • American Heart Association • American Society for Prevention of Cruelty to Animals	• Foreign organizations • For-profit groups • Homeowners' associations • Political groups • Labor unions • Chambers of commerce • Social clubs • Individuals • Civic groups

Charitable Contribution Deductions (Percent of Taxpayer's AGI)

<table>
<tr><th>Type of Property Donated</th><th>Valuation for Purposes of Charitable Deduction</th><th>Ceiling for Public Charities, Private Operating Foundations and Certain Private Nonoperating Foundations</th><th colspan="2">Ceiling for Other Private Nonoperating Foundations (PNOF)</th></tr>
<tr><td>Cash</td><td>Fair Market Value</td><td>50%</td><td colspan="2">30%</td></tr>
<tr><td>Ordinary Income Property and Short-term Capital Gain Property</td><td>Lesser of the adjusted basis or the fair market value</td><td>50%</td><td colspan="2">30%</td></tr>
<tr><td>Long-term Capital Gain property:
- Intangible</td><td>Fair market value</td><td>30%*</td><td rowspan="3">Adjusted Basis</td><td>20%**</td></tr>
<tr><td>- Tangible Personalty</td><td>Fair market value --
(a) related use
Adjusted basis --
(b) unrelated use</td><td>30%*

50%</td><td>20%</td></tr>
<tr><td>- Real Property</td><td>Fair market value</td><td>30%*</td><td>20%</td></tr>
</table>

*Taxpayer has the option to use the adjusted basis and the 50% of AGI ceiling for regular charities.

**Certain contributions of qualified appreciated stock may use the fair market value.

Charitable Contributions/Reporting

Amount or Value of Donation	Cash	Property
Under $250	Canceled check	Receipt with donee name, date, description of property
$250-$500	Contemporaneous acknowledgment from donee organization	Contemporaneous acknowledgment from donee organization
Over $500, but no more than $5,000	Same as above	Same as above plus maintain records of how and when property was acquired, its adjusted basis and file Form 8283
Over $5,000 ($10,000 for non-publicly traded stock)	Same as above	Same as above plus must obtain qualified appraisal and attach appraisal to the return

Summary of Characteristics of Charitable Remainder Trusts

	CRAT	CRUT	Pooled Income Funds (PIF)
Income Tax Deduction	Total value of property less present value of retained annuity payments	Total value of property less present value of retained unitrust payments	Total value of property less present value of retained income interest
Income Recipient	Noncharitable beneficiary (usually donor)	Noncharitable beneficiary (usually donor)	Noncharitable beneficiary (usually donor)
Income	At least 5% and no more than 50% of initial fair market value of assets paid at least annually for life or term ≤ 20 years (similar to fixed annuity)	At least 5% and no more than 50% of current fair market value of assets (revalued annually) paid at least annually for life or term ≤ 20 years (similar to variable annuity)	Trust rate of return for year
Remainderman	Qualified Charity	Qualified Charity	Qualified Charity
Additional Contributions Permissible	No	Yes	Yes
Sprinkling Provisions	Yes	Yes	No
When Income is Insufficient for Payment	Must invade corpus	Can pay up to income earned and make up deficiency in subsequent year	N/A
Can Invest in Tax - Exempt Securities	Yes	Yes	No

CRATs vs. CRUTs

Advantages	
CRATs	**CRUTs**
• Protects against declining balances • Provides a certain and fixed income stream	• Inflation protection • Can make subsequent contributions
Disadvantages	
CRATs	**CRUTs**
• No inflation protection • Income stream percentage may be limited by 5% probability test	• Require annual revaluation • Have principal erosion risk

Unlimited Marital Deduction

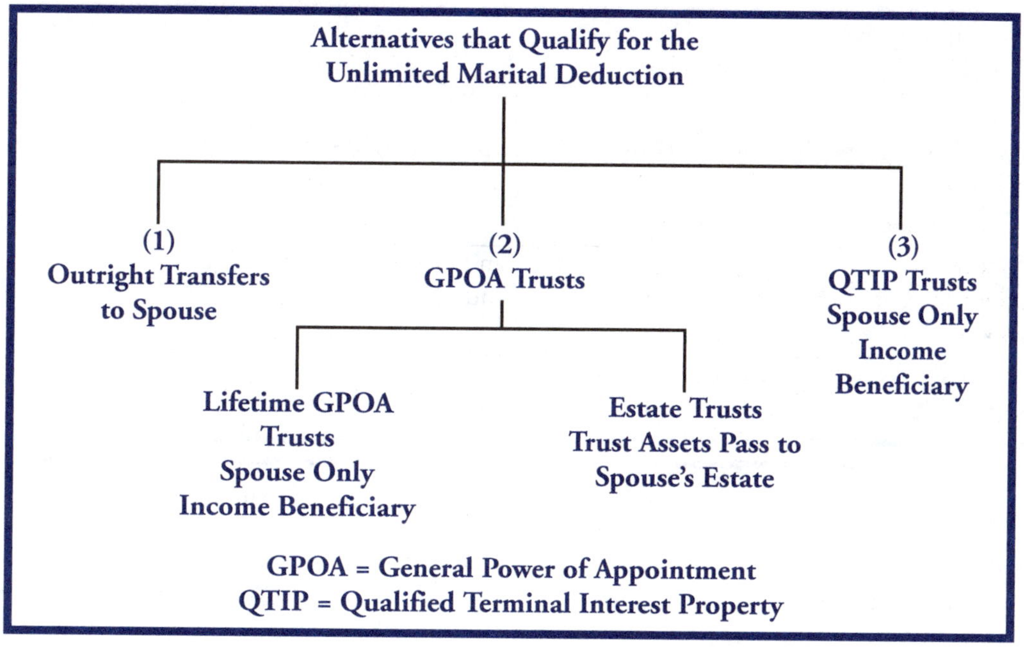

Summary of Alternative Tax Deductions

	Decedent's Income Tax Return Form 1040	Estate Income Tax Return Form 1041	Estate Tax Return Form 706	Notes
Unpaid Medical Expenses	Yes	No	Yes	Not both, but may split > 7.5% AGI (10% after 2013 or if an AMT Taxpayer)
Casualty Losses	Yes During Life	Yes After Death	Yes After Death	Not both, but may split >10% AGI if occurred before death
Executor Fees (Taxable income to the Executor)	No	Yes	Yes	May be waived for better tax result

Alternate Valuation Date (AVD)

To Qualify

1. The total value of the gross estate must depreciate after the date of death; and
2. The total estate tax must be less than the estate tax calculated using the date of death values.

Valuation if properly elected

1. All assets valued at the alternate valuation date
2. Except:
   - Assets distributed before 6 months which are valued at the date of distribution or sale; and
   - Wasting assets (annuitized annuities, patents, royalties, installment notes, lease income) which must be valued at the date of death.

Comparison of the Gift, Estate, and GSTT Tax Systems

Features	Gift Tax Transfers	Estate Tax Transfers	Generation-Skipping Transfer Tax	
			Gifts	Bequests
Applies to	Lifetime Transfers	Transfers at Death	Lifetime Transfers to Skip Persons	Transfers at Death to Skip Persons
Calculation of Transfer Includes	Value of Lifetime Transfers, plus any GSTT Paid	Value of Transfers at Death, plus any GSTT Paid	Value of Lifetime Transfers to Skip Persons	Value of Transfers at Death to Skip Persons
Annual Exclusion (2012)	$13,000	N/A	$13,000	N/A
Lifetime Exemption (2012)	$5,120,000 Cannot allocate	$5,120,000 Note: Includes Gift Transfers	$5,120,000 Can Allocate	$5,120,000 Note: Includes GST Gifts
Nature of Tax Rate	Progressive	Progressive	Highest Gift Tax Rate (Flat) 35% for 2012	Highest Estate Tax Rate (Flat) 35% for 2012
Annual Exclusion Available for Transfers under Crummey Power	Yes	N/A	Yes for Outright Transfers Possible for Transfers in Trust (See Annual Exclusions)	N/A

N/A = Not applicable

GSTT - Unrelated Persons and Nonlineal Descendents

	Age	Age Difference Between Transferor and Individual	Generations Down from Transferor
Transferor	80		0
Neighbor	67	13 Years	1
Friend	55	25 Years	1
(Neighbor's Son)	41	39 Years	2
(Friend's Son)	35	45 Years	2

Circled individuals are skip persons because they are in the 2nd generation below the transferor based on age.